STUDIES IN WELSH HISTORY

Editors

RALPH A. GRIFFITHS   KENNETH O. MORGAN
GLANMOR WILLIAMS

2

LITERATURE, RELIGION AND SOCIETY
IN WALES, 1660—1730

COFRESTR

O'R HOLL

Lyfrau Printjedig

GAN MWYAF

A GYFANSODDWYD

YN Y

Faith Gymraeg,

NEU

A gyfjeithwyd iddi hyd y Flwyddyn 1717.

Pauperis eſt numerare Pecus.

Printjedig yn *Llundain,* gan Brintwyr y Brenin, 1717.

The title-page of the cornerstone of Welsh bibliography, Moses Williams's *Cofrestr* (1717).

LITERATURE, RELIGION
AND SOCIETY
IN WALES,
1660—1730

by

GERAINT H. JENKINS

Published on behalf of the
History and Law Committee
of the Board of Celtic Studies

CARDIFF
UNIVERSITY OF WALES PRESS
1978

*Printed in Wales by Qualitex Printing Limited
Cardiff*

I'M RHIENI

EDITORS' FOREWORD

Since the Second World War, Welsh history has attracted considerable scholarly attention and enjoyed a vigorous popularity. Not only have the approaches, both traditional and new, to the study of history in general been successfully applied to Wales's past, but the number of scholars engaged in this enterprise has multiplied during these years. These advances have been especially marked in the University of Wales.

In order to make more widely available the conclusions of recent research, much of it of limited accessibility in postgraduate dissertations and theses, the History and Law Committee of the Board of Celtic Studies has inaugurated this new series of monographs, *Studies in Welsh History*. It is anticipated that many of the volumes will have originated in research conducted in the University of Wales or under the auspices of the Board of Celtic Studies. But the series will not exclude significant contributions made by researchers in other Universities and elsewhere. Its primary aim is to serve historical scholarship and to encourage the study of Welsh history.

PREFACE

This book is an attempt to fill a gap in our knowledge of religious life in Wales from the Restoration to Methodism. The archetypal view of this period is that Wales lay in a Slough of Despond. For this reason it has been sorely neglected by historians. My research, based on a wide variety of literary and ecclesiastical sources, has prompted me to take a more generous and sympathetic view of the period. It has led me to argue that there were vital forces at work which laid the foundations of the Methodist Revival. I hope the following pages will provoke some discussion, for, like Thomas Jones, the almanacer, 'I do not much fear the dispraise of the learned for what imperfections may be found herein; but from the scurrilous aspersions of the illiterate and barbarous, none shall escape'.

I am mindful of my debt to many institutions and individuals. I acknowledge my debt to the University College of Wales, Aberystwyth, for providing me with grants from various research funds towards the cost of preparing this work. I am grateful to the staff of various libraries, museums and record offices for their kind assistance. The staff of the National Library of Wales at Aberystwyth has been particularly helpful and I owe special thanks to Mr. G. Milwyn Griffiths, Mr. R. W. McDonald, Mr. Walter T. Morgan, Miss Eiluned Rees, and Mr. D. Emrys Williams for their patient replies to numerous inquiries on my part. Dr. Geoffrey F. Nuttall gave me early encouragement, and I have received much helpful and unselfish guidance from Professor J. Gwynn Williams of Bangor. I am greatly indebted to Dr. Ralph A. Griffiths of Swansea, Professor Ieuan Gwynedd Jones of Aberystwyth, and Dr. Kenneth O. Morgan of Oxford for reading the whole typescript with great thoroughness and for making many constructive comments on it. I owe an incalculable debt to Professor Glanmor Williams of Swansea: he has guided me in my work with unfailing enthusiasm, and I am deeply aware that this book would be much the poorer but for his shrewd advice and invaluable criticism. Any errors or inaccuracies which remain are entirely my own responsibility.

PREFACE

The original spelling, capitalisation, punctuation and use of italics have been modernised throughout, except in the case of book-titles in the text and footnotes. Dates are according to the Old Style of the Julian calendar, but the year has been taken to begin on 1 January rather than on 25 March.

I owe special thanks to Mr. Alun Treharne of the University of Wales Press for his kind assistance at every stage of publication.

Finally, I gratefully acknowledge my debt to my wife, Ann, not only for helping me prepare the index, but also for putting up with me and this book since the day we first met.

Geraint H. Jenkins

Department of Welsh History,
The University College of Wales, Aberystwyth.
August 1976

CONTENTS

ABBREVIATIONS

Arch. Camb.	*Archaeologia Cambrensis*
B.B.C.S.	*The Bulletin of the Board of Celtic Studies*
B.L.	The British Library, London
Bod.	The Bodleian Library, Oxford
Calamy	Edmund Calamy, *An Account of the Ministers . . . ejected after the Restoration in 1660*, 2 vols., 1713
Clement	Mary Clement (ed.), *Correspondence and Minutes of the S.P.C.K. relating to Wales, 1699–1740*, Cardiff, 1952
C.C.H.M.C.	*Cylchgrawn Cymdeithas Hanes y Methodistiaid Calfinaidd*
C.C.L.	The Central Library, Cardiff
D.N.B.	*The Dictionary of National Biography*
D.W.B.	*The Dictionary of Welsh Biography*
G.C.R.O.	The Glamorgan County Record Office, Cardiff
H.L.Q.	*The Huntingdon Library Quarterly*
H.P.N.	Thomas Rees, *History of Protestant Nonconformity in Wales*, 2nd edition, 1883
J.H.S.C.W.	*The Journal of the Historical Society of the Church in Wales*
J.W.B.S.	*The Journal of the Welsh Bibliographical Society*
N.L.W.	The National Library of Wales, Aberystwyth
N.L.W.J.	*The National Library of Wales Journal*
P.R.	Probate Records
P & P	*Past and Present*
Saunders	Erasmus Saunders, *A View of the State of Religion in the diocese of St. David's*, 1721; reprinted, Cardiff, 1949
T.H.S.C.	*The Transactions of the Honourable Society of Cymmrodorion*
T.R.H.S.	*The Transactions of the Royal Historical Society*
U.C.N.W.L.	The Library of the University College of North Wales, Bangor
W.H.R.	*The Welsh History Review*

I

PREACHING THE WORD

I. THE ESTABLISHED CHURCH

In the period before the civil wars, Wales was firmly established in puritan minds as one of 'the barren corners of the land'.[1] The impoverished established church was beset by a serious lack of preaching—a situation which zealous puritans sought to rectify. However, baulked by the intractable Archbishop Laud, their attack on the spiritual inertia of the Welsh church was effectively postponed until the revolutionary period. During the years following the Propagation Act of 1650, a new and vigorous effort was made to win men's souls by powerful preaching in the vernacular. Devout Welsh puritans like Vavasor Powell extolled the merits of their cause, while Oliver Cromwell ventured to claim that 'God did kindle a seed there indeed hardly to be paralleled since the primitive times'.[2] Their enthusiasm was understandable, for they were convinced that 'religion did grow' under the puritan regime.[3] There was a good deal of justification for this view, but contemporaries were only too painfully aware that puritan authority was based on the power of the sword. Against the joy and euphoria of puritan evangelists must be set the mood of bitterness and sense of desolation that overtook Anglicans. Their anguish found its most vivid focus in the works of Henry Vaughan, 'Silurist'. Writing plaintively 'out of that unfortunate region', Vaughan voiced the spiritual deprivation felt by those who sat 'in the shadow of death: where destruction passeth for propagation, and a thick black night for the glorious dayspring'.[4]

[1]. Christopher Hill, 'Puritans and The Dark Corners of the Land', *T.R.H.S.*, XIII (1963), 77–102.
[2] Christopher Hill, 'Propagating the Gospel', H. E. Bell and R. L. Ollard (eds.), *Historical Essays 1660–1750 presented to David Ogg* (1963), pp. 35–59.
[3] Vavasor Powell, *The Bird in the Cage* (1662), sig. B3r.
[4] L. C. Martin (ed.), *Henry Vaughan: Poetry and Selected Prose* (1963), p. 162. See also pp. 104–5, 114, 131–7, 157–61.

As a result, the memory of the Roundhead blade seared itself on the Welsh psyche and William Phylip's *cywydd* to Charles II in May 1660 breathed the widespread relief and happiness felt by Welsh royalists. Providence had rid the land of the puritan incubus and the army-trained, tub-thumping gospellers gave way to loyal and obedient churchmen:

> God, the unfailing guardian, preserve
> the King from line to line,
> and his counsellors, loyal to the faith,
> of one heart together.
> To establish learning in godly strain
> and to winnow the foolish men
> . . . .
> to have bishops, who were just,
> to preach the cream of learning.
> There will be no sorcery as there was
> nor an atheist to preach any more;
> and every official, of constitutional breast,
> to the King true and honest.[5]

But although the social and moral reformation envisaged by the puritans did not materialise, many of their distinctive values were absorbed by following generations. In particular, their traditional stress on the rôle of preaching as a crucial medium of salvation became part and parcel of Anglican *mores*.[6] A puritan necessity thus became a virtue in the eyes of the established church. After 1660, however, it remained to be seen whether the church could maintain its hold on the affections of the Welsh people by ministering effectively to their spiritual needs. In this task the rôle of the pulpit was to be vital.

The regularity with which sermons were preached from church pulpits was largely governed by economic considerations. Many of the troubles of the established church in this period stemmed from sheer poverty. The sees of St. Asaph and Bangor, each valued in the mid-eighteenth century at £1,400

---

[5] E .D. Jones, 'The Brogyntyn Welsh Manuscripts', *N.L.W.J.*, VIII (1953), 8.
[6] Christopher Hill, *Society and Puritanism in Pre-Revolutionary England* (1966), pp. 507–8.

per annum, were relatively wealthy compared with St. David's at £900 and Llandaff—'the Cinderella of all brides'[7]—at £500.[8] But, as a whole, Welsh bishoprics were pitifully poor and were widely regarded as 'no more than a stopgap, an earnest of higher promotions',[9] mere stepping-stones to richer pickings elsewhere. Few bishops, particularly Englishmen, would have disagreed with the trenchant view expressed by William Beaw, bishop of Llandaff, that a prolonged stay in the Principality was the worst 'disease' that could be inflicted upon a prelate. Marooned in Llandaff and thus in more straitened circumstances than most of his colleagues, Beaw yearned to get away from his 'little bishopric' in which, he claimed with some justice, he had 'sat stooping and bowing almost the space of the life of a man'.[10] His efforts to escape proved fruitless, however, and he, like other senile prelates put out to grass in Wales, simply lapsed into inactivity.[11]

Most ambitious young bishops avoided their dioceses in Wales like the plague. 'Some', commented Jenkin Evans ruefully, 'never go there at all, and others but once or so to take possession, to settle their rents and receive their presents; they go in snug and so they go out.'[12] Such a one was George Hooper who never visited his see at St. Asaph but still amassed profits totalling £3,600 between the time of his nomination to St. Asaph in October 1703 and his confirmation as bishop of Bath and Wells in March 1704.[13] Similarly, Benjamin Hoadly (although admittedly gravely crippled) achieved dubious fame by failing to set foot in his diocese at Bangor during his six years in office.[14] 'Many think it a degree of hardship', wrote John Ellis of Bodlew on the occasion of Hoadly's appointment in 1716, 'to have a foreigner at Bangor of which no man now

---

[7] Norman Sykes, *Church and State in England in the Eighteenth Century* (1934), p.364.
[8] Sir John Fortescue (ed.), *The Correspondence of King George the Third from 1760 to December 1783* (6 vols., 1927), I, 42–3. This valuation was made in 1762.
[9] Anon., *A Dialogue between the Rev. Mr. Jenkin Evans . . . and Mr. Peter Dobson . . . concerning Bishops, particularly the Bishops in the Principality of Wales* (1744), p. 43.
[10] Lambeth Palace MS.930, f.49; Bod., Rawlinson Letters MS.94, f.29.
[11] Bickham Sweet-Escott, 'William Beaw: a Cavalier Bishop', *W.H.R.*, I (1963), 397–411.
[12] *A Dialogue* (1744), p. 43.
[13] W. M. Marshall, 'The Life of George Hooper, Bishop of Bath and Wells, 1640–1727' (unpubl. Univ. of Bristol M. Litt. thesis, 1971), pp. 126–7.
[14] C. J. Abbey and J. H. Overton, *The English Church in the Eighteenth Century* (2 vols., 1878), I, 32.

alive can remember a resident.'[15] The fact, too, that bishops
were expected to support the government of the day in the
House of Lords meant in effect that they were non-residents for
two-thirds of the year, whilst those who failed to attend to their
duties at Westminster were generally the victims of senility and
sickness, and were consequently almost certainly guilty of
defective pastoral oversight.[16]

As we shall see, not all Welsh bishops were culpable in these
respects, but it was particularly damaging for the Welsh church
that native-born prelates, ever-mindful of the penury of their
sees, could not resist the temptation of translation to more
lucrative dioceses in England. In 1701 Humphrey Humphreys
was translated from Bangor to Hereford, and in 1728 John
Wynne of St. Asaph moved to Bath and Wells.[17] 'Very few
gentlemen,' remarked Defoe dryly, 'have died bishops of
Bangor; so that in some sense, a bishop of this see may be said
to be immortal.'[18] Jenkin Evans went further, resigning himself to a situation whereby one seldom found a Welsh bishop
'die in possession of a see in that country'.[19]

Clerical poverty was also a permanent problem in this
period. About a quarter of the benefices of the established
church were worth less than £50 in 1704.[20] Expropriation of
endowments and tithes by lay impropriators had gravely
weakened the resources of the church and the 'mean and hard
circumstances'[21] of the clergy often prevented them from
discharging their spiritual functions effectively. Even a
seasoned campaigner like Bishop George Bull was shocked to
find half the livings of St. David's in private hands on his
arrival in 1705.[22] Returns from 342 parishes in the vast and

[15] N.L.W. MS. 9070E, f.52.
[16] Some of these issues are discussed by Walter T. Morgan in G. M. Roberts
(ed.), *Hanes Methodistiaeth Galfinaidd Cymru* vol. 1 (1973), pp. 43–80. Mr. Morgan
takes a less generous view of the church in this period.
[17] W. T. Havard, 'The Eighteenth Century Background of Church Life in
Wales', *J.H.S.C.W.*, X (1955), 72.
[18] Daniel Defoe, *A Tour thro' the whole island of Great Britain* (3 vols., 2nd ed.,
1738), II, 296–7.
[19] *A Dialogue* (1744), p. 43.
[20] Alan Savidge, *The Foundation and early years of Queen Anne's Bounty* (1955), p. 9.
[21] Saunders, p. 27.
[22] Robert Nelson, *The Life of Dr. George Bull* (1714), p. 432; cf. J. Vyrnwy
Davies, 'The diocese of St. David's during the first half of the eighteenth century'
(unpubl. Univ. of Wales M. A. thesis, 1936), p. 52.

unwieldy diocese of St. David's in 1708 revealed that half the livings were nominally valued at less than £30 and a quarter at less than £10.[23] More valuable is the valuation of livings in St. Asaph, compiled in 1707, in which the real values of 118 rectories and vicarages are given: four only were returned as being worth less than £30, 33 were valued between £30 and £49, 70 ranged between £50 and £99, while eleven livings exceeded the value of £100.[24] Similarly, of valuations made in 88 livings in the diocese of Bangor in the late seventeenth century, ten were returned as being valued at less than £30, 32 were valued between £30 and £49, 40 ranged between £50 and £99, and sixteen livings exceeded the value of £100.[25] Clearly, livings in St. Asaph and Bangor were valued a good deal more realistically than those of St. David's, though it is also probable that livings in the two northern dioceses were generally more substantial since lay impropriation there had ravaged the resources of the church to a much lesser degree. It should be borne in mind, however, that valuations of livings were often kept deliberately low in order to bring as many incumbencies as possible within the terms of Queen Anne's Bounty Act of 1704, which discharged all small livings of less than £50 from having to pay First Fruits and Tenths to the royal coffers. Designed primarily to assist poor clergymen, it was not implemented swiftly enough to affect radically the problem of clerical poverty in Wales in this period.[26]

The most vulnerable section of the clergy was undoubtedly the curates. Although there were four different classes of curates,[27] virtually all of them were ill-paid and over-worked, and were, moreover, acutely aware that while rich incumbents were able to 'put Pelion upon Ossa', there were others who were 'almost in want of mere necessaries for themselves and families'.[28] The most impoverished among them were hardly better than vagrants. In 1721, William Wotton informed

[23] Ibid., p. 93.
[24] N.L.W., SA/MB/57.
[25] Bod., Tanner MS. 146, ff. 74–5.
[26] A. Savidge, op. cit., p. 115.
[27] See A. Tindal Hart, *Clergy and Society, 1600–1800* (1968), pp. 65–6.
[28] See the comments of John Jones, curate of Capel Garmon. N.L.W., SA/QA/2, no. 13; cf. Vergil, *Georgics*, I, pp. 281ff. (Mr. L. N. Wild kindly traced this source for me.)

Archbishop Wake of 'a parcel of strolling curates in south Wales, and some such there were also in north Wales, who for a crown or at most for a guinea, would marry anybody under a hedge'.[29] An Act passed in 1714 (13 Anne *c*. 11) had stipulated that the minimum salary of a curate was to be £20 and the maximum £50 per annum.[30] But this decree was seldom implemented in Wales. In St. David's it was claimed that 'a poor Curate must sometimes submit to serve three or four Churches for Ten or Twelve Pounds a Year'.[31] In St. Asaph, the annual stipend of curates ranged, on average, between £10 and £20, and it was commonly agreed that £18, together with a further £4 to £5 in perquisites, was 'a good salary for a curate in this diocese'.[32] Mocking commentators were not slow to draw attention to the augmenting of stipends with oblations and perquisites:

> Some of the most reverend rectors are dignified with a stipend of six pounds a year, besides the perquisites of a drum and fiddle; which well managed on a Holy Day, make up a very pretty thing. Others have an Augmentation of a bull or a bear, which being solemnly baited about twice in a quarter, do pick pretty comfortable tithe from the spectators' pockets, and makes the poor parson's purse to smile and mantle.[33]

It is not without significance that the common proverb, 'as ragged as a Welsh curate', dates from this period, and that both parsons and curates were becoming the favourite targets of caricaturists.[34]

The natural corollary of clerical poverty was pluralism and non-residence. It was common for Welsh bishops to augment their incomes by holding deaneries or benefices in plurality. Succumbing to the same temptations, incumbents leased their

---

[29] Christ Church Library, Oxford, Arch.W.Epist. 21, item ccxcviii, f. 419.

[30] A. Tindal Hart, op. cit., p. 65.

[31] Saunders, p. 24. Of 23 curacies whose values were given in Edward Tenison's returns for the archdeaconry of Carmarthen in 1710, none exceeded £15 and the general average was £7 per annum. G. M. Griffiths, 'A Visitation of the Archdeaconry of Carmarthen, 1710', *N.L.W.J.*, XVIII (1974), 287–311; ibid., XIX (1976), 311–26.

[32] N.L.W., SA/RD/5, 16, 17, 18, 20.

[33] William Richards, *Wallography* (1682), p. 105.

[34] *A Dialogue* (1744), p. 54.

livings, placed ill-equipped curates to serve in them, and took root in more lucrative preferments in England. Lawrence Womack, bishop of St. David's from 1683 to 1686, tarried long enough in his see to inveigh against non-residents who placed 'illiterate curates for scandalous stipends' in their Welsh livings while keeping a firm grip on livings 'of great advantage' across Offa's Dyke.[35] In a thorough-going critique of the established church in 1677, Stephen Hughes poured especial wrath on the evils of non-residence in south-west Wales,[36] whilst in 1721 Browne Willis found to his displeasure that prebends within the diocese of Llandaff were occupied by 'a parcel of non-residents' and 'mercenary remote English clergymen'.[37]

Almost inevitably, therefore, Wales became a byword for pluralism.[38] As ever, the prime cause was chronic poverty which forced impoverished clergymen to serve several churches in order to muster a competent salary. In 1707 there were 96 pluralists in the four archdeaconries of St. David's[39] and many of these found that, in attempting to minister to churches far apart from each other, they were forced to scurry frantically from one service to the next, notifying parishioners beforehand of the approximate time of their arrival.[40] The inevitable consequences were not lost on Griffith Jones, Llanddowror. In 1715, he spoke of clergymen 'pinched with poverty and forced to officiate in three or four parishes & therefore cannot pretend to do well in either, and thus are the children left uncatechised & the people in some places for months, yea for near (to say no more) twelve months together without a sermon'.[41]

Impoverishment could also mean many other things to a clergyman: it could grievously retard his advancement of learning, prevent him from buying religious literature and, as a result, seriously affect the quantity and quality of his sermons.[42] Penury inevitably bred scorn and contempt—by clergymen towards their calling and by laymen, too, towards

[35] Bod., Tanner MS. 32, f. 119.
[36] Stephen Hughes (ed.), *Cyfarwydd-deb i'r Anghyfarwydd* (1677), p. 152.
[37] Christ Church Library, Oxford. Arch.W.Epist.22, item xxx, f. 42.
[38] See the mordant comments of Thomas Brown, *Novus Reformator Vapulans: or, The Welch Levite tossed in a Blanket* (1691), p. 26.
[39] J. Vyrnwy Davies, op. cit., p. 65.
[40] N.L.W., Ottley Papers, no. 89.
[41] Ibid., no. 100.
[42] G. F. A. Best, *Temporal Pillars* (1964), pp. 13–14.

their spiritual overseers. Poverty-stricken clergymen lay at the mercy of snipers and back-biters who abused them as 'spiritual muckenders', 'sow gelders and alehouse-keepers'.[43] Many, as a result, lost the respect and approbation of their flocks. *Necessitas cogit ad turpia* was a theme taken up by an apologist of the simonist Thomas Watson, bishop of St. David's. Out of sheer economic necessity, he claimed, clerics in scandalous livings became scandalous in their deeds and habits.[44] Similarly, many small livings in the diocese of St. Asaph were said to render many clergymen 'contemptible in unwary and vulgar eyes' and likewise render 'their instructive labours less efficacious'.[45]

Allied to the twin evils of pluralism and non-residence was the growing influx of English-born prelates and clergymen into Welsh sees. During this period, fifteen Welsh bishops and nineteen English bishops, at one time or another, occupied the four Welsh bishoprics. Bangor was best provided for, with five Welsh bishops up to 1716, at which time Hoadly's appointment heralded a succession of monoglot English prelates down to 1870. In St. Asaph, four bishops were Welshmen and six were English; in Llandaff, four were natives of Wales and three were Englishmen. The diocese of St. David's was least well provided for, having only two Welshmen as against seven English bishops.[46] The majority of English bishops were appointed from the early eighteenth century onwards, when appointments were determined less by merit than by the dictates of factional politics. A distracted country parson of the diocese of Llandaff who petitioned Archbishop Tenison in 1703, stressed the fact that the intrusion of English bishops into the Welsh church deepened existing divisions:

> When we had bishops that could preach in Welsh, and did take pains to instruct the people, the generality of the people did keep the unity of the church, it may be as well as any part of the nation. But now of late there has been another course

---

[43] Anon., *North Wales defended or an Answer to an imodest and scurrilous libel, lately published, and entitled A Trip to North Wales* (1701), p. 5.
[44] Anon., *A Large Review of the Summary View, of the Articles exhibited against the Bishop of St. David's* (1702), p. 100; Saunders, p. 29.
[45] N.L.W., SA/Misc/499.
[46] M. Powicke and E. B. Fryde (eds.), *Handbook of British Chronology* (2nd ed., 1961), pp. 275–80.

taken to make choice of perfect strangers to our country, and language, who generally have large commendams in England, and seldom see us.[47]

Focusing on St. David's, Erasmus Saunders descanted on the same theme, albeit more forcefully. Dreaming wistfully of attaining a Welsh bishopric for himself, Saunders judged it monstrous 'that there should arise among the learned and the knowing, those who should not doubt of their sufficiency for, or their faithfulness in the discharge of this most solemn trust, without either understanding the language, or ever seeing the faces of those they are spiritually to feed and oversee'.[48] His pleas were echoed by a small minority of enlightened English prelates, notably White Kennett, bishop of Peterborough, and John Hough, bishop of Worcester, who argued that the appointment of Welsh bishops to Bangor would be 'much more welcome to the people and undoubtedly more useful'.[49]

The increasing tendency among churchmen to ascribe superior status to the English tongue was also a growing problem. Up to the end of the seventeenth century, the survival of the Welsh language had been largely the result of the efforts of the Welsh clergy and their flocks. By virtue of this *rapport*, ministers of religion and common people 'chiefly support the tongue, and retain the customs and traditions and principles, and proverbs of their ancestors'.[50] The language thus flourished as the medium of religion, a common link between parson and parishioner. But this happy alliance was now under threat. In 1677, Stephen Hughes issued a bitter indictment of those clergymen who pandered to the whims of an anglicized minority at the terrible price of estranging the monoglot majority.[51] Thirty years later, an Anglican minister of the same diocese claimed that some of his fellow-clergy, ensnared in the web of anglicization, were too haughty and 'puffed-up' to preach in Welsh to monoglot parishioners who had at least

[47] Lambeth Palace MS. 930, f. 33.
[48] Saunders, p. 41.
[49] Christ Church Library, Oxford. Arch.W.Epist. 9, letter 124; Arch.W.Epist. 22, letter 209.
[50] Thomas Jones, *Of the Heart and its Right Soveraign, or, an Historical Account of the title of our Brittish Church* (1678), p. 243.
[51] *Cyfarwydd-deb i'r Anghyfarwydd*, p. 152.

an equal right to the means of salvation.[52] It is improbable, however, that these strictures applied to more than a small minority. Both Stephen Hughes and Samuel Williams were rather more prone to make sweeping generalizations than to cite particular examples. The mass of the clergy was still thoroughly Welsh in speech and habit, and there were many Englishmen, too, who applied themselves to the task of learning the language of their flocks. Conversely, those who had the true interests of the Welsh church at heart would have just cause to condemn the arrival of those English clerics who, having made 'fainter applications' to learn Welsh, quickly threw in the towel, laying 'the whole blame on the uncouthness and ungrammaticalness of the language'.[53] A watchful eye needed to be kept on clerics like John Tudor of Little Stanton who, 'being loth to be at the trouble of making himself master of that uncouth ungenteel lingua',[54] were chiefly interested in feathering their own nests.

Problems such as these were not peculiar to the diocese of St. David's. In 1688, irate communicants in the parishes of Llandaff and Whitchurch in Glamorgan, of whom 'not one in ten understanding English', petitioned the Archbishop of Canterbury to secure the removal of their vicar, Thomas Andrews, 'a mere stranger to the Welsh-tongue' whose 'unreasonable and arbitrary' appointment was causing 'great danger and discomfort' to their souls.[55] In the diocese of St. Asaph, Bishop William Lloyd made strenuous efforts in the 1680s to rid his diocese of clergymen who mystified their flocks with sermons which were 'swathed in a language they do not understand',[56] but when William Fleetwood was appointed to the same bishopric in 1708 he was appalled to find clerics lapsing obsequiously into the English tongue whenever their church was blessed with the monthly presence of 'the best families in the parish'. Bishop Fleetwood was no lover of the Welsh tongue but he had an eye for social realities. 'I cannot possibly approve', he warned, 'of this respect and

---

[52] Samuel Williams, *Amser a Diwedd Amser* (1707), sig. A3v. His son, Moses, dilated on the same theme in *Pregeth a Barablwyd* (1718), p. 14.
[53] William Gambold, *A Welsh Grammar* (1727), sig. A2v.
[54] U.C.N.W.L., Penrhos (1), MS. 604.
[55] Bod., Tanner MS. 146, ff. 160–3.
[56] Bod., Tanner MS. 34, f. 33; Tanner MS. 282, f. 138.

complaisance to a few.'[57] Nevertheless, the linguistic problem was intensified in St. Asaph by the fact that some parishes were situated in England whilst others, close to the border, had become almost totally anglicized. Some parishes were bilingual while others remained thoroughly Welsh. It thus became difficult to please both sections of the community at once, and the presence of incumbents unable to preach effectively in both tongues exacerbated the situation.[58] In general, however, most arrangements for church services seem to have reflected linguistic conditions in individual parishes.[59]

Evils such as absenteeism and non-residence, the constant jockeying for lucrative positions, pluralism, nepotism and anglicisation, were all part and parcel of the structure of the unreformed church throughout the eighteenth century. Each in turn was inveighed against from time to time, but clergy and laity alike still tended to accept them as an inevitable, if unfortunate, fact of life. They were thus obliged to carry out improvements in the teeth of such abuses and learn to come to terms with the fact that the shortcomings of the unreformed church would exercise an important influence on the frequency with which sermons were preached. Evidence regarding the frequency of sermons in the Welsh church in this period is not completely reliable. Detailed information is at a premium in the terse returns presented by churchwardens, many of whom couched their replies in such vague terms as 'nothing to present', 'performs duty' or 'omnia bene'. Nevertheless, this information, if taken at face value, does provide some valuable statistical evidence.

In the diocese of St. David's, the returns for the archdeaconry of Cardigan in 1684 show that, of 69 parishes, 29 were satisfied that their ministers were fulfilling their duties. A further four parishes claimed to receive a regular Sunday sermon, four

---

[57] William Fleetwood, *The Bishop of St. Asaph's Charge to the Clergy of that Diocese in 1710* (1712), pp. 11–12. It is known, for instance, that Griffith Jones, rector of Bodfari, preached in English in the presence of the Cotton family of Lleweni. N.L.W., SA/Misc/600.

[58] For some examples, see N.L.W., SA/RD/24, pp. 82–4.

[59] W. T. R. Pryce, 'Approaches to the Linguistic Geography of Northeast Wales, 1750–1846', *N.L.W.J.*, XVII (1972), 346. In 1720 a project was launched to build a new Welsh church at Wrexham to obviate the practice of holding alternate services in Welsh and English. N.L.W., SA/Misc/586; cf. A. H. Dodd, 'Welsh and English, in East Denbighshire: an Historical Retrospect', *T.H.S.C.*, 1940, p. 55.

others received a sermon 'very often', five 'often', two 'somewhat', one 'alternately' and two 'monthly'.[60] But by 1733 a clear improvement was evident from the encouraging returns supplied by the rural deans' report for the same archdeaconry. Of 62 parishes that supplied returns, 25 received a sermon every Sunday, 27 on alternate Sundays, two every third Sunday, and three 'monthly'.[61] The returns supplied by Edward Tenison for the archdeaconry of Carmarthen in 1710 show that, of 52 parishes, only seven were blessed with a regular Sunday sermon, 23 parishes received sermons on alternate Sundays, 16 heard sermons monthly, whilst six others were fortunate to hear more than five sermons annually.[62] By 1733, however, 23 parishes could now boast a Sunday sermon whilst 29 parishes received sermons on alternate Sundays.[63]

Information for the dioceses of Bangor and Llandaff does not exist for this period and the evidence for the diocese of St. Asaph is pitifully meagre. Even so, the rural deans' returns for 1729–30 are encouraging. Of seven parishes that supplied detailed returns in the deanery of Bromfield and Yale, five received a sermon every Sunday, and two on alternate Sundays.[64] Of 18 parishes in the deanery of Rhôs, two churches received a sermon every Sunday, fifteen on alternate Sundays and one every month.[65] Of 11 parishes in the deanery of Penllyn and Edeirnion, eight received a Sunday sermon and three once a fortnight.[66] A return for the same deanery in 1732 reveals that ten churches received a regular Sunday sermon and one parish heard a monthly sermon.[67]

Clearly, the dearth of detailed information precludes confident generalisation. So many imponderables determined the frequency of sermons that conditions must have varied from parish to parish. Much depended on the circumstances of the individual clergyman: whether he was resident, how

[60] N.L.W., SD/Archdeaconry of Cardigan/Churchwardens' Returns 1684. The remaining parishes seldom heard sermons.
[61] N.L.W., SD/Misc.B/132, pp. 14–15, 20–3.
[62] G. M. Griffiths, *N.L.W.J.*, XVIII (1974), 287–311; XIX (1976), 311–26.
[63] N.L.W., SD/Misc.B/132, pp. 12, 31–4. The same pattern is evident in the archdeaconry of Brecon in the same period.
[64] N.L.W., SA/RD/15.
[65] N.L.W., SA/RD/18.
[66] N.L.W., SA/RD/21.
[67] N.L.W., SA/RD/23.

many livings he held, the standard of his education, his articulacy in the pulpit, and, in the last resort perhaps, how conscientiously he regarded his vocation. Even the weather had its say: the parishioners of Pendine in Carmarthenshire were frequently anxious lest 'very rainy weather' or some other mishap might prevent the curate of Llanddowror from making his fortnightly visit.[68] The rural dean of Penllyn and Edeirnion made the point that regular Sunday sermons were more frequent during the summer months than in winter when parishioners were often 'satisfied with a very moderate share of doctrine'.[69] Even so, the available statistics, however slender and incomplete, show that sermons were becoming more frequent in number and regular in practice. By the early decades of the eighteenth century, most parishes could at least expect a discourse on alternate Sundays and, at best, a regular Sunday sermon. In the interstices of Erasmus Saunders's generally gloomy account we find him referring to those 'many honest and good men' who were plainly responsible for this improvement in the diocese of St. David's.[70] Significantly, too, the plaintive cleric from the diocese of Llandaff who petitioned Archbishop Tenison in 1703 emphasised the presence of ministers 'of gravity & learning' who, with more encouragement from above, might be of even greater service to their country.[71] Nor should we discount effusive evidence for north Wales from Edward Samuel in 1716: rejoicing that the 'Light of the Gospel' was now shining brightly in Wales, Samuel was convinced that there were 'better preachers' at present in his native land than there had been in any age for over a thousand years.[72]

It is evident, too, that Welsh congregations had developed a taste for sermons. One of the most striking features of the Welsh from the earliest times, claimed Moses Williams, was their zeal for piety and religion.[73] It was that same zeal that prompted the inhabitants of the township of Minera in 1683 to contribute their sixpences and shillings towards the maintenance of 'an honest godly minister' to cater for their spiritual

---

[68] G. M. Griffiths, *N.L.W.J.*, XVIII (1974), 306.
[69] N.L.W., SA/RD/23; SA/RD/21, pp. 73–4.
[70] Saunders, p. 72.
[71] Lambeth Palace MS. 930, f. 33.
[72] Edward Samuel, *Gwirionedd y Grefydd Grist'nogol* (1716), p. 5.
[73] Moses Williams, *Pregeth a Barablwyd* (1718), p. 13.

needs.[74] In order to assuage their thirst for edifying discourses, parishioners in the archdeaconry of Carmarthen temporarily defected to Dissenting folds.[75] Robert Jones, curate of Bodedern, went so far as to claim that his age loved nothing else but sermons.[76] Two largely jaundiced commentators on the Welsh church in this period, William Richards and Erasmus Saunders, also found redeeming virtues in their countrymen's penchant for sermons. In 1682 the religiosity of the Welsh made a vivid impression on Richards; he found them 'pretty devout in their worship', having 'a pretty glowing zeal, though their churches are few, and at great distance'.[77] ' 'Tis almost incredible', he enthused, 'how far they are fain to trudge for a little homily.' In 1721, Erasmus Saunders paid a similar tribute, in his famous rhapsody, to the deprived inhabitants of the diocese of St. David's:

> There is, I believe, no part of the nation more inclined to be religious, and to be delighted with it than the poor inhabitants of these mountains. They don't think it too much when neither ways, nor weather are inviting, over cold and bleak hills to travel three or four miles, or more, on foot to attend the public prayers, and sometimes as many more to hear a sermon, and they seldom grudge many times for several hours together in their damp and cold churches, to wait the coming of their minister.[78]

The hunger for sermons was most clearly revealed at the advent of Griffith Jones, Llanddowror, as a popular preacher of rare quality and boundless energy. Between 1714 and 1718, Jones incurred the wrath of Adam Ottley, bishop of St. David's, for irregular preaching and for 'intruding himself into the churches of other ministers without their leave'.[79] Many of the conservatively-minded raised their eyebrows at the unorthodox activities of 'this busy enthusiast' and his abrasive criticisms of the contemporary church.[80] Jones, however, strenuously denied all charges levelled against him and, in 1715, wrote an eloquent letter of self-vindication to his bishop, the gist of which was that

[74] N.L.W., SA/Misc/517–8.
[75] G. M. Griffiths, *N.L.W.J.*, XVIII (1974), 304.
[76] N.L.W. MS. 3B, p. 113.
[77] William Richards, *Wallography*, p. 103.
[78] Saunders, p. 32.
[79] Clement, p. 72.
[80] N.L.W., Ottley Papers, no. 139.

he at least saw it as his vocation to preach salvation to those hungry sheep that cried out but were not fed.[81] In his readiness to preach in the open air, Jones stands out as a connecting link between the puritan itinerants of the Propagation period and the early Methodist evangelists. Like Wesley, he believed that he could command a larger audience in the open air than under a church roof: 'the more spacious the field the more good ground perhaps the seed of God's word may meet with'.[82]

By all accounts, Griffith Jones was a remarkably popular preacher. Excited crowds, many of them bored by the tedious homilies of their pastors, went to some pains to hear him. John Dalton estimated his congregations to be 'above five and six hundred auditors, nay sometimes 1000, a number not to [be] met with in Wales'.[83] Sir John Philipps of Picton Castle, a weighty and enthusiastic supporter of Jones's evangelising techniques, reckoned that his audiences numbered 3–4,000.[84] Fluent in speech and fervent in tone, he attracted large multitudes from neighbouring counties and from as far afield as north Wales, Herefordshire and Monmouthshire.[85] Not even the tramping propagators of the Interregnum could match his personal appeal and remarkable achievements. Widely acknowledged as 'one of the greatest masters of the Welsh tongue, that ever Wales was blessed with',[86] it was Griffith Jones who secured the conversion of the Methodist leader, Daniel Rowland,[87] and who won fulsome praise for his early pioneering zeal from Welsh Methodism's most illustrious panegyrist, William Williams, Pantycelyn.[88]

II. ANGLICAN SERMONS

The ideal which Anglican preaching set for itself in the Restoration period was simplicity and clarity.[89] This standard

[81] Ibid., no. 100.
[82] Ibid.
[83] Bod., Rawlinson MS. C.743, f. 25.
[84] Clement, p. 72.
[85] John Evans, *Some Account of the Welsh Charity-Schools; and of the Rise and Progress of Methodism in Wales* (1752), p. 19.
[86] Bod., Rawlinson MS. C.743, f. 25.
[87] Gomer M. Roberts, 'Griffith Jones' Opinion of the Methodists', *C.C.H.M.C.*, XXXV (1950), 56.
[88] William Williams, *Marwnad y Parchedig Mr. Gryffydd Jones* (1761).
[89] Richard Foster Jones, *The Seventeenth Century. Studies in the History of English Thought and Literature from Bacon to Pope* (1951), p. 113; Rolf P. Lessenich, *Elements of Pulpit Oratory in Eighteenth-Century England (1660–1800)* (1972), *passim*.

drew its motivation from a variety of sources. Anglicans had learnt from the puritans the folly of suffusing sermons with classical phrases and abstruse doctrines which the ordinary man in the pew would seldom understand. Rhetoric and eloquence for their own sake were to be sacrificed on the altar of sobriety and lucidity. Those who derived their inspiration from the cool rationalism of the Cambridge Platonists also saw their rôle as rendering religious truths intelligible, whilst the scientific bent of the preachers of the Royal Society reinforced the trend. But the distinctive Anglican 'plain style' was largely the product of the Latitudinarian school which, opposing 'enthusiasm' of all kinds, charted a middle course between the theological and cultural polarities of the day.[90] Latitudinarian preachers laid little stress on theological niceties, preferring a more functional and didactic approach. They believed that the prototypes of the budding Anglican clergyman were the patient, unambiguous sermons of John Tillotson.[91] The young clergy of St. David's were always urged to sharpen their theological teeth on the printed works of Tillotson: 'the best pattern', declared Bishop Richard Smallbrooke, 'that can be placed before us for completing a preacher, and which indeed includes all the precepts of that art, is that of the incomparable Archbishop Tillotson'.[92]

The bishops and upper clergy in Wales were strikingly unanimous in their advocacy of the 'plain style'. Bishop George Bull abhorred 'empty and frothy and trifling sermons', whilst Richard Smallbrooke advised his clergy to present their message to the meanest orders in such a way that there would be 'no overshooting of them by fine speculations, or too close and elaborate reasonings'.[93] In St. Asaph, William Fleetwood urged his clergy to avoid controversial points and to speak 'to the greatest part' of their congregation and to 'suit the matter' of their sermons to them.[94] Clear gospel truths, aimed at all

[90] B. J. Shapiro, 'Latitudinarianism and Science in Seventeenth-Century England', *P & P*, 40 (1968), 37.

[91] R. P. Lessenich, op. cit., p. 11. The best account of Tillotson's preaching style is W. Fraser Mitchell, *English Pulpit Oratory from Andrewes to Tillotson* (1932).

[92] Richard Smallbrooke, *Charge . . . to the Clergy* (1726), p. 24; cf. the comments of George Bull in Robert Nelson, op. cit., p. 420, and H. H. Henson (ed.), *Herbert Croft, The Naked Truth* (1919), *passim*.

[93] Robert Nelson, op. cit., p. 492; Richard Smallbrooke, op. cit., p. 20.

[94] William Fleetwood, *Charge* (1712), pp. 12–13; cf. George Lewis, *Pregeth* (1715), p. 6, and the views of Nathanael Jones in N.L.W. MS. 10254B, p. 2.

grades in society, were the standard to which all churchmen were expected to aspire.

Nevertheless, although preachers were widely exhorted to pitch their discourses at a level of common understanding, there must often have been a disparity between the desired ideal and the actual content, delivery and impact of the sermon. Those eager to secure better preferments would doubtless have tended to woo the attention of patrons with an amalgam of slavish and scholarly sermons. Some preachers were clearly glued to their notes, thus earning the gibes of Dissenters who portrayed the stereotype Anglican as 'poring on his notes all the while he speaks to the people, that he can scarce afford them now and then a glance for fear of being at a loss'.[95] Bishop William Lloyd of St. Asaph believed that this slender *rapport* between preachers and hearers meant that Dissenting preachers were able to make inroads into his diocese simply by virtue of their ability to preach *memoriter*.[96] It is perhaps only to be expected that a prickly Dissenter like John Wynne of Copa'rleni would rail against the 'florid affected discourses' of Anglican preachers,[97] but such strictures were also echoed by Griffith Jones, Llanddowror, who disapproved strongly of those clergymen who preached 'empty speculations, high and lofty or quaint phrases, scholastical or controversial divinity above the reach of ordinary capacities that they can't be the better nor the wiser for it'.[98] Jones was equally scathing in his criticisms of ramshackle Welsh sermons translated from the English tongue, heaped together from a dictionary 'which could make but an unsavoury discourse in any language'.[99] The most dilatory of the Welsh clergy would often substitute stereotyped readings from the Book of Homilies for sermons, whilst others, cast in a Laudian mould, were not totally convinced of the value of preaching. Samuel Williams, the enigmatic rector of Llandyfriog who translated the sermons of Tillotson, Patrick and Beveridge with consummate care in his diaries,[100] could nevertheless still be found bidding a fractious

---

[95] Charles Owen, *Some Account of the Life and Writings of . . . Mr. James Owen* (1709), p. 136.
[96] Bod., Tanner MS. 282, f. 138.
[97] N.L.W., SA/Misc/662, p. 18.
[98] N.L.W., Ottley Papers, no. 100.
[99] Griffith Jones, *Welch Piety* (1740), p.34.
[100] N.L.W., Cwrtmawr MS. 253A.

Dissenter to be 'constant in praying' and 'let preaching go to the Devil'.[101] Attitudes such as these clearly undermined loyalty towards the established church and were later to induce many to respond to the enthusiasm of Methodist preachers.

On the other hand, those Anglican sermons which have survived in manuscript show that many preachers had their fingers on the popular pulse. The urbane and carefully-modulated sermons of Richard Davies, vicar of Ruabon, are lucid and crystal-clear in their exposition.[102] Nothing could be clearer than Robert Hughes's methodical dissection of the Lord's Prayer in a sermon preached in 1710.[103] All of the sermons of Robert Roberts, vicar of Chirk, were, like his written material, characteristically limpid.[104] The sermons contained in Bangor MS. 54 are peppered with Latin, Greek and English phrases, but the style is colloquial and homely, with each point carefully explained in the minister's local dialect.[105] Richard Bulkeley, rector of Llanfechell, was given to fits of absent-mindedness in the pulpit, but his repertoire ranged from insipid homilies to clear, honest and moral discourses.[106] Robert Wynne, vicar of Llanddeiniolen, was a gifted preacher whose wide-ranging choice of texts was matched by his skilful application of scriptural language. His sermons, normally divided into two themes and often preached in serial-form on successive Sundays, were always well-organised, logical and relevant to the needs of his locality.[107]

As far as their content is concerned, Anglican sermons were designed to fulfil certain functions. In the pre-industrial world, when the spoken word was a crucial medium of communication, 'the preaching parson was the great link between the illiterate mass and the political, technical and educated world'.[108] Apart from the spiritual message, there were

[101] N.L.W., Ottley Papers, no. 126.
[102] N.L.W. MS. 7396A; U.C.N.W.L., Bangor MS. 65; C.C.L., Cardiff MS. 2.222.
[103] N.L.W. MS. 79A.
[104] N.L.W. MS. 2771B; Robert Roberts, *A Sacrament Catechism* (1720); *idem*, *A Du-Glott-Exposition* (1730).
[105] U.C.N.W.L., Bangor MS. 54.
[106] Judgment was passed on Bulkeley's sermons by the celebrated diarist, William Bulkeley of Bryn-ddu in Llanfechell, Anglesey. See U.C.N.W.L., Henblas MS. 18A, 27 July 1735; 6 November 1737.
[107] N.L.W., Bodewryd MS. 89B, parts 1–8; Bodewryd MS. 89C, parts 1–4; Bodewryd MS. 90B, parts 1–4.
[108] Peter Laslett, *The World we have Lost* (1965), p.9.

powerful social and political values to be transmitted. The anniversary sermon of Charles I's death, preached annually up and down the land on 30 January, is a prime example.[109] In an annual orgy of masochism, preachers dwelt on the themes of blood-guiltiness and humiliation, and the sinfulness of resistance to the Lord's anointed. Bitter denunciations were made of that devilish and 'bloody villainy' that had cast a blot over the nation and earned her the scorn and contempt of the civilised world. Henceforth each man's conscience bore a 'foul stain' that would not easily be shrugged off.[110]

Casting fearful eyes back to the turmoils of the revolutionary period, clergymen made strenuous efforts to instil the doctrines of non-resistance and passive obedience. Needing to re-define the traditional habits of social discipline, the Restoration church argued that churchmanship and good citizenship were synonymous. Echoes of the hackneyed notion of The Great Chain of Being reinforced these canons, and such tenets were consistently drummed out from the pulpit. Ruthlessly mauling the levelling instinct, Robert Wynne of Llanddeiniolen preached the duty of pious submission as sedulously as his Elizabethan forebears.[111] Buttressing the politico-religious props of a deferential society was a cause close to his heart, and he valiantly strove to confirm the notion of man's subjection to his superiors. 'What is poverty', he asked, 'but having to wear homespun clothes, live on modest fare, eat frugally, drink water from wooden bowls, earn bread by the sweat of one's brow, sit at the lowest end of the table, and tug one's forelock in gentle company?' God had assigned to each man a station in life, and the only real crumb of comfort offered to the poor was that the faithful in their midst would inherit the kingdom of heaven.[112]

---

[109] Helen W. Randall, 'The Rise and Fall of a Martyrology: Sermons on Charles I', *H.L.Q.* X (1947), 135–67.
[110] For some examples see George Hooper, *A Sermon preach'd before the Lords . . . on January 31st 1703–4* (1704); John Tyler, *A Sermon preach'd before the Lords . . . on 30 January 1706–7* (1707); William Fleetwood, *A Sermon preach'd before the Lords . . . on January 30th 1695–6* (1708).
[111] See especially N.L.W., Bodewryd MS. 89B, part 6: fifth sermon (no pagination). Wynne was described by his bishop as being 'sober, civil, pious . . . peaceable . . . well affected to the king, and the established Government'. Bod., Tanner MS. 36, f. 10.
[112] N.L.W., Bodewryd MS. 89B, part 6; cf. Bodewryd MS. 90B, part 2. First Welsh sermon.

Sermons of this nature voiced the unmistakable and deeply-rooted convictions of the church hierarchy and *le pays légal*. Aware of the side on which their bread was buttered, Anglican ministers desperately nourished the view of a static hierarchy which would grant no concessions to religious 'enthusiasm' nor approve of social mobility in an upward direction. Memories of the social upheaval caused by the civil wars, moreover, invested their sermons with greater urgency, and it is clear that their philosophy, preached at grass-roots level, was a crucial element in sustaining a social order in which the church had powerful vested interests. Equally important, too, was the clergyman's task of getting his flock to conceive of the church (even in post-Toleration days) as a monolithic institution to which they owed affection as well as obedience. Nine-tenths of the population of Wales were conditioned to believe that no church was adorned with lights shining more brightly than the present established church;[113] and though many may have realised in their hearts that theirs was a 'rickety and . . . scarcely seaworthy ark' it was still the sole 'vessel of salvation' for the majority of the people.[114] For one thing it was the prime bulwark against the vultures of Dissent and the locusts of Rome, standing foursquare in the face of schism and sub-version.[115] If the church, maintained the canon of St. Asaph, Robert Wynne, was based on a 'solid rock of unity and peace' then she could defy 'the confederate arts of infidels and heretics, and boldly pronounce that the gates of hell' would not prevail against her.[116]

Establishing godly discipline was also a major aim of the Anglican clergy. Although few sermons reflected contemporary behaviour in detail, most preachers descanted on the general theme of sin. Moral precepts and ethical values loomed large as preachers asked that earnest endeavour might replace back-sliding, compromise and wilful sinfulness. John Griffith, the lugubrious rector of Llanelian, preached a stern moral code,

[113] See the effusive sermon in U.C.N.W.L., Bangor MS. 362. fifth sermon (no pagination).
[114] Alan Smith, *The Established Church and Popular Religion, 1750–1850* (1971), p. 13.
[115] For some examples of anti-Popish sermons see N.L.W. MS. 68A; N.L.W. MS. 7396A; N.L.W., Bodewryd MS. 89B, part 7, first sermon; U.C.N.W.L., Bangor MS. 362, eighth sermon.
[116] Robert Wynne, *Unity and Peace the support of Church and State* (1704), title-page.

inveighing against carnal lusts, avarice, vain swearing and Sabbath-breaking, but constantly despaired of having any effect on his flock. Only the patience of Job, a fierce determination to win souls, and a dignified readiness to withstand abuse enabled him to continue to repeat his warnings.[117] Harping on similar themes, Robert Wynne of Llanddeiniolen was especially vexed by the profanation of the Sabbath, and he was joined by others who underlined the fate of those who served Mammon on the Day of the Lord.[118]

Strenuous efforts were made from the pulpit to eliminate vain swearing and excessive drinking. Cursing was variously described as the most 'reckless', 'odious' and 'atrocious' of sins,[119] and such was its prevalence that clerics, working on the principle that men were more likely to bite their tongues than open their purses, advocated the use of a sliding scale of fines to punish loose language.[120] In their strivings towards reformation, efforts were made to educate men to accept drink as a gift from God but to recoil from drunkenness as the snare of the Devil.[121] A graphic attack launched by Robert Wynne on the evils of drunkenness must surely have been based on a chapter of misfortunes which befell some of his errant parishioners.[122] Wynne described the scene when a drunken husbandman arrived home empty-handed, having squandered his money in the local tavern, to face his tearful wife and starving children who, fearful of his foul temper, hid beneath their beds until morning. But not only was a surfeit of drink a disruptive influence within the household, it also brought further disaster in its train: sued by grasping innkeepers, the wayward husbandman was plunged into bankruptcy, thrust into prison, and finally lowered into an early grave.

Having stressed moral imperatives, preachers proceeded to exhort their flocks to repent their sins and to remind them of

[117] U.C.N.W.L., Bangor MS. 95: sermons preached in the 1680s (no pagination).
[118] N.L.W., Bodewryd MS. 90B, part 4, second sermon (no pagination); N.L.W. MS. 2771B, pp. 34–5; N.L.W., Bangor/MC/408, pp. 13–15; Bangor/MC/413 (no pagination).
[119] U.C.N.W.L., Bangor MS. 54 (no pagination); N.L.W. MS. 2771B, p. 34; N.L.W. MS. 12444B, p. 57; Bodewryd MS. 90B, part 3, pp. 53–112; Bangor/MC/409, pp. 1–7.
[120] N.L.W. MS. 7396A, p. 106; U.C.N.W.L., Bangor MS. 54 (no pagination).
[121] See, for instance, N.L.W. MS. 75A and Bangor/MC/413.
[122] N.L.W., Bodewryd MS. 89B, part 6, second sermon (no pagination).

the dangers that confronted the unregenerate. Sermons on mortality—frequently preached and always foreboding in tone—emphasised the frail and tenuous existence of man, the certainty of the 'latter end', the terrible nature of Judgment Day, and the vastness of eternity.[123] A contemporary squib portrayed the typical Welsh clergyman as a 'Levite [who] fodders the poor Taffies with some melancholy tear-fetching story about a grim fellow called Death, who ambles folks on his back into another world'.[124] Romans vi 23 ('For the wages of sin is death') was a favourite text, and ministers were swift to remind men how suddenly and unexpectedly they might be dispatched to the tribunal of heaven: 'a hair in the cup, or a tile from the house, the trip of the toe, or the malice of an adversary, may dispatch hence the most daring bravado of all'.[125] The awfulness of sin, the vanity of earthly joys, the brevity of human existence, and the paramount need for repentance were themes which stocked most clerical repertoires.

The greatest stress of all, however, was laid on the terms of salvation. An anonymous clergyman in the diocese of Bangor articulated a frequent refrain in drumming out the message that religion which confined itself to outward formalities and artifices was no basis on which to build hopes of salvation.[126] Robert Wynne of Llanddeiniolen emphasised the crucial importance of man's soul, focusing in particular on the grace that abounded in the gift of the Holy Spirit. The sermons of Robert Morgan, rector of Llanddyfnan, were mostly prosaic save for those which called for a keener awareness of the state of the soul and the overwhelming necessity of regeneration.[127] The texts of Richard Davies of Ruabon were invariably Christocentric, Robert Roberts of Chirk preached Christ as 'the star of salvation', Lewis Pryse, rector of Llanfair Caereinion, urged his hearers to place their faith in Christ as the 'chief prince of salvation', and a host of others were consistent in their stress on Christ as the Redeemer.[128] But none

[123] N.L.W., Bodewryd MS. 89C, parts 4 and 5; Bodewryd MS. 90B, parts 1 and 4; Bangor/MC/416; C.C.L., Cardiff MS. 2.225.
[124] William Richards, *Wallography*, p. 104.
[125] N.L.W., Bodewryd MS. 89C, part 5, p. 163.
[126] N.L.W., Bangor/MC/413; cf. some of the sermons in Bangor/MC/411.
[127] U.C.N.W.L., Henblas MS. 9A; 10A.
[128] U.C.N.W.L., Bangor MS. 65; N.L.W. MS. 2771B, pp. 1–30; N.L.W., Peniarth MS. 325A (no pagination); N.L.W. MS. 10995A (no pagination).

of these preachers could match the impression which Griffith Jones, Llanddowror, made on his hearers. At first sight, his early sermons seem unremarkable:[129] simple, direct, soaked with copious scriptural references, one scarcely detects in them the throbbing pulse of fervent evangelicalism. But a closer reading reveals Jones's ability to drive points home by sheer repetition and insistence. Unrelenting in his stress on man's sin and the need for unqualified repentance, thriving before enormous audiences that hung on his every word, Griffith Jones's direct, sonorous and rhetorical style, allied with his 'eloquent delivery' and 'melodious voice',[130] made him one of the most effective savers of souls in pre-Methodist Wales.

III. DISSENTING PREACHING

From the beginnings of the Protestant Reformation, preaching had occupied a position at the very core of Protestant propagation. Since Calvin's time, its importance had been central to all puritan teaching. 'For', Calvin declared, 'among the many excellent gifts with which God has adorned the human race, it is a singular privilege that he deigns to consecrate to himself the mouths and tongues of men in order that his voice may resound in them.'[131] Puritans believed the pulpit to be the chief means of communication and many considered the sermon to be the most attractive and popular part of public worship.[132] For preaching, they insisted, was ordained by God as a means of bringing men to salvation. Nine out of every ten 'caught the first hints of their vocation' by listening to a sermon, and by constantly hearing good preaching they 'made their calling sure'.[133] Howell Powell of Beiliheulog went so far as to claim that without preaching and hearing there could be no religion,[134] and there is no doubt that this sentiment had been voiced on countless occasions since the earliest days of

---

[129] See N.L.W. MSS. 24B, 85A, 770A, 4495A, 5920A.
[130] *H.P.N.*, p. 315. See also Thomas Charles's description of Jones's preaching techniques in John Peter and R. J. Pryse, *Enwogion Cymru* (4 vols., n.d.), III, 78–9.
[131] John T. McNeill (ed.), John Calvin, *Institutes of the Christian Religion* (2 vols., 1961), II, 1018.
[132] The best introduction to Puritan preaching is William Haller, *The Rise of Puritanism* (1938).
[133] Perry Miller, *The New England Mind: The Seventeenth Century* (3rd ed., 1967), p. 296.
[134] Howell Powell, *Y Gwrandawr* (1709), sig. A2r.

puritanism. Dissenting ministers in this period therefore saw themselves as 'stars in the right hand of Christ', yielding to none in their efforts to carry the Gospel into 'this benighted and frozen world'.[135]

The penury which crippled the established church was also a permanent obstacle to the evangelising programme of Dissenting ministers, particularly in the pre-Toleration period. Many ejected ministers were reduced to a condition of extreme poverty and they, together with their impoverished successors, were forced to draw on the funds made available by the Congregational and Presbyterian Boards in order to subsist in their own localities and to embark on preaching tours.[136] Dissenting congregations were also expected to contribute towards the subsistence of their minister in order to enable him to carry out his public and private duties, to maintain his family, and to advance his education.[137] But some ministers clearly hovered barely above the poverty line, sustained, like James Owen of Oswestry, by 'a small pittance'.[138] Marmaduke Matthews of Swansea 'lived above the world', depending for his subsistence on 'the piety of his children' and the largesse of relatives and friends.[139] Throughout the eighteenth century, Edmund Jones of Pontypool was said to live 'very low' on £10 per annum, most of which he spent on books or gave away to the needy.[140] Generally, however, with the passing of the Toleration Act, Welsh Dissent began to breed its own peculiar brand of gentleman-preachers.[141] Lacking the benefits of parochial endowments, Dissenting ministers needed to be as self-sufficient as possible. By the early-eighteenth century, some were men of private means, holding freehold or tenant land. Many were heirs to a substantial patrimony whilst others

---

[135] Charles Owen, *Some Account*, p. 115.

[136] Alexander Gordon, *Freedom after Ejection* (1917); Isaac Thomas, 'Y Gronfa Gynulleidfaol ac Annibynwyr Cymru', *Y Cofiadur*, 28 (1958), 3–39; Walter D. Jeremy, *The Presbyterian Fund and Dr. Daniel Williams's Trust* (1885).

[137] Periodic reminders were issued to congregations, notably *Rhesswmmau Yscrythurawl, yn profi mai Dyledswydd pob maeth o Wrandawyr . . . yw cyfrannu . . . tuag at Gynhaliaeth cyssurus eu Gweinidogion* (1693) and Jeremy Owen, *Traethawd i brofi ac i gymmell ar yr holl Eglwysi y Ddyledswydd Fawr Efangylaidd o weddio dros Weinidogion* (1733).

[138] Charles Owen, op. cit., p. 77.

[139] Calamy, II, 733.

[140] *H.P.N.*, pp. 405–6.

[141] R. Tudur Jones, *Hanes Annibynwyr Cymru* (1966), p. 107.

found that a wise marriage was conducive to greater financial stability. Many were craftsmen of independent means, while others kept their heads above water by becoming schoolmasters or teachers at Dissenting academies.

The second major obstacle confronting Dissenting preachers was the series of persecuting acts which comprised the Clarendon Code. The period 1660–88 is generally known as the 'Age of Persecution', the brunt of which was borne by 'unconformed' puritans.[142] The implementation of these acts, though draconic in some parts of the country (especially at times of national crisis), was fitful since much depended on the zeal and diligence of local magistrates. With the passing of the Declaration of Indulgence in 1672, Dissenting ministers were able to organise on a more permanent basis by acquiring licences to preach in private houses and chapels. Many ejected ministers had already established unlawful conventicles in homes, barns and caves, and were now able to take advantage of this brief respite. But more rigorous persecution was still to follow until the Toleration Act of 1689 began to persuade society that persecution would not make men Anglicans any more than the puritan sword could coerce men to renounce their allegiance to the church.

Generally, however, the story is one of heroic efforts by Welshmen who, under the shadow of economic and political disabilities, formed that faithful band of preachers whom Joseph Alleine liked to call 'the men of Macedonia'.[143] Such men were as industrious as bees: 'preach these fellows do every where', muttered the disgruntled bishop of St. David's, William Lucy, in 1673.[144] In the forefront of early Congregational preachers stood Henry Maurice, erstwhile conformist, who had re-entered the Dissenting fold in 1671.[145] From the end of 1672 until his premature death ten years later, Maurice was the major propagator of the Gospel in Breconshire and neighbouring counties. Courageous and indefatigable, his fame as a preacher spread so widely that poor people were wont to travel

---

[142] See especially Gordon R. Cragg, *Puritanism in the period of the Great Persecution* (1957) and Thomas Richards, *Wales under the Penal Code, 1662–87* (1925).
[143] Charles Stanford, *Joseph Alleine: his Companions and Times* (1861), p. 308.
[144] Bod., Tanner MS. 146, f. 113.
[145] Thomas Richards, 'Henry Maurice: Piwritan ac Annibynwr', *Y Cofiadur*, 5–6 (1928), 15–67.

far to hear him.[146] Equally tireless was Hugh Owen of Bronclydwr, a humble, self-effacing minister of low estate who ministered to five or six meeting places within a twenty mile radius of his home in Merioneth. In spite of poor health, he braved all sorts of weather and travelling conditions—often riding at night—in order to spread, in a three-monthly circuit, religious knowledge in the neighbouring counties of Caernarvonshire and Montgomeryshire.[147] The doyen of Welsh Congregational ministers, however, was Stephen Hughes, the 'apostle of Carmarthenshire'. A constant and tireless traveller, Hughes retained eight churches under his pastoral charge and was often obliged to ride eight or ten miles between sermons on Sundays.[148] Although Hughes was an avowed Dissenter, he was also an occasional conformist who was prepared to woo the 'sober part of the gentry' so that he might preach in parish churches which 'were much thronged by the vast numbers that came to hear him from the neighbouring parishes'.[149] His most enduring work, however, was as mentor and guide to promising young Calvinist ministers; at his feet sat James Owen, William Evans, David Penry, Daniel Phillips and others who were later to build on his early missionary work.[150]

Singleness of purpose and indefatigability characterised the careers of so many Dissenting preachers. Even among the second generation of Congregational ministers, Edmund Jones, 'the old Prophet', showed himself to be as restless a spirit as his predecessors, tramping the Principality with boundless energy and noting in his diary the text and place of each sermon.[151] By ministering, with the aid of two colleagues, to the needs of five churches in the upper reaches of the rivers Aeron and Teifi, Philip Pugh, the staunch Calvinist of Cilgwyn, was able to muster a thousand hearers by 1715.[152] Among the Baptists, that rigorous and enterprising evangelist, William Jones of

---

[146] See extracts from Maurice's diary reproduced in *H.P.N.*, pp. 211–8.

[147] Calamy, II, 710–2. Owen was also described as 'a burning and shining Light in a dark cold and barren country; one eminently self-denying, and mortified to the things of this world'. William Tong, *An Account of the Life and Death of ... Matthew Henry* (1716), p. 277.

[148] Calamy, II, 718; *H.P.N.*, p. 222.

[149] Hughes set out his doctrinal position in *Gwaith ... Mr. Rees Prichard* (Part IV, 1672), p. 577; Calamy, II, 718.

[150] Each of these ministers is noted in *D.W.B.*

[151] N.L.W. MSS. 7022A–7030A.

[152] Dr. Williams's Library MS. 34, f. 138.

Cilymaenllwyd, built up a network of Baptist causes in south-west Wales almost single-handed.[153] Among his successors, Enoch Francis, a gentle, serene preacher, sought to cover the Baptist chapels of south Wales on an annual preaching tour and still found time to preach in Presbyterian chapels, where he was always accorded a warm welcome.[154] Methodist evangelists, too, were thankful for his labours, and on lamenting Francis's death in 1740, Howel Harris prayed 'that God would repair his loss among the Baptists, and not suffer Satan to make havoc'.[155] By sheer diligence, application and enthusiasm, Dissenting ministers of this period exercised an influence which was entirely disproportionate to their numbers.

IV. DISSENTING SERMONS

The 'plain style' of the Dissenting preachers lay at the very heart of the puritan tradition. Deriving its impetus and justification from the logic of Ramus, this particular style was deliberately cultivated until it became part and parcel of the pulpit technique of Dissent.[156] Verbal gymnastics were eschewed since the basic aim was to reveal God's will in intelligible forms.[157] Nor were involved and mysterious doctrines thought suitable. 'He is a good minister', argued Matthew Henry, 'who fills not your heads with airy notions, nor troubles your minds with matters of doubtful dispensation.'[158] Welsh Dissenting sermons were thus a judicious admixture of erudition, clarity and common sense. The keynote was always explicitness, and whenever ministers found themselves increasingly immersed in abstruse doctrinal matters, as did a knot of refractory Baptists in the 1720s, they were swiftly brought to heel and told to preach 'plain, clear gospel, and not puzzle the people with inexplicable mysteries'.[159]

---

[153] William Jones is noticed in *D.W.B.*
[154] Joshua Thomas, *Hanes y Bedyddwyr* (1778), p. 386.
[155] Tom Beynon, *Howell Harris's Visits to Pembrokeshire* (1966), p. 25.
[156] Perry Miller, op. cit., pp. 331–62.
[157] Richard Steele of Hanmer urged that 'we may not fill our sermons with sapless niceties, impertinent quotations, choleric reflections, or with that unquiet controversial divinity . . . which hardly ever produce any effect, save exasperation'. *The Husbandmans Calling* (1668), sig. A4v.
[158] Matthew Henry, *A Sermon preach'd at the Funeral of . . . James Owen* (1706), p. 29.
[159] Joshua Thomas, *A History of the Baptist Association in Wales, 1650–1790* (1795), p. 43.

Essentially practical men, Welsh Dissenters made a point of preaching plainly and methodically, always pitching their discourses within the capacity of the meanest.[160] Great care was taken in the preparation of sermons, and if the net result was a seemingly endless reiteration of numbered points, objections and answers, this was precisely because it was known that subdividing a sermon had distinct mnemonic advantages. Dissenters appreciated the pedagogic value of adhering to the traditional pattern of dividing sermons under the sub-headings of doctrine, reasons and uses, and they were perfectly prepared to sacrifice a certain measure of literary merit in order to ensure that their hearers were able to grasp the issues involved. 'We should not', urged James Owen, 'offer to God the half and the lame, or that which costs us nothing . . . nor crude and un-digested matter to our people.'[161] Delivering a sermon 'raw and undigested' was reckoned a cardinal sin,[162] for pulpit material needed to be well-organised in order to facilitate note-taking. Members of congregations, especially heads of households, were expected to become experienced and pro-ficient note-takers during sermons. Other members of the household, particularly the illiterate, were also expected to follow the sermon, to memorise the salient parts, and to reveal their knowledge when the *paterfamilias* came to rehearse his household in the major points of the minister's discourse.

Dissenting sermons were consistently drenched in torrents of scriptural language and references. The Bible was the 'heavenly armoury'[163] from which ministers selected appro-priate weapons to press home their mission. Most of them were absolute masters of the scriptures, taking delight in interlacing their sermons with biblical threads. James Owen's proficiency in the scriptures was so remarkable that he could, when tested, quote chapter and verse at the drop of a hat.[164] In a sermon preached at Llangloffan in 1729, Enoch Francis quoted

[160] For descriptions of the style of Stephen Hughes, see Calamy, II, 718; for James Owen, see Charles Owen, op. cit., p. 72; for Morgan Griffiths of Hengoed, see William Richards, *The Welsh Nonconformists' Memorial* (1820), pp. 257–8.
[161] Charles Owen, op. cit., p. 72.
[162] Matthew Henry, *The Life of the Rev. Philip Henry*, ed. J. B. Williams (1825), p. 193.
[163] Jeremy Owen, *Traethawd i brofi*, p. 82.
[164] Charles Owen, op. cit., p. 71.

references or made allusions to over 150 verses from the Bible.[165] Similarly, Stephen Hughes's *forte* was his ability to weave into his sermons familiar images drawn from everyday occurrences, from nature and from the environment, thus enabling his rural audiences to feel some identity with his pastoral analogies, homely comparisons and measured asides.[166]

Dissenting ministers demanded strict ethical behaviour and high moral standards from their flocks. Admonitions and exhortations to live moral and pious lives were rife, and sinners were left in no doubt that persistent delinquency would lead to excommunication from chapel society. 'The end of our ministry', claimed James Owen, 'is the destruction of sin.'[167] Sin, thundered Abel Francis, was the worst evil in the world, blacker than the devil and hotter than hell.[168] No minister worth his salt could ignore the deeds of unrepentant sinners who, hardening their hearts against God, worshipped the golden calf. Hugh Owen's dying advice to his followers was to 'beware of worldliness, for I fear, least the world, like a canker, should eat up all the good that is in many, and leave their souls like dry shells'.[169] Faithful attention was thus paid to eliminating those sins which had provided perennial themes for preachers of all religious persuasions. However, profanation of the Sabbath, drunkenness and vain swearing commanded much less attention from Dissenting preachers since it was generally agreed that standards of discipline within their congregations were higher than those of their Anglican counterparts. Moral imperatives preached from Dissenting pulpits were more often directed to the world at large, though reminders of the nearness of mortality were designed for each individual. 'We must forsake sin', warned James Owen, 'before sin forsakes us.'[170] Preaching dolefully on the inevitability of death and Judgment Day, the Dissenting preacher, boot-maker-cum-poet of Tre Wen, Jenkin Thomas, and the tender-conscienced minister of Pencader, James Lewis, were both

---

[165] Enoch Francis, *Gwaith a Gwobr Ffyddlon Weinidogion yr Efengyl* (1729).
[166] For some examples see *Gwaith Mr. Rees Prichard* (part 3, 1672), sig. A4v; *Cyfarwydd-deb i'r Anghyfarwydd*, p. 145; cf. Calamy, II, 719.
[167] Charles Owen, op. cit., p. 133.
[168] N.L.W. MS. 9913A. tenth sermon (no pagination).
[169] *H.P.N.*, p. 283; cf. 'Cyfarwyddiadau' Thomas William of Mynydd Bach. N.L.W. MS. 368A (no pagination).
[170] Charles Owen, op. cit., p. 59.

ominously terse in reminding their hearers of the reckoning that awaited all men.[171]

In the final analysis, Dissenting preachers were obsessed with the need to save souls. However forceful their discourses on morality and their forebodings on mortality might be, such precepts were secondary to the central issues of salvation and regeneration. The purpose of the sermon, insisted Howell Powell, was not to satisfy the idle fancies of men but to save their souls.[172] The conversion of 'one poor sinner' was thought to be 'worth an age's preaching'.[173] Sermons were thus not merely a string of moral platitudes or tedious exhortations to guard against the sniping Devil. It is a fallacy to suppose that Dissenters were obsessed with the rational and intellectual content of their sermons. It is equally wrong to suppose that Methodist preachers were the first to dedicate themselves to the task of penetrating the heart through the medium of the spoken word. The foremost Dissenting preachers of this period were painstakingly searching in their discourses and skilled practitioners in the art of touching the affections. Invariably preaching Christ and his merits, Henry Maurice retained 'a wonderful skill in unravelling the very thoughts and inward workings of men's hearts, and was very particular and convincing as well as affectionate in his applications to the consciences of his hearers'.[174] Vavasor Powell used similes and parables in inviting sinners to Christ, while Stephen Hughes seldom preached 'without melting into tears, which often drew tears from his auditors'.[175]

Many sermons adhered closely to the Calvinist formula of election, vocation, justification, sanctification and glorification. But the overwhelming emphasis was invariably placed on the rôle of Christ as Redeemer and the manner and process of regeneration. Jeremy Owen rejoiced in the frequency with which preachers chose 'awakening texts' to explain to sinners the necessity of a rebirth to facilitate their entry into the

[171] N.L.W. MS. 368A (no pagination); N.L.W. MS. 9913A, eighteenth sermon.
[172] *Y Gwrandawr*, p. 8.
[173] Charles Owen, op. cit., p. 72.
[174] *H.P.N.*, pp. 220–1.
[175] Anon., *The Life and Death of Mr. Vavasor Powell* (1671), pp. 108–9; Calamy, II, 718.

kingdom of heaven.[176] Dissenting ministers knew that regeneration could be achieved by a moving of the spirit, and that their discourses were thus invaluable media for the Holy Spirit. Most vital of all was their emphasis on the atoning work of Christ, stressing the rôle of revelation in the inner recesses of man's soul. Preaching to a wet-eyed congregation at Rhydwilym in 1723, Enoch Francis urged his hearers to anatomise their souls, to probe the symptoms and effects of grace, and to rejoice in the knowledge that salvation was available to sinners whose repentance and faith qualified them for a new life.[177] Preaching memorably on the latter part of Colossians iii 11 ('but Christ is all, and in all') at Mynydd Bach in 1722, William Davies stressed the crucial process of regeneration, the need for a lively and fruitful faith, and the joy and contentment of those who inherited the kingdom of Christ.[178] He and his colleagues would have agreed wholeheartedly with the anonymous Dissenting preacher who insisted that of all the fools on earth, the greatest fool was the unregenerate man.[179]

There is no doubt that Dissenting preachers retained great pride in their rôle as converting ministers. 'Converting preachers', sang Vavasor Powell, 'shall shine for they are wise.'[180] It is true that many of their sermons lacked the spontaneity and infectious enthusiasm of early Methodist discourses, but the vast bulk of them succeeded in probing depths of feeling in mind and soul, touching the affections and exhorting inwardly. And though most Dissenting ministers were self-effacing men, they took great pride in 'capturing' sinners to the cause of Christ. Indeed, old Dissent seldom forgot its successes. Those 'great numbers' whom Stephen Hughes 'reclaimed from their sinful and wicked ways' remained true to their newly-acquired faith and told their sons and daughters of the charismatic qualities of the 'apostle of

---

[176] *Traethawd i brofi*, p. 99.
[177] N.L.W. MS. 10589A (no pagination). According to Joshua Thomas, Francis's sermons seldom failed to move his audience to tears. *Hanes y Bedyddwyr*, p. 386.
[178] N.L.W. MS. 368A (no pagination). For further collections of Dissenting sermons see N.L.W. MS. 5465A; N.L.W. MS. 11076A; N.L.W. MS. 12298A; N.L.W., E. Francis Davies, Blaendyffryn, MS. 216.
[179] N.L.W. MS. 75A, p.71.
[180] *The Life and Death of Mr. Vavasor Powell*, p. 97.

Carmarthenshire'.[181] Some of the igneous sermons on regeneration, preached by David Lewis at Henllan Amgoed,
stood out vividly in Matthias Maurice's mind over twenty
years later.[182] Edmund Jones of Pontypool catalogued the
experiences of those in his locality (including amongst them
the 'new birth' of his father) whom Dissenting preachers had
set on the right road to Christ.[183] It is of no small significance
that Evan Williams, the Congregational minister and influential revivalist of Cwmllynfell, publicly denied that Howel
Harris was his 'spiritual father'. When Harris claimed him as
his 'convert and son in the faith', Williams refuted the claim,
insisting that his most powerful 'convictions and awakenings'
had come from hearing the sometime Congregational pastor of
Llanedi, Lewis Jones.[184] Evan Williams had clearly done
something more than establish the root of his conversion: he
had protected the identity and achievements of old Dissent.

[181] Calamy, II, 718. For an example of how Hughes's conversions passed into
popular mythology see the forged letters in *Yr Ymofynnydd*, 1871–2, *passim*.
[182] Matthias Maurice, *Y Wir Eglwys* (1727), pp. 41–2.
[183] Edmund Jones, *A Geographical, Historical and Religious Account of the Parish of
Aberystruth* (1779), pp. 112–60.
[184] Edmund Jones, *A Sermon preached . . . occasioned by the death of Mr. Evan
Williams . . . to which is added some Account of his Life and Death* (1750), p. 97.

II

WELSH PRINTED BOOKS:
CLASSIFICATION AND MOTIVES

In 1716, Robert Lloyd, rector of Hirnant, printed his Welsh translation of the sermon *The Christian's Way to Heaven* (1700) with one avowed purpose: that it might dwell longer in the minds and hearts of men.[1] There were others like he who clearly felt that the transmission of Reformation truths by oral delivery of sermons was, by itself, an inadequate means of moulding the true Christian. Some, like Griffith Jones, Llanddowror, became convinced that 'without catechising . . . preaching is in a manner lost and thrown away'.[2] The inculcation of the basic Christian axioms was thus one crucial prerequisite. But experience also taught other reformers that the printed book was an indispensable adjunct to preaching. In short, they argued that oral transmission and the reading of printed books were two sides of the same coin. Many seventeenth-century puritans, however, were persuaded that the eye 'took in sentiments more effectually than the ears'.[3] In a memorable observation made in 1621, Samuel Ward claimed that sermons were 'as showers of rain that water for the instant, books are as snow that lies longer on the earth'.[4]

Religious reformers in Wales, too, were learning from experience that a lack of basic grounding in Christian truths among parishioners meant that too many sermons went in through one ear and out through the other. Taking the maxim *Vox audita perit, sed littera scripta manebit* as his touchstone, David Maurice, vicar of Abergele, argued that the eye was a more faithful guide than the ear since it committed the Word not

---

[1] Robert Lloyd, *Ffordd y Cristion i'r Nefoedd* (1716), p. 3.
[2] Griffith Jones, *Welch Piety* (1740), p. 16.
[3] One notable example was Richard Baxter. F. J. Powicke, 'The Reverend Richard Baxter's Last Treatise', *Bulletin of John Rylands Library*, X (1926), 182.
[4] Quoted in H. S. Bennett, *English Books and Readers, 1603 to 1640* (1970), p. 114.

only to the memory but also to the heart as well.[5] While not for one moment belittling the crucial rôle of preaching, Welsh religious reformers realised that the printed book offered the reader the opportunity to pore over it at will, to refer backwards and forwards, and to ponder and meditate upon its contents. 'Faith cometh by hearing' was a cardinal and ever-popular tenet, but without printed books the Reformation could not possibly achieve its full realisation in Wales or elsewhere. The educationalist, Griffith Jones, understood this point better than most. In a fiery dispute with Howel Harris over the most effective techniques of evangelisation, Jones insisted that 'all should be stirred up to read else they may come to follow their experiences and not the Word'.[6] Protestantism, after all, is a religion of the Word. There is an air of finality about the way William Lloyd, bishop of St. Asaph, succinctly summed up the whole argument:

> Is not preaching enough, what need we reading?
> Is not one eye enough, what need we two?[7]

One of the most vital features of this period—so often unrecognised—is the astonishing increase in the number of printed books in Welsh. From 1546 to 1660, *circa* 108 separate Welsh titles were published.[8] But from 1660 to 1730 at least 545 separate Welsh titles were published, that is, over five times as many titles within seventy years as had been published during the previous 115 years. It must also be borne in mind that many books, particularly the products of the provincial presses, have vanished without trace. This is particularly true of the more ephemeral literature—almanacs and ballads especially—which, though avidly read, were seldom carefully bound and were consequently the most perishable commodities. This hidden dimension is not expressed in the following table which is based only on those books which have been seen or are

[5] David Maurice, *Cwnffwrdd ir Gwan Gristion* (1700), p. vi. For similar evidence see the comments of John Jones, curate of Capel Garmon, N.L.W., SA/QA/3, and the ballad-monger, Richard Parry, *Dihuniad Cysgadur* (1723), p. 5.
[6] Tom Beynon, 'Howell Harris' Visits to Kidwelly and District (1743–1746)', *C.C.H.M.C.*, XXV (1940), 20.
[7] N.L.W. MS. 11313D, p. 46.
[8] I am indebted to Professor R. Geraint Gruffydd for supplying me with statistics for the period before 1660.

known to have existed:

Decade	Number of books published	Percentage of the total figure (i.e. 545)
1660–1669	10	1·8
1670–1679	39	7·2
1680–1689	47	8·6
1690–1699	43	7·9
1700–1709	76	14·0
1710–1719	150	27·5
1720–1730	180	33·0
Total	545	

With the exception of the decade 1690–9, the number of Welsh books multiplied in each successive decade. Ten books (1·8 per cent of the total number of books published in the whole period) were published between 1660 and 1669, a comparative dearth that reflects twin constraints: the severe licensing laws and the political and religious disabilities imposed on Dissenters. Thirty-nine books (7·2 per cent) were published during the following decade, 1670–9, an upsurge which was largely the result of the formation of the Welsh Trust and, in particular, of the unselfish labours of Stephen Hughes. This impetus was maintained during the next decade, 1680–9, when 47 books (8·6 per cent) were published. Four fewer books (7·9 per cent) emerged from the press during the following decade, 1690–9. This minor setback, however, was essentially short-term, and it is significant that 74·5 per cent of all the books published in this period appeared after 1700. The crucial factor behind this acceleration was the relaxation of the licensing laws in 1695 which opened the way for the growth of the provincial press. As a result, the dramatic increase in the publication of Welsh books after 1700 was partly a consequence of the patronage of the S.P.C.K., but mainly the fruit of publishing activity at Shrewsbury from 1696 onwards, at Trefhedyn from 1718, and at Carmarthen in the period after 1721. Seventy-six books (14 per cent) were published between 1700 and 1709, and this number nearly doubled in the next decade, reaching 150 (27·5 per cent), and rising again to 180 (33 per cent) between 1720 and 1730.

TABLE ONE

Decade	Bibles (whole or in part)	Book of Common Prayer and 39 Articles	Psalms and Matins	Catechisms and Explanations	Didactic and Devotional	Controversial Books	Religious Verse	Almanacs	Religious History	Miscellanea
1660–69		2	1		4	1			1	1
1670–79	3	1	2	3	18	6	2		3	1
1680–89		3	2	4	17	2	4	11		4
1690–99	3		1	4	15	3	4	12		1
1700–09		3	2	6	37	4	2	19	1	2
1710–19	3	6	5	10	54	10	38	18	2	4
1720–30	2	4	5	5	60	8	67	21	2	6
Total:	11	19	18	32	205	34	117	81	9	19
% of Total No. of Books	2%	3·5%	3·3%	5·9%	37·6%	6·2%	21·5%	14·9%	1·6%	3·5%

Of the 545 books published, at least 260 (47 per cent) were works translated from English. This figure is probably an underestimate since it is not always easy to discover whether or not some Welsh books were original works or translations.[9] Welsh literary critics have tended to bemoan the fact that so much Welsh literature of the seventeenth century was translated work. But translations were evidently the easiest means of getting saving knowledge to Welsh people in the shortest possible time. Moreover, there were powerful factors militating against the publication of original works. In spite of the successes of Welsh Renaissance scholars in the Tudor and early Stuart periods, it is clear that there was still no guarantee that the Welsh language was universally accepted as a medium of intellectual discussion. In terms of patronage by the gentry, the Welsh language had most certainly lost ground by the Restoration period and, even at this advanced stage, there were many who were still not persuaded that it was a suitable medium for theological controversy or politico-legal protest. Thomas Williams, vicar of Llanrwst, was voicing a widespread anxiety when he claimed in 1691 that his mother tongue was bound in captivity and wanting in many things pertinent to learning.[10]

Moreover, the attitude of charitable bodies towards the Welsh language was an open secret: it was, at best, a nuisance and, at worst, a pernicious relic of barbarism. It is plain that the policy of the Welsh Trust and the S.P.C.K. of distributing religious literature in Welsh was essentially a short-term expedient calculated to save the souls of those monoglot Welshmen who were poised on the brink of everlasting damnation; they believed their more enduring function to be the rearing of a new generation of English-speakers in the network of charity schools which they had established in the Principality. Many, indeed, were convinced that the Welsh would soon 'entertain the speech of the conquerors', having seen their 'lingua . . . English'd out of Wales, as Latin was barbarously Goth'd out of Italy'.[11] Prominent religious

---

[9] I have simply relied on personal judgement when in doubt.
[10] Thomas Williams, *Ymadroddion Bucheddol ynghylch Marwolaeth* (1691), sig. A2r.
[11] Jeremy Owen, *The Goodness and Severity of God* (1717), p. 9; William Richards, *Wallography* (1682), p. 63.

reformers in Wales were not slow to voice their misgivings about this policy. Always alive to social realities, Stephen Hughes knew that his countrymen could be turned into readers of the English tongue overnight only by divine intervention. 'But O Lord', he pleaded, 'how could this come about? unless you were to fashion miracles?'[12] Rees Prydderch of Ystradwallter stated flatly that efforts to persuade monoglot Welsh children to rehearse set prayers in English smacked heavily of the *opus operatum* of Popery,[13] whilst John Morgan, vicar of Matchin, pungently railed against teaching poor children 'in a foreign tongue . . . for . . . they are as wise after five or six years' schooling as they were before, whereas were they taught in the mother's tongue, it would take but little time and charges'.[14]

In spite of these problems, Welsh books were published with increasing regularity throughout this period. The bulk of them were religious, didactic and utilitarian in character, and brief, plain and succinct in presentation.[15] From the very outset it was felt that books were needed to supply the groundwork of Christian worship. Churchmen and Dissenters alike would have needed no reminding that the Protestant faith was still not a rock-hard, indestructible force in Wales, and that not only had the practice of formal worship broken down during the revolutionary period but that there were also many uncommitted and uninstructed Welshmen still to be effectively won over to the Christian faith. Necessity thus forced them to place major emphasis on the basic principles of Protestantism. Eleven editions of the Welsh Bible (whole or in part) were published in this period, together with nineteen issues of the Welsh Prayer Book (including three separate issues of the Thirty Nine Articles). Eighteen issues of the Psalms in prose and metre (including two translations of the Book of Matins) were published. Crucial, too, to the performance of ecclesiastical duties were the thirty-two issues of the catechism (including explanations of the catechism) which were designed as aids to

---

[12] Stephen Hughes (ed.), *Tryssor i'r Cymru* (1677), sig. A6v.
[13] William Evans (ed.), Rees Prydderch, *Gemmeu Doethineb* (1714), p. 131.
[14] N.L.W. MS. 17B, pp. 12–13. The impracticability and absurdity of the language policy within charity schools was best revealed, however, by Griffith Jones, Llanddowror. See *Welch Piety* (1740), pp. 29–62.
[15] See Table One.

both clergymen and laymen. In all, bibles, prayer books, psalms and catechisms comprised 14·7 per cent of the total number of Welsh books published in this period. Even so, these books were not published solely to facilitate the smooth running of church services. Indeed, the basic single unit at which the vast majority of these books—together with the didactic and devotional books and books of religious verse—were aimed was the family. The general pattern in early modern Europe was for privileged classes to have large families whilst the poorer classes had fewer children.[16] On average, the mean household size in England from the earliest period of calculation up to 1911 has been estimated as remaining fairly constant at 4·75.[17] Some examples in this period come fairly close to that mark.[18] The mean size of households in the diocese of St. Asaph (covering the counties of Flintshire, Denbighshire, Montgomeryshire and parts of Merioneth) from 1681–6 was 4·40,[19] which suggests that the family in Wales was very much the same as it was in England in the late-seventeenth century. Although our knowledge of the family in pre-industrial Wales is lamentably small, it would seem that it was in the seventeenth century that this crucial cell became a miniature church, assuming definite moral and spiritual functions. One of the major achievements of the Protestant Reformation was to domesticate religion by elevating the status of the home and involving this vital unit in spiritual affairs. Among the most striking features of this period is the way in which those whose doctrinal beliefs were often in bitter conflict were united in their awareness of the paramount rôle of the household in moulding religious attitudes.[20]

Prior to the Reformation, the spiritual overseer of each community was the parish priest. But the strong patriarchal bent implicit in Protestantism meant that duties previously

[16] Henry Kamen, *The Iron Century. Social Change in Europe, 1550–1660* (1971), p. 16.
[17] Peter Laslett, 'Size and Structure of the Household in England over Three Centuries', *Population Studies*, XXIII (1969), 200.
[18] See the examples in Peter Laslett and John Harrison, 'Clayworth and Cogenhoe', *Historical Essays, 1660–1750*, ed. H. E. Bell and R. L. Ollard (1963), p. 166.
[19] J. Gwynn Williams, 'Rhai Agweddau ar y Gymdeithas Gymreig yn yr Ail Ganrif ar Bymtheg', *Efrydiau Athronyddol*, XXXI (1968), 44.
[20] Levin L. Schücking, *The Puritan Family* (1969), p. xiii.

entrusted largely to priests were now assigned to parents within the home.[21] Although a great mass of pious literature had been circulated in the middle ages and was intended for laymen and heads of families, its circulation in manuscript form had inevitably been restricted. Protestantism, on the other hand, was able to reap the benefits of the printing press to the full and, as a result, the head of the household—the *paterfamilias*—was elevated into a figure of sovereign importance: he became the priest and Christian magistrate within the family, a paragon of piety, virtue and rectitude whose example children and servants were expected to follow.[22] Indeed, when we recall that some 44 per cent of the total population was under sixteen years of age,[23] the importance of parental example assumes major significance. As Edmund Jones shrewdly argued, 'Children will take more notice of their parents' faults and virtues than their parents are aware of'.[24] 'If the root be holy', affirmed Matthias Maurice, 'so likewise are the branches.'[25] As a result, the head of the household was a prime target of much printed literature, since he was the focal point of a virile oral tradition. He was enjoined to read the Bible and extracts from devotional books aloud to the rest of the household, particularly to the illiterate members, and also to catechise them regularly. On their return from church on the Sabbath he was also expected to rehearse the whole family in the text and content of the minister's sermon.[26] Erasmus Saunders was articulating the accumulated experiences of many reformers when he urged that, without complementary instruction within the household, preaching could have no more than a fleeting and superficial influence on the lives of individuals:

> Now, though the blessed communications of books have in a great measure eased us . . . yet by reason of the weak capacities

[21] Christopher Hill, *Society and Puritanism in Pre-Revolutionary England* (Mercury Books, 1966), p. 446.

[22] Stephen Hughes (ed.), Rees Prichard, *Canwyll y Cymru* (1681), pp. 193–204.

[23] D. V. Glass, 'Gregory King's Estimate of the Population in England and Wales in 1695', *Population Studies*, III (1949–50), 338–74.

[24] Edmund Jones, *A Geographical, Historical and Religious Account of the Parish of Aberystruth* (1779), pp. 148–9.

[25] Matthias Maurice, *Social Religion Exemplify'd* (3rd ed., 1759), p. 412.

[26] For the ideal performance of closet duties see William Tong, *An Account of the Life and Death of the late Reverend Mr. Matthew Henry* (1716), pp. 123–30. Cf. William Shepard, *Camrias Light, being two of Mr. Rees Prichard's Divine Gems* (1716).

of many, and for the more effectual obedience that the oral precepts, especially of such as are in authority, are like to be met with, this duty is not to be omitted, as being of unspeakable use and benefit: for the advice and direction of a serious parent or master, will be much sooner taken notice of, than the information of the press or the pulpit; or it may be a good book they don't understand, and their minister they don't care for: in this case the mercy of their household-governor must relieve them, or they are utterly undone.[27]

Particular stress was laid on the need to implant the faith early in the minds and hearts of children. Sensitive to the potential sinfulness of children, authors emphasised the importance of cultivating the tender mind. Behind this concern lay Solomon's wisdom: 'Train up a child in the way he should go, and when he is old he will not depart from it'. Anglicans and Dissenters alike urged the head of the household to nourish the future generation with the cardinal Christian truths.[28] 'It is', argued Erasmus Saunders, 'in the growing or spring-time of our age, that we receive the first impressions and seeds of virtue and vice, and according to these first seeds will the general fruits and issues of our lives be: either vicious or virtuous.'[29] 'Fill the vessel', urged Richard Steele, 'something will stick.'[30] Furthermore, given the brevity of human life, parents needed to be reminded that their children were not exempt from hell's fires and everlasting perdition. It was imperative, therefore, that the household should be a refuge from the sins of society, a nursery for the young and, ideally, both a model and a bastion of Church and State.

The elevation of the home as a focal point of religious inculcation also meant that a greater emphasis was laid upon the private worship of the individual. It is of the utmost significance that 205 books (37·6 per cent) were didactic and devotional in character. This is clearly the largest single group, and the vast majority of these books were aimed at the individual layman or the household unit. Conversely, only

[27] Erasmus Saunders, *A Domestick Charge, or, The Duty of Household-Governours* (1701), pp. 56–7.
[28] For two good examples see James Owen, *Bedydd Plant or Nefoedd* (1693), Preface, and George Lewis, *Cyngor Difrifol i Geidwaid Tai* (1704).
[29] Saunders, *A Domestick Charge*, p. 103.
[30] Richard Steele, *The Husbandmans Calling* (1668), p. 260.

thirty-four controversial books (6·2 per cent) were published in this period.[31] There were, as we shall see, passionate doctrinal vendettas in this period and these often spilled over into print, but polemical works were generally directed towards better educated social groups, notably clergymen, ministers and learned laymen. What needs to be explained is the striking output of didactic and devotional literature—four books in the first decade and thenceforward 18, 17, 15, 37, 54 and 60 in each subsequent decade—as opposed to the relative paucity of polemico-doctrinal literature which ran from one in the first decade to 6, 2, 3, 4, 10 and 8 respectively in later ones.

It is manifest that strong ideological considerations lay behind the dissemination of devotional and didactic literature. These find their sharpest focus in the charitable enterprises of the Welsh Trust and the S.P.C.K. But even before the foundation of these bodies, immense sums of money for educational purposes had been poured into the Principality by London philanthropists, many of whom had been born in Wales and were now part of a highly articulate and powerful merchant class that had retained a deep and abiding interest in Welsh affairs.[32] As a group they believed themselves to have been among the greatest beneficiaries of the Acts of Union and many of the political sentiments expressed in the writings of Charles Edwards represent the views of gentlemen and businessmen who held that their association with England was an invaluable means of advancement. In Edwards's eyes, the activity of the Welsh Trust was the apogee of union, meriting a fulsome paean: the English, he maintained, 'having once been ravenous wolves are now become as embracing shepherds, almost as dear to us as we are to each other'.[33] Edwards believed that the merging of Wales with a wider and more advanced unit was a precondition for the creation of a God-fearing literate nation. Providence had decreed that the English were now kindly benefactors, eager to save the souls of their former enemies.[34] These same chords of contentment were struck by Jeremy Owen

---

[31] By controversial books I mean polemico-doctrinal literature that is essentially contentious.

[32] W. K. Jordan, *The Charities of London, 1480–1660* (1960), p. 313.

[33] Charles Edwards, *Y Ffydd Ddi-ffuant* (1677), p. 210.

[34] Rowland Vaughan, *Yr Ymarfer o Dduwioldeb* (1675), sig. Ee7r; Richard Jones, *Hyfforddiadau Christianogol* (1675), sig. T8v.

in 1717, when he rejoiced that erstwhile foes were now generously contributing to charitable concerns in 'poor Wales', where they had once 'driven on furiously the chariots of death and destruction'.[35]

Yet human dispensations as well as the impulses of providence moulded the attitudes of these men. They were bound together by a powerful puritan ethos. When the Act of Uniformity of 1662 established the Church of England into a monopoly, plans for comprehension went by the board and the puritan saint now became the Nonconformist. Fears were widely expressed at that time that those who chose not to conform would become social and religious Ishmaels. 'Ah, thou old whore of Babylon', exclaimed the frustrated Welsh puritan, Jenkin Jones, training his trusty shotgun on the door of Llanddety church, 'thou wilt have it all thy own way now!'[36] Substantially, Jones's forebodings were justified, but it is also remarkable how much of the social and religious doctrine of puritanism cleared the formidable obstacle of the Restoration and remained embedded in the interstices of Anglican dogma. In particular, a puritan ethos survived and manifested itself as a deep religious mood or an intense emotional tone.[37] It was this ethos that made many Anglicans and Nonconformists play down their theological differences and subscribe to John Tillotson's ecumenical wisdom: 'charity', he argued, 'is above rubrics'.[38]

Not surprisingly, therefore, the books disseminated by the Welsh Trust were not intended to foment contention and strife. Anxious to collaborate in benevolent projects in order to deflect men from fractious controversies, men who differed doctrinally over a wide spectrum were generally motivated by a desire 'not to intoxicate . . . brains with notions . . . but to reform men's lives, and purify their natures'.[39] Books published by the Trust were thus of a moral, practical, didactic and devotional bent. From 1699 onwards, too, the S.P.C.K. was equally determined to eschew divisive religious controversy

[35] Jeremy Owen, *The Goodness and Severity of God*, p. 16.
[36] Charles Wilkins, *The History of Merthyr Tydfil* (1908), p. 303.
[37] M. G. Jones, *The Charity School Movement* (1938), *passim*.
[38] Quoted in C. J. Abbey and J. H. Overton, *The English Church in the Eighteenth Century* (2 vols., 1878), I, 126.
[39] Edward Fowler, *The Principles and Practices of certain moderate Divines of the Church of England* (1670), part 1, p. 18.

and, by distributing non-polemical books designed to promote practical piety and good works, it hoped to foster a common Protestant Christianity. But how far both bodies were able to sustain an identity of interests is problematic. In referring to the publications of the Welsh Trust, Edmund Calamy argued that there was 'not one that persuades people to Nonconformity, but they contain such practical duties as all good Christians are and must be agreed in'. On balance, Calamy was probably right, but some diehard Anglicans had clearly smelt a rat, for he went on to point out that if the growth of Dissent in Wales was 'an effect of the increase of knowledge there, we can't help that'.[40] In the case of the S.P.C.K., the boot was on the other foot, for even though their devotional manuals, family prayers and practical treatises were non-polemical in character, all were uniformly and self-consciously Anglican. Even so, the puritan ethic that sustained a powerful non-party and ecumenical strain in this period made it possible for men who were poles apart in their theology to cooperate in worthwhile literary endeavours. Nor was this a feature confined to charitable institutions: in 1733, Jeremy Owen paid tribute to the 'catholic spirit, Christian liberty and ties of amity' which had prompted churchmen and Dissenters to work together in the localities in order to spread saving knowledge.[41]

The publication of didactic and devotional literature was also determined by a further ideological consideration. For at least two generations men remembered the civil wars, and nervous recollections of the wranglings and upheavals of the revolutionary period caused them to look constantly and fearfully over their shoulders. It was their *damnosa haereditas*. 'Rebellion', claimed William Lloyd, bishop of St. Asaph, 'though it blaze for a time, and give a glorious light: yet goes out in a snuff, and leaves an odious scent to posterity.'[42] Thoughts of further revolutionary turmoil chilled the marrow of those with vested interests in the established order. In the Restoration decade, William Roberts, bishop of Bangor, could hardly bring himself to mention the name of 'the usurper Oliver',[43] and memories of Cromwellian rule were seared so

[40] Calamy, II, 10.
[41] R. T. Jenkins (ed.), Jeremy Owen, *Golwg ar y Beiau, 1732* (1950), p. 26.
[42] N.L.W. MS. 11302, p. 29. Cf. Charles Edwards, *Y Ffydd Ddi-ffvant*, p. 148.
[43] Bod., Tanner MS. 45, f. 21.

deeply in the popular consciousness that the passing of a generation scarcely began to erase experiences suffered under heavy-handed sequestrators ('the Boars of the Forest') and upstart committeemen ('Arbitrary and Republican Hoghens Moghens').[44] As late as 1710 when the Sacheverell Affair evoked a clutch of loyal addresses from the counties of north Wales, men inveighed against 'those pernicious and fatal doctrines that paved the way to the execrable murder of your Majesty's royal grandfather, and laid these kingdoms in desolation and ruin'.[45]

As a result, 30 January, the anniversary of the death of the 'Royal Martyr' who had fallen innocent victim to rebellious subjects, became a day of fasting, lamentation and humiliation. 'The guilt of innocent blood', grieved Humphrey Humphreys, bishop of Bangor, 'leaves a deep and lasting stain; not only upon the persons that shed it, but upon the place where it was shed.'[46] Moreover, the more scurrilous of Welsh churchmen grasped their opportunity to blacken the name of Dissent. John Thomas, rector of Penegoes, went into the most lurid detail in recording the evil deeds of 'king-killers' and 'sons of Belial'; Welsh preachers bitterly denounced those 'wicked men' who had publicly topped the king; poets recalled the 'heavy-handed oppression' of puritan regicides; and Ellis Wynne's famous satire was riddled with pejorative references to Cromwell and 'murderous Roundheads'.[47] Dissenters, for their part, probably shifted uncomfortably in their seats whenever such emotional issues were discussed. Philip Henry, who shuddered when the axe fell, confessed in his diary his abhorrence of the deed but 'like(d) not' the annual commemoration, though he supposed that 'many good men' did.[48] But whilst most Dissenters bit their tongues and left a good deal unsaid, there were also some who blurted out underlying resentments

---

[44] David Lewis, 'A Progress through Wales in the Seventeenth Century', *Y Cymmrodor*, VI (1883), 146.
[45] Geoffrey Holmes, *The Trial of Doctor Sacheverell* (1973), p. 250.
[46] Humphrey Humphreys, *A Sermon preach'd before the House of Lords . . . on . . . the 30th day of January, 1695–1696* (1696), p. 2.
[47] John Thomas, *Unum Necessarium* (1680), p. 34; N.L.W. MS. 3B, pp. 144–5; Edward Lloyd, *Egwyddor i rai Jeuaingc* (1662), sig. A6r; David Jenkins, 'Bywyd a Gwaith Huw Morys, Pontymeibion (1662–1709)' (unpublished Univ. of Wales M.A. thesis, 1948), p. 56; Gwyn Thomas, *Y Bardd Cwsg a'i Gefndir* (1971), p. 16.
[48] M. H. Lee (ed.), *Diaries and Letters of Philip Henry* (1882), p. 284.

against those clergymen who used the event to 'sow the seed of bigotry' and to re-fortify men's hatred against innocents who had played no part in the execution of the king.[49]

Even following the embarrassment aroused by the deposition of James II, Whig attacks on puritan doctrines and their past record continued.[50] Memories of the puritan sword clearly died hard. But after 1688 the drum-beats of passive obedience and non-resistance were reduced to faint echoes. Emphasis was now laid on obedience to the 'good' monarch and the laws of the nation. Law, order, and the new spirit of rationalism demanded that men should detest enthusiasm, shrink from fanaticism and do their utmost to maintain the *status quo*.[51] Within the established church it was necessary to douche the fires of enthusiasm and eliminate needless quarrels and strife. Descanting on the theme of pious submission, John Thomas quoted from Proverbs xx 3 to remind men of the 'honour' of ceasing from 'strife'; Robert Wynne, vicar of Llanddeiniolen, wearily declared that disputes over religion had over-stepped the bounds of propriety and good order; and the same dread of turmoil lay behind Samuel Williams, vicar of Llandyfriog's plea for unity and stability in three printed sermons based on Psalms cxxxiii 1 ('Behold how good and how pleasant it is for brethren to dwell together in unity').[52]

Inevitably, therefore, much of the literature published in this period, particularly that of a didactic and devotional character, bore a heavy socio-political motive. Social discipline and submission could be inculcated not only through sermons but also by distributing literature of a practical bent. The best way of exorcising the traumas of the past was to nurture the present generation in such a way that they would become 'a real treasure to the next age'.[53] Although false principles propagated during the revolutionary period had made men proud and intractable and a threat to order and stability, that

[49] N.L.W. MS. 17054D, p. 203; N.L.W. MS. 9167A, pp. 97–8.

[50] Byron S. Stewart, 'The Cult of the Royal Martyr', *Church History*, XXXVIII (1969), 175–87.

[51] B. Behrens, 'The Whig Theory of the Constitution in the Reign of Charles II', *The Cambridge Historical Journal*, VII (1941), 44.

[52] Thomas, *Unum Necessarium*, sig. A2r; N.L.W., Bodewryd MS. 89C, part 4, p. 146; Samuel Williams, *Undeb yn Orchymynedig i Ymarfer* (1710).

[53] Samuel Crossman, *The Young Mans Monitor* (1664), p. xvii.

situation could be speedily reversed by providing them with books that preached the virtues of a healthy saving knowledge and true holiness.[54] Devotional literature thus carried a two-edged message: it could nourish God-fearing, literate Christians and also build a nation of faithful citizens to whom the very thought of rebellion would be anathema.

Such books were also salutary inoculations against the disease of Popery. Even though members of the Roman Catholic faith in Wales were declining in numbers and influence after 1660, the dread of the religious and political implications of Popery remained an obsession. From pulpit and press a national stereotype of the Papist and his faith was deeply instilled into the popular consciousness and did much to fan the paranoiac fears which emerged at times of national crisis.[55] Emphasis was laid not so much on the falsehood of the Roman Catholic religion but on the cruelty and treachery of its adherents. Episcopal charges dilated on the horrible deeds committed in the past in the name of Rome, whilst commemorative services held regularly throughout the land constantly reminded society of the fearful link between Popery and 'foreign arbitrary power'. Welsh literature in this period is shot through with the most vigorous anti-Roman animus: poets and authors warned against the 'cruel hand' of Papists, religious reformers thundered against the 'devilish ways' of the great enemy, and, most important of all perhaps, the annual chronologies published in Welsh almanacs listed the evil acts perpetrated by Catholics since Mary's day, and did much to foster popular hatred towards 'the French monster', Louis XIV.[56] In these ways, Welshmen were taught to believe that Spaniards were heinous butchers, that Catholic priests were insidious fanatics, that the Jesuits were 'the Devil's own imps' or, more strikingly, 'the last vomit of Satan', and that their Irish *confrères*—the dreaded *Gwyddelod*—were devilish barbarians beyond the pale

---

[54] Edward Morris, *Y Rhybuddiwr Christnogawl* (1689), p. 53.
[55] For the background, see John Miller, *Popery and Politics in England, 1660–1688* (1973), and John Kenyon, *The Popish Plot* (1972).
[56] N.L.W. MS. 5A, pp. 99, 327; David Jenkins, op. cit., p. 292; E. D. Jones, 'The Brogyntyn Welsh Manuscripts', *N.L.W.J.*, VII (1953), 30n.; Stephen Hughes (ed.), *Mr. Perkins His Catechism* (1672), sig. A5v; *idem, Gwaith Mr. Rees Prichard*, IV (1672), Preface; Edwards, *Y Ffydd Ddi-ffvant*, pp. 108–50; Thomas Jones, *Newyddion Mawr oddiwrth y Ser* (1691), sig. A2r–A7r.

of civilisation.[57] There can be little doubt that thinking men in seventeenth-century Wales were well aware that conquest by a foreign power would mean Popery, rape and wooden shoes: the three badges of slavery.

In order to present a united and effective front against Popish battalions, more was needed than a well-stocked arsenal of virulent polemics and pious prognostications. Dousing the flames of Popish affections was more likely to be achieved by ensuring a ready flow of the calming waters of Protestant literature. Papists were widely believed to have a vested interest in ignorance; without it, it was thought, their faith could not possibly exist. Ignorance, chuckled Protestants, was one of the 'main hinges that support Popery, or the poles on which it turns',[58] but it was no joking matter to Welsh reformers to know that their province was one of the 'barren corners of the land' and dangerously vulnerable to Popish infiltrations. As a result, one of the major objectives of churchmen and Dissenters alike was to ward off the evils of Popery by distributing literary bromides outlining the fundamental tenets of Protestantism. Hence the vast numbers of practical, didactic and devotional books published. The ideal was that every man and child, armed with the Bible, the Book of Common Prayer, a catechism and devotional books of the nature of *The Practice of Piety* and *The Whole Duty of Man*, would effectively man the barricades against external threats, forming 'frontier garrisons'[59] against Popery and rendering both church and state inviolable.

The most compelling reason, however, for publishing books of a practical, didactic and devotional nature was the level of understanding prevailing among the majority of society. Although Christianity was 'the only totalizing force in the popular experience of the sixteenth and seventeenth centuries'.[60] it does not follow that the canons imposed by the Anglican establishment were accepted and absorbed at all levels. The rôle of the church as a teaching institution still left a lot to be desired and, at the lowest level of society, religion

---

[57] *Morris Letters*, I, 36, 52; U.C.N.W.L., Mostyn Correspondence, V, no. 49; N.L.W. MS. 17054D, p. 507; G. H. Hughes, 'Cefndir Meddwl yr Ail Ganrif ar Bymtheg: rhai ystyriaethau', *Efrydiau Athronyddol*, XVIII (1955), 33.

[58] Anon., *The Condemnation of the cheating Popish priest* (1679), p. 3.

[59] G. V. Bennett, *White Kennett, 1660–1728, Bishop of Peterborough* (1957), p. 190.

[60] John Bossy, 'Early Modern Magic', *History*, 57 (1972), 401.

and its practice were often haphazard affairs, owing little or nothing to creed, conviction or spiritual commitment. To many country folk, the Christian framework into which they had been born was not lightly to be renounced, but neither was it deeply understood or revered. Indeed, many of them were more prepared to place their faith in the influence of superstition and magic than in the official culture of Protestant Christianity. Several factors contributed towards the stubborn persistence of magical cults: the tenacity of rural values and needs; the innate conservatism and sheer inertia of peasant life; the dearth of surgeons, doctors and adequate medical knowledge; the paucity of popular entertainments and amenities; and the relative failure of successive waves of Protestant reforming activity to wipe out the protective rites of Catholicism at the lowest levels. Throughout this period and beyond, the esoteric, vestigial remains of pre-Reformation days were still widely cherished and easily perpetuated in an environment where the casting of charms and spells, the converse with spirits and demons, the belief in omens and apparitions, the pursuit of magic and astrology, and recourse to the milder forms of witchcraft were as much part of popular *mores* as Easter communion and catechising at Lent.[61] 'People will not be taken off their old groundless observances', noted Philip Henry mournfully.[62] That same chord of despair was to be sounded many times long after the Methodist revival.

When David Maurice claimed in 1700 that there were 'more sparrows than eagles, more bruised reeds than cedars, and more babes in Christ than strong, well grown Christians in God's family',[63] he was voicing sentiments widely shared by fellow ministers. Conscious of the limited levels of literacy and hence the paramount need to suckle the weak, reformers were chiefly concerned with presenting the basic substance of Christianity in clear and intelligible form. In the Interregnum period, that doughty puritan warrior, Colonel John Jones of Maesygarnedd, had mildly reproved Morgan Llwyd, the Welsh mystic, for not adapting his books to the needs and

---

[61] I have discussed this theme more fully in a forthcoming article in the *Bulletin of the Board of Celtic Studies.*
[62] M. H. Lee (ed.), *Diaries and Letters of Philip Henry* (1882), p. 240.
[63] David Maurice, *The Bruised Reed* (1700), p. 26.

capabilities of the people. 'Babes', he urged, 'must be fed with milk.'[64] That favourite metaphor of St. Paul echoes throughout this period. Countless authors made the point that the foundations of Protestantism were more important than subtle points of doctrine or abstruse controversy. It is significant that virtually none of Morgan Llwyd's work was reprinted until 1715. Stephen Hughes did flirt briefly with his work and, after some trepidation, published part of *Llyfr y Tri Aderyn* in 1688— but only a small portion of it since, as he explained, it demanded so much more time and space to elucidate than he could afford.[65] It evidently did not meet the needs or realities of the time. 'One must crawl before walking', murmured Rowland Vaughan, pressing the need for palatable literature and necessary truths.[66] Practical didacticism, rather than rousing polemic, was the order of the day.

None showed a keener awareness of the limited capacities of the potential reading public in Wales than Stephen Hughes. In the early 1670s Hughes confessed that two decades' experience of propagating the gospel had taught him that controversies and mysteries were barriers rather than aids to true spiritual edification and that the primary aim of a minister should be to present Christian knowledge in forms intelligible to the lowest levels of society.[67] Naturally, therefore, he judged that publishing practical books was simply a matter of horses for courses. When problems of translation and elucidation taxed his patience, he never shirked his responsibilities. Prior to preparing a translation of Bunyan's *Pilgrim's Progress* in 1688, Hughes had nursed doubts regarding the book's use of allegory as a means of revealing scriptural truths and had wondered whether such a technique smacked too heavily of prose fiction.[68] However, with his customary eye for clarity and common sense, Hughes left nothing to chance and ensured that the text of his translations was suffused with running interpolations, marginal notes and scriptural references. In this

---

[64] N.L.W. MS. 11440D, p. 149.
[65] Stephen Hughes (ed.), *Taith neu Siwrnai y Pererin* (1688), sig. A3v.
[66] G. H. Hughes (ed.), *Rhagymadroddion, 1547–1659* (1967), p. 142.
[67] Stephen Hughes (ed.), *Gwaith Mr. Rees Prichard*, IV (1672), 273–4, 286; cf. ibid., 111, 1672, sig. A2r–v.
[68] Hughes, *Taith . . . y Pererin*, sig. A2r.

way, he achieved outstanding success in bringing the Protestant faith within the compass of the most humble reader.

Hughes's techniques and enthusiasm rubbed off on his contemporaries and successors, for it is striking how many authors were prepared to cultivate a style suited to the limitations of their audience. Aiming for the 'uneducated peasantry', few authors bothered to dally with speculative notions or doctrinal niceties. When Ellis Wynne translated Jeremy Taylor's much-esteemed *Holy Living* in 1701, he went to great pains to eliminate many cloudy phrases and classical references in order to cater for his audience.[69] Popular works like the translations of *The Practice of Piety* and *The Whole Duty of Man* were couched in clear, intelligible language and were aimed at the poorest readers. The anonymous author of *Cristionogrwydd yn Gynnwys* (1703) felt it a great shame that anyone, except children, should require his book—but he knew full well of its need among adults and its guaranteed reception.[70] Scores of authors, particularly those who published under the auspices of the Welsh Trust and the S.P.C.K., repeated the same phrases as they focused their undivided attention on the fundamentals of religion and took pains to ensure that the style and manner of their work were geared to the capabilities of the reading public.

Strenuous efforts were also made to ensure that, in spite of their various dialects, readers in different parts of the country would be able to read practical and devotional books with little difficulty. In bemoaning the dearth of preaching ministers in north Wales, Thomas Baddy claimed that Dissenting ministers who had arrived from south Wales were 'differing much in their dialect from us' and were consequently 'not so acceptable or useful and upon their first coming are discouraged and so go off'.[71] Similar problems confronted Welsh translators. In 1714, Thomas Price of Merthyr, airing the peculiar grievances of the fraternity which spoke Gwenhwyseg (i.e. the

[69] Gwyn Thomas, op. cit., pp. 139–72.
[70] Anon., *Cristionogrwydd yn Gynnwys* (1703), sig. A2r; cf. Walter Price, *Godidowgrwydd, Rhinwedd ac Effaith yr Efengyl* (1707), sig. alv; Enoch Francis, *Gair yn ei Bryd* (2nd ed., 1839), p. xxi; Samuel Williams, *Amser a Diwedd Amser* (1707), sig. A5r.
[71] W. A. Evans, 'Thomas Baddy ac Ymddiriedolwyr Cronfa Dr. Daniel Williams', *Y Cofiadur*, 27 (1959), 25.

dialect of south-east Wales), complained in exaggerated language to the S.P.C.K. that it was 'the unhappiness of south Wales that there has hardly ever been any book translated into such Welsh as the inhabitants there understand'.[72] Although it was accepted that it was impossible to meet the dialectic needs of each community, attempts were nevertheless made to bridge the linguistic gap that divided north and south Wales. Under the auspices of the Welsh Trust, Stephen Hughes and Charles Edwards sought, by careful editing and revising, to transform manuscripts into printed books that could be fairly easily read throughout the Principality. Classical phrases were ruthlessly eliminated, complex words and phrases were couched in more intelligible and homely language, and a convenient list of synonyms was appended to many of their tracts. Their successors followed similar policies and, by the end of the seventeenth century, Welsh books were available for sale in every county in Wales.

Up to a point, it could be argued that the dissemination of didactic and devotional books—the largest single category of literature in this period—reflected ideological considerations and cultural patterns not wholly rooted in Welsh soil. But this does not mean that the books were either alien or unacceptable to the reading public. On the contrary, it is clear that such literature was deliberately geared to meet the needs and aspirations of that public. The second major category of books, religious verse, can confidently be said to have stemmed very largely from the popular religion of the Welsh people. 117 books (21·5 per cent) of religious verse and epigrams, together with 81 almanacs (14·9 per cent) formed the bulk of the popular market. During the latter half of the seventeenth century printed religious verse was largely confined to issues of Rees Prichard's *Canwyll y Cymry*, but it is clear that a good deal of material also circulated in manuscript form. Once the provincial presses were established, particularly the press at Shrewsbury, the floodgates were opened and ballad-mongers took full advantage of their opportunity to cater even more widely for the popular market. At least 105 books of religious verse and sayings were published between 1710 and 1730, and most of these comprised popular ballads.

[72] Clement, p. 69.

Erasmus Saunders was right when he observed that Welsh-men were 'naturally addicted to poetry'.[73] Religious verse always had been a *genre* close to their hearts. Its popularity in this period was often indicative of an active and personal spiritual fervour, and it would probably be fair to say that this form of literature reflected an indigenous culture better attuned to the national temperament than most other cultural patterns. Moreover, although much of the printed verse was often unsophisticated and crude, it was strikingly effective in its didacticism. When Robert Jones, the Methodist of Rhoslan, sneeringly observed that a religious verse or carol was reckoned in pre-revival Wales to be equal to a sermon he was being unwittingly perceptive.[74] For many Welsh religious reformers, notably Rees Prichard and Stephen Hughes, had realised that the easiest and most natural way of instilling Reformation truths was by casting scripture, private devotion and moral codes into popular verse-form. Among semi-literate folk in particular, popular verse had the mnemonic advantages of rhythm and rhyme. That is why so many authors chose to turn the catechism, the decalogue, the Lord's Prayer, and even parts of devotional books into verse, thus presenting the meanest orders of society with relatively cheap books couched in intelligible language.

The final two categories of books included works on religious history and miscellaneous subjects, the latter group largely comprising aids for reading and treatises on Welsh grammar and language. Nine books (1·7 per cent) were published on religious history, and it should be borne in mind that these, too, were of a didactic bent, for most interpretations of the past were couched in spiritual and moral terms. At the helm sat the inscrutable God of Hebrew invention, sustaining a moral code which, once broken, led inevitably to divine wrath. Welsh readers were soon to familiarise themselves with the pattern of lapse and recovery, backsliding and repentance, falling away and a return to obedience among their ancestors, and they themselves were duly urged to heed the appropriate lessons that might be derived from studying the past. Some of the works in this category—Charles Edwards's *Y Ffydd*

---

[73] Saunders, p. 33.
[74] G. M. Ashton (ed.), Robert Jones, *Drych yr Amseroedd* (1958), p. 27.

Ddi-ffvant (1677) and Theophilus Evans's *Drych y Prif Oesoedd* (1716)—are classics in their own right.[75] The same could be said of some of the more substantial volumes of miscellaneous interest: Edward Lhuyd's *Archaeologia Britannica* (1707) is a monumental feat of scholarship by one of Europe's most brilliant polymaths, while Moses Williams's *Cofrestr* (1717) is the cornerstone of Welsh bibliography.

The vast majority of Welsh books published in this period, however, are undistinguished in terms of literary excellence and academic attainment. They stand generally at a much more mundane level and have consequently been largely ignored by Welsh scholars. But what is prosaic and uninspiring to the modern reader was often of the utmost significance to our ancestors. There is no doubt that these books served a deliberate social and religious purpose and filled an acute spiritual need. To ignore their presence or to underestimate their importance is to misunderstand the course of the campaign, first started in the mid-sixteenth century, to instil into Welshmen the values of Protestantism. One of the salient features of this period is that the central doctrines of the Reformation were disseminated intensively in print, in intelligible and popular forms, for the first time in Wales.

[75] The literary merits of these works are discussed in Geraint Bowen (ed.), *Y Traddodiad Rhyddiaith* (1970), pp. 213–30, 262–75.

III

BIBLE, PRAYER BOOK AND CATECHISM

I. THE BIBLE

Protestant reformers in Wales were agreed that the foundation stone on which the edifice of literacy was to rest was the Welsh Bible. This period therefore witnessed a large-scale attempt to diffuse Welsh Bibles for private use, penetrating beyond the parish church and the vicarage into the homes of the laity. Not until 1630 had a Welsh Bible been made available to the reading public in a size handy for the pocket and relatively cheap at five shillings, and this essentially puritan venture had been further extended during the revolutionary period when an edition of the New Testament in Welsh was issued in 1647 and again in 1654, together with a new edition of the Welsh Bible. Although, according to Vavasor Powell, 'at least . . . 5 and 6,000' of the latter editions were 'sold off',[1] popular demand remained unsatisfied, and in the Restoration decade the chronic need for a new edition of the scriptures in Welsh once more called for attention. Stephen Hughes could lay his hands on fifty Welsh Bibles only in London and he feared that even those were so costly as to be beyond the means of the lowest stratum in Welsh society.[2] Similarly, Welsh mercers claimed that 'not one Welsh Bible' was available 'to be bought at any rate, although greatly desired by persons of all ranks and conditions'.[3] Whilst English Bibles poured forth from London presses, mourned a jealous Charles Edwards, Welshmen were deprived of God's Word and allowed to languish in spiritual torpor.[4]

Once Welsh Nonconformists had weathered the early rigours

---

[1] Vavasor Powell, *The Bird in the Cage* (1662), sig. B3r.
[2] Stephen Hughes (ed.), *Gwaith Mr. Rees Prichard*, Part IV, (1672), sig. A3r–v; Samuel Clarke, *The Lives of Divers Eminent Divines of this Later Age* (1683), p. 205.
[3] M. G. Jones, 'Two Accounts of the Welsh Trust, 1675 and 1678', *B.B.C.S.*, IX (1937), 72.
[4] Charles Edwards, *Y Ffydd Ddi-ffuant* (1667), p. 88.

of persecution in the 'sixties, further efforts were made to organise the publication of a new edition of the scriptures. The moving spirit behind the venture was Stephen Hughes, whose greatest ambition was to provide his countrymen with a complete and inexpensive edition of the Bible in the vernacular.[5] Like all puritans, Hughes regarded the Bible as the supreme and decisive authority and he shared the Erasmian ideal that 'all the communication of the Christian should be of the Scripture'. His own works were always generously furnished with copious scriptural references as he urged the cardinal necessity and all-sufficiency of God's Word. But Hughes knew also that his mission was rendered doubly important by the threat posed by the Roman Catholic religion. He was deeply conscious that the dearth of Protestant literature left a free field for the mischievous labours of lurking Papists who 'sowed their poisonous seeds throughout Wales whilst the servants of God lay dormant'.[6] Thrown into something of a panic by the publication of the Catholic devotional, *Allwydd neu Agoriad Paradwys i'r Cymrv*, in 1670, Hughes promptly riddled his new version of Rees Prichard's poetry with virulent attacks on the elevation of the church above the Bible, 'the fiction of transubstantiation', praying to the saints and for the dead.[7] Hughes saw his work as a short-term prophylactic to counter Catholic arguments and to protect the innocent from the wiles of the 'devilish' enemy. He certainly had cause to be alarmed, for several passages in *Allwydd Paradwys* would have raised the temperature of any strenuous puritan, and none more so than those which insisted on the necessity of confining the interpretation of the scriptures to the priesthood.[8] The use of the scriptures was, in fact, one of the major bones of contention dividing Protestants and Catholics. Whereas Papists were expected to accept their faith without question, Protestants firmly believed in *sola scriptura* as the prime source of revealed truth and they urged that God's disciples should be literate, Bible-reading people. Thus, drawing a wealth of evidence

---

[5] For the fullest account of Hughes's publications see G. J. Williams, 'Stephen Hughes a'i Gyfnod', *Y Cofiadur*, IV (1926), 5–44.
[6] *Gwaith Mr. Rees Prichard*, Part IV, sig. A5r.
[7] Stephen Hughes (ed.), *Catecism Mr. Perkins* (1672), sig. A5v–A6r; *Gwaith Mr. Rees Prichard*, Part IV, Preface and pp. 301–18.
[8] See, for instance, *Allwydd neu Agoriad Paradwys*, pp. 215–6.

from the scriptures and from that pungent store of anti-Romanist rebuttals, the *Theses Salmurienses*, Stephen Hughes laboured hard to expose the Catholic heresy of semi-Pelagianism and to extol the virtues of the gospel of justification by faith alone.[9] He knew full well that the creation of a Bible-reading public would sound the final death-knell of the cause of Rome in Wales.

Stephen Hughes went some way toward satisfying popular demand in 1672 when he published a new edition of the New Testament in Welsh, preceded by the Psalter and followed by Edmund Prys's translation of the metrical Psalms. But since this edition comprised 2,000 copies only and was priced at four shillings, it was clearly a stop-gap production designed to meet the most pressing need.[10] For some time Hughes had been formulating plans for the publication of a new edition of the Welsh Bible, but he encountered many daunting problems that threatened to frustrate his ambition. Dogged by refractory printers and publishers in London, hampered by lack of funds,[11] shunned by diehard churchmen who suspected his motives, Hughes trod a wary and wearisome path during the early 'seventies. Characteristically, he sought to win over Welsh prelates by courting the support of sympathetic Anglicans like William Thomas, precentor of St. David's (who was made bishop in 1677) and dean of Worcester, together with conformist puritans who had made their peace with the Anglican establishment in order to exert a purifying influence on the Church.[12] Men such as these were convinced that benevolent

[9] Hughes quoted at length from sections XXIV–XXX of *Syntagma Thesium Theologicarum in Academia Salmvriensi Variis Temporibvs Dispvtatarvm* (2 vols., 2nd ed., Saumur, 1665), vol. 1, pp. 72–3. I am grateful to Dr. G. F. Nuttall for drawing my attention to a copy of this work in Dr. Williams's Library.

[10] *Gwaith Mr. Rees Prichard*, Part IV, sig. A3r; Edward Arber (ed.), *The Term Catalogues, 1668–1709* (3 vols., 1903–6), I, 102; *Y Gwyddoniadur Cymreig*, I, 639.

[11] Hughes outlines these problems in *Gwaith Mr. Rees Prichard*, Part 3, 1672, sig. a4v; Part IV, 1672, sig. a4v.

[12] Hughes dedicated the fourth part of Rees Prichard's Works, published in 1672, to William Thomas and four ministers, Hugh Edwards of Llangadog, William Lloyd of St. Petrox, David Thomas of Margam, and Samuel Jones of Llangynwyd, who had generously helped to finance the publication of the Welsh New Testament and a translation of Perkins's Catechism. For William Thomas see *D.N.B.* and Francis Green (ed.), Edward Yardley, *Menevia Sacra*, suppl. to *Arch. Camb.*, 1927, p. 115. For Edwards and Lloyd see Thomas Richards, *Religious Developments in Wales, 1654–1662* (1923), p. 455 and *idem*, *Wales under the Indulgence, 1672–1675* (1928), p. 117n. For David Thomas and Samuel Jones (the only Dissenter among them) see *H.P.N.*, p. 239.

schemes—even those sponsored in the name of Dissent—
should not be frozen by icy episcopal indifference or narrow
doctrinal prejudice. Stephen Hughes was also fortunate in
being able to call on the financial support of the Welsh Trust
after 1674. Whilst he exhorted the rich, badgered bishops and
cajoled clergymen and ministers, he was joined by Thomas
Gouge, who circularised his friends in London and made
annual visitations to Wales to collect funds.[13] Another ejected
minister, Charles Edwards, a superb biblical scholar, took on
the task of reading the proofs and guiding the edition safely
through the press.[14]

In 1678, the Welsh Bible, was eventually published, along
with the Prayer Book, Apocrypha and the Book of Psalms.
Stephen Hughes's earlier pleas for financial assistance had not
fallen on barren ground, for contributions to the scheme had
been received from:

> charitable persons of all ranks and conditions, from the
> nobility and the gentry of Wales and the neighbouring counties,
> and several of that quality in and about London; from diverse
> of the right reverend bishops, and of the clergy; and from that
> perpetual fountain of charity the city of London, led on and
> encouraged by the most bountiful example of the right
> honourable the lord mayor and the court of aldermen.[15]

The contribution from the nobility and gentry of Wales
reflected a growing response on their part to the impassioned
pleas of religious reformers and a widening sensitivity to the
argument that it was their moral obligation to ameliorate the
social and religious woes of the nation. The flow of munificence
issuing from London was not surprising: not only was it a
deeply-rooted custom among gentlemen and merchants, but
it was further swollen by the affluence and connexions of the
members of the Welsh Trust. Most of the Welsh bishops
reluctantly swallowed their misgivings and subscribed to what
was still, in their eyes, a highly-suspicious venture. Memories

---

[13] *D.N.B.*
[14] G. J. Williams (ed.), Charles Edwards, *Y Ffydd Ddi-ffvant, 1677*, (1936),
pp. xxxvii–xxxviii.
[15] John Tillotson, *A Sermon preached at the Funeral of the Reverend Mr. Thomas
Gouge . . . with a brief account of his Life* (1682), p. 88.

of the revolutionary régime died hard amongst those of them who gazed longingly back to the palmy days of Laud. Humphrey Lloyd, bishop of Bangor, was notoriously prone to see hell's fires in any puff of smoke. Expressing his fears privately in Virgil's famous phrase, *timeo danaos et dona ferentes*, he believed that Gouge and his colleagues were covertly seeking to draw 'credulous common people . . . into a disaffection to the government and liturgy of the church'. Fears of an aftermath of ignominy and shame, however, persuaded him not to voice publicly his objection to the scheme, but his episcopal blessing nonetheless carried a somewhat hollow ring.[16]

The cost of this major undertaking—the most sizeable edition of the Welsh Bible hitherto published—is difficult to establish precisely. When Stephen Hughes made his initial estimate he calculated that an edition of 6,000 copies, printed in larger type, would cost around £1,500. In 1676, Thomas Gouge informed Bishop Humphrey Lloyd that he had already collected subscriptions amounting to £1,000 and that a further £400 would be sufficient to 'perfect the work'. It is probable, however, that more funds were raised than had first been thought likely since the eventual size of the edition was 8,000 copies. Three years after publication, Stephen Hughes calculated that the cost of the edition had been close to £2,000.[17] 7,000 copies, 'well bound in good calf-leather and clasped', were sold in Wales for a relatively modest sum of 4s. 2d. each, whilst the remaining copies were distributed gratuitously to 'such poor families and persons as are not able to buy a Bible, and yet can read, and are like to make good use thereof'.[18] The last clause was no mere after-thought: here we have the nature of puritan philanthropy writ large. Far from distributing relief and educational opportunities at random, puritan philanthropy was consciously discriminating and purposeful.

Popular demand for Welsh Bibles was such that the edition of 1678 was swiftly exhausted. But Stephen Hughes had shrewdly anticipated this and was already engaged in preparing

---

[16] Bod., Tanner MS. 40, f. 18–19r.

[17] *Gwaith Mr. Rees Prichard*, Part IV, sig. a5r; Bod., Tanner MS. 40, f. 18r–v; Stephen Hughes (ed.), *Canwyll y Cymru* (1681), sig. A3r.

[18] M. G. Jones, *B.B.C.S.*, IX (1937), 77.

a new edition when he died in 1688. The project was not allowed to languish, for David Jones of Llandysilio followed the blueprint laid down by his predecessor. In order that Welsh Bibles might be printed in greater numbers and be disseminated even more widely among the poor, Hughes had decided to excise the Prayer Book and the Apocrypha—and Jones duly complied with his wishes.[19] In 1689–90, he published an edition of 10,000 copies, many hundreds of which were 'given to the poor of the Welsh Protestants'.[20] Much of the financial assistance for this edition came from 'persons of quality' in London, erstwhile supporters of the now defunct Welsh Trust, and those who had retained connexions with Wales. The fourth Baron Wharton, for instance, had long been aware of the need for missionary work in Wales and had entered into correspondence with Joseph Alleine to that effect. Widely known as 'Good Lord Wharton', he was prompted to render generous support to David Jones by his close family links with Wales and his genuine interest in charitable work.[21]

The next edition of the octavo Welsh Bible did not appear until 1717–8. This lapse of a generation is not easily explained. The gap cannot be attributed to the vicissitudes of war since issues of the English Bible, often more than three editions per year, flowed unabated from the major presses in this period.[22] The most plausible explanation is that Wales was cast adrift between two tides at this time. Following a relatively smooth passage for a decade, the Welsh Trust had finally run aground in 1684. Conversely, the S.P.C.K., founded in 1699, did not raise sufficient steam to embark on the task until the second decade of the eighteenth century. To some extent, also, the hiatus may be attributable to a lack of leadership and drive. There was no ready-made successor to Stephen Hughes and David Jones, men who had spent a good deal of time in London and who were familiar with the machinations of London booksellers. More crucial, however, was the lack of

[19] Calamy, II, 720; Stephen Hughes (ed.), *Taith neu Siwrnai y Pererin* (1688) sig. A2v.
[20] Edward Arber, op. cit., II, 516.
[21] Charles Stanford, *Joseph Alleine: his Companions and Times* (1861), p. 308. For Wharton see E. R. Wharton, *The Whartons of Wharton Hall* (1898), and Bryan Dale, *The Good Lord Wharton* (1906).
[22] T. H. Darlow and H. F. Moule (eds.), *Historical Catalogue of the Printed Editions of the Holy Scriptures* (2 vols., 1903), I, Part one, *passim*.

ready cash. The purse strings of an anglicising gentry could be unloosed only at the behest of an organised and socially acceptable enterprise. Without this *primum mobile*, any scheme designed to produce a large edition of the Welsh Bible could not hope to succeed.

Not until 1714, through the initiative of the S.P.C.K., were proposals published for the printing of a new octavo edition of the Welsh Bible, together with the Welsh Prayer Book.[23] This project received the official sanction and warm approval of the four Welsh bishops and also the bishops of Hereford and Worcester, who not only subscribed to the issue but also vowed 'earnestly to recommend it to the clergy, gentlemen, and other well dispos'd persons in our respective dioceses'. Such open and unrestrained episcopal approbation would have warmed the heart of Stephen Hughes in the 1670s. The proposals undertook to print the new edition 'on good paper, and a new letter', and to sell unbound copies for 4s. 6d., a shilling less than copies bound in calf. Individuals worked hard to make the venture a success. Erasmus Saunders and Griffith Jones, Llanddowror, both expressed their readiness to assist in preparing the edition and to use their influence to elicit subscriptions from their friends.[24] Addressing the Society of Antient Britons in 1716, Philip Phillips urged that subscribing to the new edition would be the 'best test of our being true sons of the Church of England', and within a few hours of his sermon over 1,200 copies of the proposed Welsh Bible had been subscribed for.[25] The overall success of the venture, however, was largely the fruit of the uncommon industry of Moses Williams, vicar of Defynnog. Although Williams knew that a copy of the proposals had been sent to each member of the S.P.C.K. and that a favourable response had been received, he could still see the value of the personal touch. Thus, from his appointment as editor of the proposed edition in May 1714, he embarked, like some latter-day apostle, on an itinerary of north and south Wales, spreading the good news of the Gospel

[23] *Proposals for reprinting the Holy Bible and Common Prayer Book in the British or Welsh Tongue in Octavo* (1714).
[24] Clement, p. 282.
[25] Philip Phillips, *Ufudd-dod i Lywodraeth a Chariadoldeb* (1716), pp. 19–20; Clement, p. 283. For a list of eminent supporters, see Bod., MS. Rawlinson D839, f. 67.

and urging a wide range of subscribers to dig deeply into their pockets. By October 1715, the subscription list totalled 5,000, and advance money had been received for over 1,400 copies.[26] Eventually, issues of the Welsh Bible of 1718 were published to suit all tastes. Copies of the first issue comprised the Old Testament, the Apocrypha, the New Testament, a Scripture index, and Prys's Book of Psalms. Churchmen were accommodated with an issue that included the Prayer Book, whilst copies issued exclusively for Dissenters omitted the Apocrypha and the Scripture index. The whole edition numbered 10,000 copies, a thousand of which were distributed gratuitously among the deserving poor.[27] A year later, Griffith Jones, Llanddowror, was moved to remark that those Bibles which Sir John Philipps of Picton had distributed among his 'poor tenants in that neighbourhood and elsewhere, prevailed with many to learn to read that before could not, and in some respects to reform'.[28] Indeed, so eagerly was this edition welcomed by the literate and illiterate alike that a new edition, again edited by Moses Williams, was urgently commissioned and published by the S.P.C.K. in 1727. Sold at four shillings each, the new Bibles were less popular than those of the previous edition since the dictates of economy had resulted in the omission of the synopsis of the content of each chapter and the marginal references.[29] Even so, demand inevitably exceeded supply. Although Griffith Jones bought over 2,000 copies 'by the bountiful assistance of good persons', these were still insufficient for his needs.[30] The growing numbers of literate Welshmen were only too anxious to buy copies of the primary source of God's will, and securing a Bible-reading market was now the least of the worries facing religious reformers in Wales.

Prior to 1660, nine editions of the Welsh Bible (or parts of it) had been published, giving a total of around 15,000 copies. But in the period 1660 to 1730, six major editions (together with revisions and indices) produced 40,000 copies, largely

---

[26] N.L.W., Llanstephan MS. 105B, p. 6; Clement, pp. 70, 75, 78, 282.
[27] Griffith Jones, *Welch Piety* (1741–2), p. 15.
[28] Clement, p. 103.
[29] William Rowlands, *Cambrian Bibliography* (1869), p. 346n. See the complaints aired in Joshua Thomas, *Golwg ar Destament Newydd* (1728), sig. A4v, and Griffith Jones, op. cit., p. 15.
[30] Griffith Jones, *Welch Piety* (1740), p. 11.

through the benevolence of public and private charity.[31] In comparison with the annual sale of 30,000 English Bibles, this would seem to be very small indeed. However, it must be borne in mind that English Bibles were heavily subsidised, sold to relatively wealthier and more densely populated communities, and made available to much wider markets, including Scotland. Furthermore, it was always possible for bilingual Welshmen to avail themselves of English Bibles, thus enabling precious Welsh Bibles to be distributed among the monoglot poor. The crucial point is that Welsh Bibles were now increasingly available to laymen. Only Bishop William Lloyd's folio Bible of 1690, an edition of a thousand copies, was specifically designed for the parish pulpit. Abel Morgan had just cause to rejoice in 1730 that the Welsh scriptures were now not only in the hands of the rich and the learned but also of the common people who, like the inhabitants of Berea, could now 'search the scriptures daily, whether these things were so'.[32]

It must be realised, too, that religious reformers waged a constant campaign throughout this period to convince their countrymen that the Bible was the *unum necessarium* of laymen as well as clergymen.[33] Many of them urged Welshmen to take a proper pride in the spiritual release afforded by the 're-flowering' of Protestantism and to make the most of their privilege of having God's Word in their own tongue.[34] It was inevitable that worshippers within the parish church would swiftly become familiar with the scriptures. Congregations derived an intimate knowledge of the Bible from sermons which were drenched with scriptural references and allusions, whilst the prayer book and catechism were heavily furnished with scriptural proofs of doctrine. Devotional literature, moreover, constantly stressed the importance of reading the Bible within the home. To be without a Bible in the house, claimed Richard Steele, was as 'unfit' as to be 'without a fire

[31] The best bibliographical account is John Ballinger, *The Bible in Wales* (1906).
[32] Abel Morgan, *Cyd-Gordiad Egwyddorawl o'r Scrythurau* (1730), p. 7.
[33] *Gwaith Mr. Rees Prichard*, Part IV, sig. A6v–A10r; U.C.N.W.L., Bangor MS. 95, no pagination (sermons of John Griffith, rector of Llanelian); *Cymorth i'r Cristion* (1704), pp. 104–5; *Cyfoeth i'r Cymru* (1706), p. 175; Walter Price, *Godidowgrwydd, Rhinwedd, ac Effaith yr Efengyl* (1707), sig. a3r; Samuel Williams, *Amser a Diwedd Amser* (1707), p. 230.
[34] Simon Thomas, *Hanes y Byd a'r Amseroedd* (1718), p. 191; Griffith Jones, *Welch Piety* (1743–4), pp. 28–9.

or without your household bread'.[35] Rowland Vaughan urged
that by reading three chapters of the scriptures daily, one in
the morning, one at noon, and one at night, a man could read
all but six chapters of the Bible within a year.[36] That ideal, no
doubt, was beyond the capabilities of humbler folk, but many
of them were being instructed in the value of the Bible as a
means of stimulating literacy. It was not merely discerning
poets like Henry Vaughan who took their first faltering steps
towards achieving literacy through an early acquaintance
with the Bible:

> Though wert the first put in my hand,
> When yet I could not understand,
> And daily didst my young eyes lead
> To letters, till I learnt to read.[37]

Young children were encouraged to learn words from the
Bible, starting always with the large capitals at the beginning
of each chapter.[38] Where there were many illiterate members
within a household there lay a particular obligation on the
paterfamilias to read parts of the Bible aloud to them. Each
family cell was thus supplied with a common code of familiar
reference based on the scriptures. The result was that biblical
narratives might circulate orally, becoming part of people's
vocabulary. For the Bible, with its code of images, tales and
examples, could epitomise the daily experiences of most men,
especially in a largely pastoral society where many resem-
blances and points of contact could be found with the society
which had existed in Palestine in Old and New Testament
times.

It is difficult to avoid the conclusion that literate people
viewed the Bible as a precious and sacred possession. It is
remarkable how many individuals made a point of mentioning
the Bible in their wills and who went to some pains to ensure

---

[35] Richard Steele, *The Husbandmans Calling* (1668), p. 264.
[36] Rowland Vaughan, *Yr Ymarfer o Dduwioldeb* (1675), pp. 129–30.
[37] L. C. Martin (ed.), *Henry Vaughan: Poetry and Selected Prose* (1963), p. 378.
For similar testimonies by Welsh poets, see N.L.W., Peniarth MS. 124D, p. 174,
and David Jenkins, 'Bywyd a Gwaith Huw Morys' (unpubl. Univ. of Wales M.A.
thesis, 1948), p. 3.
[38] This tradition is best revealed in J. H. Davies (ed.), *The Life and Opinions of
Robert Roberts, a Wandering Scholar* (1923), p. 13.

that their copy was safely bequeathed. In many households the Bible was a family heirloom to be cherished and handed down through a line of descendants. Many of them often contained a family record of births, marriages and deaths. When Robert Davies of Llannerch prepared a separate codicil for his library in 1706, he stipulated that his 'Bible and about half a score of other books which I used to write in may never go out of my house'.[39] Even Bibles on loan seldom slipped through the net: in 1698, Hugh Hughes of Segrwyd recalled his Welsh Bible borrowed by Robert Owen of the same parish in order to bequeath it to his son.[40] The more affluent members of the society might own more than one Bible. Richard Edmunds, a gentleman of Pool, left his son his 'best Bible', whilst Randolph Parry, a tanner of the same parish, bequeathed his 'large Bible' to his wife.[41] Rice Powell, vicar of Lampeter, shared his Welsh Bibles among his children,[42] whilst Thomas Price, vicar of Meidrim, thoughtfully bequeathed the sum of 3s. 6d. to his grandson 'to buy him a Bible'.[43] Bible-owning yeomen and craftsmen of modest wealth were not uncommon. Thomas Morris, an impoverished yeoman of Bagillt, Flintshire, boasted a Welsh Bible and Prayer Book worth nine shillings in a meagre estate valued at £9 6s. 5d.; Morgan Thomas, yeoman of Llanfihangel Abercywyn, owned one old Welsh Bible which figured prominently in his personal estate valued at £13 2s. 6d.;[44] the inventory of goods in the possession of Thomas David, a cobbler of Carmarthen, included one English Bible and one testament worth five shillings.[45] The wills and inventories of small farmers and labourers in the upland and middle regions of Glamorgan in this period show

[39] Gwilym A. Usher, *Gwysaney and Owston* (1964), p. 113.
[40] N.L.W., St. Asaph P.R. 1698. I owe this reference to Professor J. Gwynn Williams.
[41] N.L.W., St. Asaph P.R. 1744; St. Asaph P.R. 1735.
[42] N.L.W., Archdeaconry of Cardigan P.R. 1681.
[43] N.L.W., Archdeaconry of Carmarthen P.R. 1710. The only book owned by Griffith Jones, vicar of Silian, on his death in 1731 was an old Welsh Bible worth a shilling. Archdeaconry of Cardigan P.R. 1731.
[44] N.L.W., St. Asaph P.R. 1735; Archdeaconry of Carmarthen P.R. 1739. For other examples see Peter Jones of Brymbo, St. Asaph P.R. 1729; Thomas John Owen of Llanfairmathafarn, Bangor P.R. 1695; Ffoulke Roberts of Llansantffraid Glyn Ceiriog, St. Asaph P.R. 1729; David Lloyd, Llansannan, St. Asaph P.R. 1744.
[45] N.L.W., Archdeaconry of Carmarthen P.R. 1735.

that Bibles were widely-owned and much-prized.[46] There ma‧
be some truth in Richard Steele's impressionistic remark tha‧
the gentry might own finer Bibles but that the commo‧
husbandman would 'use it oftner to his comfort'.[47] Certainl‧
many poor people received Bibles as gifts from charitabl‧
organisations or from local clergymen.[48] Significantly, too
the traditional *cywydd gofyn* (poem of request) was bein‧
utilised by poets in this period as a means of procuring Welsh
Bibles from wealthy dignitaries for the use of humble people.[4]
It is likely that many at these levels were men of one book
finding, like Howel Harris, 'very great love to the Bible a‧
God's Word'.[50] The inventory of goods owned by Willian
John Hugh, a fisherman of Llangynnwr, is eloquent in it‧
bleakness: when he died in 1720 he left behind him one ol‧
Welsh Bible worth a shilling.[51]

II. THE BOOK OF COMMON PRAYER

The ordinance of the Long Parliament in 1645 abolishing
the Book of Common Prayer was abrogated by the fourth Ac‧
of Uniformity of May 1662. Recalling the 'blood and confusion
of the previous two decades, the preamble of the newly revised
edition of the Prayer Book defended the need for a commor‧
liturgy and mourned recent schisms.[52] Spurred on by the
spectre of Roundheads, churchmen in the Restoration period
were determined to revive the formal procedure of public
devotion and to reinstil the virtues of the set form of prayer. A

[46]M. I. Williams, 'A general view of Glamorgan houses and their interiors in
the seventeenth and eighteenth centuries', Stewart Williams (ed.), *Glamorgan
Historian*, X (1974), 169.

[47] Richard Steele, op. cit., p. 43. When Randolph Wynne wrote to Sir Robert
Owen of Porkington in August 1691, he referred to the purchase of a family Bible
which, he claimed, had 'so fine an outside that it is pittie to sullie it with dayly use
and if posteritie be as carefull as you no doubt but the booke may last many
generations in your familie'. N.L.W., Brogyntyn MS. 905.

[48] One good example is John Robinson, vicar of Ruabon (d. 1703), who
bequeathed to his successor £40 yearly in Bibles and Prayer Books to be
distributed among poor people. N.L.W., SA/MB/9, p. 103.

[49] N.L.W., Nantglyn MS. 2, pp. 243–8, 280–1; David Jenkins, op. cit., pp. 1–3;
John Edwards, 'Edward Samuel: ei Oes a'i Waith' (unpubl. Univ. of Wales M.A.
thesis, 1925), Appendix 1, pp. 1–3. It is significant that the poetry written from
the latter half of the seventeenth century onwards was increasingly suffused with
biblical allusions.

[50] Tom Beynon, *Howell Harris's Visits to Pembrokeshire* (1966), p. 5.

[51] Archdeaconry of Carmarthen P.R. 1720.

[52] *An Act for the Uniformity of Publick Prayers* (1662).

eep revulsion had set in against the puritan practice of
xtempore prayer and many had come to the conclusion that
ast upheavals were the direct result of neglecting the Prayer
ook.[53] Moreover, it was believed that further turmoil would
e avoided only if the traditional duties of prayer and due
ubordination were replanted in men's minds. Urging his
ontemporaries to eschew fruitless dissension, John Thomas,
ector of Penegoes, emphasised strongly that prayer was the
num necessarium of the age and that the Prayer Book itself was
he sturdiest of crutches to support crippled men.[54]

There were powerful reasons, therefore, for ensuring the
teady publication of Welsh Prayer Books for the pulpit and
or the layman's hearth. By the Act of Uniformity of 1662, the
our Welsh bishops and the bishop of Hereford were enjoined
o see that a Welsh translation of the revised Prayer Book of
hat year be prepared—a task that was completed in 1664. This
vas the third great revision of the Welsh Prayer Book and it
emained the standard edition until 1710.[55] Even more
mportant, however, were the pocket-sized Prayer Books
ublished for the benefit of laymen in this period. In 1678,
under the auspices of Stephen Hughes, an octavo Prayer Book
vas published with the Welsh Bible, and this edition served
s a model for a further Welsh edition published at Oxford
n 1683. These issues were followed by a series of unauthorised
ditions (curtly dismissed by Moses Williams as being
miserably altered and mangled throughout')[56] published by
Thomas Jones in 1687, 1700, 1708 and 1712. Even so, these
atchwork issues were evidently a response to a growing public
lemand: cheap, pocket-sized and of a fair letter, they were
nade available throughout the Principality.

It was the call for more Prayer Books which prompted the
.P.C.K. to publish a new octavo edition in 1709 which was
ffered to subscribers at 'eighteen shillings per dozen'.[57] In the

---

[53] *Anon., Ffordd y Gwr Cyffredin* (1683), p. 21. See also the sermon on John v 14
n Cardiff MS. 2.226.
[54] John Thomas, *Unum Necessarium* (1680), sig. A3v.
[55] A. O. Evans, *A Chapter in the history of the Welsh Book of Common Prayer* (3 vols.,
922), I, Introduction.
[56] N.L.W., Llanstephan MS. 105B, p. 9. For similar comments by Bishop
Humphrey Humphreys, see Clement, p. 262.
[57] Clement, pp. 255-6, 271, 324-5; G. M. Griffiths, 'Eight Letters from
dmund Gibson to Bishop Humphreys, 1707-9' *N.L.W.J.*, X (1958), 365-74.

following year, too, the second major revision of the Welsh
Prayer Book was completed by Ellis Wynne of Lasynys and
printed in folio in London.[58] This edition became the prototype
for a spate of unauthorised octavo editions published subsequently at Shrewsbury. Such issues were evidently calculated
to answer the needs of the reading public. George Bull, bishop
of St. David's, saw that they were very 'much wanted' in his
diocese and he urged his clergy to buy copies in bulk from
Shrewsbury and London so that 'they may quickly and easily
be dispersed through the whole diocese'.[59] Brimming with
defects and tarnished by errors, the issues of John Rogers in
1711 and 1724 and Thomas Durston in 1718 and 1730 were
nevertheless cheap and convenient. And when Moses Williams
published revised issues of the Welsh Prayer Book in 1718 and
1727 he did so in the knowledge that there was a ready market
at his disposal.[60]

The main use of the Book of Common Prayer was in public
worship. The very rubric—*common* prayer—symbolised the
collective nature of the act, and the ordered, uniform nature
of the service, the sense of tradition refined and hallowed
since apostolic times, together with the very beauty of the
liturgy, seized the imagination of Welsh authors.[61] But they
also emphasised that the Prayer Book was a priceless boon to
private worship. Indeed many books of private devotion were
based on the prayers and collects of the Prayer Book, since
private worship was a means of preparing for and supplementing church services.[62] Besides regular and punctual
attendance at public worship, prayers should be conducted
by the head of the household three times a day or, at the very
least, in the morning and at night. Private devotions were
believed to be crucially important since formal conformity
was of no consequence without the inward, subjective piety
which stemmed from regular devotional exercises within the
home.

[58] A. O. Evans, op. cit., I, xxv.
[59] George Bull, *A Companion for the Candidates of Holy Orders* (1714), p. 63.
[60] A. O. Evans, op. cit., I, pp. xxv–xxvi.
[61] *Ffordd y Gwr Cyffredin* (1683); *Pregeth ynghylch Godidowgrwydd a Defnyddiaeth neu Lesioldeb Llyfer y Gweddiau Cyffredin* (1693), Theophilus Evans, *Prydferthwch Sancteiddrwydd yn y Weddi Gyffredin* (1722).
[62] See, for instance, Evan Evans, *Y Llyfr Gweddi Gyffredin, y Cydymmaith Goreu* (1693; reprinted 1711).

The distribution of Welsh Prayer Books was also crucial to the proper administration of the sacrament of the Lord's Supper, which many judged to be the climax of Anglican worship. Frequenting holy communion had fallen into desuetude during the revolutionary period and earnest efforts were made to revive the practice after the Restoration. However, the frequency with which holy communion was celebrated during this period should not be judged by modern standards. Canon 21 demanded a minimum of three celebrations a year within each parish, and most rural communities did not aspire to exceed this norm. These celebrations tended to coincide with the three great festivals of the church: Christmas, Whitsun and Easter. Frequently a further sacrament might be held in the autumn, a sacred thanksgiving to celebrate the ingathering of the harvest.[63] Although churchwardens' returns for the diocese of St. David's in the late-seventeenth century are frustratingly vague, it is evident that the maximum number of sacraments in most parishes seldom exceeded three a year.[64] Even so, wide variations were always possible. Archdeacon Edward Tenison's returns for the archdeaconry of Carmarthen in 1710 reveal that each parish, except one, held communion sometime during the year.[65] Of 24 parishes for which precise returns are given, six held an annual sacrament, four celebrated twice a year, six conformed to the canonical minimum of three a year, and seven celebrated on four occasions. The parish of Laugharne excelled all others with twelve sacraments annually. Clearly, some efforts were being made to encourage more regular sacraments. From the beginning of the eighteenth century, the societies for reformation had persuaded local clergy and laity in parts of the dioceses of St. David's and St. Asaph to organise monthly sacraments and lectures on a peripatetic basis.[66] In 1710, William Davies, rector of Llanwrin

---

[63] Norman Sykes, *Church and State in England in the Eighteenth Century* (1934), 250.
[64] N.L.W., SD/Archdeaconry of Cardigan/Churchwardens' returns 1684/1–69; SD/Archdeaconry of St. David's/Churchwardens' returns 1678/1–75; 1688/76–109; 1691/110–44; SD/Archdeaconry of Carmarthen/Churchwardens' returns 1705/7–154.
[65] N.L.W., SD/Misc. B/131, pp. 7–79.
[66] D. W. R. Bahlman, *The Moral Revolution of 1688* (1957), pp. 39–40, 61.

in the deanery of Cyfeiliog, estimated that six out of eight parishes in that deanery celebrated a regular monthly communion.[67] By 1729, eight parishes in the deanery of Rhôs held communion four times a year, whilst eight parishes in the deanery of Penllyn and Edeirnion celebrated a monthly communion.[68]

Such improvements often depended on the presence of a resident curate, for non-residence and pluralism meant that even the basic minimum of thrice-yearly celebration might prove unmanageable for some of the more penurious and over-worked clergy. Impoverished neighbourhoods often suffered most. The minister of Freystrop in the archdeaconry of St. David's complained in 1678 that he would willingly celebrate the sacrament thrice-yearly or oftener on condition that his parishioners fulfilled their obligation of buying the elements for the communion service.[69] James Langford, rector of Llansanffraid in the deanery of Penllyn and Edeirnion, confessed in 1732 that communion was available at Easter only, since they had no church tax to pay for the wine.[70] Conversely, better-placed incumbents often bore the financial burden themselves: at Loveston in the archdeaconry of St. David's in 1678 the minister bought the bread and wine himself at Easter lest his forty communicants be disappointed.[71] Furthermore, the presence of a resident and scrupulous bishop might set higher standards to which clergymen could aspire. William Lloyd, bishop of St. Asaph (1680–92), called a synod of his clergy at St. Asaph in July 1683 and instructed them to prepare communicants properly, to preach at least twice a year on the proper preparation for the sacrament or to read in Welsh the two relevant homilies concerning Common Prayer and the worthy receiving of the sacrament.[72] Eager to keep his diocese in 'the strictest regulation',[73] Lloyd urged the clergy to give due notice before each sacrament, to turn away scandalous people, to present those who failed to conform, and

[67] Clement, pp. 29–30; N.L.W., SA/Let/702.
[68] N.L.W., SA/RD/18; SA/RD/21; SA/RD/23.
[69] N.L.W., SD/Archdeaconry of St. David's/Churchwardens' returns 1678/13
[70] N.L.W., SA/RD/23, p. 70b.
[71] N.L.W., SD/Archdeaconry of St. David's/Churchwardens' returns 1678/37
[72] N.L.W., SA/Misc./520–1.
[73] Robert Wynne, *A Short Narrative of the Proceedings against the Bishop of St. Asaph* (1702), p. 1.

to carry out a weekly inspection of the bread and wine. Similar efforts were made by George Bull, bishop of St. David's (1705–10), to instruct the clergy in their duties, to cajole magistrates to support the clerisy, and to set a personal example by employing only those servants who were constant communicants.[74]

But although the frequency with which holy communion was celebrated varied in the localities, most parishes could boast a popular and heavily-attended communion at Eastertide. In response to the close supervision exercised by Bishop William Lloyd, every single adult communicant in the parish of Northop, comprising 231 families or 945 souls in 1686, received the sacrament either at Easter or Whit Sunday, 'when there have been the greatest communions that have been known in that parish'.[75] With the coming of toleration the number of communicants decreased, sometimes quite sharply in rural areas, but the general pattern of relatively high attendance at Easter persisted. Edward Tenison's returns for the arch-deaconry of Carmarthen in 1710 reveal that only a small proportion of communicants at Easter attended the other celebrations. At Llanboidy, a parish of 240 families, 300 communicants attended at Easter, but only 40 attended at other times during the year. At Trelech, a parish of 64 families, holy communion was celebrated thrice-yearly, but whereas only 30 communicants attended at Christmas and Whitsun, 150 did so at Easter.[76] It should be borne in mind that the pattern of infrequent sacraments during the year coupled with high attendance at Easter was a common phenomenon in England. Indeed, Wales compares relatively favourably with conditions in rural dioceses in England.[77] The visitation returns of the diocese of York in 1743 reveal that, of 836 churches, only 72 held a monthly communion. 764 parishes celebrated on six or fewer occasions and, of these, 208 parishes did not achieve a quarterly sacrament.[78] In Wiltshire, a

---

[74] Robert Nelson, *The Life of Dr. George Bull* (2nd ed., 1714), p. 452.
[75] N.L.W., SA/Misc/1463.
[76] N.L.W., SD/Misc. B/131.
[77] Attendances, however, did not match the remarkable 99 per cent attendance at Easter boasted by Catholic France in the late-seventeenth century. Gabriel le Bras, *Études de Sociologie Religieuse* (2 vols., 1955), I, 275–7.
[78] Norman Sykes, op. cit., p. 251.

thrice-yearly sacrament was the norm, and only by the mid-
eighteenth century had Devon attained a general standard of
four celebrations annually.[79] But while the number of Easter
communicants in York was often remarkably high, numbers
in Devon remained low throughout the eighteenth century.

How far the spate of prayer books and commentaries
published in this period served to encourage regular attendance
at holy communion is impossible to calculate. Clerics constantly
aired their frustrations in bringing their parishioners 'to their
duty',[80] and the fact that much of the literature on the subject
was specifically directed at poor people suggests that they
were not regular communicants. Tracts were always 'fitted to
the meanest capacities', and in his preface to Thomas Williams's
translation of William Assheton's *Brief Exhortation to the Holy
Communion* in 1710, Edward Tenison suggested that the poor
were the least aware of their obligations to attend the sacrament, and he urged the clergy of the archdeaconry of
Carmarthen to distribute copies among those 'as can read,
especially the poorer sort'.[81] John Vaughan of Derllys disseminated 5,000 copies of the Welsh translation of John
Tillotson's *Persuasive to Frequent Communion* among the deserving
poor of Carmarthenshire.[82] In north Wales, too, Welsh prayer
books and commentaries were assiduously distributed among
the poor and found to be 'very acceptable' in their midst.[83]

Further evidence that a special effort was being made to
instruct poor rural communities may be inferred from the
common objections raised against frequenting the Lord's
Supper.[84] Many books devoted attention to the objections of
honest, common folk, the hewers of wood, and drawers of water,
and sought to dispel their fears and scruples. Many of the lower
orders clearly felt a sense of unworthiness and inferiority,
judging, as Archbishop Secker observed, that the sacrament

---

[79] Anne Whiteman, 'The Church of England 1542–1837', *A History of Wiltshire*
(1956), III, 45; Arthur Warne, *Church and Society in Eighteenth-Century Devon*
(1969), p. 45.

[80] For one striking example, see a letter written by Benjamin Conway, vicar of
Northop, in 1729. N.L.W., SA/Let/827.

[81] Thomas Williams, *Annogaeth Ferr i'r Cymmun Sanctaidd* (1710), p. 4. Both
Welsh and English versions were issued in the same year.

[82] Clement, pp. 252–3.

[83] Ibid., pp. 25, 28, 33–4.

[84] These were specifically dealt with in Michael Jones, *Attebion i'r Holl Wag
Escusion a wnae llawer o bobl yn erbyn dyfod i dderbyn y Cymmun Bendigedig* (1698).

belonged 'only to persons of advanced years, or great leisure, or high attainment in religion, and is a very dangerous thing for common persons to venture on'.[85] Rural inhabitants also argued that their daily preoccupation with making ends meet left them with no time to prepare themselves adequately for communion and thus they felt no benefit from attending. Welsh authors went to some pains, therefore, to emphasise that the sacrament was not the monopoly of the privileged few, but was a necessary act of worship for high and low, rich and poor, literate and illiterate alike.[86] To this end, several devotional manuals contained simple private prayers that might become part of every person's closet duty.[87] Welsh translations of William Viccars' *Companion to the Altar* in 1715 and 1721 were key works in 'influencing many to communicate more frequently than they do' and in pointing out the merits of worthy communicating.[88] Since there were sacred obligations involved in the sacrament, the prospective communicant was exhorted to examine his spiritual condition thoroughly and to scrutinise his soul in preparation. Moreover, since the sacrament was a reminder of Christ's sacrifice, it should not become a mere outward profession, a pharisaical compliance, or a sign of lip-service to a political régime, but a voluntary, sincere and humble act of will by each individual. Exhortations such as these may have fallen on deaf ears amongst large sections of the rural communities, yet it is significant that religious reformers were no longer content with a general reception at Easter but were prepared to raise their standards and make earnest efforts to bring their parishioners to the altar and prepare them for the act of communion.

Since they were fewer in numbers, Dissenters were able to achieve more rigorous supervision of their communicants. It was expected of Dissenters that they should be able to give a proper account of their convictions, and the strict discipline involved had always been the envy of churchmen. Dissenters

---

[85] Cited in S. C. Carpenter, *Eighteenth Century Church and People* (1959), p. 188.

[86] George Lewis, *Annogaeth i Gymmuno yn fynych* (1704); Michael Jones, *Y Cymmunwr Ystyriol* (1716).

[87] David Maurice, *Arweiniwr Cartrefol i'r Iawn a'r Buddiol Dderbyniad o Swpper yr Arglwydd* (1700); Thomas Williams, *Annogaeth Ferr i'r Cymmun Sanctaidd* (1710); John Rhydderch, *Dwyfolder Gymmunol neu Ddefosiwnau Sacramentaidd* (1716); Edward Samuel, *Prif Ddledswyddau Christion* (1723).

[88] Clement, p. 113.

normally held communion on the first Sunday of the month and usually held a preparatory prayer meeting prior to the sacrament.[89] None was admitted to the Lord's Table without an exhaustive knowledge of the obligations involved, and ministers like Philip Henry went to great pains to coax the 'weak and timorous' with 'much mildness and humility and tenderness, and endeavour to make the best of every body'.[90] Authors, too, stressed the scrupulous preparation and tireless self-examination required of communicants. The self-interrogation called for in Thomas Baddy's *Pasc y Christion neu Wledd yr Efengyl* (1703) was vigorously incisive, calling for a relentless self-scrutiny which reflected the contempt which Dissenters reserved for all lax or lukewarm communicants.[91]

III. CATECHISM

In 1749, Griffith Jones, Llanddowror, maintained that the result of neglecting the catechism would be that 'the most laborious preaching, and all other methods of reforming the poor and ignorant will be lost labour upon them'.[92] But although Jones had been the most determined and eloquent champion of regular catechising since the 1730s, it should not be thought that his predecessors had not arrived at similar conclusions. It was commonly known that many sermons fell on stony ground simply because many worshippers were ill-versed in first principles and unable to digest pulpit language. There were many clergymen like David Maurice, vicar of Abergele, who grasped the inefficacy of preaching to those who were bereft of a sound catechetical base and who, therefore, arranged the distribution of catechisms among the lame ducks of his parish.[93] 'Preaching', claimed William Thomas, bishop of St. David's, 'without the auxiliary catechetical preparation may prove like sounding brass, like a tinkling cymbal.'[94]

[89] R. Tudur Jones, *Hanes Annibynwyr Cymru* (1965), p. 115.
[90] J. B. Williams (ed.), Matthew Henry, *The Life of the Rev. Philip Henry* (1825), pp. 195, 237–8.
[91] Thomas Baddy, *Pasc y Christion neu Wledd yr Efengyl* (1703), pp. 59–65; cf. James Owen, *Hymnau Scrythurol, yn cynnwys achosion perthynasol o foliant yngweinidogaeth y Sacrament o Swpper yr Arglwydd* (1705).
[92] Griffith Jones, *Welch Piety* (1740), p. 16.
[93] David Maurice, *Cwnffwrdd ir Gwan Gristion* (1700), p. iv.
[94] William Thomas, *The Bishop of Worcester. His Letter to the Clergy of his Diocese* (1689), pp. 7–8; cf. William Nicholson, *A Plain, but full Exposition of the Catechism of the Church of England* (1678) and William Beveridge, *The Church-Catechism explained* (1704).

Religious reformers were thus fully aware of the importance of thorough catechetical preparation. With echoes of the civil wars still resounding in their ears, they were understandably conscious of the need to cultivate the tender mind. Educating children was 'a matter of the highest trust',[95] and the stock philosophy of authors was invariably enshrined in Proverbs xxii 6 ('Train up a child in the way he should go, and when he is old, he will not depart from it') and ii Timothy i 13 ('Hold fast the form of sound words, which thou hast heard of me, in faith and love which is in Christ Jesus').[96] A solid knowledge of the catechism would not only provide a child with a clear explanation of church doctrines but also protect him from corrupt influences. Without it, claimed William Rowlands, the mind became like a ship with neither rudder nor sail, thrown to and fro by every puff of doctrine and always in peril of being overturned.[97]

Ideally, catechising involved obligations for the minister, parents and children. The 59th canon of the established church required the curate of each parish to instruct and examine in some part of the catechism those of the parish who had been sent to him. This was to be carried out diligently on Sundays and holy days after the second lesson at Evening Prayer. Parents were also expected to send their children, together with servants and apprentices resident within their households, to church at the appointed time to be catechised prior to their confirmation. But how far these obligations were fulfilled is difficult to determine precisely. The churchwardens' returns for the diocese of St. David's in the late-seventeenth century are too imprecise and stereotyped to allow for a thorough assessment of the degree of catechising carried out at church and in the home. It is clear, however, that most clergymen called children and catechised those who came. The negligent among them were usually either non-residents or men who were unable to perform their duty for lack of a competent salary. But the major problem was convincing

---

[95] N.L.W., Picton Castle MS. 1669.
[96] G. F. Schochet, 'Patriarchalism, Politics and Mass Attitudes in Stuart England', *The Historical Journal*, XII (1969). See also the pithy remarks of William Evans (ed.), Rees Prydderch, *Gemmeu Doethineb* (1714), p. 53, and Moses Williams, *Y Catecism* (1715), title-page.
[97] William Rowlands, *Catechism yr Eglwys* (1713), Sig. A2v.

parents of their duty to send children and servants to be catechised. According to churchwardens, children were 'slow and faulty' or 'very remiss', largely owing to the ignorance, indifference or sheer obduracy of their parents. Poverty, too, was a basic obstacle, for rural householders were often forced, through economic necessity, to deprive their offspring of the opportunity of attending church services. The churchwardens of Letterston in Pembrokeshire reported in 1678 that most householders fulfilled their obligation save for those 'who by reason of their poverty are forced to put their children to such employs that they cannot be spared'.[98] That same lament rang down the decades in so many reports.

In the early decades of the Restoration period, churchmen also pointed to other factors that adversely affected the fulfilment of catechetical duties. It was widely believed that puritan 'sermonising' in the revolutionary period had relegated the practice of catechising to an inferior status, with the result that men had become 'possessed with strange errors in religion, and hurried on by the spirit of giddiness, of faction, of rebellion'.[99] In 1673, William Lucy, bishop of St. David's, ascribed the 'backwardness' of parents in sending their children to be catechised to 'the general looseness in the manners of men and those evil principles formerly instilled during the late rebellion'.[100] By 1710, Edward Tenison's returns for the archdeaconry of Carmarthen reveal that restricting catechising to Lent had become a common phenomenon. Only three parishes—Cyffig, Laugharne and Llandeilo Fawr—could boast of regular catechising on Sundays, and the same pattern prevailed at Llanddowror during the summer months.[101]

Far more striking success in the field of catechising was achieved in the diocese of St. Asaph following the appointment of Bishop William Lloyd in 1680. Anxious to establish catechising as a regular Sunday afternoon activity, Lloyd immediately urged his chancellor to 'press all the clergy very earnestly to catechise and to expound the catechism'.[102] The evidence available suggests that he met with no small success.

[98] N.L.W., SD/Archdeaconry of St. David's/Churchwardens' returns 1678/25.
[99] William Nicholson, op. cit., Epistle Dedicatory.
[100] Bod., Tanner MS. 146, f. 138r–v.
[101] N.L.W., SD/Misc. B/131.
[102] Lloyd-Baker MSS., Letter no. 6 (xerox copy in N.L.W.).

Although there were clearly some clergymen who found it difficult to live up to his expectations,[103] remarkable success was achieved within the parish of Northop where, by 1686, every child between the age of nine and sixteen, with the exception of two poor children, was able to say his catechism.[104] One swallow does not make a summer, but there were a good many clergymen who were eager to enforce Lloyd's injunctions and also use their own initiative. William Foulkes, rector of Llanfyllin (1661–91), catechised the youth of his parish with solemn care, edited Welsh sermons by Bishop George Griffith, and published a Welsh translation of a catechism by Thomas Ken.[105] Similarly, David Maurice, vicar of Llanasa (1666–84), vicar of Abergele and Betws (1681–1702) and sinecure rector of Llanarmon-yn-Iâl (1695–1702), worked industriously to instruct the youth of his parishes by translating sermons for 'weak Christians' and by employing schoolmasters to teach both young and old in his neighbourhood.[106] Rondl Davies, vicar of Meifod (1660–97), much troubled by the eroding influence of Dissent, prepared for the press his translation of Richard Sherlock's enormously popular *Principles of Holy Christian Religion*, and urged Bishop Lloyd to take steps to ensure that licensed schoolmasters were settled in every parish so that, by teaching poor children to read English and Welsh, they might more easily learn the catechism.[107] Fired by the same enthusiasm, William Williams, rector of Bodfari (1672–81), not only catechised the eligible members of his parish but sought also to confer further benefits on more impoverished children who, although able to recite the Lord's Prayer, the Creed and the Ten Commandments, were in no position to advance their knowledge since their parents were unable 'to instruct them further and their circumstances not affording them any means for school improvements'. Williams thus informed Bishop Lloyd of his willingness to devote one or two days each week to catechising the poor and ensure their attendance by warning neglectful parents that uncatechised children would no longer

[103] See, for instance, N.L.W., SA/Misc/1369; SA/Misc/1437–8.
[104] N.L.W., SA/Misc/1463.
[105] N.L.W., SA/Misc/1401; *Gueddi'r-Arglwydd wedi ei Hegluro* (1685); *Esponiad ar Gatechism yr Eglwys* (1688).
[106] N.L.W., SA/Misc/1368; *Cwnffwrdd ir Gwan Gristion* (1700).
[107] N.L.W., Llanstephan MS. 23A; SA/Misc/1452.

be recipients of public alms distributed within his parish.[108]

There is no reason to suppose that the industry and commitment of these clergymen were not shared by their fellows, for Bishop William Lloyd was a rigorous overseer of his clergy and as intolerant of negligence as any Welsh prelate in the seventeenth century. The indications are that he established so sound and efficient a catechetical activity within his diocese that it managed to survive the maladministration of his less capable successor, Edward Jones (1692–1703). On his appointment to St. Asaph in 1704, Bishop William Beveridge found, to his 'great comfort', that the duty of catechising was 'generally practised throughout the diocese every Lord's Day'.[109] For the benefit of his clergy, Beveridge published *The Church Catechism explained for the use of the Diocese of St. Asaph* (1704), a work translated into Welsh by Thomas Williams, rector of Denbigh, and published in 1708.[110] Beveridge's successor, William Fleetwood (1708–15), applied similarly strict standards, exhorting his clergy to catechise children and servants as much for social reasons as for their spiritual improvement: 'the whole parish', he urged, 'is better for dutiful children and honest servants; and much the worse for disobedient, false, lying, and thievish ones'.[111]

However, there are indications that by the second and third decades of the eighteenth century, the clergy were finding increasing difficulty in persuading parishioners to fulfil their obligations, and that the vast majority of rural parishes had lapsed into the habit of catechising only at Lent. The rural dean's report for the deanery of Rhôs in 1729 reveals that fifteen parishes were catechised only at Lent, and three only during the spring and summer seasons.[112] Similarly, each of the ten parishes in the deanery of Penllyn and Edeirnion was catechised at Lent only.[113] Most clergymen complained

---

[108] N.L.W., SA/Misc/1308. Williams was held in such esteem as to earn a fulsome elegy from the poet, Edward Morris. Gwenllian Jones, 'Bywyd a Gwaith Edward Morris, Perthi Llwydion', (unpubl. Univ. of Wales M.A. thesis, 1941), pp. 431–2.

[109] William Beveridge, op. cit., sig. A2v.

[110] Thomas Williams, *Eglurhaad o Gatechism yr Eglwys: wedi ei gyfieithu, er mwyn a lles Escobaeth Llanelwy* (1708).

[111] William Fleetwood, *The Bishop of St. Asaph's Charge to the Clergy of that Diocese in 1710* (1712), p. 35.

[112] N.L.W., SA/RD/18.

[113] N.L.W., SA/RD/21.

bitterly that parents were remiss in their duties and, by 1742, Thomas Jones, rector of Llandderfel, was able to report that catechising at Lent had become 'a custom . . . in most if not all country parishes in north Wales . . . when the country people think themselves more particularly bound to resort to the church and send their youth to be instructed'.[114] The confinement of regular catechising to Lent was not, however, peculiar to Wales for a similar pattern had emerged in rural parishes in England.[115] The tenure of Bishop William Lloyd at St. Asaph shows that there was no substitute for proper episcopal supervision, and the appointment of non-resident Englishmen of dubious merit to the dioceses of Bangor and St. Asaph under the early Hanoverians may have hastened the process. Without rigorous supervision from above, many of the clergy were disinclined to follow up their public exhortations by persistently hectoring errant parents within their parishes. Persuading parishioners of their duty remained an obligation that was rather more easily imposed than accepted.[116]

Catechetical instruction was often augmented by various forms of private enterprise. Although such agencies were not at work in all areas or at all times during this period, where they did exist an undoubted influence was exercised on popular religious instruction. Some lasting results were achieved by clerical societies at the turn of the century. In July 1700, Thomas Thomas of Carmarthen reported that clergymen in his county were working as a unit and had distributed 'many good books and revived catechising'. In the same year, John Price, vicar of Wrexham, recorded that the clergy of Flintshire and Montgomeryshire had joined in societies and were resolved to spend the summer catechising their youth, whilst in spite of the 'miserable neglect' of parents, 'catechumens' were also increasing in numbers in Caernarvonshire.[117] Such improvements were chiefly responses to the guide-lines laid down by Thomas Tenison, Archbishop of Canterbury,[118] and the newly-formed S.P.C.K. Catechetical lectures were also encouraged

[114] N.L.W., SA/QA/1, no. 69.
[115] Norman Sykes, *William Wake, Archbishop of Canterbury 1657–1737* (2 vols., 1957), I, 183.
[116] For a similar situation see John Bossy, 'The Counter-Reformation and the People of Catholic Europe', *P & P*, 47 (1970), 65.
[117] Clement, pp. 3, 5–6, 8, 11.
[118] N.L.W., Plasgwyn MS. 6, no. 144a–b, p. 7.

for the mutual benefit of clergy and parishioners. Catechising at Ruthin and Erbistock, for instance, was conducted for 'most part of the year' chiefly because a former vicar, John Robinson, had bequeathed in his will in 1703 the sum of £12 per annum to finance a catechetical lecture 'to the capacity of the meanest' every Sunday from March to the end of October.[119]

There are grounds for thinking, too, that the growing number of charity schools and small reading-schools were beginning to usurp the traditional catechetical duties of the clergy and certainly to compensate for ministerial deficiencies. The very presence of these schools improved enormously the social opportunities offered in backward rural areas and market towns.[120] There is no doubt, moreover, that they were in-valuable stimulants in the growth of literacy. But the advantage of having a charity school in a particular locality was often sullied by the use of English as the official medium of instruc-tion. This evidently made no difference in some of the more anglicised market towns, but there could be little hope of any dramatic improvements in the state of primary education in monoglot rural areas. As a result, perceptive clergymen and schoolmasters in north Wales chose to teach in the vernacular in order to achieve more lasting success. But English seems to have been the dominant language in the schools established in south Wales, and it is scarcely surprising, therefore, that patrons like Sir John Philipps of Picton should find that pupils might often recite the catechism perfectly but were 'literally ignorant of the meaning of the words, resurrection, saint, grace &c'.[121] Griffith Jones, Llanddowror, aired similar criticisms,[122] and the cardinal motive that prompted him to establish his Welsh circulating schools in the 1730s was his decision, based on years of practical experience, that the poor could not afford either the time or the money to spend long periods in charity schools where teaching was conducted through the medium of English. As a result, his schools were more successful than those of his predecessors simply because he had grasped the essential point that instilling a certain

---

[119] N.L.W., SA/MB/9; SA/RD/15, p. 3.
[120] For some rhapsodical remarks on the success of S.P.C.K. schools, see Clement, p. 97.
[121] Clement, p. 265.
[122] Griffith Jones, *Cyngor Rhad yr Anllythrennog* (1737), pp. 1–2.

measure of understanding and awareness was inseparable from the process of instructing children in the fundamental tenets of Christian doctrine.[123]

Nevertheless, the publication of a constant stream of expositions of the church catechism in this period did much to foster popular understanding of the rudiments of Christianity within schools and households. These 'sums of divinity' multiplied rapidly after 1660 as supplements to the prayer book,[124] and their translation into Welsh reflected a growing awareness of the pitfalls of learning by rote. Clerical authors knew from their own teaching experience that learning the catechism parrot-fashion was easily accomplished by the young; more taxing than this outward recognition was a degree of inner comprehension and a proper application of the doctrines embodied in the catechism. Most expositions, usually best-sellers in England, were thus aimed at 'babes in Christ' and were generally divided and sub-divided into subsidiary questions and answers. Particularly influential were William Foulkes's translation of Thomas Ken's *Exposition on the Church-Catechism, or the Practice of Divine Love* (1685), published in 1688, and John Morgan's translation of John Williams's *Brief Exposition of the Church Catechism* (1689), published in 1699. Both translations were immediately brought into use by the clergy of the dioceses of Bangor and St. Asaph, and were still key works in catechising programmes in the 1730s.[125]

With the formation of the S.P.C.K. in 1699 the number of Welsh catechisms and expositions multiplied rapidly. In 1708, Thomas Williams's translation of William Beveridge's popular exposition was dispersed throughout the four Welsh dioceses. Most expositions were designed for the use of householders and schoolmasters. None was more popular than John Lewis's *Church Catechism Explain'd* (1700), a work which ran through seven English editions of 12,000 copies each by 1714, and which was translated into Welsh in 1713.[126] Books explaining the duties

---

[123] See the comments of E. Le Roy Ladurie, *Les Paysans de Languedoc* (2 vols., 1966), I, 649.

[124] H. R. McAdoo, *The Spirit of Anglicanism* (1965), p. 324.

[125] William Foulkes, *Esponiad ar Gatechism yr Eglwys* (1688); John Morgan, *Eglurhad Byrr ar Gatechism yr Eglwys* (1699); N.L.W., Plasgwyn (Vivian) MS. 1, no. 21; Clement, p.6; N.L.W., SA/QA/1.

[126] Bod., MS. Rawlinson D.376, f. 105b; William Rowlands, *Catechism yr Eglwys* (1713).

involved in confirmation were also set out in catechetical form in 1706, a Welsh translation of Robert Nelson's *Instructions for them that come to be confirmed* (1706?) was published, and in 1711 Moses Williams translated and published Nelson's *Exercise for the Charity-Schools explaining the Nature of Confirmation* (1711).[127] In 1715, Moses Williams also published a thousand Welsh catechisms for the immediate benefit of his parishioners at Llanwenog in Cardiganshire.[128] Such basic text-books were further supplemented throughout this period by a battery of small, elementary primers designed to guide children along the path of literacy and true understanding. Bought by householders and read aloud to weak and illiterate members of the family, such works went a long way to furthering popular understanding of the fundamental principles of the Christian religion.

Although Dissenters considered catechising to be generally inferior to preaching,[129] it was still afforded a prominent position in their worship. In particular, Dissenters appreciated the need for heads of households to catechise their children and servants. To them, the home was a 'little church' as well as a nursery, where the *paterfamilias* was the chief director of catechetical activity and where each member of the household was bound to submit willingly to regular catechising. Special emphasis within schools and households was laid on fostering 'heart knowledge', for teaching by rote was entirely foreign to Welsh Dissenters and they frowned heavily on techniques that served to nurture mere 'parrots or popinjays'.[130] It was not enough, insisted Jenkin Jones, for children to acquaint themselves merely with the sounds and echoes of words, for ministers and parents had a duty to 'set things home upon the heart'.[131]

[127] Anon., *Naturiaeth Conffirmasiwn: wedi ei hegluro drwy Holi ac Ateb* (1706); Moses Williams, *Ymarferol-Waith i'r Elusen-Ysgolion* (1711); cf. *Cyngor yr Eglwyswr: i wr ieuangc newydd dderbyn Conffirmasiwn gan yr Esgob* (1703); *Catechism Sacramentaidd a amcanwyd er cyfarwyddyd i wasanaeth-ddynion tlodion* (1711).
[128] Clement, p. 82. A second edition was also issued in 1716. Other unpublished catechisms and expositions were clearly drawn up and used by clergymen and householders. See N.L.W. MS. 527A; N.L.W. MS. 13077B; N.L.W., Llanstephan MS. 23A; Llanstephan MS. 107B.
[129] Christopher Hill, *Society and Puritanism in Pre-Revolutionary England* (1966), p. 70.
[130] J. Lewis Wilson, 'Catechisms and their use among the Puritans', *One Steadfast High Intent* (The Puritan and Reformed Studies Conference, 1966), p. 42.
[131] Jenkin Jones, *Llawlyfr Plant sef Catecismau neu Hyfforddiadau yn Egwyddorion y Grefydd Gris'nogol* (1732), pp. iii–x.

Thus, works like William Evans's *Egwyddorion y Grefydd Cristionogawl* (1707)—dedicated to heads of households in the parishes of Pencader, Llanybri and Carmarthen—were composed in such a manner as to persuade families to rehearse the whole catechism regularly within a single month.[132]

The principal catechism employed by Dissenters during this period was the Shorter Catechism, prepared by the Westminster Assembly in 1647. After the Restoration it became 'the most widely recognised manual of instruction' among orthodox Dissenters.[133] In essence, the Shorter Catechism laid great stress on the condition of the individual believer and the means of his salvation through justifying faith. It figured prominently in the syllabus of unlicensed Dissenting schools in the years of persecution,[134] and most expositions, especially those published by the Welsh Trust,[135] were based upon it. The Shorter Catechism also appealed to moderate churchmen. William Evans's exposition in 1707 was financed by Anglican patrons, printed and published by an Anglican, John Rhydderch, and eventually issued with a copy of the Thirty-Nine Articles. Expositions of the catechism were also reckoned to be an invaluable means of promoting knowledge of the scriptures, and when Iaco ab Dewi's long-awaited translation of Matthew Henry's *Scripture-Catechism* (1702) was published in 1717, it was prefaced by an epistle of commendation signed by a number of overjoyed Dissenting ministers.[136] In 1719, too, the tiny press at Trefhedyn issued a Welsh translation of Thomas Vincent's *Explicatory Catechism* (1673), a bulky exposition designed to plant the basic rudiments and resolve cases of conscience.[137]

Even so, there were many percipient Dissenters who felt that the Shorter Catechism and expositions of that work were too demanding for children. It was widely thought that the

---

[132] William Evans, *Egwyddorion y Grefydd Gristianogawl* (1707), sig. A1v-A2r.
[133] Alexander F. Mitchell, *Catechisms of the Second Reformation* (1886), p. xxix; cf. S. W. Carruthers, *Three Centuries of the Westminster Shorter Catechism* (1957).
[134] Bod., Tanner MS. 146, f. 138r-v; John Davies, *Y Lloffyn Addfed* (1852), p. 20.
[135] William Jones, *Principlau neu Bennau y Grefydd Gristianogol* (1676); Thomas Gouge, *The Principles of Christian Religion* (1679); Charles Edwards, *Gwyddorion y Grefydd Gristianogol* (1679); Charles Edwards, *Catecism yn cynwys Pyngciau y Grefydd Gristianogol* (1682).
[136] William Evans (ed.), *Iaco ab Dewi, Catecism o'r Scrythur* (1717).
[137] J. P. and T. J., *Eglurhaad o Gatechism Byrraf y Gymanfa* (1719).

Catechism was too long for them and, in parts at least, 'too abstruse and quite above their capacity'.[138] Thus, in 1708 and again in 1727, Jenkin Evans's Welsh translation of Matthew Henry's *A Catechism for Children* (1700) was published for the benefit of those children who had not made sufficient progress to be able to master the Assembly's Catechism[139] The Arminian minister, Jenkin Jones, also believed that the 107 questions and answers in the Shorter Catechism were far too burdensome a load to place on frail shoulders. Declaiming strongly against forcing children to cut their teeth on nuts and almonds, he voiced the common concern that all possible avenues should be explored in order that catechumens be able to understand the principles of their faith.[140] Clearly, the achievement of a basic level of understanding was a problem common to churchmen and Dissenters in this period. Without this foundation, religious reformers held out little hope of leading their flocks on to bigger and better things.

[138] William Tong, *An Account of the Life and Death of . . . Mr. Matthew Henry* (1716), p. 211.

[139] Jenkin Evans, *Catecism Byrr i Blant* (1708; 1727).

[140] Jenkin Jones, *Llawlyfr Plant*, pp. iii–x.

IV

MORAL IMPERATIVES

Throughout this period religious reformers of different persuasions were greatly preoccupied with what appeared to them to be the sinfulness of Welshmen. Many commentators, nursed carefully in the puritan tradition that saw every sin as a rebellion against God's will, couched their accounts in terms both lugubrious and general. In 1661, Elis Lewis's indictment of the sins and sinfulness of his countrymen was heightened by his bitterness over the turmoils of the past two decades. Men, he grieved, were idle, unruly, pretentious, arrogant, stubborn, proud and boastful.[1] In 1681, that tireless moralist, Stephen Hughes, voiced the rigorous standards set by old Dissent in a lengthy catalogue of the sins of the world: cursing, swearing, adultery, hypocrisy, malice, lying, perjury, slander and mockery.[2] Similarly, the satirical portraits painted in Ellis Wynne's famous trilogy of visions in 1703 reflected the universal sins of mankind not merely the moral shortcomings of his own society.[3]

Gloomy accounts such as these were made by men who, captured by the strictest puritan ethics, were profoundly suspicious of worldly pleasures and were bent on inculcating the habits of moral and social discipline, efficiency and restraint, decorum of bearing and propriety of speech, sobriety, caution and thrift. Fortified by their firm, and often high-minded, spiritual principles, they consciously waged war upon sin and wickedness. Essentially spiritual warriors, they attacked the eternal enemy, Satan, and vowed to rid the world of corruption and evil. The flow of moralising literature was increasing rapidly in this period, and although Welsh authors inveighed against sins which were universal in their application, they were also agreed that three major sins were widely

---

[1] Elis Lewis, *Ystyriaethau Drexelivs ar Dragywyddoldeb* (1661), sig. A3v–A4r.
[2] Stephen Hughes, *Adroddiad Cywir o'r Pethau pennaf* (1681), p. 12.
[3] Ellis Wynne, *Gweledigaetheu'r Bardd Cwsc* (1703).

prevalent within their own society. These were Sabbath breaking, drunkenness and vain swearing. Profaning the Lord's Day, claimed John Rhydderch in 1716, was the principal sin of his countrymen.[4] 'Swearing and drunkenness' thundered William Powell in 1727, were 'the bane of society.' Special efforts were thus made to seek to eradicate the grosse aspects of these sins, and the torrent of Welsh literature published on these subjects suggests that the printing press had a major rôle to play in this task.

I. SABBATARIANISM

Religious reformers who were anxious to elicit a more rigid adherence to the fourth commandment were confronted with two major problems: enforcing attendance at church and eradicating the more boisterous recreations that interfered with Sunday worship. The exigencies of poverty kept many of the poorer elements from the church door on the Sabbath, and *douceurs* of various kinds were often required to bring them to some form of religious worship.[6] Moreover, church authorities knew that it was scarcely worth presenting the poor before church courts for non-attendance since few of them could afford to pay the ensuing fines. Apart from those browbeaten into obedience by their landlords most of the poor remained preoccupied with either their struggle to make ends meet or their delight in the wide variety of Sabbath recreations. After 1689, the problem seems to have worsened, for many rural inhabitants simply contracted out. The slender number of regular communicants at Sunday worship[7] in this period suggests that a growing proportion of the population never darkened the church door, and the establishment of licensed Nonconformist chapels underlined the fact that Dissenting ministers were now able to compete lawfully and openly with clergymen for the allegiance of parishioners.

---

[4] John Rhydderch, *Cilgwth neu Ergyd at Halogedigaeth a Llygredigaeth* (1716) title-page.
[5] William Powell, *Swearing and Drunkenness, the Bane of Society, and Destructive to Body and Soul* (1727), title-page.
[6] Clement, p. 53; Robert Nelson, *The Life of Dr. George Bull* (2nd ed., 1714) pp. 450–1.
[7] See pp. 71–2.

Among those who did attend church, a wide range of motives and standards of behaviour prevailed. There were, of course, large numbers who fulfilled their duties unostentatiously, worshipping regularly and in a spirit of true devotion and seriousness.[8] To others attendance at divine service was simply a matter of habit.[9] Some ventured to church merely to catch up with the latest gossip, and many others came 'to see and be seen'.[10] Irreverent behaviour during services was a constant irritant to clergymen. Men whispered and laughed, fidgeted and itched, burped like babies, quarrelled and fought during sermons.[11] Among the least attentive were young maidens on the look out for a likely husband, and libidinous males who ogled back at the prettiest among them.[12] The more cynical came to chortle over the minister's shortcomings whilst others, happy to let 'the devil rock their cradle', simply fell asleep.[13]

The Sabbath, moreover, was still a day of recreation in rural areas. Many of the traditional sports survived the restrictive puritan legislation of the Interregnum. The ball-game known as *knappan* retained its buoyancy in the shires of south-west Wales and was particularly popular on Sundays and Holy Days.[14] In early-eighteenth century Anglesey, dancing, leaping, wrestling and football in the churchyard were regular preliminaries to divine service.[15] The traditional centre of recreation was the churchyard and, in many areas, the most exciting of popular spectacles—cockfighting—was held in cockpits situated on the northern (and traditionally the least holy) side of the churchyard.[16] The records of the

[8] Ellis Wynne, op. cit., p. 36.

[9] Richard Parry, *Dihuniad Cysgadur* (1723), p. 4.

[10] Stephen Hughes (ed.), Henry Evans, *Cynghorion Tad i'w Fab* (1683), p. 59; anon., *A Journey to Llandrindod Wells* (2nd ed., 1746), p. 45.

[11] N.L.W. MS. 6900A, pp. 10–11; N.L.W., Llandaff/CC/G/407, 417; Llandaff/CC/G/208.

[12] N.L.W. MS. 11991A, p. 25; *C.C.H.M.C.*, no. 1 (1917), 11–14; Ellis Wynne, op. cit., p. 36.

[13] John Thomas, *Unum Necessarium* (1680), p. 13.

[14] H. M. Waddington, 'Games and Athletics in Bygone Wales', *T.H.S.C.*, 1953, pp. 89–90.

[15] Hugh Owen (ed.), *The Life and Works of Lewis Morris, 1701–1765*(1951), p.141.

[16] M. H. Lee (ed.), *Diaries and Letters of Philip Henry*, p. 170; N.L.W., Bodewryd (Sotheby) Correspondence, no. 169; N.L.W., Penrice and Margam MSS. A98–100; Elias Owen, 'Churchyard Games in Wales', *The Reliquary and Illustrated Archaeologist*, 1–2 (1895–6); I. C. Peate, 'The Denbigh Cockpit and Cockfighting in Wales', *Denbighshire Hist. Soc. Trans.*, 19 (1970), 125–32.

church courts reveal that persistent offenders might master a
wide range of sports: Evan Treharne and David Williams of
Llanharan were presented in May 1726 for playing 'tennis
ball, fives ball, bowls, quoits, skittles, and other idle and
unlawful games'.[17]

Dancing to the tunes of pipers, fiddlers, harpists and minstrels
was also a particularly popular recreation on Sundays. After
1660 the maypole once more became a striking feature of
village greens and a focal point for companies of Morris
dancers.[18] In 1679, Thomas Wynne, the Quaker barber-
surgeon of Caerwys, spoke out against the 'great meetings' on
Sundays in his neighbourhood, 'with fiddlers, to revel and
roar, swear, dance and sing, yea, the same up and down the
country, and Morris dances, waxes, interludes, football,
ninepins and tennis'.[19] Such recreations lost little of their
popularity during this period,[20] particularly among 'uneducated, poor, and labouring people'.[21] Many of these
revelries were encouraged by excessive drink consumed on
Sundays. Erasmus Saunders was convinced that the irregularity
with which church services were held in parts of the diocese of
St. David's meant that congregations were 'too apt to think
themselves at liberty to spend the remaining part of the day at
an alehouse, or at some pastime or diversion'.[22] Moreover, a
surfeit of drink often meant that fairly innocuous revelries
degenerated into unseemly quarrels and brawls within church-
yards. In 1722, Thomas Miller of Pentyrch was presented
before the ecclesiastical authorities for assaulting David John
of Pendeulwyn in a churchyard and beating him 'upon his
head, face, and other parts of his body, even to the effusion
of his blood'.[23] Similarly, David Jones, a tiler of Abergavenny,

[17] N.L.W., Ll/CC/G/427–8. For other examples see SD/CCB/55; SD/CCB(G)/
389; SD/CCB(G)/556–7.
[18] For some examples of reformers' complaints against the maypole see N.L.W.,
SA/Misc/1346; SA/Misc/1369; SA/Misc/1481; Friends' House Library, Kelsall
MSS. Diaries, 1, p. 208.
[19] Thomas Wynne, *An Antichristian Conspiracy Detected* (1679), p. 17.
[20] For various examples see N.L.W., Wynnstay MS. 6, pp. 238–40; SD/CCB(G)/
137; SD/CCB/55; SA/RD/17; SA/RD/21, p. 23; SA/QA/1, nos. 60, 88; SA/QA/2,
no. 11.
[21] William Fleetwood, *The Bishop of St. Asaph's Charge to the Clergy of that Diocese
in 1710* (1712), p. 33.
[22] Saunders, p. 25.
[23] N.L.W., Ll/CC/G/278.

was accused in 1727 of having assaulted David Morris in the belfry of St. Mary's, Abergavenny, and of having lashed him with the rope of one of the bells until it twisted around his neck and almost strangled him.[24] How far behaviour of this kind was common to all grades in society is difficult to assess. One suspects that church courts prosecuted only persistent offenders, especially those who deliberately and mischievously interfered with church services by their revelries.[25] The poor were undoubtedly culpable, and the number of labourers, husbandmen and yeomen who appeared before the church courts and who became the errant subjects of cautionary tales peddled by ballad-mongers suggests that they, too, were by no means blameless. The most that can be said is that although Sunday was a day of devotion and rest for the pious, it was also a day of diversion and boisterous merriment for many sections of society.

Sober-minded Anglicans and Dissenters were not prepared to dismiss such profaneness as inconsequential. 'He is blind' pronounced James Owen, 'that sees not this [Sabbath-breaking] to be one of the crying sins of the land.'[26] As a result, authors of Sabbatarian literature were anxious to graft the values and standards of puritanism on to more rustic, backward communities.[27] The Sabbath, it was stressed, was 'the market-day of the soul', 'the queen of days, the pearl of the week'.[28] The seventh day belonged to God: it was his *rightful* day, and men were expected to perform specific duties in obedience to Him. No manner of work, save for deeds of the utmost necessity and acts of compassion, might be carried out. Sabbath-breaking thus entailed ploughing, sowing, reaping, harvesting, and any other worldly employments or pleasures.[29] Recreations on Sundays, moreover, were judged to be flagrant breaches of the puritan moral code. If God, urged Richard Jones in 1675, had proscribed the practice of honest and legal callings on the

---

[24] N.L.W., Ll/CC/G/445 a–b. For further examples see SD/CCB(G)/550; Ll/CC/G/189–189a; Ll/CC/G/491a–d.
[25] See, for instance, N.L.W., SD/CCB(G)/651; SD/CCB(G)/540.
[26] Charles Owen, *Some Account of . . . James Owen*, p. 50; cf. Jeremy Owen, *Traethawd i brofi . . .* (1733), p. 32.
[27] Christopher Hill, *Society and Puritanism in pre-revolutionary England* (1964), p. 191.
[28] Richard Jones, *Hyfforddiadau Christianogol* (1675), p. 97; J. B. Williams (ed.), Matthew Henry, *The Life of the Rev. Philip Henry* (1825), p. 80.
[29] James Owen, *Trugaredd a Barn* (1715), p. 46.

Sabbath, then so much more would he deplore unlawful and unnecessary recreations on His day.[30]

Although religious reformers were eager to establish the Sabbath as a day of rest, they were even more concerned that it should become a day of spiritual labour and dedication. Virtually all the major devotional and didactic books published in this period devoted some part of their content to stressing the duties implicit in the fourth commandment. Every minute of the Lord's Day was thought to be precious, for time was a sacred, God-given gift. For every twenty years of our lives, claimed Philip Henry, 'we enjoy above a thousand Sabbaths, which must all be accounted for in the day of reckoning'.[31] Rees Prydderch, an equally thorough-going puritan, offered no loophole for either the slothful or the profane: it was worse, he maintained, to be idle than to work on the Lord's Day—but both were evil in themselves.[32] Sunday, claimed Edward Samuel, was the most profitable day of the week, a day indeed of spiritual harvest.[33]

Keeping the Sabbath holy depended on proper preparation and diligent performance.[34] The true Christian was expected to retire early to bed in order to rise early on the Sunday morning. While dressing, the worshipper should engage in morning prayers and meditations, and, before setting off for the church, he was urged to adopt a devotional frame of mind so that he might profit more from divine service by being 'in the spirit'. The whole household was expected to attend church—and each individual should do so willingly and joyfully. Within the church, each member was to pray earnestly and listen attentively to the minister. On their return home, it became the special duty of the head of the household to call his family together to discuss the day's sermon with them. The *paterfamilias* was expected also to read parts of the scriptures, to catechise the children and servants, and lead them in psalm-singing and evening prayers.[35] True religion, it was widely

[30] Richard Jones, op. cit., p. 37; Jeremy Owen, op. cit., p. 33; Charles Owen, op. cit., p. 84.
[31] Matthew Henry, op. cit., pp. 81, 192.
[32] William Evans (ed.), Rees Prydderch, *Gemmeu Doethineb* (1714), p. 74.
[33] Edward Samuel, *Holl Ddyledswydd Dyn* (1718), p. 52.
[34] Richard Steele, *The Husbandmans Calling* (1668), p. 272.
[35] This paragraph is based on the duties outlined in Robert Lloyd's *Duwioldeb ar Ddydd yr Arglwydd* (1698) and Richard Jones's *Hyfforddiadau Christianogol* (1675).

believed, never flowered in those households where the Sabbath was disregarded and where family duties were ignored.

An even more substantial body of literature sought to instil into the reader's mind the penalties that befell Sabbath-breakers. Not only did idle and immoderate persons automatically end their days in a state of poverty and squalor,[36] but they might also be the butt of God's wrath on several occasions. In 1678, Edward Roberts, vicar of Capel Garmon, showed how God struck down those who worked, travelled, swam, played or drank heavily on the Sabbath.[37] Similarly, Rowland Vaughan's popular translation of *The Practice of Piety* included a wealth of biblical and contemporary tales that illustrated God's methods of punishing Sabbath-breakers.[38] James Owen's monitory *Trugaredd a Barn*, published in 1687, 1715 and 1722, contained not only material culled from works such as William Twisse's *The Christian Sabbath Defended* (1652) but also local examples related to him by word of mouth.[39] One of his most arresting examples was that of a hapless sawyer of Nantwich who, on cutting wood for a maypole on the Sabbath, collapsed and died suddenly. It was hoped that such exemplars might discourage others, and when Philip Henry noted the same incident in his diary, he fervently expected that 'all who might hear might fear, and do no more so wickedly'.[40] It was inevitable, however, that the achievements of reformers fell short of their intentions in this period. The Methodist revival did a good deal to encourage a stricter adherence to the fourth commandment, but, even at the end of the eighteenth century, preachers and authors were still fulminating against the abuse of the Sabbath. In the last resort, it was the growth of a powerful Nonconformist conscience which succeeded in enforcing the austere conception of a biblical Sabbath that had been so diligently promulgated by early puritan reformers.

[36] Edward Morris, *Y Rhybuddiwr Christnogawl* (1689), p. 19.
[37] N.L.W. MS. 527A, pp. 96–101.
[38] Rowland Vaughan, *Yr Ymarfer o Dduwioldeb* (1675), pp. 224–6. Other tracts, no longer extant, probably contained their quota of punishments doled out to Sabbath-breakers. In 1672, Stephen Hughes received a Welsh translation of William Gouge's *The Sabbath's Sanctification* (1641). Stephen Hughes (ed.), *Mr. Perkins His Catechism* (1672), sig. A6v. Another Sabbatarian tract no longer extant is R. Jones, *Rheol i wasanaethu Duw ar Ddydd Sul* (1705).
[39] James Owen, *Trugaredd a Barn*, pp. 46–51.
[40] M. H. Lee, op. cit., p. 288.

II. DRUNKENNESS

Alcoholic beverages figured prominently in most public and private ceremonies, at fairs and markets, at christenings, weddings, funerals, wakes and revels. The staple drink was beer, on which, according to one estimate, something like one-seventh of the nation's total income was expended.[41] A good deal of beer was also brewed privately and varied greatly in quality: William Bulkeley, squire of Bryn-ddu in Anglesey, was something of an expert at spicing and sweetening home-brewed ale which might supplement, as in other gentle households, imported claret and wines.[42] Buttermilk and mead were also popular beverages, whilst in the heather moorlands and hillier districts, honey was available for the making of metheglin—'the wine of Wales', which was tartly dismissed as 'Welsh hogs' wash' by Englishmen.[43] Nevertheless, beer was the standard beverage and was drunk in particularly large quantities at fairs and markets (which were exempt from the normal licensing hours) and festive gatherings. According to Lewis Morris, most guests at christenings in eighteenth-century Anglesey ended the day helplessly drunk. Weddings, too, were occasions for 'drinking, wooing, dancing . . . fighting'.[44] Prior to a funeral, friends and acquaintances kept vigil throughout the night, 'smoking and drinking about a long table and the dead corpse under it', and, on the day of the burial, they adjourned to the tavern to await the time of the service.[45]

As always, taverns were seductive and popular social centres. In a society bereft of alternative social amenities, they offered refreshment, light, heat, relatively comfortable furniture, recreation and amusement, news, gossip and a communal spirit. Within their walls many people escaped, if only briefly, from the sheer drudgery of their daily toil. The indications are

---

[41] Charles Wilson, *England's Apprenticeship, 1603–1763* (1971), p. 22.

[42] G. Nesta Evans, *Social Life in mid-Eighteenth Century Anglesey* (1936), pp. 73–4; P. R. Roberts, 'The Social History of the Merioneth Gentry, c. 1660–1840', *Journal Merioneth Hist. & Rec. Soc.*, IV (1963), 218; Gareth H. Williams, 'A Study of Caernarfonshire Probate Records, 1630–1690' (unpubl. Univ. of Wales M.A. thesis, 1972), p. 130.

[43] R. F. Bretherton, 'County Inns and Alehouses', in R. Lennard (ed.), *Englishmen at Rest and Play. Some Phases of English Leisure, 1558–1714* (1931), pp. 172–3. The poorer sorts drank beer made of oaten malt. David Lewis, 'A Progress through Wales in the Seventeenth Century', *Y Cymmrodor*, VI (1883), 147.

[44] Hugh Owen, op. cit., p. 142.

[45] N.L.W. MS. 10B, p. 91; N.L.W. MS. 559B, p. 35.

that unlicensed alehouses—so strictly repressed in Cromwellian times—were increasing rapidly in numbers, attracting a disreputable clientèle that was more prone to self-indulgence and wild behaviour.[46] But visiting taverns was not, in itself, frowned upon. 'Men may certainly go thither', assured William Powell, 'and yet continue very innocent; it is the too frequent resort, and the excess that is committed there, that is to be condemned.'[47] Alcoholic liquor was thus an essential ingredient in men's diet. This was partly owing to a dearth of adequate substitutes: water, for instance, was rarely safe to drink, while the drinking of tea and coffee—the butt of much good-humoured banter by ballad-mongers—was restricted to the tables of gentle ladies. Drink as such, then, was not outlawed, for the virtues of total abstinence were not extolled until the nineteenth century. But drunkenness was an affront to the puritan conscience, and sermons and printed literature constantly stressed the duty of moderation. In calling for a greater degree of sobriety and restraint, reformers always made a sharp distinction between drinking and being given to drink. In a memorable phrase, Bishop William Lloyd urged men to 'dabble a little, but not be drowned'.[48]

It is not easy to assess the prevalence of drunkenness. During festive occasions it was probably not confined to any particular social class. And since the normal price of ale was a penny a quart, a state of intoxication could be achieved relatively cheaply by those who were able to afford to buy alcohol regularly. On the basis of his experiences in London, Daniel Defoe feared that drunkenness was fast becoming part of 'the nation's character', and the much-travelled Welsh drover, Edward Morris, was not inclined to disagree.[49] None clung to their drinking habits more tenaciously than the gentry. Many of them were imprudent spenders whose delight in rakish

---

[46] J. Gwynfor Jones, 'The Caernarvonshire Justices of the Peace and their Duties during the Seventeenth Century' (unpubl. Univ. of Wales M.A. thesis, 1967), pp. 161–2. For efforts to suppress the activities of illicit alehouses in the diocese of St. David's, see N.L.W., SD/CCB(G)/351; SD/CCB(G)/361; SD/CCB(G)/391.

[47] William Powell, *Swearing and Drunkenness*, p. 37.

[48] N.L.W. MS. 11303D, f. 86v.

[49] D. W. R. Bahlman, *The Moral Revolution of 1688* (1957), p. 2; Gwenllian Jones, 'Bywyd a Gwaith Edward Morris' (unpubl. Univ. of Wales M.A. thesis, 1941), p. 300.

frivolities and self-indulgence often led them to an early grave.[50] Philip Henry's diary was significantly littered with examples of gentleman acquaintances of his who died of 'a surfeit of drink'.[51] More disturbing were those cases of drunkenness involving clergymen. The traditional portrait of beer-bellied parsons is often overcoloured, but it is nevertheless clear that many clergymen, for various reasons, were 'too apt to sip'.[52] Many of those who were anxious to gate-crash the circle of polite society and thereby rid themselves of the stigma of poverty unashamedly consorted with the local squirearchy, sharing their tables and 'cherishing their spirits' with ale and wines.[53] Consequently, many clergymen became liable to intoxication and the indiscretions which stem from excessive drink. Curates were duly warned in 1729 by Roger Kynaston, rector of Llanfechain, to spend less time 'in public conversation or at the tables of the laity, where generally speaking they meet with nothing else but either bad principles or intemperate practices'.[54] In addition to those who chafed against the restraints which poverty imposed upon them were those clergymen who, aware of their own personal shortcomings, took to drink because of their inability to live up to the increasingly high standards of personal morality and pastoral care demanded of them.

As for the rest of society, the reply of the churchwardens of Llangain in the archdeaconry of Carmarthen in 1705 probably reflected the situation in most rural parishes: 'as for common swearers and drunkards we cannot say they are very notorious sinners of that kind, but are aware too many are highly blameable in this parish as most parishes'.[55] The age-old instruments of punishment and coercion—whipping-posts,

---

[50] Joseph Cradock, *Letters from Snowdonia* (1770), pp. 80–1; H. P. Wyndham, *A Tour through Monmouthshire and Wales 1774* (2nd ed., 1781), p. 123; P. R. Roberts, 'The Decline of the Welsh Squires', *N.L.W.J.*, XIII (1963–4), 164.

[51] M. H. Lee, op. cit., *passim*.

[52] For some examples of clergymen guilty of intemperance, see N.L.W. SD/Misc. B/131, pp. 22, 28, 33, 54, 62, 66–7; Ll/CC/G/272; Ll/CC/G/550 a–b; Ll/CC/G/487; Ll/CC/G/620 a–b; SA/RD/21, pp. 97, 113, 132, 142, 145.

[53] A good example of this kind of hob-nobbing was the relationship between Richard Bulkeley, rector of Llanfechell, and William Bulkeley, squire of Brynddu. G. N. Evans, 'Llanfechell Church, 1734 to 1760', *Trans. Anglesey Antiq. Soc.*, 1947, p. 83; cf. A. Tindal Hart, *The Country Priest in English History* (1959), pp. 85–7.

[54] N.L.W., SA/RD/17, p. 14.

[55] N.L.W., SD/Archdeaconry of Carmarthen/Churchwardens' returns 1705/119.

ducking-stools and stocks—were still used to bring habitual drunkards to heel, but it is probable that heavy drinking was confined to the week-end, together with wakes and festivals. Frequenting 'Satan's Exchange'[56] on the Sabbath was itself a release from tensions and was often the only day in the week on which men succumbed to heavy tippling. Richard Steele believed that most frugal husbandmen were 'in exceeding fault' only at the 'great festivals and yearly wakes'.[57] Similarly, in industrial communities, intemperance was rife only on those occasions when workers were released from the grinding monotony of their labour.[58] At the lowest levels, drink provided an essential anodyne for those sunk in misery and deprivation, but even so alcoholic intake cannot have been all that heavy in view of the constant dearth of ready cash. It is, perhaps, rather too easy to exaggerate the number of people who dedicated a substantial portion of their lives to Bacchus.

Nevertheless, puritan reformers were determined to augment moral imperatives against intemperance from the pulpit with a solid battery of didactic books. The general message was that the drunkard was a social nuisance and that intemperance was both wasteful and ruinous. Much stress was laid on the excesses that inevitably accompanied merry-making at alehouses, and graphic portraits were painted of the self-indulgence and licentiousness of the tavern.[59] According to Rees Prichard, the drunkard's God was Bacchus, his church was the tavern, the innkeeper's spouse was his priest, and the pipe and the beer-glass were the equivalent of the elements.[60] Intemperance, it was claimed, sapped man's intelligence, drowned his judgment and reduced him to the level of a vile and bestial creature.[61] The drunkard's appearance was surely a deterrent to others:

> One might naturally expect, that the very sight of a drunken man, the seeing what a trifling, vain, weak, and contemptible

[56] Erasmus Saunders, *A Domestick Charge* (1701), p. 84.
[57] Richard Steele, op. cit., p. 208.
[58] Friends' House Library, Kelsall MSS. Diaries, V, p. 143; N.L.W., Penrice and Margam MS. 5555.
[59] A good portrait of carefree and often unruly roistering is drawn in Thomas Jones (ed.), *Carolau a Dyriau Duwiol* (1696), pp. 309–14.
[60] Stephen Hughes (ed.), Rees Prichard, *Canwyll y Cymru* (1681), p. 162.
[61] Richard Jones, *Traethawd ar Feddwdod* (1675), p. 2; E. J., *Annogaeth yn erbyn y Pechod o Feddwdod* (1720), pp. 7–8; Gwenllian Jones, op. cit., pp. 300–1.

figure he makes, should be a powerful restraint to keep all others from falling into the same deplorable weakness, and from being the scorn and derision of very boys. Look upon the drunkard, when his eyes stare, his mouth drivels, his tongue falters, and his feet reel; how ugly, how loathsome, how monstrous does he seem to thee?[62]

Authors made the further point that drunkenness gave a free rein to baser instincts. Insobriety, maintained Edward Morris, was the mother of sin.[63] Every time a man became drunk he became more and more likely to commit the same sin again and then graduate to other excesses. 'Where wine gets the mastery', warned John Copner, 'all the ill that before lies hidden breaks out.'[64] One of James Owen's most telling examples in *Trugaredd a Barn* was the tale of the young man of unblemished character who was tempted by the devil to choose one of three sins: to become drunk once, to lie with his neighbour's wife, or to kill his neighbour. In his quandary, the young man chose what he judged to be the least offensive sin— to become intoxicated; but having done so, he went on to sleep with his neighbour's wife and to kill his neighbour.[65] It was also argued that intemperance was an exercise in self-destruction since, among other things, it might bring on dropsy and consumption. Where the sword had killed thousands, urged one author, drunkenness had been responsible for the death of tens of thousands.[66]

Such prudential morality was best expressed in Edward Morris's translation of John Rawlet's *The Christian Monitor*, published in Welsh in 1689, 1699 and 1706. Preaching the virtues of thrift, frugality, sobriety and moderation, Morris dwelt on the familiar tale of the habitual drunkard who dissipated his income, found himself in prison for bankruptcy, and who eventually died, leaving a penniless widow to support his family.[67] Drunkenness could thus ruin families, reducing them 'to the lowest ebb of misery and want',[68] and those who

[62] William Powell, op. cit., p. 29.
[63] Gwenllian Jones, op. cit., p. 301; cf. anon., *Testament y Dauddeg Padriarch* (1700), p. 60; Edward Samuel, *Holl Ddyledswydd Dyn* (1718), p.192.
[64] N.L.W. MS. 2905A, p. 140.
[65] James Owen, *Trugaredd a Barn*, p. 68.
[66] N.L.W. MS. 9A, p. 266; *Annogaeth yn erbyn y Pechod o Feddwdod*, p. 10.
[67] Edward Morris, op. cit., pp. 18–19.
[68] William Powell, op. cit., p. 31.

might still doubt the wisdom of that creed were plied with scriptural evidence ('he that loveth wine and oil shall not be rich', Prov. xxi 17;, for the drunkard and the glutton shall come to poverty', Prov. xxiii 21) that pointed unmistakably to the dangers of prodigality.[69] It was widely held that poverty stemmed from intemperance rather than *vice versa*, and only those who preached the puritan ethic in a shrewder manner sought to solve the problem at its roots. Rees Prydderch, for instance, earnestly prevailed on brewers to make bread from corn and barley to sell or distribute among the starving poor.[70] Similarly, Ellis Wynne fired some of his most prickly barbs into the corpulent flesh of grasping innkeepers and publicans who figured prominently in his Street of Profit.[71] Most authors, however, preferred to show drunkards the error of their ways and warn those who stubbornly chose to wallow imprudently in a state of inebriation that retribution was swift, if not on this earth, then in the next.

III. VAIN SWEARING AND CURSING

Commentators in this period were pretty well agreed that cursing and swearing had been invented by 'the rich, the easy, and the thoughtless great men of the world'.[72] Isaac Barrow reckoned that vain swearing carried 'a genteel and graceful quality, a mark of fine breeding and a point of high gallantry'.[73] 'Many think to swear is gentleman-like', claimed John Bunyan, whilst Richard Steele found 'witty wicked heads' most culpable.[74] But it was also widely known that poorer orders were indulging in the same sins, and it was feared that vain swearing had become almost ineradicably woven into the fabric of men's lives. 'What oaths', mourned James Owen, 'what blasphemies, what immoralities abound among us.'[75] 'Is it not strange', asked Bishop William Fleetwood, 'to hear poor

---

[69] Cited in *Traethawd ar Feddwdod*, p. 5.
[70] Rees Prydderch, op. cit., p. 159.
[71] Ellis Wynne, op. cit., p. 19.
[72] William Fleetwood, *A Sermon upon Swearing* (1721), p. 28.
[73] Isaac Barrow, *Several Sermons against Evil-Speaking* (1678), p. 26.
[74] Cited in Christopher Hill, *The World turned Upside Down* (1972), p. 162; Richard Steele, op. cit., p. 214.
[75] James Owen, *Salvation Improved* (1696), p. 23; cf. Richard Steele, op. cit., p. 215.

people swearing at the plough, and at their daily labour, swearing at their horses, cattle, and anything that comes in their way?'[76] Cases of defamation were endemic in the consistory courts, with careless talk especially common among the highest and lowest orders. Churchmen generally admitted that Dissenters were innocent of this sin. 'Whence is it', complained William Powell, 'that we who have the best religion should deform it with the worst manners?'[77]

Vain swearing, in contemporary language, normally entailed common oaths, expletives, curses and blasphemies. At the most extreme level the Welsh equivalents of English 'four-letter' words were well-established in the Welshman's vocabulary. Welsh clergymen were appalled by the number of 'accursed' English oaths that had penetrated thoroughly Welsh communities and become absorbed in a corrupt and stilted form.[78] When John Wesley trekked north to Anglesey in 1750 he found 'sons of Belial' whose daily conversation in Welsh was riddled with oaths and curses in broad English.[79] Among the most prevalent oaths and blasphemies were 'Od's Buds' or 'Sbuds', 'Od's Zownds', 'Od's Life' or 'Slife', 'Od's Zooks' and 'Od's me'. In truly monoglot areas the current oaths were 'Myn Duw' (By God), 'Myn chwys Duw' (By the sweat of God), 'Duw'n farn' (As God is my judge), and 'Myn Crist' (By Christ). At fairs and markets men were prone to invoke God or Christ whilst buying and bargaining, whilst the invocation of favourite saints was deeply-embedded in their daily conversation.[80] To some extent, as Hill suggests, swearing was 'an act of defiance', a tangible protest by 'vulgar sorts' against the puritan ethic.[81] By and large, however, most common expletives were uttered almost unconsciously, particularly those 'dreadful oaths and curses' heard among children at play.[82] Moreover, few understood or reflected on the profane words that they uttered.

[76] William Fleetwood, A Sermon, p. 28.
[77] William Powell, op. cit., p. 11; cf. the view of Richard Davies, vicar of Ruabon, N.L.W. MS. 7396A, p. 100.
[78] Simon Jones, Dr. Wells's Letter to a Friend (1730), p. 18; John Prichard Prŷs, Difyrrwch Crefyddol (1721), pp. 103–4; John Jones, Cennad oddiwrth y Ser (1721), pp. 7–10; N.L.W., B/MC/409; N.L.W. MS. 2771B; N.L.W. MS. 12444B.
[79] A. H. Williams (ed.), John Wesley in Wales, 1739–1790 (1971), p. 47.
[80] Simon Jones, op. cit., pp. 17–18; Henry Evans, op cit., p. 58; Iaco ab Dewi, Llythyr y Dr. Well's at Gyfaill (1714), p. 14; Rees Prydderch, op. cit., p. 172.
[81] Hill, The World turned Upside Down, p. 162.
[82] William Powell, op. cit., p. 23; Clement, p. 90.

James Owen noticed how some of his countrymen used the expletive 'Godsowns' without having the slightest inkling of its true meaning.[83]

How far blasphemous statements were the fruit of scepticism or open infidelity is hard to judge. There must have been disbelievers, particularly among the educated who, when called before their betters to answer for their oral indiscretions, may well have voiced the apathy and atheism that was shared by a small, but often vocal, minority. In 1698, William Morgan, a gentleman of Neath, was presented before the court of Great Sessions as 'an impious, profane and irreligious person', one who had not 'the fear of God in his heart'. It was claimed that Morgan, having been seduced by the devil, had vilified the Christian religion in the most blasphemous terms. 'This world', he had stated precociously, 'was not made by God, but was made before there was a God; nor do I believe the Scripture which is an old book; for we are not to believe old books. And Moses was either a fool or a liar, and he made the Scripture, which is but a fable.'[84] Morgan's fulminations may have been the garbled outpourings of an unbalanced mind, but his views may also reflect a rational denial of orthodox Christianity. We should bear in mind the suggestion that 'the actual volume of disbelief'[85] may have been greater than the surviving evidence would indicate.

Nevertheless, religious reformers suckled on the most rigorous puritan ethics were determined to combat vain cursing and swearing from the pulpit and through the press. Literature specifically designed to stress the cogency of the third commandment reiterated the point that vain swearing was a 'horrid', 'atrocious' and 'accursed' practice 'so fatal to the souls of men'.[86] Emphasising Psalms xxxiv 13 ('Keep thy tongue from evil and thy lips from speaking guile'), Richard Jones maintained that even the smallest oath was a cardinal sin and that, in God's eyes, profane swearers were as culpable as murderers, adulterers and idolators.[87] Some English best-sellers, well-

[83] James Owen, *Trugaredd a Barn*, p. 38.
[84] J. H. Matthews (ed.), *Records of the County Borough of Cardiff* (6 vols., 1898–1911), II, 183–4.
[85] Keith Thomas, *Religion and the Decline of Magic* (1971), p. 169.
[86] William Fleetwood, op. cit., sig. A2r.
[87] Richard Jones, *Hyfforddiadau Christianogol*, p. 21.

known for their success in stemming the tide of profanity, were
swiftly deemed worthy of translation. The Welsh translation of
Josiah Woodward's much-vaunted work, *A Kind Caution to
Prophane Swearers*, in 1707, was popularly considered to 'promote
God's glory and the good of souls'.[88] Both a Dissenter, Iaco ab
Dewi, and a clergyman, Simon Jones, published translations
of Edward Wells's *Letter to a Friend concerning the Great Sin of
taking God's name in vain*. Welsh Quakers, too, took part in the
onslaught against coarse language and blasphemy as part of
their general refusal to swear oaths. James v 12 showed that
Christ had declared categorically, 'Swear not at all', and this
command, they believed, applied to judicial oaths and vain
swearing. One of the motives behind the publication of a Welsh
translation of John Kelsall (senior)'s *Testimony* (1682) in 1705
was to censor vain swearing and 'peoples calling upon God to
damn them'.[89] Similarly, Roger Jenkin's translation of John
Barcroft's *Faithful Warning to the Inhabitants of Great Britain and
Ireland* (1720) in 1721 was designed to combat 'profane
swearing, cursing, drunkenness and debauchery'.[90]

Strenuous efforts were also made in printed books to spell
out the likelihood of divine retribution for such evil deeds as
blasphemy and cursing. Not only were the most lurid
scriptural testimonies invoked, but so also were cautionary
anecdotes which often fulfilled a valuable didactic rôle. In his
collection of tales of judgments upon sinners, James Owen told
the story of Oliver Woodall, a bailiff of Llanfyllin who, having
lost a velvet cap, asked a bellman, Cadwalader Rowland,
whether he had seen it. Rowland replied on solemn oath that
had he seen the cap, God should strike him dead at the bailiff's
door. Within three months, Rowland was found dead outside
Woodall's front door, wearing the cap he had stolen.[91]
Anecdotes of this kind, in which the hand of God was always
to be detected, served to reinforce the puritan moral code and
authors were never loath to leave profane swearers in any doubt
of their eventual lot.

[88] *Rhybudd Caredig i bob Tyngwr ofer* (1707); Clement, p. 42.
[89] G.C.R.O., D/DSF 379, p. 69.
[90] Friends' House Library, Kelsall MSS. Diaries, IV, pp. 50–1; G.C.R.O.,
D/DSF 320, p. 172.
[91] James Owen, *Trugaredd a Barn*, pp. 32–3. For a similar example in ballad-
form, see Richard Parry, *Rhybudd Benywaidd* (1727).

V. MORAL RESTRAINTS

The want of data makes it virtually impossible to assess the impact of moralising literature on the reading public. But it is surely significant that the torrent of literature published against Sabbath-breaking, drunkenness and vain swearing was disseminated far more intensively than ever before and was evidently reinforcing the code of morality preached from the pulpit. Possibly the most effective books were those which centred on God's judgment upon sinners. James Owen's *Trugaredd a Barn*—a collection of divine punishments on sinners and mercies to the pious—was based on the motto, 'Happy is the man who accepts a warning when he sees another under judgment'.[92] Throughout the eighteenth century, successive editions of Owen's work left their mark on readers, causing apprehension, unease and many sleepless nights.[93] Equally influential were the *exempla* incorporated in *The Testament of the Twelve Patriarchs* (1575), published in Welsh in 1700 and 1719, and their grinding emphasis on the fact that, whilst the virtuous received their just deserts, the wicked never went unpunished. Works that focused exclusively on the appalling horrors of hell caused more than a few tremors in readers' minds.[94] It was common, too, for reformers to impress on people that dearth and famine, epidemics, fires and earthquakes were tangible signs of God's anger. A spectacular event like the great storm of November 1703 provided moralists with a classic opportunity to fulminate, with varying degrees of vehemence, against the sins of the flesh and to interpret the widespread devastation as the direct result of the Almighty's displeasure with the prevailing laxity of the times.[95] And where men drew the appropriate conclusions from such calamities, a sudden, if fleeting, wave of piety and moral rectitude might follow.

[92] Many of Owen's most graphic examples were garnered from popular English best-sellers, notably Thomas Beard's *The Theatre of God's Judgments* (1597) and Samuel Clarke's *A Mirrour or Looking-glass both for Saints and Sinners* (1646).
[93] See the evidence of those august compilers of *Enwogion y Ffydd*, John Peter and Gweirydd ap Rhys, vol. 3, pp. 30–31n.
[94] See below, pp. 141–2.
[95] N.L.W., Bodewryd MS. 69, f. 67; Thomas Williams, *Pregeth o Achos y Dymmestl Ddinistriol* (1705); David Rees, *A View of the Divine Conduct in the Government of this Lower World* (1730), p. 30.

It would, however, be idle to pretend that attempts to reform society could rely on oral and printed exhortations, exemplars and warnings of judgment. Enforcing the moral code within each diocese depended on important local factors. The presence of resident bishops was a fundamental prerequisite since they were in a position not only to throw their own weight into the struggle for godly reformation, but also to exercise tighter control over their clergy and embolden them to take rigorous action in matters pertaining to morality. Unfortunately, Wales in this period had its share of time-servers and birds of passage. Those whose attitude towards their sees was generally compounded of indolence and disdain wove their way through their impoverished dioceses only when the butterflies were in season. Some were deflected from pastoral concerns by their persecuting zeal and by their political obligations at convocation—twin evils which often vitiated attempts to establish an effective pastoral relationship with both clergy and laity. But not all Welsh bishops by any means carried tarnished reputations. Prelates in the early decades of the Restoration period did their best to pick up the pieces broken during the revolutionary upheaval, and some of their successors proved sticklers for discipline. In the diocese of Bangor, Humphrey Humphreys, successively dean (1680–9) and bishop (1689–1701), not only constantly exhorted his clergy to beat down the strongholds of Satan, but also absorbed himself in the activities of reforming societies together with a series of enlightened administrative reforms.[96] At St. Asaph, Bishop William Lloyd (1680–92) also proved an enormously forceful bishop, voicing an early determination to ensure that 'the Ark of God' should not 'like old Eli' be lost on account of flagrant behaviour by drunken clerics. Lloyd ruled his diocese with a firm hand, bringing the errant to justice, rooting out persistently scandalous clerics, replacing them with 'painful and deserving pastors' and altogether achieving remarkable success in coordinating reforming endeavours.[97] Some of his successors, notably William Beveridge (1704–8), William Fleetwood

[96] E. G. Wright, 'Humphrey Humphreys, Bishop of Bangor and Hereford (1648–1712)', Trans. Anglesey Antiq. Soc., 1949, pp. 61–76.
[97] N.L.W., Lloyd-Baker Letters, no. 6; Bod., Tanner MS. 30, f. 124; Robert Wynne, A Short Narrative of the Proceedings against the Bishop of St. Asaph (1702), pp. 1–2; A. Tindal Hart, Bishop William Lloyd, 1627–1717 (1952), pp. 40–86.

1708–14) and John Wynne (1715–27) also strove hard to earn
sense of loyalty from their clergy, to eradicate common vices
nd to promote practical piety.[98] Similarly, post-toleration
ishops in the diocese of St. David's were not disposed to
bdicate their responsibilities. Bishop George Bull (1705–10),
lways the most vigorous of episcopal greybeards, revived the
ffice of rural dean in order to exercise proper surveillance over
ne 'conversation, sobriety and diligence' of both clergy and
uity.[99] His enthusiasm was sustained by Adam Ottley (1713–23)
vho, by regulating the conduct of his clergy and advancing in
articular the careers of able native Welshmen, laboured hard
p weed out 'public disorders, sins and offences'.[100]

In spite of the growing measure of supervision, however,
here were undeniably far too many clergymen who were
tterly unfit to carry out their spiritual obligations. The
requency with which charges of drunkenness, immorality,
candalous behaviour and neglect were made against clergymen
n the consistory courts, particularly in the diocese of St.
David's, reveals that corrupt and immoral clerics were
mbarrassingly numerous.[101] Several factors encouraged this
tate of affairs. Firstly, it is clear that scholarship and integrity
vere no guarantees of promotion in St. David's; most of the
rofitable livings were filled by men selected by private patrons,
vhilst the most impoverished livings were left to the rank and
le of the clergy who, miserably thwarted owing to their
enury and lack of connexions, joined the ranks of backsliders
nd profligates. Secondly, the negligent exercise of patronage
nabled many immoral men to be admitted to livings, whilst
thers 'of no meaner parts but more sober and likelier to do
ood are rejected and laid aside'.[102] Thirdly, efforts to raise
tandards of pastoral care were often choked by the fact that
nany clergymen viewed their benefice as a piece of freehold
roperty that afforded them an income from tithe rather than

[98] D. R. Thomas, *History of the Diocese of St. Asaph* (3 vols., 1908–11), I, 139–43.
[99] Robert Nelson, op. cit., pp. 418, 430; J. Vyrnwy Davies, 'The diocese of
t. David's during the first half of the eighteenth century', (unpubl. Univ. of
Vales M.A. thesis, 1936), pp. 33–4.
[100] N.L.W., Ottley Papers No. 1045; J. V. Davies, op. cit., pp. 38–44.
[101] Walter T. Morgan, 'Yr Eglwys Sefydledig yng Nghymru', in Gomer M.
toberts (ed.), *Hanes Methodistiaeth Calfinaidd Cymru* (1973), pp. 68–9.
[102] N.L.W., Ottley Papers No. 100; E. E., *Ymddiddan rhwng Gwr o gyfraith ar
ngeu* (1728), p. 7.

as a cure of souls. Where some were cynically obsessed with th
church's loaves and fishes, the most impoverished clergy wer
through sheer necessity, forced to supplement their slend
stipends by devoting more time to agricultural pursuits than t
their pastoral obligations. Not a few of the clergy, therefor
thoroughly disgruntled with their social status and smoulderin
helplessly before the apathy and obstinacy of some of the
parishioners,[103] simply surrendered to these overwhelming odd
by lapsing into inertia, wanton neglect or profligacy.

But there is another side to the coin. It is easy to exaggerat
the dramatic examples of clerical misdemeanour in th
records of the church courts. In the nature of things, suc
evidence deals primarily with black sheep. We should recognis
that clergymen who fall from grace always attract mor
attention than the faithful shepherds who struggle to kee
themselves and their flocks on the straight and narrow. Muc
of the immorality was the indirect result of sheer poverty, an
it is perhaps more remarkable that so many clergymen wer
able to surmount successfully the combined obstacles c
penury, calumny and apathy. Erasmus Saunders acknowledge
the labours of those clergymen who 'by their virtue and stead
application, surmount the difficulties they meet with, fin
means to be well accomplished, and to adorn their station fo
the sake of well-doing, and to be no less eminent for thei
pastoral care and diligence than others are for their neglec
and scandal'.[104] The records of the S.P.C.K. reveal a leave
of pastorally-minded clergymen who strove to eradicate th
most shameful abuses in their localities by assiduously dis
tributing moralising literature designed to promote practica
piety.[105] There is a real danger, too, of ignoring the self-effacin
industry of those faithful pastors who left no written memorial
but who, unprodded by fastidious bishops and undeterred b

---

[103] Some of this frustration comes through in the sermons of John Griffit
rector of Llanelian 1683-9. U.C.N.W.L., Bangor MS. 95. One can imagine th
feelings, too, of the parson who was stoned by a certain Edward Edwards
Llangollen for having chided him for profaning the Sabbath. G. M. Griffith
'Glimpses of Denbighshire in the Records of the Court of Great Sessions', *Denb.*
Hist. Soc. Trans., 22 (1973), 114.

[104] Saunders, p. 27. Elsewhere, Saunders claimed that 'have we not a numbe
of pious and able Divines, not inferior when proportioned to any age or country
A Domestick Charge (1701), p. 85.

[105] See Clement, *passim*.

piteful gibes at their lowly status, fulfilled their spiritual obligations to the best of their ability. The poet, R. S. Thomas, recalls these forgotten men best:

> . . . . They left no books,
> Memorial to their lonely thought
> In grey parishes; rather they wrote
> On men's hearts and in the minds
> Of young children sublime words
> Too soon forgotten. God in his time
> Or out of time will correct this.[106]

It is significant, too, that clergymen in this period were increasingly voicing their contempt towards lapsed colleagues and were anxious to whittle them down to a small minority. Religious reformers were well aware that clergymen who flouted ethical scruples and neglected their pastoral concerns were serious obstacles to a true reformation. If they themselves were not moral exemplars, they could scarcely expect to win the respect of their flocks or persuade the errant to heed their sermons. Never one to suffer clerical fools gladly, Griffith Jones, Llanddowror, warned that 'some profligates have owned that nothing promoted their profaneness so much as the immorality of clergymen'.[107] 'The reproofs of a guilty man', agreed John Copner, vicar of Abergwili, were of necessity 'indecent and ineffectual.'[108] Nothing was 'more nauseous', pleaded Erasmus Saunders, than 'the moral lessons of an immoral man.'[109] Many other clergymen descanted on the same theme, and their concern clearly testified to a considerable appreciation of the improved standards demanded not only of themselves but also of those placed under their care.[110] Moreover, the fact that many of them felt morally obliged to reinforce their moral imperatives by translating pious and moral tracts specifically for their own parishioners is itself earnest

---

[106] R. S. Thomas, *Poetry For Supper* (1958), p. 28.
[107] N.L.W., Ottley Papers No. 100.
[108] N.L.W. MS. 2905A, p. 28.
[109] Erasmus Saunders, *The Divine Authority and Usefulness of the Pastors of the Christian Church Vindicated* (1713), p. 28.
[110] N.L.W., Llanstephan MS. 146E, no pagination; William Powell, *A Sermon preach'd at the Visitation of the Lord Bishop of St. Asaph* (1742), p. 14; N.L.W. MS. 2444B, p. 176.

of a profound regard for the salvation of souls.[111]

Even so, additional coercive powers were required to punish and deter those who persistently infringed the moral code. An important rôle was played by the consistory courts which could punish offenders either by subjecting them to the humiliation of a public penance or by excommunication. It was also possible, on rare occasions, to 'signify' those who refused to pay costs or perform the prescribed penances to the secular authorities, who could then imprison them until such time as they agreed to obey the mandates of the ecclesiastical authorities.[112] The efficacy of the church courts depended to a large extent on the readiness of churchwardens to perform their duty of presenting offenders. Acting as unpaid moral policemen, they were, at best, erratic social regulators. Saddled with a wide and burdensome variety of responsibilities, they were not always able to keep a vigilant eye on offenders. In 1720, the churchwardens of Llangain in Carmarthenshire complained that those who sold intoxicating liquor on Sundays lived so far from the church 'that we cannot attend the worship of God and search their homes'.[113] Desperately seeking to enforce the moral code, the churchwardens of Llanfair Discoed in Monmouthshire scrawled permanent reminders to Sabbath-breakers on the churchyard stile:

> Who ever here on Sunday
> Will practise playing at ball
> It may be before Monday
> The Devil will have you all.[114]

Some churchwardens were understandably nervous about prying too intensely into their neighbours' moral peccadilloes whilst others were only too delighted to present offenders 'out

---

[111] For some examples, see Edward Wynn, *Trefn Ymarweddiad gwir Gristion* (1662); Robert Lloyd, *Duwiolder am Ddydd yr Arglwydd* (1698); David Maurice *Cwnffwrdd ir Gwan Gristion* (1700); Robert Robert, *A Sacrament Catechism* (1720) Alban Thomas, *Llythyr Bugailaidd* (1729).

[112] Walter T. Morgan, 'The Consistory Courts in the diocese of St. David's' *J.H.S.C.W.*, VII (1957), 18; *idem.* 'The Prosecution of Nonconformists in the Consistory Courts of St. David's, 1661–88', ibid., XII (1962), 28–54.

[113] N.L.W., SD/Archdeaconry of Carmarthen/Churchwardens' returns 1720, 166.

[114] John Fisher, 'The Religious and Social Life of Former Days in the Vale of Clwyd', *Denbighshire Free Press*, 10 February 1906, p. 6.

of spleen, malice and revenge'.[115] Some were not averse to taking bribes,[116] but whilst most did not seriously neglect their duties they were rather too prone to take their responsibilities lightly and pin their 'faith and consciences upon Laodicean sleeves'.[117] Caught in the crossfire between hectoring clergymen and quibbling parishioners, it is probable that churchwardens concentrated mainly on ensuring that at least the most flagrant and persistent offenders were not permitted too wide a latitude to practise their indiscretions.

The campaign against immorality and wickedness was also intensified by the passing of a series of statutes and proclamations designed to strengthen the hand of the church courts. By the end of the seventeenth century there were twelve statutes against the profanation of the Lord's Day on the statute book, the chief of which was the Sunday Observance Act of 1677 which prohibited any tradesman, artificer, workman or labourer from exercising any worldly labour or business on the Sabbath.[118] Also on the statute book were six laws against drunkenness, five against swearing and cursing, one against blasphemous oaths, and eight against lewd and disorderly practices. The monarchy, too, played its part in buttressing the moral sanctions of the church. In February 1689, William III and Mary issued a proclamation instructing all officers of the law to enforce existing laws against profaneness and vice. In February 1698, a further proclamation urged that the curing of social evils was the responsibility of judges, mayors, justices of the peace and sheriffs. Judges of assizes and local justices were to ensure that the proclamation was read at both assizes and quarter sessions. Moreover, clergymen were ordered to read the proclamation after divine service on four separate occasions each year, and also to take care that the document be displayed in prominent places. A further proclamation in 1699 reaffirmed these directions, and three similar edicts followed during the first half of Anne's reign.[119]

---

[115] N.L.W., SD/CCB(G)/593.
[116] In his biting version of 'The Poor Man's Ten Commandments', Lewis Morris advised: 'Thou shalt not break ye Sabbath without feeing the constables & churchwardens'. Hugh Owen, op. cit., p. 69.
[117] N.L.W., SA/Misc/527.
[118] D. W. R. Bahlman, op. cit., p. 14; W. B. Whitaker, *The Eighteenth Century English Sunday* (1940), pp. 11–13.
[119] D. W. R. Bahlman, op. cit., pp. 14–16.

Publishing a spate of laws and proclamations, howeve
commendable, was a fairly straightforward exercise; mo
exacting, as Bishop Bull impressed on his clergy and magi
trates,[120] was the task of enforcing them in the localitie
Sceptics might justifiably point to the fact that the ver
renewal of such diktats was itself an admission of failure, an
many reformers feared that they had become 'baubles an
banters, the laughter of the lewd party'.[121]

   More penetrating efforts to raise moral standards were mad
in the provinces by the societies for the reformation of manner
These societies were convinced that the most effective means o
rendering the nation inviolable to the Popish threat was b
raising the moral tone and eliminating wickedness and vic
An important by-product, too, would be the inculcation o
the virtues of subordination and submission as a means o
guarding against social upheaval and maintaining an orderl
and quiescent society. The work of the reforming societies wa
further reinforced in April 1699, when Archbishop Teniso
published a letter to the bishops of his province urging them t
declare 'a national war on vice'.[122] A special effort was made t
inspire clergymen to renew their sense of vocation and joi
with laymen of repute to form societies to combat vice.[12]
Tenison's exhortations were swiftly heeded by Bishop Humphre
Humphreys of Bangor, who issued his own directives, divide
his diocese into three deaneries and formed monthly societie
in each, and outlined the respective duties of clergymen
churchwardens and parishioners.[124] Fired by the enthusiasm
of the newly-formed S.P.C.K., London-based reformin
societies spread into the provinces and took root in Caernarvon
shire, Carmarthenshire and Pembrokeshire. Their immediat
effect was often striking: Thomas Thomas was happy to repor
from Carmarthen in May 1701 that 'drunkenness, swearing
profanation of the Lord's Day, etc. are generally suppressed
and the state of religion very much mended'.[125] How lastin

---

[120] Robert Nelson, op. cit., p. 451.
[121] Stuart Andrews, *Methodism and Society* (1970), p. 69.
[122] D. W. R. Bahlman, op. cit., p. 74.
[123] N.L.W., Plasgwyn (1924) MS. 6, No. 144.
[124] N.L.W., Plasgwyn (1924) MS. I, no. 24. For the reaction of the clergy o
the deanery of Tindaethwy and Menai, see nos. 19 and 20.
[125] Clement, p. 11.

their work proved to be remains a problem, and it is more likely that the most enduring success was achieved by the schools of the S.P.C.K. which, by inculcating pupils from an early age with rigorous moral standards, helped to raise standards of popular morality.

The rôle of secular authorities was also beginning to assume greater prominence in the localities. Clergymen were increasingly convinced that, without the support of influential laymen, they were unable to impose lasting discipline on their flocks. Edward Samuel, vicar of Betws Gwerful Goch, argued that the natural rulers of society were the most 'lasting' preachers; for whilst men's eyes were often closed to the admonitions of the clergy, their eyes were always open to perceive and to ape the moral code of their social betters. We may advise and warn, he went on, but the gentry were in a position to *compel* the populace to live according to the Gospel of Christ.[126] Thus, men with a sizeable stake in society, particularly those who were magistrates, were constantly pressed to advance the reforming campaign. 'With one warrant', ventured Erasmus Saunders, magistrates could work 'a more visible reformation than may be effected by some hundreds of sermons upon some people.'[127] The magistrate's bench, however, was normally made up of men of diverse capacities and moral fibre, and many of them must have found some difficulty in setting their face against vices to which they themselves were all too often susceptible. Even so, as property-owners, it was in their interest to maintain an orderly, disciplined society. The well-being of their estates and businesses depended heavily on the industry and sobriety of the lower orders and, by clamping down on disruptive elements, they guarded against the possibility—however remote—of popular tumult.

For economic as well as moral reasons, therefore, many substantial gentlemen were prepared to enforce coercive

---

[126] Edward Samuel, *Prif Ddledswyddau Christion* (1723), sig. K6v. For similar comments by Samuel see N.L.W. MS. 2026B, f. 66v; by Bishop Humphrey Humphreys to Lord Bulkeley, N.L.W. MS. 9070E, f. 24; and by Thomas Hancorne, *The Right Way to Honour and Happiness. A Sermon preach'd at the Assizes held at Cardiff* (1710), p. 14.
[127] Erasmus Saunders, *A Domestick Charge*, sig. C8r; cf. William Powell, *Swearing and Drunkenness*, p. 4; Clement, p. 144.

measures and forward the aims of reforming societies. The S.P.C.K. took special advantage of their assistance to distribute practical literature—usually among the poor—at the assizes.[128] In October 1708, six magistrates in Carmarthen publicly voiced their determination to execute the statutes against immorality and profaneness, and framed their intentions within a notice board ordered to be hung at the church door at Whitsun, Easter and Christmas. Their attempts to eliminate the most flagrant abuses, claimed Bishop Bull, had a 'wonderful influence upon the lives and manners of the people', and he urged justices in other counties within his diocese to follow suit.[129] William Powell, too, found the example set by the justices of Carmarthen 'very worthy of imitation', and he encouraged their counterparts in Denbighshire and Shropshire to illustrate how the secular arm could underpin the moral sanctions of the church.[130]

How far all these sanctions were successful in raising moral standards is hard to assess. Tracing changes in moral attitudes— themselves often will-o'-the wisp affairs—is an elusive task. Even so, the evidence suggests that the puritan message found its most receptive ears among serious-minded farmers, self-made merchants and sturdy artisans. Their economic independence, together with their independence of mind and spirit, meant that the virtues of moderation, prudence, frugality and industriousness counted a good deal in their lives. And although many of the gentry never lost their zest for worldly comforts, the shrewdest of them knew that they had much to lose from following dissolute ways and, moreover, that they had a responsibility to keep the mass of the population in line. Conversely, the poorer elements in rural society resisted most efforts to bring them under the umbrella of upper-class respectability. In particular the profane unregenerate mass remained implacably hostile to the puritan reformist diktats. This is not surprising. Considering the lot to which many of them had been born, they could well be forgiven for judging themselves to be more sinned against than sinning. After all, sin, like beauty, is in the eye of the beholder. Moreover, it is important to evaluate

[128] N.L.W., Plasgwyn (1924) MS. 3, no. 94.
[129] Robert Nelson, op. cit., pp. 451–5.
[130] William Powell, *Swearing and drunkenness*, p. 10.

their moral norms according to the social context and thinking of the time, rather than through the interpretative blinkers of nineteenth-century nonconformity. The sins of most rural folk were the simple sins of a basically untrammelled society. Alcohol was an intrinsic part of their diet and drunkenness at weekends was a way of letting off steam.[131] Following the burdens of arduous and sustained labour over six days, men felt entitled to recreational activity on the seventh.[132] Sport on the Sabbath brought a dash of colour into their lives and helped to prop up morale when economic pressures were barely tolerable. Weekend recreations and the periodic celebration of festivals performed a necessary social function in that they broke up the monotony of the struggle for survival.[133] Most moral lapses were thus determined by the prevailing agricultural pattern and the progress of the seasons. It is clear, therefore, that acceptance of the puritan ethic would have entailed a profound disruption of traditional ways of life. Many of the values so dear to middle-class puritans ran counter to the ritualistic and parochial morality of rural inhabitants. Traditionally conservative and gregarious in their habits, they would not readily accept change.

Inevitably, therefore, there remained a gap between the aspirations of religious reformers and their capacity to control moral habits. Progress was essentially piecemeal, depending largely on the cumulative effect of successive waves of reformist activity. Within small rural communities, moral standards were subject to conflicting pressures and varying standards of behaviour were always possible. What is clear is that parishioners were now being made aware of the required moral standards with increasingly consistent vigour. Overt coercion could never be employed effectively, for the experience of Cromwellian intrusiveness, having proved intolerable to the bulk of society, had taught religious reformers the value of circumspection and patience. More obvious success was

---

[131] R. W. Malcolmson, *Popular Recreations in English Society, 1700–1850* (1973), p. 76.

[132] William Fleetwood, *The Bishop of St. Asaph's Charge*, p. 33.

[133] R. W. Malcolmson, op. cit., pp. 14, 170–1; Keith Thomas, 'Work and Leisure in Pre-Industrial Society', *P & P*, 29 (1964), 50–62; E. O. James, *Seasonal Feasts and Festivals* (1961); G. J. Williams, 'Glamorgan Customs in the Eighteenth Century', *Gwerin*, I (1957), 99–108.

achieved by the early Methodists, but even they would have conceded that tenacious, if outworn, conventions could not be chopped down root and branch by one blow. Most rural 'sins' lingered on, particularly in the more remote and secluded parts of Wales,[134] obstinately resisting the eroding influence of Methodist culture well into the nineteenth century.

---

[134] E. Gwynne Jones (ed.), Edmund Hyde Hall, *A Description of Caernarvonshire* (1809–11) (1952), pp. 316–20; John Hughes, *Methodistiaeth Cymru* (3 vols., 1851–6) I, 52.

V

DEVOTIONAL LITERATURE

Religious reformers of different persuasions found a common bond in this period in their desire to emphasise the importance of Christian duties within the household. A substantial proportion of the letters sent by John Vaughan of Derllys to the S.P.C.K. was concerned with the necessity of promoting family devotions in every parish throughout the kingdom.[1] 'It is not so much what we are at church', observed Philip Henry, 'as what we are in our families. Religion in the power of it will be family religion.'[2] Public and private worship was widely considered to be complementary and, although the parish church or chapel remained the major centre of worship, the home also was 'a little church' where each member of the household, under the watchful guidance of the *paterfamilias*, took part in devotions designed to supplement his public worship and stiffen his own faith. It was this performance of family devotion, claimed James Owen, that distinguished the Christian from the pagan families.[3] He spoke for scores of his reforming brethren who appreciated that the promotion of piety and devotion within the domestic circle was heavily dependent on their ability to ensure a regular flow of Welsh literature specifically designed for that purpose.

I. DEVOTIONAL MANUALS

The growth of family devotion was stimulated largely by the publication of Welsh translations of the most popular and influential English devotional books. The major works were Lewis Bayly's *Practice of Piety* (1611), a phenomenally successful book that reached its 58th English edition by 1734;[4] Richard

---

[1] Clement, pp. 18–19, 113–4, 116; cf. Robert Nelson (ed.), *The Life of Dr. George Bull* (1714), pp. 443–6.
[2] J. B. Williams (ed.), Matthew Henry, *The Life of the Rev. Philip Henry* (1825), p. 69.
[3] James Owen, *Moderation a Virtue* (1703), p. 12.
[4] C. J. Stranks, *Anglican Devotion* (1961), p. 36.

Allestree's *Whole Duty of Man* (1658), which ran through 25 editions between 1658 and 1700; and John Rawlet's *Christian Monitor* (1686), of which 29 editions had been published by 1703.[5] These best-sellers also became enormously popular among the Welsh reading public. Rowland Vaughan's translation of Bayly's work, published five times during this period, was clearly popular at all levels: it found its way regularly into gentry households; it provided a wealth of *exempla* for sermons; it fortified the faith of Welsh settlers in America; and it nourished the devotions of a wide cross-section of the Welsh reading public, notably the poorer orders who received 2,500 free copies of the 1675 edition sponsored by the Welsh Trust.[6] The Welsh translation of Allestree's familiar work, first produced by John Langford in 1672, reprinted in 1711, and joined in 1718 by a new translation completed by Edward Samuel, was equally well-received. Its popularity is best reflected in Samuel's list of patrons which numbered 233 subscribers drawn mostly from among clergymen, gentry and yeomen.[7] Gentry families bought their copies faithfully and Allestree's work significantly headed most lists of books recommended for the education of their sons and daughters.[8] *The Whole Duty of Man* evidently patched many threadbare sermons and was reckoned by the clergy to be an indispensable guide to moral conduct and family worship.[9] But it was also warmly commended to the poorer sorts.[10] 500 copies of the

[5] Donald Wing (ed.), *Short-title Catalogue, 1641–1700* (1945).
[6] N.L.W., Esgair and Pantperthog MS. 2; N.L.W., Nantglyn MS. 6, p. 127 N.L.W., E. Francis Davies (1962) MSS. (books owned by William Roberts o Bodwenni); U.C.N.W.L., Bangor MS. 54; Mary Clement (ed.), *Correspondence and Records of the S.P.G. relating to Wales, 1701–1750* (1973), pp. 33–4; N.L.W., Bangor P.R. 1690, Henry Williams, apothecary of Clynnog; Archdeaconry of Carmarther P.R. 1695, William Morgan Evan, yeoman of Swansea; M. G. Jones, 'Two Accounts of the Welsh Trust, 1675 and 1678', *B.B.C.S.*, IX (1937), 73.
[7] Edward Samuel, *Holl Ddyledswydd Dyn* (1718). See the analysis in chapter ten.
[8] N.L.W., Nantglyn MS. 8; U.C.N.W.L., Penrhos (1) MS. 975; N.L.W. Bodewryd (Sotheby) MS. 98B.
[9] Robert Nelson, op. cit., p. 436; N.L.W. MS. 9102A; *C.C.H.M.C.*, no. 1 (1917), 16. A copy of the English folio edition of 1687 was secured by lock and chain in the parish church of Llanfyllin and was made available on loan to ministers or 'any person of quality' on surety of £5. Robert Williams, 'A history of the parish of Llanfyllin', *Mont. Colls.*, III (1870), 72.
[10] Anon., *Ffordd y Gwr Cyffredin* (1683), p.5; Edward Morris, *Y Rhybuddiw Cristnogawl* (1689), p. 57; Ellis Wynne, *Rheol Buchedd Sanctaidd* (1701), sig. A4r anon., *Cymorth i'r Cristion* (1704), p. 142; Alban Thomas, *Dwysfawr Rym Buched Grefyddol* (1722), pp. 104–8.

1672 edition were distributed solely among the literate poor by the Welsh Trust.[11] When William Wenlock of Colemear bequeathed sums of money in 1691 to buy books for the poor of the parishes of Ellesmere, Holywell, Mold and Northop, *The Whole Duty of Man* and *The Practice of Piety* were his first recommendations.[12] Edward Morris, the drover-poet, piously wished that every single poor family in the kingdom might receive a copy and, fired by similar enthusiasm, Griffith Jones of Bodfari published a Welsh translation of Edmund Stacy's abridged version of Allestree's work so that it might be more widely bought and read by the poor.[13] In the same category, Edward Morris's translation of *The Christian Monitor*, published in rapid succession in 1689, 1699 and 1706, was couched in 'a very plain and easy style' and was clearly geared to the level of common understanding.[14]

These popular manuals had several common features.[15] Firstly, they were designed for family and personal use and were especially concerned with fostering devotional habits. Bayly's work placed enormous stress on the need for daily prayers and meditations both within the family circle and by the individual in the privacy of his room. Allestree's work was divided into seventeen chapters in the hope that, by reading a chapter each Sunday, the whole book might be completed by families three times a year. Similarly, Rawlet's work contained guides to devotional practice and a medley of prayers and meditations for domestic use. Secondly, these works were essentially non-controversial 'home-helps' to godly living. By emphasising the sinfulness of man, Bayly was concerned to impress the virtues of a godly and ethical life on his reader. In outlining the right way of living, Allestree laid a threefold stress on man's duty to God, to himself and to his neighbour, whilst Rawlet's work was a self-styled 'exhortation to an holy

[11] *B.B.C.S.*, IX (1937), 73.
[12] N.L.W., SA/Misc/863.
[13] Edward Morris, op. cit., p. 57; Griffith Jones, *Y Llyfr a elwir Holl Ddyledswydd Dyn* (1722).
[14] Edward Morris, *Y Rhybuddiwr Cristnogawl*, title-page.
[15] Some of these features are discussed in C. J. Stranks, *Anglican Devotion* (1961); H. C. White, *English Devotional Literature, 1600–1640* (1931); Louis B. Wright, *Middle-Class Culture in Elizabethan England* (1935); Douglas Bush, *English Literature in the earlier seventeenth century, 1600–1660* (2nd ed., 1962); H. R. McAdoo, *The Spirit of Anglicanism* (1965).

life'. Thirdly, each work preached a practical and prudential morality. The respective duties of superiors and inferiors, and the merits of holiness and moral rectitude, were spelled out simply because it was felt that they made for greater quiescence and stability within the kingdom. It was also strongly hinted that the want of godliness not only made men poor and wretched but also contentious and unruly. Social unrest was held to be a direct result of collective moral disorder, and a thorough knowledge of Christian duties would necessarily render men pious and holy, sober and chaste, humble and content with their station in life.

Even the Catholic works which managed to evade the restrictive licensing laws in this period were avowedly concerned with kindling the spirit of devotion and godliness in their readers. The major Catholic publication was Hugh Owen's translation of Thomas à Kempis's *De Imitatione Christi* in 1684.[16] Kempis's book is a classic of its kind. A product of the *devotio moderna* of the fifteenth century, it stood out as a lighted beacon in reaction to the theological disputations of that age. Its universal appeal stemmed from its eschewal of abstruse polemics, its emphasis on the twin themes of devotion and grace, and its seemingly ageless relevance to the everyday lives of people.[17] In 1723, a new Welsh edition of the same work was published, but on this occasion the author, William Meyrick, had transformed the work into a Protestant devotional text by adapting or omitting parts of Hugh Owen's translation and by consciously laicising Catholic terms and doctrines.[18] The tailoring of Catholic doctrines by Protestant authors was not a new practice. In 1584, a Protestant rector, Edmund Bunny, had 'neutralised' the offending passages in the work of the Jesuit author, Robert Parsons, and his ensuing edition, *A Book of Christian Exercise, appertaining to Resolusion* (1584) at once became enormously popular among Protestants.[19] It was

[16] This was a printed edition of a manuscript bequeathed by Hugh Owen of Gwenynog to his son, John Hughes. G. Bowen, 'Llyfr y Resolusion neu Directori Christianogol Huw Owen o Wenynog', *N.L.W.J.*, XI (1959), 147.

[17] Thomas à Kempis, *The Imitation of Christ*, translated by Betty I. Knott (1963), Introduction.

[18] William Meyrick, *Pattrwm y Gwir-Gristion* (1723); cf. Saunders Lewis, 'Thomas à Kempis yn Gymraeg', *Efrydiau Catholig*, IV (1949), 36–41.

[19] Robert McNulty, 'The Protestant Version of Robert Parsons' The First Book of the Christian Exercise', *H.L.Q.*, XXII (1959), 271–3.

translated into Welsh by John Davies, Mallwyd, in 1632[20] and republished in 1684, 1711 and 1713. Ironically Hugh Owen, the translator of the *Imitatione*, had also translated Parsons's original work into Welsh around 1602. Now, in 1723, by a strange twist of fate, his translation of the *Imitatione* suffered a similar transmogrification, for the Roman Catholic doctrines implicit in à Kempis's work had now been neutralised and turned into a non-polemical Protestant manual.[21]

These major devotional texts were also reinforced in this period with a veritable torrent of small devotional books made up mainly of moral theology, prayers and meditations.[22] Tracts of this nature were largely aimed at those with slender purses, short memories and little leisure time to read weighty tomes. Some editions were fairly substantial: 3,500 copies of Richard Jones's *Hyfforddiadau Christianogol* were published in 1675;[23] 2,000 copies of the Welsh translation of *Family Devotions* were published in 1726;[24] in 1706, Caleb D'Avenant, a prominent English patron of Welsh literature, claimed to have been instrumental in the publication of between eight and nine thousand devotional books, including works such as *Cristion-ogrwydd yn Gynnwys* (1703) and *Cymorth i'r Cristion* (1704).[25] Most of these works stressed the social obligations of the Christian, his duty towards church and state, and his responsibilities towards his wife, children and neighbours. Also, by attacking worldly pleasures, vice and depravity, they sought to implant the desire to live a holy, pious life. Essentially terse in presentation and unambitious in aspiration, they concentrated on those things that a Christian should believe in and practise, avoid and fear, work and hope for.[26] The

[20] John Davies, *Llyfr y Resolusion* (1632).
[21] G. Bowen, 'Rhai o Lyfrau Defosiynol Reciwsantiaid Cymru yn yr ail ganrif ar bymtheg', *N.L.W.J.*, XI (1960), 362–3. The final *reductio ad absurdum* occurred in the Welsh edition of 1730, which bore Hugh Owen's name on the title-page but included the first chapter only of his work, the remainder being a reprint of Meyrick's edition of 1723.
[22] Among the most prominent were *Cyngor y Bugail iw Braidd* (1700); *Blaenor i Ghristion* (1701); *Cristionogrwydd yn Gynnwys* (1703); *Cymorth i'r Cristion* (1704); *Hynodeb Eglwysydd Cywir* (1712); *Holl Dd'ledswydd Christion* (1714).
[23] Richard Jones, *Hyfforddiadau Christianogol* (1675), sig. T8v.
[24] Clement, p. 104.
[25] N.L.W., Bodewryd (Sotheby) Correspondence, no. 230. For the edifying effect of *Cymorth i'r Cristion* on the Methodist preacher, John Thomas of Rhaeadr, see J. D. Owen (ed.) *Rhad Ras* (1949), p. 32.
[26] *Blaenor i Ghristion* (1701), title-page.

succinct instructions issued in the translation of Clement Ellis's *Christianity in Short* (1682) in 1703 give a fair indication of the demands which these simple manuals made on their readers: men were urged to consider seriously, learn industriously, pray devoutly, believe firmly, repent sincerely, love unfeignedly, resolve deliberately, practise constantly, hope patiently, receive thankfully—and enjoy eternally.[27]

II. PRAYER

Those books dealing with devotional practice were augmented by a regular flow of works designed to enable readers to understand the nature and purpose of prayer. Churchmen persistently maintained that the only sure way of safeguarding family godliness was by conducting morning and evening prayers at fixed times daily under the supervision of the head of the household.[28] Many of the most popular works included prayers designed for the household as a whole, for individual members of the family, and for children and servants.[29] It was hoped that, by mastering the art of prayer at home, public worship might also benefit. The Lord's Prayer, of course, had traditionally served as the most popular pattern to direct men in their prayers at church, but George Griffith, bishop of St. Asaph, was not alone in thinking that many parishioners recited the Lord's Prayer parrot-fashion, without truly recognising the meaning of their incantations. Such misgivings prompted Griffith to write a detailed exposition of the Lord's Prayer, a work which was later published by William Foulkes in 1685.[30] Others also felt that reciting the Lord's Prayer might easily become a mechanical, unthinking habit unless works were at hand in the home to explain its significance. In 1677, Stephen Hughes re-edited the Welsh translation of William

[27] *Cristionogrwydd yn Gynnwys* (1703), title-page.
[28] John Thomas, *Unum Necessarium* (1680), p. 9; *Cymorth i'r Cristion* (1704), p. 71; *Holl Dd'ledswydd Christion* (1714), p. 11; Alban Thomas, *Dwysfawr Rym Buchedd Grefyddol* (1722), pp. 61–103; Lewis Evans, *Dwyfolder-Teuluaidd* (1726), p. 17.
[29] Edward Wynn, *Trefn Ymarweddiad Gwir Gristion* (1662); George Lewis, *Cyngor Difrifol i Geidwaid Tai* (1704); *Boreuol a Phrydnawnol Weddiau iw harfer mewn Teuluoedd* (1711); N.L.W., Llanstephan MS. 146E (an unpublished translation by Samuel Williams of Erasmus Saunders's *Domestick Charge to Householders*).
[30] William Foulkes (ed.), George Griffith, *Gueddi'r Arglwydd wedi eu heglurâ* (1685).

erkins's *An Exposition of the Lord's Prayer* (1592),[31] whilst in
733, Theophilus Evans, a doughty champion of the 'set'
rayer, published a translation of Offspring Blackall's *Practical
iscourses on the Lord's Prayer* (1727).[32]

Anglicans expected that the household unit and private
ndividuals should also touch on the state of the nation and the
stablished church in their prayers. Prayers of this kind were
enerally formal, orthodox and stereotyped, for their common
orm was thought to make for greater stability and unity. Most
nglican devotional manuals and guides to prayer also
ontained set forms of prayers. This was partly a means of
uiding the weaker sort: hobbling with crutches was thought
o be better than not walking at all.[33] Basically, however,
hurchmen were distinctly loath to grant any elbow room for
nstable ideas or unruly zeal in their prayers. Dissenters
egularly poured scorn on this attitude, maintaining strongly
aat an imposed liturgy and 'set' prayers were responsible for
aapkining' men's talents and denying them any degree of
ontaneity in their petitions.[34] Reformers were increasingly
rging their readers to be fervent, earnest and warm in their
rivate prayers.[35] Prayer, argued John Thomas, was the ladder
y which we poor worms climbed to heaven to glorify God, to
eg his forgiveness, to petition for faith and perseverance, and
o so in a fervent but reverent manner.[36] It was widely
ressed that prayer was so much more than a moving of the
ps in a formal, parrot-like incantation—it needed to be a
ncere profession from the depths of the soul. By opening the
eart, concealing nothing, and allowing the Holy Spirit to
ove the soul, repentant sinners could petition God in a truly
ncere and humble fashion.[37]

How far the duties of family devotion and prayer were
ctually performed is difficult to assess. There was inevitably

[31] *Agoriad byrr ar Weddi'r Arglwydd*, translated by Robert Holland and first
ublished in 1600.
[32] *Pwyll y Pader* (1733).
[33] *Cymorth i'r Cristion*, sig. A2v.
[34] James Owen, *Moderation a Virtue*, p. 12; Simon Thomas, *Hanes y Byd a'r
mseroedd* (1718), pp. 157–8.
[35] See some of the prayers in Thomas Jones (ed.), *Llyfr o Weddiau Duwiol* (1707).
[36] John Thomas, op. cit., p. 2.
[37] *Rheol Buchedd Sanctaidd*, p. 207; *Cymorth i'r Cristion*, p. 74; *Holl Dd'ledswydd
hristion*, p. 12; Theophilus Evans, *Cydwybod y Cyfaill Gorau ar y Ddaear* (1715),
g. B4r.

some disparity between the demanded ideal and the actual practice. As might be expected, household religion was practised within gentry households. Daily prayers based on a Welsh translation of *Gerard's Prayer or a Daily Practice of Piety* (1631) were conducted at Plas Nantglyn, Denbighshire, and the prayers, meditations and reflections that figure among some of the manuscripts of the Bodewryd, Nannau and Penrhos families reveal that domestic devotions were faithfully observed.[38] It is clear, too, that the pious *materfamilias* was often as diligent as her husband in conducting the spiritual side of domestic affairs. Lady Price of Newtown Hall, Montgomeryshire, acted 'like a guardian-angel to her family' organising family prayers and devotions and generally shaping the religious life of the household.[39] The most earnest and diligent of the clergy would always look to provide members of their family with spiritual nourishment and strive to persuade heads of households that devotional schooling was both necessary and good.[40] Dissenting ministers discharged their family duties with relish, urging their members never to neglect their 'secret duty'.[41] Fired by his belief that 'apostasy generally begins at the closet-door', Philip Henry used to rehearse not only his family but also servants, sojourners, workmen and day-labourers.[42]

It is less easy to assess the reaction of other grades in society to what was preached and practised by their social betters and their spiritual shepherds. There is a strong likelihood that family devotions were less prominent within village communities, where more boisterous social activities afforded opportunities for communal life but also served to preclude the growth of family solidarity.[43] Conversely, the well integrated, self-sustaining farmhouses in pastoral areas made for more compact family units where domestic devotion might flourish. It is evident that some of the guides to prayer and

---

[38] B. F. Roberts, 'Defosiynau Cymraeg', in Thomas Jones (ed.), *Astudiaethau Amrywiol* (1968), p. 109; N.L.W., Bodewryd (Sotheby) MSS. 94B, 96B, 97A, 98B; N.L.W., Peniarth 373B.

[39] Thomas Richards, *The Happiness of Good Christians after Death* (1733), p. 21.

[40] See note 29.

[41] Charles Owen, *Some Account of . . . James Owen* (1709), pp. 83–4; John Roberts, *Ychydig o Hanes y Diweddar Barchedig Lewis Rees* (n.d.), pp. 21–2.

[42] Matthew Henry, op. cit., p. 73.

[43] Joan Thirsk, 'The Family', *P & P*, 27 (1964), 122.

meditation were specifically directed towards husbandmen and yeoman farmers. Moses Williams's translation of Edward Welchman's *The Husbandman's Manual* (1695) in 1711 was designed to improve the husbandman's calling by providing him with short prayers and lessons, couched in a parable-form readily understood by men of the soil, to accompany him in his daily labour.[44] It is significant, too, that of 689 subscribers to *Trefn Ymarweddiad Gwir Gristion* (1723–4) and 352 subscribers to *Defosiwnau Priod* (1720) a substantial proportion were yeoman-farmers.[45] Books of devotion and prayer were clearly in heavy demand within those cohesive family units that were neither lacking in material comforts nor deprived of the opportunity to buy books. It may be, also, that those dwelling in farmhouses most distant from the parish church would rely a good deal on devotional literature, especially during the winter months when harsh weather conditions might keep them indoors on the Sabbath. In particular, servants and labourers employed in these households were heavily dependent on their masters for religious instruction, especially since they themselves were allegedly 'wholly unsupplied with private prayers'. One imagines that a sensitive and persuasive *paterfamilias* could convey a good deal of the comforting message contained in such books as Iaco ab Dewi's *Cyfeillach Beunyddiol* (1714). This work told the remarkable life story of Armelle Nicolas—'la bonne Armelle'—a poor, illiterate servant girl in rural France who, in spite of her lack of schooling, had established a true spiritual companionship with God by her sheer devotion and constancy in prayer and meditation.[47]

On the other hand, those who belonged to a less integrated family circle—particularly the poor—were least likely to have imbibed any basic religious knowledge and were often abysmally ignorant of, or deaf to, the need to conduct regular devotions. William Foulkes, rector of Llanfyllin, believed that

---

[44] Moses Williams, *Llaw-Lyfr y Llafurwr* (1711). See also the books recommended to the husbandman by Richard Steele, *The Husbandmans Calling* (1668), pp. 263–5.
[45] See chapter ten.
[46] Clement, p. 94.
[47] This translation was based on part of *Daily Conversation with God, exemplify'd in the Holy Life of Armelle Nicolas, a poor ignorant country maid in France* (1st extant ed., 1754). See also Edward Morris's advice to maid-servants in Gwenllian Jones, 'Bywyd a Gwaith Edward Morris' (unpubl. Univ. Wales M.A. thesis, 1941), pp. 428–9.

common people were ignorant and remiss in their duties of prayer, excusing themselves on the grounds that they had never been taught to pray and that their memories anyway were poor.[48] The deep-seated persistence of magic cults meant that the credulous among them would often blur the distinction between a prayer and a charm.[49] But the major and perennial obstacle to family devotion among the poor was their miserably deprived social status. Living in cold, dimly-lit and wretched hovels of one room, they lacked the material comfort and privacy which were indispensable to regular devotional practice. They lacked, moreover, the spare cash necessary to buy even the simplest guides to prayer and devotion, whilst their children were not able to attend school because their labour was needed to supplement, however meagrely, the family income. Given these circumstances, the illiterate poor were probably the least able to transform their homes into 'little churches'.

III. THE LITERATURE OF INWARD EXPERIENCE

In the post-Methodist revival era, critics ranging from Robert Jones, Rhoslan, to Lewis Edwards of Bala attacked what they considered to be the deficiencies of the manuals of popular theology and devotion which we have discussed. They maintained (and more than faint echoes of their criticisms may still be heard) that Anglicanism and old Dissent laid inordinate stress on the will and the understanding, on formal conduct and outward conformity and sanctity. In their view, books like *The Practice of Piety*, *The Whole Duty of Man*, *Holy Living* and similar devotional works so popular in pre-Methodist days lacked passion, emotion and depth. Fortified by his evangelical commitment, Lewis Edwards argued that such books had no fire in their bellies and could thus never hope to provoke a true revival.[50]

It is true that the major devotional books of this period did

---

[48] William Foulkes, *Esponiad ar Gatechism yr Eglwys* (1688), p. 2.

[49] *Arch. Camb.*, III (1848), 245–6; 'Parochialia', Suppl. to *Arch. Camb.*, 1909–1 part 1, p. 146; B. F. Roberts, 'Rhai Swynion Cymraeg', *B.B.C.S.*, XXI (1965), 19

[50] G. M. Ashton (ed.), Robert Jones, *Drych yr Amseroedd* (1958), pp. 26–7 Lewis Edwards, *Traethodau Llenyddol* (n.d.), pp. 297–8; Henry Lewis, 'Perla Benthyg', *T.H.S.C.*, 1930–1, pp. 36–61.

not aspire to much beyond inculcating the basic tenets of Protestantism, the practical duties incumbent on the Christian, and the spiritual and prudential virtues of holiness and moral propriety; but what Lewis Edwards and his fellow critics did not understand was that the kind of religious drama of intense soul-searching and subjective conversion that Methodists were accustomed to think of as normal could only come about after a long preliminary period during which the major emphasis was laid on rudimentary moral and religious instruction. The value of didactic and devotional books was never in doubt at the time, particularly among those who were striving to achieve literacy and a proper understanding of the faith they professed. Moreover, reformers were aware of the crucial influence of the practical writings of puritan divines on those who wrestled inwardly with their consciences. Bayly's *Practice of Piety*, together with Dent's *Plaine Man's Pathway to Heaven*, had been responsible for begetting within the sinful John Bunyan 'some desires to religion'.[51] Reading *The Book of Resolution* had such an effect on Richard Baxter that 'the same things' that he knew before 'came now in another manner, with light, and sense and seriousness' to his heart.[52] The Welsh experience was similar: Thomas Jones of Shrewsbury was prepared to claim that *Llyfr y Resolusion* had been as efficacious as any book of its type in persuading men to seek salvation.[53] Judging by the amount of puritan literature read by the early Methodists, puritan teaching on inner experience and conversion was an indispensable guide in their own lives. After all, by his own evidence, Howel Harris was called 'from death to life' through reading 'that most excellent book', *The Whole Duty of Man*.[54] The early devotional experiences of Methodists owed much to the pervasive influence and spiritual guidance of puritan literature.

Lewis Edwards proclaimed a second indictment of the religious reformers of the pre-Methodist age: he charged them

---

[51] John Bunyan, *Grace Abounding to the chief of Sinners* (1666; reprinted 1970), pp. 4–5. The famous Lutheran pietist, Philipp Jakob Spener, was also deeply influenced by Bayly's book. F. E. Stoeffler, *The Rise of Evangelical Pietism* (1965), p. 231.

[52] Matthew Sylvester (ed.), *Reliquiae Baxterianae* (1696), p. 3.

[53] Thomas Jones (ed.), John Davies, *Llyfr y Resolusion* (1711), sig. A2r.

[54] Howel Harris recorded his spiritual conversion with minute precision. See *C.C.H.M.C.*, I (1917), 10.

with having failed to supply their countrymen with books dealing with the essential sinfulness of man and the availability of God's grace as a means of rescuing him from his pitiful condition.[55] How much substance lies in this accusation is something which can now be considered in dealing with the literature that emphasised inward experience and the need to regenerate the soul of sinful man.

Man, it was made clear in a wide range of devotional and doctrinal works, was congenitally sinful and corrupt.[56] Ever since the Fall, he had alienated himself from God and dedicated himself to 'lower fleshly things'. Poisoned by original sin, his natural depravity had been inherited by successive generations of mankind. Man's condition was thus base and miserable; ensnared by Satan, he had become the victim of passion, worldliness and self-interest. His natural condition, consequently, was a state of sin and death. Weak, fearful and obstinate in his fallen and rebellious state, he was in no position to reconcile himself to God and was at the same time totally incapable of saving himself. Recovery was possible only through God's second Covenant with man. Since man had no powers of recovery from his wretched condition, God had allowed his son to take the world's debt on his shoulders and, by voluntarily sacrificing his own life, give full atonement and satisfaction for the sins of the world. As a result, through the imputed righteousness of Christ, man now had the means of redemption.

Having made this cardinal point clear, authors were concerned to implant within the reader's mind and heart the need for regeneration, the need to be converted and made a new man. The most crucial occurrence in a man's life, they insisted, was the bestowal of divine grace by God. Without regeneration, conformity, morality and sanctity remained leaky vessels in which man could never hope to sail to heaven. Among the most popular works that stressed the necessity of regeneration was Thomas Gouge's *A Word to Sinners and a Word*

[55] Lewis Edwards, op. cit., p. 298.
[56] See, for instance, William Jones, *Gair i Bechaduriaid a Gair i'r Sainct* (1676) pp. 18–20; Charles Edwards, *Y Ffydd Ddi-ffvant* (1677), pp. 260–80; Richard Jones, *Galwad i'r Annychweledig* (1677), pp. 21–9; anon., *Tystiolaeth o Gariad a Ewyllys Da* (1683), pp. 4–5; anon., *Hyfforddwr Cyfarwydd i'r Nefoedd* (1693), pp. 1–3 anon., *Cyngor y Bugail iw Braidd* (1700), pp. 3–10; anon., *Y Cywyr Ddychwelw* (1727), pp. 18–73.

to Saints (1668) which, translated by William Jones in 1676, figured prominently among the texts favoured by the Welsh Trust.[57] Even more popular and persuasive was Richard Baxter's *Call to the Unconverted* (1658), translated into Welsh by Richard Jones and published in 1659 and 1677.[58] Intended for families 'where none are converted', the English version sold phenomenally, running through 20,000 copies within a year of its publication, and Baxter himself was gratified to learn that 'almost whole households' had been converted by his book.[59] One of its chief rivals was Joseph Alleine's *An Alarm to the Unconverted* (1673), a book which Calamy believed stood next to the Bible in its selling capacity. Under its original title, it sold 20,000 copies, and a further 50,000 were sold when the work was more comfortingly retitled *A Sure Guide to Heaven* (1688).[60] Alleine had shown a keen interest in the evangelisation of Wales and it is not surprising that his work was translated into Welsh, published in 1693 and reprinted in 1723.[61]

As their titles suggest, these works urged the reader to repent his wickedness, to reject the ephemeral pleasures of the flesh, to seek salvation, and then to wage war wholeheartedly upon sin. William Jones called on men to renounce the ways of the world, to follow Christ's call and become new men in Him. This could be done only by making a conscious choice: between Christ and the world, holiness and sin, life and death.[62] Similarly, Alleine made it abundantly clear that regeneration involved a spiritual rebirth, whilst Richard Jones, concentrating on some of Baxter's more 'vehement persuasions', persistently underscored the message that the wicked shall live if they will but turn and avail themselves of God's offer of salvation.[63] Better, they all agreed, never to have been born than not to be born again, and, judging by the annotated

---

[57] William Jones, *Gair i Bechaduriaid a Gair i'r Sainct* (1676). See the well-thumbed and annotated copy of Gouge's English edition of 1683 in N.L.W. MS. 11030A.
[58] Richard Jones, *Galwad i'r Annychweledig* (1659; 1677).
[59] *Reliquiae Baxterianae*, p. 115.
[60] Calamy, II, 577.
[61] Charles Stanford, *Joseph Alleine: his Companions and Times* (1864), p. 308; *Hyfforddwr Cyfarwydd i'r Nefoedd* (1693; 1723).
[62] *Gair i Bechaduriaid*, pp. 58, 81.
[63] *Hyfforddwr Cyfarwydd* (1693), pp. 64–92, 126–32; *Reliquiae Baxterianae*, p. 114; *Galwad i'r Annychweledig, passim.*

reflections on several extant copies of these works, their poignant aspirations were shared by many of their readers.[64]

The price of conversion was unwavering vigilance over the state of the soul. It was paramountly important to prepare the heart for grace.[65] The penitent sinner was required to subject his soul to a psychological inspection in order to detect hidden sins, to examine the motives for his deeds, and to discover his true spiritual condition. This vigorous self-scrutiny and unsparing heart-searching had become thoroughly rooted in the puritan mentality by the seventeenth century. Only medieval or counter-reformation mystics plumbed the depths of man's soul as fastidiously as the puritans, and the various techniques of self-appraisal which they employed in their daily lives were made available to the reading public at large through the printed book.

Whatever means of scrutiny might be used, all were agreed that the more rigorous the examination the greater the benefits. An outward show of sanctity clearly fell well short. It was not enough to attend church regularly every Sabbath with a prayer book tucked dutifully under one's arm, nor was it enough to shed the occasional tear during the sermon or to canter briskly through public and private prayers.[66] Hypocrites and simulators would find the path to heaven too narrow for them, for they were the 'almost Christians' who observed the conventional shell of Christian duty and worship in a self righteous, pharisaical manner. Men who washed the outsides of cups and saucers but left the insides soiled deceived none but themselves. Too many men, argued Jenkin Jones, could be likened to pepper: hot in the mouth but cold in the belly.[6]

[64] Copies of *Gair i Bechaduriaid* in Bangor University Library are copiousl annotated with reflections and verses, whilst an interesting note is contained in th copy at Swansea University Library: 'A booke bestowed to me by Thomas Goug the 20th day of July 1676. Hugh Roberts'.

[65] In preparing what follows I have benefited generally from reading th following works: William Haller, *The Rise of Puritanism* (1938); Perry Mille *The New England Mind: The Seventeenth Century* (1939); Geoffrey F. Nuttall, *Tl Holy Spirit in Puritan Faith and Experience* (1946); C. H. and K. George, *Tl Protestant Mind of the English Reformation, 1570–1640* (1961); A. W. Brink, 'A Stud in the Literature of Inward Experience, 1600–1700' (unpubl. Univ. of Londo Ph.D. thesis, 1963); Norman Pettit, *The Heart Prepared: Grace and Conversion Puritan Spiritual Life* (1966); Owen C. Watkins, *The Puritan Experience* (1972).

[66] *Y Cywyr Ddychwelwr* (1727), pp. 95–6, 108–12, 121–30.

[67] Jenkin Jones, *Llun Agrippa* (1723), pp. 50–1, 174–86; cf. Joshua Thoma *Llyfr Du y Gydwybod* (1723), p. 9.

Formal conformity, insisted Samuel Williams, was merely the corpse of religion—pipes without water, breasts without milk, sails with no wind.[68] This made religion a skeleton of dry bones, lacking the flesh, blood, nerves and sinews that gave it life.

In their inward scrutiny, Anglican authors placed heavy emphasis on the response of the soul to the pinpricks of conscience. 'Conscience', claimed William Lloyd, bishop of St. Asaph, was 'the rudder of all men's actions.'[69] 'It either acquits or condemns', agreed John Copner, 'shines or burns, refreshes or torments according to the innocence or guilt of men's actions.'[70] Conscience thus lay within all men, acting as God's faithful messenger in the soul, probing into man's anatomy and 'searching all the inward parts of the belly'. Works such as Theophilus Evans's translation of Henry Stubbe's *Conscience the best Friend upon Earth* (1677), published in 1715, were designed to jog the sleepy consciences of the most wilful sinners,[71] whilst Joshua Thomas's translation of Andrew Jones's popular *Black Book of Conscience* (6th ed., 1658), published in 1723, was aimed directly at those who had hardened their consciences against God's summons.[72] What influence such works had we cannot tell, but those readers who were weighed down by guilty consciences must surely have squirmed anxiously under the aggressive onslaught of questions and accusations.

Dissenting authors employed more ingenious techniques in the task of self-examination. Probably the most effective and penetrating analysis of the microcosmic human soul is the third part of Charles Edwards's *Y Ffydd Ddi-ffuant* (1677), in which the author invokes a wealth of figurative allusions to reveal the activity of the Holy Spirit in the soul.[73] Feverishly translating, editing and publishing literature for the Welsh Trust, Stephen Hughes was particularly anxious to show his readers different ways of appraising the soul. He nursed a fond regard for works of a Theophrastan character whereby each

[68] Samuel Williams, *Amser a Diwedd Amser* (1707), p. 38.
[69] N.L.W. MS. 11302D, f. 52v.
[70] N.L.W. MS. 2905A, p. 162.
[71] Theophilus Evans, *Cydwybod y Cyfaill Gorau* (1715).
[72] Joshua Thomas, *Llyfr Du y Gydwybod* (1723).
[73] See, in particular, D. L. Morgan, 'A Critical Study of the Works of Charles Edwards (1628–1691?)' (unpubl. Univ. of Oxford D.Phil thesis, 1967); Saunders Lewis, 'Arddull Charles Edwards', *Efrydiau Catholig*, IV (1949), 45–52.

figure typified a particular quality or fulfilled a certain social rôle.[74] For instance, Oliver Thomas's *Drych i dri math o Gristion*, published in 1677, was designed in such a way as to enable the reader to establish his true spiritual condition by finding his soul reflected in one of three mirrors.[75] Similarly, Hughes saw the value of written dialogue as a means of stripping down the conventional outer image, exploring the darkest recesses of the soul, and establishing who were true Christians and who were not. By publishing translations of works like Vavasor Powell's *Saving Faith set forth in Three Dialogues or Conferences* (1651) in 1677 and Arthur Dent's *Plaine Man's Path-way to Heaven* (1601) in 1682, Stephen Hughes was able to impress on his readers the exhaustive self-examination needed to ascertain whether Christ was within them.[76]

Hughes's successors were equally vigorous in stressing that only by coming to know oneself could man come to know God, to become aware of his sinful nature and his need for salvation. Thomas Baddy's influential translation of Thomas Wadsworth's *Serious Exhortation to an holy life* (1660) in 1713 was marked by a mood of uneasy restlessness, with the reader granted not a moment's peace. He was urged to probe inwardly, burrow down into every nook and cranny of the soul to uncover his sins and look for signs of grace. Examine yourselves, exhorted Baddy, examine your heart and your soul.[77] Similarly, Iaco ab Dewi liked to employ a dramatic, staccato form of questioning which was as persistent and remorseless as a pecking gull: 'what are you doing, and what have you been doing since you were born? what is the condition of your soul? what spirit are you in? where are you going? what are you? do you know yourself?'[78] The same pattern recurs in the Welsh translation of William Dyer's *Christ's Famous Titles* (1663), now shrewdly titled *Cyfoeth i'r Cymru* and a popular work published in 1688, 1706, 1714, 1731 and 1740. Consciously playing down the

---

[74] For the background to this type of literature see Benjamin Boyce, *The Theophrastan Character in England to 1642* (1947).

[75] Stephen Hughes (ed.), *Tryssor i'r Cymru* (1677), p. 226.

[76] The translation of Powell's work was included in *Cyfarwydd-deb i Anghyfarwydd* (1677); Robert Llwyd, *Llwybr Hyffordd yn cyfarwyddo yr anghyfarwyd i'r Nefoedd* (1682).

[77] Thomas Baddy, *Dwys Ddifrifol Gyngor* (1713).

[78] Iaco ab Dewi, *Llythyr at y Cyfryw o'r Byd* (1716), pp. 7–8. See also the same author's *Meddyliau Neillduol ar Grefydd* (1717; 1726).

ntellectual side of religion, this work called for an unrelenting
issection of the soul and stressed the value of personal
xperience in spiritual matters. Better a heart full of grace
han a head full of knowledge was the message, and, in focusing
n the subjective qualities of emotion and heat, such authors
vere anticipating much of what early Methodists had to say.
Many works, therefore, bore a strong hint of evangelical
ervency. By laying stress on justifying faith and Christ's
edemptive mercies, and by reducing the intellectual bent to
bare minimum, the fruits of experience were thrown into
harper relief. Here, too, lies the key to the phenomenal success
f John Bunyan's books in Wales throughout the eighteenth
entury. Stephen Hughes's translation of *The Pilgrim's Progress*
n 1688 was reissued in 1713 and 1722, whilst Thomas Jones of
hrewsbury also published his own translation of the work in
699. The second part of *The Pilgrim's Progress*—the pilgrimage
f Christiana and her children—was published in verse in 1713
nd in prose in 1730. A year later, Thomas Lewis referred
lowingly to the welcome hitherto afforded by the Welsh
eading public to Bunyan's major work and its dramatic
mpression upon readers.[79] Indeed, the influence of *Taith y*
ererin—published at least 41 times between 1688 and 1934[80]—
n independent religious thinking in Wales is incalculable. One
f the most prominent features of Welsh Dissent from its
nception was a resilient self-sufficiency, much of which might
e fortified by reading of the obstacles that Christian
urmounted bravely on his arduous journey between the City
f Destruction and the Celestial City.[81] Welsh Dissenters, whose
igorous moral code was second to none, found comfort from
dentifying themselves with the wayfaring pilgrim—the arche-
ypal Christian—who had thwarted the wiles of Satan and
roved that courage and steadfastness could bring its rewards
n a world riddled with backsliders and compromisers.
Methodists, too, like Dafydd Cadwaladr, learned Bunyan's

---

[79] Thomas Lewis, *Bywyd a Marwolaeth yr Annuwiol dan enw Mr. Drygddyn* (1731),
. 2.
[80] Mairwen Lewis, 'Astudiaeth gymharol o'r cyfieithiadau Cymraeg o rai o
veithiau John Bunyan, eu lle a'u dylanwad yn llên Cymru' (unpubl. Univ. Wales
M.A. thesis, 1957), p. 98.
[81] R. Tudur Jones, 'Agweddau ar Ddiwylliant Ymneilltuwyr', *T.H.S.C.*,
art 2, 1963, p. 179.

most famous work off by heart and took great pride in settii
it next to the Bible on their book-shelves.[82]

Much of Bunyan's appeal also lay in his broader churchma
ship. Although his doctrinal standpoint was set in a Calvin
mould, it was also strongly permeated with the Lutheran stro
on justifying faith.[83] Similarly, Stephen Hughes, who nursed
deep attachment to Bunyan's work, sought to harness the o
doctrinal viewpoint to the other to the advantage of both. I
employing shrewd marginal references and interpolatior
Hughes clearly showed the importance of justifying faith in I
Welsh edition of *The Pilgrim's Progress*.[84] Other authors la
similar stress on the imputation of Christ's righteousness to tl
sinner. In his translation of Bunyan's *Come and Welcome*
Jesus Christ (1678) in 1719, Iaco ab Dewi's basic theme was tl
doctrine of the grace of God as revealed in Christ.[85] Focusing
John vi 37 ('. . . him that cometh to me I will in no wise ca
out'), he preached the gospel of hope and consolation, showir
that Christ would not cast out even blood-red sinners, crimsc
sinners or sinners of a double dye. Christ's redemptive gra
was also the most prominent theme in Bunyan's *Good News*
the Vilest of Men (1688), translated by Benjamin Meredith
1721, and in which Welshmen were urged to draw comfo
from the fact that even the vilest sinners would not be cast o
provided they became justified in Christ.[86]

In an age when the written word was deeply reflected upc
by the literate, the effect of some of these dramatically per
etrating works could often be startling. The effect of Iaco a
Dewi's *Tyred a Groesaw at Iesu Grist* (1719) is well-attested. Bot
Methodists and Dissenters professed a genuine admiration ar
affection for the book and commended it warmly to the
brethren. Howel Harris confessed to having received gre
personal benefit from reading 'that extraordinary book',

[82] Richard Bennett, 'Richard Tibbott (1719–1798)', *C.C.H.M.C.*, II (1916), 3
Tom Beynon, *Howell Harris's Visits to Pembrokeshire* (1966), p. 35; J. D. Owen (ed
John Thomas, *Rhad Ras* (1949), p. 36; *Gwaith Barddonol Sion Wyn o Eifion sef J*
Thomas, *Chwilog* (1861), p. 70; anon., *Ychydig Gofnodau am Fywyd a Marwola*
Dafydd Cadwaladr (1836), pp. 9–10.
[83] Richard L. Greaves, *John Bunyan* (1969), pp. 153–6.
[84] Stephen Hughes (ed.), *Taith neu Siwrnai y Pererin* (1688), pp. 21–43.
[85] Iaco ab Dewi, *Tyred a Groesaw at Jesu Grist* (1719).
[86] Benjamin Meredith, *Pechadur Jerusalem yn Gadwedig* (1721).
[87] Tom Beynon, op. cit., p. 53; *C.C.H.M.C.*, VII (1961), 190.

whilst Edmund Jones claimed that many besides himself had reason 'to bless God that such a book was wrote'.[88] This book was also one of the catalysts that precipitated the conversion of Evan Williams of Cwmllynfell, the youthful Independent minister who flirted briefly with Methodism and who, until his tragically early death at the age of 29, won widespread acclaim as a revivalist preacher of uncommon fervency. Williams was reputed to have valued the work second only to the Bible; carrying a copy in his pocket wherever he went, he read and absorbed its content to such a degree that its substance proved a considerable help to him in preaching the Gospel.[89] Even more remarkable was the glowing testimony which David Jones of Dygoed, Llanlluan, revealed to Howel Harris:

> . . . I were in a field reading Mr. Bunyan's book, come and welcome to Jesus. I cannot tell what was the words but God Almighty pleased to show me a great light as I thought that the heaven was opened, and the son of God shining but not very clear; and the voice was, I am willing to receive thee, come to me, and that made me very willing to be his.[90]

Further to the left of the Lutheran-Calvinist orthodoxy stood the Welsh Quakers, whose central doctrine, to which the church, scripture, liturgy and all else were deemed subordinate, was that the light of truth was within man. By virtue of this belief, Welsh Friends were in the van of those groups in this period who, by expressing subjective states of mind and inward conviction, sought to probe the springs of action in men's souls.[91] They laid particular emphasis on the cleansing powers and redemptive cures of the Spirit within, and employed characteristically startling language to convey the effect of 'the heavenly power' which 'burned like a fire' and provoked much quaking and trembling.[92] Clearly, the shades of difference over types of inward experience among Protestants of different

---

[88] Edmund Jones, *A Sermon preached from John v 28, 29. Occasioned by the death of Mr. Evan Williams* (1750), p. 82.

[89] Ibid., pp. 83–4. For Williams, see *D.W.B.*

[90] G. M. Roberts, 'Letters written by David Jones, Dygoed, Llanlluan, to Howell Harris', *C.C.H.M.C.*, XXI (1936), 71–2.

[91] See especially John ap John, *Tystiolaeth o Gariad ac Ewyllys Da* (1683); Owen Lewis, *Agoriad yn agor y ffordd i bob dealltwriaeth cyffredin* (1703); Ellis Pugh, *Annerch ir Cymru* (1721).

[92] For a striking account of a Quaker conversion, see Thomas Wynne, *An Antichristian Conspiracy Detected* (1679), p. 24.

complexions often merged imperceptibly into one another. I particular, the emphasis on the subjective awareness of sin ar salvation bound together individuals over a wide spectrum religious beliefs and experiences.

If the step from sinfulness to contrition and repentan needed grace to nudge it forward, so too did the presence faith necessarily lead the regenerate on to good works. Th most genuine conversion was thought to have begun with mustard seed of faith; but, in time, that seed began to grov swelling from a tender bud and blossoming into fruit.[93] Ever Calvinist believed that his faith was revealed in his good dee which, although not in themselves guarantees of salvatio were nevertheless manifest proof of his conversion. Regene ation thus inevitably involved a growth in grace in terms sanctification or godliness. For the faith of the Christian w revealed in his works. Once man was fully reconciled to Chris new and more pressing demands were made on his commitmen devotion and zeal. The regenerate became elevated to a high moral plane than ordinary mortals, and this was reflected i his daily life. His joyous spiritual experience had the effect transforming his whole outlook and liberating his enti personality—a catalysis which did not go unnoticed amon contemporaries. Malicious men, observed Charles Edward became loving citizens, attackers became protectors, tl depraved became chaste, the drunk were made sober, and tl clenched fist poised to strike in anger was now opened in spirit of benevolence and charity.[94] Regeneration, howeve did not mean that man had attained a state of perfection—r man had claims to that condition. But it did mean that he w. no longer possessed by sin; indeed, he was now committed wage war on sin and depravity. When a man, claimed Jenki Jones, had been drawn from darkness to light, from th vice-like grip of Satan to the protective bosom of God, an when the mind had been enlightened, the will revealed, inn sensibilities and affections totally and irrevocably touche then he was a true Christian indeed.[95] Joyfully reborn, he wa

[93] Anon., *Gronyn o Had Mwstard neu'r messur lleiaf o Ras* (1722); David Mauri Cwnffwrdd ir Gwan Gristion (1700), p. 3.
[94] Charles Edwards, op. cit., p. 343.
[95] Jenkin Jones, *Llun Agrippa*, p. 112; cf. *Gair i Bechaduriaid*, pp. 86–11 *Hyfforddwr Cyfarwydd*, pp. 13–35.

ow a new spiritual creature who, blessed with the final
ssurance of salvation, would inherit not only fulness of life
n earth but also eternal bliss.

In an earnest appeal to his readers to read both sound
evotional manuals and searching, penetrating books, Iaco ab
)ewi recommended the Welsh translations of Dent's *Plaine
Mans Path-way to Heaven*, Bayly's *Practice of Piety*, Bunny's
Book of Resolution, Allestree's *Whole Duty of Man*, Baxter's *Call
) the Unconverted*, Shephard's *Sincere Convert*, all of Thomas
Gouge's books, together with Rees Prichard's *Canwyll y Cymry*
nd Charles Edward's *Y Ffydd Ddi-ffuant*.[96] This judicious
malgam of godly manuals, devotional 'home helps' and more
esting works which focused on sin, conversion and salvation,
vas the literate Welshman's 'five-foot shelf' of popular religious
terature. Looking back in 1750, Edmund Jones, too, singled
ut those awakening tracts that had led many sinners to
eassess their spiritual condition:

> . . . such books as Arthur Dent's (i.e. *Plaine Mans Pathway to
> Heaven*), Shephard's *Sincere Convert*, Allen's *Sure Guide to Heaven*;
> Gouge's *Word to Sinners* and *Word to Saints*; Baxter's *Call to the
> Unconverted*; Dyer's *Christ's famous Titles*; Wadsworth's *Self-
> Examination*; Doolittle on the Sacrament translated into Welsh,
> have been blessed of God to do good to many souls in Wales.[97]

ll these works were standard treatises on conversion, all were
vorks by those whom Richard Baxter liked to call 'affectionate
ractical' writers,[98] and all were published in the years between
he Restoration and Methodism. What is particularly striking
bout these books is that they were not content to scratch the
urface in spiritual matters; in fact, they deplored the dry
norality and bland, self-satisfied piety of the 'almost Christian'.
ndeed, the bulk of the literature of inward experience

---

[96] Iaco ab Dewi, *Llythyr at y Cyfryw o'r Byd*, p. 58. An indication of the lasting
opularity of some of these works may be gained from the observations of Robert
oberts (Y Sgolor Mawr, 1834–85): he believed that books normally found in
Velsh farmhouses were the *Bible*, *The Whole Duty of Man*, *Y Ffydd Ddiffuant*, *The
ilgrim's Progress* and *Canwyll y Cymry*. J. H. Davies (ed.), *The Life and Opinions of
obert Roberts* (1923), p. 17.
[97] Edmund Jones, op. cit., p. 82. Richard Steele's recommended books to
Velsh farmers were of the same character. *The Husbandmans Calling* (1668),
p. 264–5.
[98] Richard Baxter, *A Christian Directory* (1673), part 3, p. 922.

published in this period was outstanding in its emphasis c
the 'psychological vivisection' of the soul,[99] on the subjectiv
awareness of sin, on the Christocentric nature of faith, and c
the practical fruits of the growth of grace in the regenerate
soul. Such works made it clear that spiritual matters were
personal responsibility, a two-way relationship between Gc
and the individual. By a process of restless and uncompromisir
self-scrutiny, testing the state of mind and soul, these bool
helped to prepare men as they wrestled to attain salvatior
There is no doubt, too, that they helped to foster some of tho:
attitudes and habits which became bound up in the Methodi
psyche. For a good deal of this literature of inward experienc
is strongly redolent of the characteristically intense pr
occupation with the state of the soul—almost to the point
morbidity—which was part and parcel of early Methodism
Wales.

IV. MORTALITY AND JUDGMENT

The melancholy, and sometimes obsessive, concern with dea
in the religious literature of this period largely reflected 'tl
hazards of an intensely insecure environment'.[100] From bir
many people's lives were insecure in the extreme and we
made more so whenever calamities such as disease and sicknes
famine and plague, fire or bankruptcy struck. Illness ar
suffering were constant companions in seventeenth-centu
life, and when John Rhydderch claimed that good health w
a God-given gift, a rare blessing that made men happy, l
voiced a commonly-held sentiment.[101] Few people enjoy
complete health, and most were racked with violent pains ar
distempers for which they had no adequate remedies. Eve
those whose diets were relatively well-balanced could ho
for little more than 'some intervals of respite'[102] from chron
illnesses, whilst the poorer orders, lacking the benefits
proper nutrition and made vulnerable by rudimenta
standards of hygiene and sanitation, were peculiarly prone

[99] Perry Miller, op. cit., chapter ten.
[100] Keith Thomas, *Religion and the Decline of Magic* (1971), p. 5.
[101] Hugh Owen (ed)., *Additional Letters of the Morrises of Anglesey (1735–176*
(1947), p. 2.
[102] Thomas Richards, *The Happiness of Good Christians*, p. 10.

ialadies and disease. Only the wealthy could afford the
:rvices of the few qualified physicians resident in Wales,
·hilst those much-maligned sellers of medical nostrums,
pothecaries, were rarely held in high esteem.[103] As a result,
iany preferred to rely on palliatives, usually age-old herbal
:medies, handed down through the ages, or take their chance
ith the local cunning man, a wise woman, or an itinerant
iedical quack.[104]

In what was an overwhelmingly rural society, men's lives
·ere often indirectly determined by the quality of successive
arvests. Against the 27 good harvests which occurred in
ngland and Wales between 1660 and 1729 must be set the
) that were singularly deficient, particularly during the years
695–8, 1708–11 and 1727–8.[105] Bad harvests invariably meant
)aring food prices which immediately caused economic crises
i those communities where resources were already thin.[106]
or society at large, dear food meant dearth and malnutrition
hich, aggravated by infective diseases, notably smallpox,
·phus, scrofula, tuberculosis and dysentery, resulted in higher
iortality rates.[107] A smallpox infection—generally despised as
he coldest of conquerors'[108]—might often descend on small
>mmunities with devastating consequences, ravaging even
·ell-nourished families and proving particularly virulent
mong children. It accounted for the death of sixty people in
enmachno within a period of fourteen months between 1705
nd 1706, whilst of 104 people who died in Carmarthen
etween July 1722 and March 1723, 71 were victims of
nallpox.[109]

[103] For petitions urging the need for physicians and surgeons see N.L.W.,
)/Misc/512; SD/Misc/1196; anon., *A Journey to Llandrindod Wells* (2nd ed., 1746).
). 64–5; Gwyn Thomas, *Y Bardd Cwsg a'i Gefndir* (1971), p. 74.
[104] Glyn Penrhyn Jones, 'Folk Medicine in Eighteenth Century Wales', *Folk
fe*, VII (1969), 60–74; Thomas Jones, *Newyddion Mawr oddiwrth y Ser* (1699),
z. A1v–A5v.
[105] W. G. Hoskins, 'Harvest Fluctuations and English Economic History,
i20–1759', *Agricultural History Review*, 16 (1968), 15; John Oliver, 'Tywydd
ymru yn y cyfnod hanesyddol', *Y Gwyddonydd*, IV (1966), 72–80.
[106] This subject is particularly well treated in a French context by Pierre
oubert, *Beauvais et le Beauvaisis de 1600 à 1730* (1960), pp. 45–59.
[107] G. Penrhyn Jones, *Newyn a Haint yng Nghymru* (1963); Charles Creighton,
History of Epidemics in Britain (2 vols., 2nd ed., 1965).
[108] Dafydd Jones, *Blodeu-gerdd Cymry* (1779), p. 377; James Owen, *Hymnau
rythurol* (2nd ed., 1717), pp. 99–100.
[109] G. Penrhyn Jones, op. cit., p. 36; William Spurrell, *Carmarthen and its
eighbourhood* (2nd ed., 1879), p. 14.

A combination of harsh weather, crop failures, dearth, hi
prices, smallpox, and an epidemic of fever made the year 17
one of particularly high mortality. Indeed, the last three yea
of that decade witnessed 'the last catastrophic epidemic'
pre-industrial times.[110] The 'general sickness', described
Griffith Jones, Llanddowror, as 'a nervous kind of fever', see
to have 'raged mightily' in most counties, bringing sudd
death to the majority of sufferers.[111] In Anglesey, Ow
Davies, vicar of Llanbadrig, feared that the distemper w
'very deceitful & flattering, one thinks living is pretty jo
today & tomorrow is ready to make his exit'.[112] 'Are not o
neighbours', preached Griffith Jones, rector of Denbig
'daily dropping round about us, who having equal advantag
of health, strength and vigour with ourselves, had as lit
reason to expect death as any of us?'[113] The epidemic clea
had a crushing effect on the vulnerable poor who were drive
by a combination of dearth and the exorbitant price of whe
to live on bad bread, thereby rendering themselves even mo
susceptible to crippling fevers and sudden death. 'The gent
in general are pretty hearty in the country', wrote Ow
Davies laconically in March 1729, 'it's the common sort th
drop off.'[114]

Even so, every Christian was conditioned, by his unblinki
faith in the doctrine of providence, to accept every advers
that overtook him as a manifestation of God's will.[115] God w
the most active power in man's affairs and nothing on ear
happened without His having ordained or willed it. T
adversities that befell man were not the products of chan
and since God had a purpose in sending both blessings a

[110] J. A. Johnston, 'The Impact of the Epidemics of 1727–30 in South W
Worcestershire', *Medical History*, XV (1971), 278; R. S. Schofield, 'Crisis Mortali
Local Population Studies, no. 9 (1972), 10–22; A. Gooder, 'The Population Crisi
1727–30 in Warwickshire', *Midland History*, I (1972), 1–22.
[111] Clement, pp. 153, 163; U.C.N.W.L., Henblas MS. 18A, p. 4; B.L., A
MS. 14866, f. 304v; W. Spurrell, op. cit., p. 14; E. D. Jones, 'Copi o Lyfr Egl
Pant-teg, Abergwili', *Y Cofiadur*, 23 (1953), 65; O. S. Ashton, 'Eighteenth Cent
Radnorshire: a Population Survey', *Trans. Radnorshire Soc.*, XL (1970), p.
Friends' House Library, Kelsall MSS. Diaries, Transcript Series, V, pp. 181–2
[112] Leonard Owen, 'The Letters of an Anglesey Parson, 1712–1732', *T.H.S*
1961, p. 89.
[113] Griffith Jones, *A Sermon preach'd at St. Hilary's Chapel in Denbigh on occasio
the late General Mortality* (2nd ed., 1730), p. 22.
[114] Leonard Owen, op. cit., p. 89; cf. *Morris Letters*, I, 63, 74.
[115] Keith Thomas, op. cit., pp. 78–112.

punishments, man was able to come to terms with the pain and misfortune which dogged his life.[116] Jeremy Owen had experienced both sides of the coin when he beheld 'the goodness and severity of God',[117] for the Almighty's interventions on earth were designed either to awaken a sense of shame and contrition in the hearts of the sinful or to subject the righteous to trial. 'God', wrote Philip Henry soothingly, 'hath sent the one over against the other, prosperity over against adversity, sweetly intermixing the one with the other & all for the good of his chosen.'[118]

Thus, whenever local or even European disasters caught the public imagination, a rash of tracts and ballads betrayed the tensions within society. When the dreaded bubonic plague—the *peste*—made one of its last appearances in western Europe at Marseilles and Provence in 1720–2, claiming over 128,000 victims, Welsh reformers drew the appropriate moral: plague and mortality were divinely-ordained as a judgment for sin, and, if He so desired, God could destroy the whole world by the sword, by famine or by plague.[119] Similarly, John Thomas of Bodedern saw the harrowing epidemic of 1729 as a function of the wrath of God, a punishment for sin on wilful men who deserved no better fate.[120] In 1730, Thomas Richards took up the same theme in his translation of Edmund Gibson's *Advice to Persons recovered from Sickness*, 4,000 copies of which were distributed among those who had either survived the epidemic or were still in the throes of mortal sickness. Richards viewed the epidemic as a visitation prompted by God as a timely reminder to sinners and also as a means of giving man a closer look at death so that he might test his readiness for his appointed fate.[121]

---

[116] N.L.W. MS. 510A, p. 166; N.L.W. MS. 3B, p. 10; Thomas Wynne, *The Evidences of an Over-ruling Providence in defeating the Conspiracies of Cunning and Ungodly Men* (1722).
[117] Jeremy Owen, *The Goodness and Severity of God* (1717), p. 19.
[118] M. H. Lee (ed.), *Diaries and Letters of Philip Henry*, p. 263.
[119] Jean-Noel Biraben, 'Certain Demographic Characteristics of the Plague Epidemic in France, 1720–1722', *Daedalus*, Spring 1968, pp. 536–45; Dafydd Thomas, *Hanes y Pla yn Ffraingc* (1721); R. Prichard and T. Dafydd, *Y Newydd ychyrynadwy o Ffraingc neu Ddiflaniad Marsailles* (1721); *Gair i Gymru . . . ar achos y Pla yn ffraingc* (1722); Friends' House Library, Kelsall MSS. Diaries, IV, p. 102.
[120] John Thomas, *Dwy o Gerddi Newyddion: sef, Pennillion yn gwahodd pobl i droi at Dduw yn y dyddiau enbyd hyn gan draethu ynghylch y Drudaniaeth Clefydon ar Marwolaethau sydd yn ein plith* (1729).
[121] Thomas Richards, *Cyngor Difrifol i un ar ol bod yn Glaf* (1730); Clement, p. 306.

Adversities that befell the godly were explained away a God's means of measuring the pulse of the faithful. After al gold was no worse for being tested.[122] The more we fly in th face of providence, maintained Robert Lloyd, the mor uncomfortable adversities turn out to be.[123] Every trial an tribulation was thus to be accepted and borne without demu since the decrees of providence were absolute. At first sigh this doctrine appears essentially gloomy and repellent. But was also a doctrine of comfort and consolation which save many from utter despair. 'I thank God', mused the affluer and melancholy industrialist, John Wynne of Copa'rlen 'that all the help and comfort that a man has comes to pa only and altogether by the providence of God.'[124] In particula submission to divine providence helped to inure men family sickness and bereavement. On the occasion of her son illness in 1726, Ann Owen of Penrhos, sick at heart and bare able to conceal her fears for the worst, was neverthele prepared to resign herself totally to God's impenetrable wil 'God's will be done', she wrote bravely, 'to him & us all.'[1] Complete reliance on the inscrutable ways of providence help(to smooth away the wrinkles and bring peace of mind.

Authors inevitably belaboured the obvious when they dre their readers' attention to the universal fate of mankind. Apa from nature around them, men learnt from their Bible that a creatures, without exception, were liable to mortality and deat None escaped the 'common prison of all mankind: the grave'.[1] 'Time', wrote Bishop William Lloyd, 'with his vast scytl mows down all things: death sweeps away his mowings.'[1] Mortality, moreover, acknowledged no class distinctions—a men were equal before death: beggars and kings, fools ar wise men, the oppressed and their oppressors, all becan

[122] N.L.W. MS. 1446A, p. 15.
[123] Robert Lloyd, *Cyssur i'r Cystuddiedig* (1723), p. 9; cf. Bishop Humph: Humphreys's letter to the palsied Lord Bulkeley. N.L.W. MS. 9070E, f. 24. ° also Edward Roberts, *Llaw Lyfr yw Ddarllen ir Cleifion gida Myfyrdodau peraid(gweddiau iw harfer yn amser Clefyd* (completed in 1671 but first published in 175(
[124] N.L.W., SA/Misc/662, p. 3.
[125] N.L.W., Bodewryd (Sotheby) Correspondence, no. 966. For simi sentiments see N.L.W., Penrice and Margam MSS. L266; N.L.W. MS. 15! M. H. Lee, op. cit., p. 161; David Jenkins, 'Bywyd a Gwaith Huw Mor Pontymeibion' (unpubl. Univ. Wales M.A. thesis, 1948), pp. 164–9.
[126] N.L.W. MS. 12444B, p. 184.
[127] N.L.W. MS. 11302D, f. 58v.

nutual bedfellows in the grave.[128] Earnest clergymen like
John Morgan, vicar of Aberconwy, reflecting murkily on 'the
unavoidableness of man's mortality', found some comfort from
quoting James Shirley:

> Sceptre and crown
> Must tumble down
> And in the dust be equal laid.[129]

But it was presumably the poorer orders who drew most
consolation from the knowledge that death was the greatest
eveller. Those who secretly nursed some notion of eternal
revenge on their oppressors must have laughed up their
sleeves in the certainty that cheeseparing squires, rack-renting
andlords, bullying stewards and grabbing lawyers would, in
ime, share the same ineluctable fate as themselves. Born into
poverty and hardship, the poor were expected to work out
heir own salvation within their appointed station in the world.
Barely responding to their distress signals, clergymen assured
hem that their inheritance and consolation were not of this
world:

> Those, for instance, who are placed in the lowest class of life
> here, and groan under the hardships of poverty and want, cold
> and nakedness, should comfort themselves with this considera-
> tion, that when they have ended the days of their pilgrimage
> here upon earth, and are returned to their Father's house, they
> shall hunger no more, neither thirst any more—and that God
> shall wipe away all tears for ever from their eyes.[130]

Although it was known that death overtook all men in the
fullness of time, no one could be sure when each individual's
time would come or whose turn came next. It is hardly
surprising that special intercessions for preservation from
sudden death were incorporated in the Litany of the Prayer
Book. Even within gentry families, where life expectancy was
generally higher than among most other grades in society,

---

[128] Anon., *Cadwyn Euraidd o Bedair Modrwy* (1706), p. 3; John Morgan,
Myfyrdodau Bucheddol ar y Pedwar Peth Diweddaf (1716), p. 4; Robert Lloyd,
Llaw-Lyfr y Gwir Gristion (1716), p. 8.
[129] U.C.N.W.L., Bangor MS. 421, pp. 423–4.
[130] Thomas Richards, *The Happiness of Good Christians*, p. 12.

men of gentle birth, bearing in mind 'the uncertain state of this transitory life', prepared draft wills many years before the onset of death.[131] Those melancholic souls who were obsessed with mortality knew that death came in various guises and owing to its 'delusive approaches', it was thought sheer folly to rely on some providential portent since death might come stealthily with no warning at all.[132] But even if men had no means of telling when death's arrows might strike, they needed no reminder of the brevity of life. At the end of the seventeenth century the average age of the population was twenty-seven and the expectation of life at birth was around half of what it was for males in Britain in the 1950s.[133] The average expectation of life was kept low by high infant mortality rates which could decimate even the offspring of gentry households. Of twelve children born to Robert and Ann Owen of Penrhos six died in their infancy and only one of the remaining six survived their mother.[134] Similar traumas befell the families of ministers: of seven children born to James Owen by his first marriage, only two survived their infancy.[135] If such tragedies were common among the relatively well-to-do, infant mortality rates among the poor, especially at times of famine and disease, must have been appalling. Generally, however, surmounting the crucial years of infancy was the real test, and those who survived childhood, provided they did not suffer constantly from malnutrition or fall prey to disease, had every chance of prolonging their lives. Returns sent in response to Edward Lhuyd's inquiries in the 1690s reveal that most parishes sported sprightly octogenarians—the oracles of their localities—and the occasional soul who topped the hundred mark.[136] Of

---

[131] U.C.N.W.L., Mostyn MS. 183.

[132] Bangor P.R. 1702, John Morgan, Aberconwy; John Morgan, *Myfyrdod Bucheddol*, p. 4; *Y Cofiadur*, 23 (1953), 60–2; Friends' House Library, Kelsall MS, Book of Poems, p. 10; Elis Lewis, *Ystyriaethau Drexelivs ar Dragywyddoldeb* (1661), p. 234.

[133] D. V. Glass, 'Gregory King's Estimate of the Population of England and Wales, 1695', *Population Studies*, II (1950), 338–74. But see also the estimate for Colyton, Devon, which puts the expectation of life at 36.9 between 1625 and 1699 and 41.8 between 1700 and 1774. E. A. Wrigley, 'Mortality in pre-industrial England: the example of Colyton, Devon, over three centuries', *Daedalus*, Spring 1968, pp. 546–80; Peter Laslett, *The World we have Lost* (1965), p. 93.

[134] N.L.W., Bodewryd (Sotheby) Documents, no. 1075, p. 6.

[135] Charles Owen, op. cit., p. 21.

[136] 'Parochialia', Suppl. to *Arch. Camb.*, 1909–11, *passim*.

the whole, however, as Welsh authors untiringly insisted, man's span on earth was exceedingly brief, passing by like a speedy messenger or a fleeting shadow.[137] Our lives, warned Thomas Williams in his translation of William Sherlock's popular and consolatory *Practical Discourse concerning Death* (1689), fade like the flowers of the field.[138] We live, confirmed Elis Lewis in his most foreboding tone, on the very doorstep of eternity.[139]

Under the influence of Robert Bolton's popular work,[140] many books fixed their attention on the 'four last things': death, judgment, hell and heaven. God's judgment, warned John Thomas ominously, hangs over us, suspended by a thin thread, like Dionysius' sword over Damocles.[141] The apocalyptic expectations of Jenkin Jones and John Harri enabled them to view life on earth as merely an ignoble prelude to the 'Day of the Lord', which would herald the advent of a new heaven and a new earth.[142] It was ordained that all of Adam's seed should appear before God and Christ at the *Dies Irae*, and on that fateful day the omnipotent and inscrutable Judge dispensed life or eternal reward to the righteous and death or eternal punishment to the reprobate. Woe betide those who arrived before the great tribunal in an unregenerate state for, as so many lurid and horrific descriptions revealed, God would expose the iniquities of the sinful and wreak his vengeance upon them.[143]

Hell was the ultimate repose of the sinner through all eternity. Cast into the yawning, bottomless pit where the devil was the jailer, hell the prison, damnation the punishment, and eternity the fate, death to the hapless reprobate was a dreadful

---

[137] Anon., *Ymadroddion Mr. Dod* (1692), p. 11; Samuel Williams, *Amser a Diwedd Amser*, sig. A5r; Robert Lloyd, *Llaw-Lyfr y Gwir Gristion*, p. 12.

[138] Thomas Williams, *Ymadroddion Bucheddol ynghylch Marwolaeth* (1691), p. 29. Sherlock's work ran through ten editions prior to 1700 'and continued to console and sustain readers like Mrs. Veal and Mrs. Bargrave in the next century'. James Sutherland, *English Literature of the late Seventeenth Century* (1969), p. 314.

[139] Elis Lewis, *Ystyriaethau Drexelivs*, p. 16.

[140] Robert Bolton, *Mr. Bolton's Last and Learned Worke of the Foure Last Things, Death, Ivdgement, Hell and Heaven* (1633). See Charles A. Patrides, 'Renaissance and Modern Thought on the Last Things', *Harvard Theological Review*, Ll (1958), 169–85.

[141] John Thomas, *Unum Necessarium*, sig. A4r.

[142] Jenkin Jones, *Dydd y Farn Fawr* (1727); John Harri, *Rhai Datguddiadau o'r Nefoedd Newydd ar Ddaear Newydd* (1725).

[143] See, for instance, John Morgan's terrifying description in *Bloedd-nad Ofnadwy yr Udcorn diweddaf* (1704), p. 38.

curse which brought untold misery.[144] In painting their gruesome portraits of hell, authors lingered fondly on the physical torments that befell those who descended to the regions of eternal punishment. In this world, observed John Morgan, one might experience intense pain from breaking a limb or dislocating a bone, but this pain was never as excruciating as that felt continuously by those cast into the fire and brimstone of hell.[145] Stephen Hughes admitted that it was a traumatic experience for a man to spend a year locked in a dark prison, or to have his hand forcibly held in a fire for fifteen minutes, or to have his body eaten by insects; but the actual pain felt, he insisted, was no more than a pinprick compared with the torments of hell which lasted through all eternity.[146] In hell, therefore, there could be no release from pain, no comfort or sleep, only darkness and sorrow, much wailing, wringing of hands and gnashing of teeth.

Yet the emphasis was not always morbidly focused on the dreadfulness of judgment and hell, for authors were also fond of drawing comparisons between the eternal torture of hell and the eternal joys of heaven. Heaven was the reward in the hereafter for the godly and the righteous. For them, therefore, death was a glorious event, and authors did their best to coax their readers into righteousness by painting seductive portraits of the heavenly community. In heaven there was joy without sadness, light without darkness, pleasure without pain, life without death, rest without labour, plenty without poverty and gain without loss.[147] Mundane pleasures could never match the Elysian joys of heaven and it would be a foolish man indeed who would spurn such an opportunity by wilfully hardening his heart to the need for redemption. The material wealth, entertainment and pleasures of the earth were essentially perishable commodities, ephemeral delights which could never offer complete fulfilment, mere straws in comparison with the glories of heaven. Thus, if death opened the way to a heaven of spiritual delights to be blissfully enjoyed for all eternity, was it not worth seeking and striving for such an inheritance?[148]

[144] *Cadwyn Euraidd o Bedair Modrwy*, pp. 5–6.
[145] *Bloedd-nad Ofnadwy*, p. 64.
[146] Stephen Hughes (ed.), *Tryssor i'r Cymru* (1677), sig. A3v.
[147] *Cadwyn Euraidd*, p. 10; *Myfyrdodau Bucheddol*, pp. 13–17.
[148] Edward Lloyd, *Meddyginiaeth a Chyssur* (1722), pp. 28–9.

Scores of authors made it perfectly clear then that life was no more than a short prelude to eternity. It followed, therefore, that time on earth was precious and to be accounted for almost as a sacred trust between man and God. Inspired by the growth of puritanism, those tracts which sought to teach men how to die well formed a major pillar of the devotional book-trade.[149] They decreed that life was meant to be a meditation of death, a probationary period and not an end in itself.[150] For the godly the prospects were bright, since he that lived well could not die ill. For sinners the matter was urgent, for there was no worse fate than to be struck down in an unregenerate condition. But preparing for death was not a task that could be hastily accomplished overnight or reserved for the death-bed. It was, in fact, a lifetime's work. Since death might strike at any moment, immediate repentance was a crucial necessity, for the tears of the reprobate after death would be unavailing.[151] If the foundations of your home home had rotted away, urged Edward Lloyd, and the building threatened to collapse upon you, would you not hasten to leave that house at speed?[152] By the same token, it was in the sinner's interest to hasten his repentance and to prepare for his inevitable fate by learning to die joyfully and willingly.

It is difficult to gauge how various grades in society reacted to the morbid concern over death found in so much of the literature of this period, and how far the personal implications of mortality were grasped. Sensitive and perceptive men would doubtless have taken these issues to heart as they filtered through from parish pulpits and printed books. Possibly the most efficacious books were those which riveted men's attention to the harrowing fate awaiting the reprobate. Most didactic books that aspired to make men pious were generally content to apply a little gentle persuasion on the reader or at least to hector him persistently to think about his ultimate end. But those books which dealt with the eternal issues of death,

[149] F. M. M. Comper, *The Book of the Craft of Dying and other early English tracts concerning Death* (1917).

[150] See especially, *Ystyriaethau Drexelivs ar Dragywyddoldeb* and *Amser a Diwedd Amser*.

[151] *Ymadroddion Bucheddol ynghylch Marwolaeth*, pp. 17–32; *Amser a Diwedd Amser*, pp. 194–8; *Myfyrdodau Bucheddol*, p. 7; anon., *Myfyrdodau Duwiol i'n cymhwyso erbyn awr Angeu* (1727), *passim; Cyngor difrifol i un ar ol bod yn Glaf*, pp. 11–12.

[152] *Meddyginiaeth a Chyssur*, p. 98–9.

judgment and hell were a good deal more intimidating. The graphic and lurid imagery employed in the descriptions of hell and its eternal torments was clearly an attempt to frighten men into being godly. In their different ways, puritans like Stephen Hughes and Ellis Wynne (and many others) made the fear of hell a living reality, not out of a perverse and gloomy delight in casting pessimism and despair, but as a means of persuading their readers to fix their minds and hearts on eternity and to grasp the absolute necessity of a speedy repentance. There can be no doubt that they believed that the idea of an eternal hell acted as a deterrent from sin, and some of their more fearsome and grimly-worded *exempla*, told and re-told around the hearth throughout the eighteenth century, drove not a few readers to distraction.[153]

Memento mori was doubtless a motto never far from the thoughts of serious-minded gentry, lachrymose ministers and the pious middling sorts. Those rooted in the faith and therefore liberated from the fear of death were happy in the certainty that, since they were to join their 'dear Redeemer', death was a gain and not a loss.[154] Conversely, those who repudiated the Christian faith probably experienced death-anxiety least; for them, mortality remained a curious mystery. Those who had become long hardened to the thunderings of the clergy on the subject of hell's fires and damnation were also rarely prone to great crises of doubt and apprehension. It might be expected, too, that many would be more disposed to heed the advice of magicians and astrologers and believe that forces such as the constellation of the stars at birth, the movements of the planets, or the phases of the moon could neither be influenced nor changed and were inextricably bound up with man's ultimate destiny.[155] In some localities, moreover, uninstructed rural folk hopefully relied on the notorious 'sin-eater' who, at the risk of social ostracism, performed a cathartic deed which posthumously wiped away the sins of the deceased.[156]

[153] *Ychydig Gofnodau am Fywyd a Marwolaeth Dafydd Cadwaladr*, pp. 9–10; Mairwen Lewis, op. cit., p. 322.

[154] See the confessions, hopes and expectations of Dissenters on their death-beds in *Y Cofiadur*, 23 (1953), 18–70.

[155] Helmer Ringgren (ed.), *Fatalistic Beliefs in Religion, Folklore, and Literature* (1967), p. 14.

[156] T. M. Owen, *Welsh Folk Customs* (2nd ed., 1968), p. 183. According to John Aubrey, the 'sin-eater' was prevalent as late as 1686 in parts of Wales.

The thoughts of the poorer orders on the subject, their hopes and fears, remain for the most part unrecorded. In a society racked by illness and disease, famine and dearth, it is likely that those on whom these burdens pressed more than ordinarily hard would fitfully turn their minds to the fragility of man's existence and the significance of eternal things. Yet the 'plain country fellow' was rarely troubled by fears of death, for, provided his harvest was gathered, he would, with serene indifference, 'let it come when it will'.[157] Loath to resign themselves to the inscrutable ways of providence, the attitude of unlettered and unreflecting folk was generally one of careless stoicism.[158] They believed their fate to be 'as natural and unavoidable as the course of the sun and river, or the growth of the grass in the field'.[159] Edward Lhuyd's informant at Walwyn's Castle, Pembrokeshire, reckoned that 'the opinion of fatality prevails as amongst most of the vulgar of this country'.[160] Like Brendan Behan, most of them would rather be dead than think about death. Many, too, retained a limitless capacity for self-deception. The timorous in their midst may have objected that preparation for death actually hastened the event, and they would need a good deal of persuasion before accepting that a conscience purged by repentance was more likely to extend their lives and eventually open the way to eternal happiness.[161] Deaf to all homilies on the insufficiency of man, the emptiness of this fickle and corrupt world, and the incontrovertible justice and eternal torments of hell, they were prepared to take their chance. 'God is merciful'[162] was their optimistic retort to the most earnest attempts to convince them that they lived in a fool's paradise and that, at a time known only to God, they would be called before Him to account for their deeds on earth.

---

[157] John Earle, *Microcosmography: or, a piece of the World discover'd in Essays and Characters* (1732), pp. 76–7.
[158] Keith Thomas, op. cit., p. 17.
[159] N.L.W. MS. 10B, p. 80.
[160] 'Parochialia', Suppl. to *Arch. Camb.*, 1909–11, p. 84.
[161] N.L.W. MS. 9070E, f. 24.
[162] See *Ystyriaethau Drexelivs*, pp. 86–7 and *Tryssor i'r Cymru*, p. 45.

VI

RELIGIOUS VERSE AND SAYINGS

As late as the Restoration period, religious reformers were still struggling to carve out a respectable niche for religious verse in the framework of Christian worship. The value of poetry as the handmaiden of divinity was still denied by those dissident voices that looked upon verse as an inferior medium of didacticism. In his work on the efficacy of prayer, John Thomas muzzled his penchant for verse rather than offend those who judged poetry to be an improper means of conveying religious truths.[1] 'Poetry', sighed John Kelsall, 'is much disesteemed by many.'[2] Most objections, however, were provoked by the misapplication and abuse of verse. Men of puritan persuasion were not, as royalist hyperbole and Victorian fiction would have it, philistine in their attitudes towards music and verse. But they did nurse a long-standing suspicion of frivolous, profane and shallow material that lured men away from the paths of true godliness. In order to counter this trend, a growing emphasis was placed on the didactic merits of religious verse and its potential advantages. Sir John Philipps of Picton combed his Bible to find examples of 'the good effect divine hymns have had', whilst the poet, John Prichard Prŷs, invoked the Psalms as the most irrefutable vindication of songs of praise.[3] Stephen Hughes pointed to the wealth of poetry in the Bible which all right-thinking men, he insisted, should view as a divine sanction for human poetry.[4] 'Much of God's mind' agreed Philip Henry, 'is revealed in scripture by songs.'[5] Poets too, naturally stood shoulder to shoulder in defence of their craft, happily proclaiming that verse was a talent 'of the Lord's giving'.[6]

[1] John Thomas, *Unum Necessarium* (1680), sig. A1v.
[2] Friends' House Library, Kelsall MSS. Diaries, 1, p. 94.
[3] Clement, p. 152; John Prichard Prŷs, *Difyrrwch Crefyddol* (1721), sig. A4v.
[4] Stephen Hughes (ed.), *Rhan o Waith Mr. Rees Prichard* (1658), sig. A4r.
[5] J. B. Williams (ed.), Matthew Henry, *The Life of Philip Henry* (1825), p. 193.
[6] N.L.W. MS. 559B, p. 10; Thomas Jones (ed.), *Carolau a Dyriau Duwiol* (1696), p. 56; Kelsall MSS. Diaries, 1, p. 94.

Moreover, the addiction of most Welshmen to verse was proverbial. Nothing was more agreeable to his countrymen, wrote Thomas Jones in 1696, than reading and singing Welsh verses.[7] Echoing Erasmus Saunders, Iolo Morganwg wrote effusively of the 'national passion for poetry among the Welsh which has a very good effect upon their minds and general disposition'.[8] Religious reformers fully appreciated the crucial didactic rôle which religious verse could play in winning the affections of bruised reeds and young people. Puritans like Richard Jones and Stephen Hughes, deeply committed to the pragmatic approach, knew that not only should their books make no demands on the reader that were beyond his competence, but also that many underprivileged folk might gain far more benefit from reading or hearing one memorable line of edifying verse than a hundred lines of heavy prose.[9] Ever perceptive to the mnemonic merits of rhythm and rhyme, Philip Henry composed short synopses of his sermons in verse form for the benefit of the youthful members of his congregation, 'many of whom wrote them, and learned them, and profited by them'.[10] The sermons set to verse by Thomas William of Mynydd Bach were so popular among the Dissenting fraternity that they swiftly embedded themselves in the oral tradition of the locality.[11] Among the beleaguered Catholic minority, William Pugh, the last in a long and illustrious line of Papist poets in Wales, desperately sought to arrest the decline of his faith by disseminating popular verses among 'all classes of the population'.[12] Moreover, the increasing availability of printed books meant that those who lacked the means to buy prose, or the sustained concentration to read it, were provided with versified digests of the catechism, the decalogue, the Lord's Prayer and popular devotional books.[13] In a variety of ways, religious verse served an invaluable function in

---

[7] *Carolau a Dyriau Duwiol*, p. 3.
[8] Saunders, p. 33; N.L.W. MS. 13121B, p. 476.
[9] See Richard Jones's sentiments in *Perl y Cymro: neu Cofiadur y Beibl* (1655), sig. B4r; *Testun y Testament Newydd* (1653), p. 136.
[10] Matthew Henry, op. cit., p. 193.
[11] John Peter and R. J. Pryse, *Enwogion y Ffydd* (4 vols., n.d.), 111, p. 114.
[12] N.L.W. MS. 4710B.
[13] For some examples, see John Powell of Tredwstan's versified digests of works by Perkins and Alleine in James Owen, *Hymnau Scrythurol* (1717), pp. 103–118; cf. Joshua Thomas, *Golwg ar Destament Newydd ein Harglwydd a'n Jachawdwr Iesu Grist* (1728).

spreading the doctrines of the Christian faith in popular forms, both in public and private worship.

I. PSALMODY AND HYMNODY

Edmund Prys's celebrated *Book of Psalms* enjoyed enormous popularity in this period. First published in 1621, Prys's work had been written in popular metres so that it might be sung and committed to memory by whole congregations,[14] and, in the period after 1660, it was normally published with some part of the scriptures or prayer book.[15] The constant flow of issues of Prys's work helped to make psalm-singing an increasingly attractive feature of public worship. In 1718, James Harries of Llantrisant found that psalm-singing during morning and evening service had attracted 'a greater number of people at church' than before.[16] Reformers were also acutely aware of the need to persuade men, especially heads of households, of the benefits of psalm-singing within the domestic circle. In 1677, Charles Edwards suggested that Welshmen were far more skilled in singing wanton poems than praising the Lord in psalms,[17] and it was in response to such reproaches that ministers exercised their initiative in exhorting their flocks and producing material for daily worship. William Foulkes reminded readers of the pristine days of the early church, when common people learnt their psalms at home and repeated them constantly at the plough and in the workshop.[18] Matthew Henry believed that psalm-singing would 'warm and quicken' domestic devotions, especially among young children.[19] Michael Jones, vicar of Llanbrynmair, composed a metrical setting of Psalm 148 for the use of youths in his parish, and it was in the same spirit that 'private hands' in the neighbourhood of Llantrisant set the Psalms of David to 'good tunes' to the 'great advantage' of worshippers.[20] Works such as these,

[14] Edmund Prys, *Llyfr y Psalmau* (1621), sig. A2r.
[15] Prys's work was published in 1672, 1678, 1687, 1690, 1700, 1708, 1709, 1710, 1712, 1713, 1717, 1718, 1722 and 1727 (twice).
[16] Clement, p. 96.
[17] *Y Ffydd Ddi-ffuant* (1677), p. 271.
[18] William Foulkes, *Esponiad ar Gatechism yr Eglwys* (1688), p. 21.
[19] Matthew Henry, *A Church in the House* (1704), p. 30.
[20] U.C.N.W.L., Penrhos MS. 8, no. 722; Clement, p. 11; cf. Edward Wynn, *Trefn Ymarweddiad Gwir Gristion* (1662), pp. 129–40; *Y Psaltar neu Psalmau Dafydd yn Cymraeg* (1711).

circulating in manuscript and in print, achieved a good deal in edifying public and private worship.

In England, psalm-singing was firmly established in the formal worship of the established church, and the transition from psalmody to hymnody was neither swift nor painless. Unlike song-loving Lutherans, Calvinists would have no truck with hymnody that was not solidly based on scripture, and their attachment to the metrical psalms was therefore fond and enduring. Even so, hymns for the purpose of parochial use were published during the seventeenth century, with those of Thomas Ken and John Mason figuring prominently in Anglican hymnody, and the collections of Benjamin Keach winning popular esteem among Baptists.[21] But these works were never able to compete with, let alone supplant, psalmody, and modern English hymnody did not really begin until the advent of the Congregationalist, Isaac Watts.[22] Watts believed that hymns should express and evoke spiritual experiences, and although he understood the value of a scriptural basis to hymns, he was also eager to invest them with a new and more invigorating subjectivity. In Wales, too, Welsh Dissenters were beginning to reject the outmoded doggerel of psalm-metres in favour of subjective hymnody. The pioneers in this field were Thomas Baddy, Presbyterian minister at Denbigh and author of *Pasc y Christion* (1703) and *Caniad Salomon* (1725), and James Owen, Presbyterian minister-cum-academy tutor at Shrewsbury and author of *Hymnau Scrythurol*, published in 1705 and 1717.[23] Although the work of these pioneers, when set beside the supreme craftsmanship of Williams, Pantycelyn, amounts to no more than the plodding efforts of honest artisans, their hymns (and those of their successors) were significant pointers on the road to Methodist hymnody.

The most arresting feature of early-eighteenth-century hymnody was the stress laid on the inestimable virtues of Christ. Only through Christ, insisted Thomas Baddy, whose pleadings in this quarter were not far removed from those of

[21] C. S. Phillips, *Hymnody Past and Present* (1937), pp. 161–6.
[22] H. A. L. Jefferson, *Hymns in Christian Worship* (1950), p. 42.
[23] For descriptive studies, see M. H. Jones, 'Emynyddiaeth Gynnar y Ddeunawfed Ganrif', *J.W.B.S.*, 111 (1928), 191–204; H. Elvet Lewis, 'Emynwyr Cynnar yr Annibynwyr yng Nghymru', *Y Cofiadur*, 8–9 (1932), 3–17; G. H. Hughes, 'Emynyddiaeth Gynnar yr Ymneilltuwyr', *Llên Cymru*, II (1953), 135–46.

his wistful evangelical successors, could man attain salvation.[2] He and his colleagues were especially enamoured of the Song of Solomon, which not only formed a popular corner-stone for many hymns, but also stood in its own right as a collection of love poems that revealed Christ's love for his church and his people.[25] This Christocentric emphasis was further deepened by the growing attention paid to the rôle of Christ as the suffering Redeemer. The spiritual hymns of David and Evan Thomas, published in 1730, focused sharply on Christ's sufferings on the road from Gethsemane to the Cross and on the physical torments of his crucifixion.[26] Similarly, some of Thomas Baddy's meditations on the Cross and reveries on the blood of sacrifice were afforded a prominent place in all his work.[27] Indeed, in their obsession with the distress and anguish of the Lamb of God, his excruciating torture, his wounds and flowing blood, many of the early Dissenting hymns are not only redolent of the rood-poems of medieval times but also point forward to the more subjective and poignant emotionalism of Methodist hymnody.

II. CANWYLL Y CYMRY

No other single work, with the exception of the Welsh almanac, was published as frequently in this period as Rees Prichard's *Canwyll y Cymry*: the publication of fourteen editions between 1658 and 1730 is eloquent testimony to its enormous appeal. Incomplete selections from Prichard's work were published by Stephen Hughes in 1658–9 and, once the persecuting zeal of the Restoration decade had slackened somewhat, Hughes went on to publish fuller editions in 1672.[28] Still anxious to swell his collection, he then continued, with typically beaver-like industry, to search out lost manuscripts, and a more comprehensive edition duly emerged in 1681. Death overtook Hughes before he was able to produce a cheaper version, but David Jones of Llandysilio, fired by the same enthusiasm for

---

[24] Thomas Baddy, *Pasc y Christion* (1703), pp. 185–7.
[25] Dafydd Lewis, *Caniadau Nefol* (1714); Thomas Baddy, *Caniad Salomon* (1725), pp. 4–50; Enoch Francis, *Gwaith a Gwobr Ffyddlon Weinidogion yr Efengyl* (1729), p. 1.
[26] David and Evan Thomas, *Hymnau Ysprydol* (1730).
[27] *Pasc y Christion*, p. 179.
[28] For the dating of these editions see Eiluned Rees, 'A Bibliographical note on early editions of *Canwyll y Cymry*', *J.W.B.S.*, X (1968), 36–41.

Prichard's work, published a new edition in 1696. Once Thomas Durston had published a popular edition at Shrewsbury in 1713, the floodgates opened, bringing further editions in rapid succession in 1714, 1715, 1721 (twice), 1724, 1725 and 1730.[29] The drawing-power of Rees Prichard's book may also be gauged from the fact that it was one of those rare works that reformers felt might be worth translating into English. In 1724, Adam Ottley, bishop of St. David's, suggested to the S.P.C.K. that since Prichard's verses were 'very much esteemed for the vein of piety and good sense in them', an English translation might prove highly popular among monoglot Englishmen. Although the S.P.C.K. was never wholly convinced of the value of verse as a means of instruction, an edition of some 600 copies was decided upon. But the whole scheme died of inanition when the appointed translator, John Morgan of Matchin, found himself dogged by ill health, onerous parish duties and barely lukewarm encouragement from headquarters.[30]

Even so, there is no doubting the popularity of the original Welsh version. At bottom, it contained the sum and substance of the Christian faith. Studiously avoiding theological subtleties and intricate metaphysical problems, Prichard poured out verses full of 'the cream of the Bible'.[31] His primary purpose was to hammer furiously at the gates of Satan's kingdom and convert sinners out of the world. His lament over the degeneracy of early-Stuart society was just as appropriate for this period since most of the evils he inveighed against were running sores. Much of his language was couched in the 'gird up your loins' and 'be on your guard for Satan never sleeps' style, and his anxiety to convey the fearful implications of the human condition meant that few pages went by without a reminder of the brevity and frailty of life. Striking telling blows in the campaign for godly reformation, Prichard undermined the stubborn resolution of 'unclean people', exposed the shallowness

---

[29] John Ballinger, 'Vicar Prichard: a study in Welsh Bibliography', *Y Cymmrodor*, XIII (1900), 1–75.
[30] Clement, pp. 137–8, 144, 291. A certain William Shepard had translated two of Prichard's 'Divine Gems' in 1716. *Camrias Light, being two of Mr. Rees Prichard's British Divine Gems* (1716). I am grateful to the Rev. Gomer M. Roberts for allowing me to see his copy of this work.
[31] This was Peter Williams's view. See *Enwogion y Ffydd*, I, 176n.

of rival creeds and superstitions, spelled out the duties of public and private worship, and sharpened men's awareness of the virtues of justification by faith.

The success of *Canwyll y Cymry* also owed much to the catchy, homespun carol metres and the rough and ready colloquialisms which Prichard employed. He believed that only three readings were required to commit his verses to memory, and religious reformers found from experience that that was no idle boast.[32] Prichard's verses lay in the same tradition as the godly *cwndidau* which edified the reading public of south Wales in the sixteenth century, and it is significant that he was known in his day as 'y Cwndidwr du'.[33] But although he rubbed shoulders with popular free-metre rhymesters, his work differed in that it was meant to be read not sung. His style moreover, was based on the familiar daily vocabulary of common folk, with the sheer earthiness of his expressions and his use of anglicised Welsh verbs such as 'singco', 'excepto' and 'protecto' reflecting the language of his community. Explicitness and intelligibility were Prichard's prime considerations and his occasional lapses into vagueness were swiftly ironed out by that marvellously perceptive editor, Stephen Hughes.

One of Lewis Morris's favourite hobby horses was to disparage the popular literature of his day, and Welshmen's attachment to Prichard's work constantly evoked his scorn 'God help silly people', he groaned, 'an excellent book, they say, is the Vicar's Book, yes by God say I, it is a fine book indeed. Was not the world also so—more geese than swans? . . The Lord have mercy upon us, what a stupid stock we are.'[34] Morris's characteristic bursts of uppish indignation usually reflected not only his snobbish disdain for literary work published in south Wales, and especially those that were couched in what he considered to be the most undignified and corrupt forms, but also his traditional inability to measure the pulse of his countrymen. Less myopic commentators were acutely aware of the real worth of Prichard's work. Stephen Hughes was astonished by its catalytic effect on literacy rate.

[32] Stephen Hughes (ed.), Rees Prichard, *Canwyll y Cymry* (1681), p. 237.
[33] L. J. Hopkin James and T. C. Evans, *Hen Gwndidau, Carolau, a Chywydd* (1910); Glanmor Williams, *The Welsh Church from Conquest to Reformation* (1962) pp. 417, 423, 427; Bod., Welsh f. 6, p. 3.
[34] *Morris Letters*, I, 489–90.

Flushed with success, he maintained in 1672 that, following the publication of the editions of 1658–9, many thousands had learnt to read Welsh and gone on to buy Welsh Testaments and Bibles.[35] Again in 1681, buoyed up by the vigour with which Prichard's work had renewed the reforming cause, he affirmed that readers of the vicar's book had become more faithful and attentive hearers during sermons.[36] Robert Nelson found that Prichard's poems were 'in very great repute' throughout the country and was particularly surprised to discover that 'even those that are illiterate are so well versed that they will very pertinently quote authorities out of this book for their faith and practice'.[37] When Robert Roberts recorded his own and his great-grandmother's debt to Vicar Prichard, he was also voicing the enormous obligation of many others whose enlightenment stemmed from following that faithful lantern:

> This book, next to the Bible, was my earliest reading book. I read and re-read its homely rugged rhymes till I could repeat the greater part off by heart. It was my great-grandmother's constant companion. In spite of her great age she could read large print without glasses, and the Vicar's Book was seldom out of her hands, except when she was knitting.[38]

Prichard's book left a profound impression not only on readers in this period but also on succeeding generations. It seems to have attracted readers over a wide spectrum of society, finding a happy niche in Welsh affections as 'the Vicar's Book'.[39] It won universal respect among Methodist reformers, whilst Griffith Jones, Llanddowror, introduced a synopsis of the poems into the syllabus of his circulating schools.[40] Clergymen and ministers alike found that Prichard's voice, used as a

---

[35] Stephen Hughes (ed.), *Gwaith Mr. Rees Prichard*, IV (1672), 580.
[36] *Canwyll y Cymru* (1681), sig. A2v.
[37] Robert Nelson, *The Life of Dr. George Bull* (2nd ed., 1714), p. 475.
[38] J. H. Davies (ed.), *The Life and Opinions of Robert Roberts* (1923), p. 17.
[39] See the will of John Thomas of Cadoxton-juxta-Neath. N.L.W., Llandaff P.R. 1735. M. I. Williams, 'A General View of Glamorgan houses and their interiors in the seventeenth and eighteenth centuries', Stewart Williams (ed.), *Glamorgan Historian*, X (1974), 170.
[40] Tom Beynon, *Howell Harris's Visits to Pembrokeshire* (1966), p. 325. For Thomas Charles of Bala's view, see N.L.W. MS. 128C, f. 64r; Griffith Jones, *Pigion Prydyddiaeth Pen-Fardd y Cymry* (1749), pp. x–xi.

powerful antidote to immorality, was one not easily stilled.[41] More importantly, his work was now meat and drink for common people. It had always been Prichard's dream that his work would become the common man's song-book of the Reformation,[42] and when we consider that even beggar women were able to recite his verses on the duty of charity to householders (and also, of course, an appropriate verse for those miserly citizens who 'stopped up their ears' to the plea of paupers),[43] it is clear that his work had penetrated to lower levels than did most printed books. The flames of Rees Prichard's candle burned strongly on Welsh hearths for over two centuries and his work counts as much in the religious history of Wales as the hymns of Williams, Pantycelyn.

III. CAROLS AND GODLY POEMS

By the latter part of the seventeenth century, free-metre verse was fast becoming one of the most effective didactic media. Circulating constantly in manuscripts and by oral transmission, and further spurred on by the development of the printing press, carols and godly poems retained a special appeal in that they were meant to be sung, with the result that conventional rhymes and *cynghanedd* were augmented by a musical appeal.[44] Many carols were written specially for the seasonal feasts and festivals upon which the rhythm of rural life depended. May Day was ushered in with the singing of May carols, which were sung either within the domestic circle or from door to door.[45] This was generally an occasion for revelry and good cheer, a time for courtship and love-making. It was also an opportunity for thanksgiving. Carols portrayed spring as representing the rebirth of nature and, after a winter that was usually long and hard, it was only right that men should welcome fine weather

[41] John Rhydderch (ed.), *Canwyll y Cymru* (1714), p.v; William Evans (ed.), *The Welshman's Candle* (1771), sig. A2r; see the will of Morgan Williams, vicar of Myddfai. N.L.W., Archdeaconry of Carmarthen P.R. 1732, and the library of Thomas William of Mynydd Bach. C.C.L., Cardiff MS. 2. 197.

[42] *Gwaith Mr. Rees Prichard*, IV (1672), Sig. *8r.

[43] *Enwogion y Ffydd*, I, 176n.

[44] The most substantial and popular printed collection in this period was Foulke Owen (ed.), *Cerdd-Lyfr* (1686), re-edited by Thomas Jones, *Carolau a Dyriau Duwiol* (1696) and by John Rhydderch, *Llyfr Carolau a Dyriau Duwiol* (1729).

[45] T. M. Owen, *Welsh Folk Customs* (2nd ed., 1968), p. 100.

by praising God. Moreover, authors insisted that this time of rejoicing was also an opportunity for the community to express its solidarity by solemnly professing its loyalty to church and state.[46] This more serious didactic element was clearly meant as a counterweight to the more frivolous aspects of the celebrations.

Equally popular were the Christmas carols sung either around the hearth or from door to door on frosty December nights, and the matin carols sung by candlelight before dawn at Christmas.[47] These carols generally followed a stereotyped pattern, beginning with man's Fall, the story of Christ's birth, the miracles and deeds of Christ during his lifetime, his suffering on the Cross, his promise that the faithful shall live, and the overwhelming need for sinners to repent. In a modest way, therefore, this type of carol was a valuable way of spreading biblical knowledge, and poets certainly strove hard to satisfy public needs in this direction. Huw Morys wrote at least thirty matin carols and John Rhydderch included eighteen matin carols by different authors in his edition of *Carolau a Dyriau Duwiol* in 1729.[48] With the aid of such works, parishioners in parts of north Wales learnt to sing psalms, hymns and carols 'with great devotion and earnestness' in church, whilst even those disabled 'through age and infirmity . . . never fail to have prayers or carols on our Saviour's nativity at home'.[49]

Apart from those exclusively devoted to seasonal festivities, a substantial number of carols and poems were strongly Christocentric in character. Man, they claimed, was a fallen 'loathsome monster' whose only redemption lay in Christ. What was needed most was a 'sincere', 'undeceitful' and 'steadfast' faith which would sail men on the vessel of repentance to the land of Canaan.[50] Meanwhile, moral rectitude was advocated under all circumstances. Poets were particularly

[46] For some examples of 'carolau haf' see *Carolau a Dyriau Duwiol* (1696), pp. 265–84.
[47] Gwynfryn Richards, 'Y Plygain', *J.H.S.C.W.*, I (1947), 53–71; Enid P. Roberts, 'Hen Garolau Plygain', *T.H.S.C.*, 1952, pp. 51–70; David Jenkins, 'Carolau Haf a Nadolig', *Llên Cymru*, II (1952–3), 46–54; D. Roy Saer, 'The Christmas Carol-Singing tradition in the Tanad Valley', *Folk Life*, 7 (1969), 15–42.
[48] *Llên Cymru*, 1952–3, p. 52; *Llyfr Carolau a Dyriau Duwiol*, pp. 321–431; cf. John Prichard Prŷs, *Difyrrwch Crefyddol* (1721), pp. 17–20, 79–82.
[49] N.L.W. MS. 2576B, no pagination.
[50] *Carolau a Dyriau Duwiol*, pp. 5–11, 59–61, 77–9, 148–9, 160–1, 177–80.

fond of making the point that man had three enemies upon which to wage war: the world, the flesh, and the devil. Striving earnestly to instil the prudential virtues of sobriety, patience, honesty and righteousness, they were not loath to remind wrongdoers of the condign doom that awaited them.[51]

Generalised moral imperatives were sometimes narrowed down into more pointed social criticisms. Religious verse was not merely an outpouring of didactic instruction or a reflection of spiritual values. In a deferential society it provided one of the few outlets for the airing of social and economic grievances. Some quite striking social comment was contained in poetic indictments of rapacious landowners and grasping lawyers. Carols and poems were often littered with spiky references to the 'covetous mighty gentry', to 'the oppressors of the land', and to rack-renting profiteers who always took more than their share and spared no thought for their poor victims.[52] Edward Morris was furiously incensed that the gentry were never held accountable for their treacherous treatment of the poorer members of society. In legal matters, for instance, the gentry, ever adroit exploiters of the system, grew fat on their ill-gotten spoils, whilst their victims, duly fleeced, became less and less inclined to expect justice in court. No matter how truthfully the poor litigant might speak in court, sniffed Morris, nobody heeded his plaintive cry.[53] The poor man who dared to challenge the 'proud gentry', agreed Thomas Jones the almanacer, was seen as an impudent knave who laid himself open to violent retribution, unemployment and beggary:

> Everything that a landowner says is true:
> If a common man from the parish
> challenges his social better,
> he is judged a shameless knave
> and even worse than that,
> His skull is broken
> for disputing with his natural master,

[51] Ibid., pp. 216–62, 301–4; *Difyrrwch Crefyddol*, pp. 153–74.
[52] *Carolau a Dyriau Duwiol*, pp. 314, 366; *Cân ar fesur Triban ynghylch Cydwybod a'i Chynheddfau* (1718), p. 8; *Cyngor i Ddychwelyd at yr Arglwydd* (1728), p. 2; *Llyfr Carolau a Dyriau Duwiol*, pp. 374–92; David Jenkins, 'Bywyd a Gwaith Huw Morys, 1622–1709' (unpubl. Univ. Wales M.A. thesis, 1948), p. 462; Gwyn Thomas, 'A Study of the Changes in the Tradition of Welsh Poetry in North Wales in the Seventeenth Century' (unpubl. Univ. of Oxford D.Phil. thesis, 1966), p. 440.
[53] *Carolau a Dyriau Duwiol*, pp. 67–70.

One of his limbs is broken,
And rest assured sir
if he says any more
his forehead is broken.
If he argues that the crow is black
he'll be in prison tomorrow
If he litigates for justice
he'll lose his employment;
If he sues for his own property
he'll be reduced to beggary.[54]

Small wonder, therefore, that some poets, surely reflecting the unuttered aspirations of oppressed social orders, were wont to dream of more just and equitable times. Just as devotees of the myth of the Norman yoke harked back to the simplicity and justice of Anglo-Saxon laws,[55] so did poets like Ellis ab Ellis, in castigating the Welsh Leviathans, gaze back wistfully to the halcyon days of Hywel Dda, when good will and justice were part of the fabric of society.[56]

Whilst musing on mortality, poets liked to contrast the fate of the rich and the poor at death. It did not pass their notice that when a poor man died there was often the problem of rallying men to wrap the deceased in his winding sheet and carry him to his grave. But when a gentleman died, his interment was invariably an elaborate and dignified affair, complete with fulsome sermons, lengthy funeral processions and plaintive elegies. Even so, they hastened to add that inequality at funerals did not imply that the next world was also to be monopolised by the affluent. Like their medieval forebears, poets never ceased to remind the poor that death was the great leveller and that Christ, who had traditionally shared his secrets and privileges with the lowliest of men, would allow them to come into their own in the after-life.[57] This was, perhaps, pretty cold comfort for the disaffected poor, but at the very least they would derive a kind of etherealised revenge from reading and hearing verse which assured them

---

[54] Thomas Jones, [*Almanac*] (1693), sig. A1v.
[55] Christopher Hill, 'The Norman Yoke', *Puritanism and Revolution* (1965), pp. 50–122.
[56] *Carolau a Dyriau Duwiol*, pp. 11–14.
[57] Many examples may be found in *Carolau a Dyriau Duwiol* and *Difyrrwch Crefyddol*.

that the privileged and the poor would be in the same boat on Judgment Day. Indeed, they were led to believe that God had vouchsafed his vengeance on their oppressors, who would in time inherit the horrifying torments of the bottomless pit. As long as captious social criticism and terse warnings of this kind were couched in fairly nebulous terms—no names, no pack drill—there could be little hope of making the author, who often in any case shielded himself under a cloak of anonymity, pay for his temerities.

IV. HALSINGOD

The fourth type of religious verse circulated more in manuscript form and oral tradition than in print. This was the *halsingod* or carols which were composed mainly in the virile cultural communities of the Teifi valley and south Cardiganshire generally.[58] Described by Erasmus Saunders as 'a kind of divine hymns or songs', they were composed largely by 'the more skilful and knowing' of the populace, chiefly clergymen and men of letters. They were performed within the home, but more especially at wakes, funerals, festivals, holy days and after (or as a substitute for) the Sunday service. Within the church the practice was for eight to ten people to divide into two equal groups which would proceed to chant the *halsing* alternately and finish in unison with a chorus. The actual process of learning these works was never a chore; indeed public performances seem to have stimulated the competitive instincts of young people, who went to some pains to learn them thoroughly in order both to emulate their neighbours and to make their own spiritual sentiments manifest.[59]

Like the godly *cwndidau*, *halsingod* were drenched in scriptural references. Some were set out in sermon-form, but the vast majority were dramatised renderings of biblical stories, notably some of the celebrated allegories of the Old Testament. Many, too, contained an astonishing amount of deuterocanonical or apocryphal material, reflecting possibly the growing interest,

[58] G. H. Hughes, 'Halsingau Dyffryn Teifi', *Yr Eurgrawn*, CXXXIII (1941), 58–63, 89–91, 126–7; Geraint Bowen, 'Yr Halsingod', *T.H.S.C.*, 1945, pp. 83–108. *Halsingod* also spread farther north in Cardiganshire. See Harold Cohen Library University of Liverpool MS. 2.69.

[59] Saunders, pp. 33–4.

accelerated during the revolutionary period,[60] in such texts. Evidently local clergymen were prepared to use religious verse as a means of spreading biblical knowledge in graphic and intelligible forms to socially deprived members of society. It is highly significant that clerical authors like Samuel Williams, vicar of Llandyfriog, and Dafydd Lewys, curate of Llanllawddog, were composers of *halsingod* as well as prolific translators of devotional books.[61] Such men were consciously supplying the needs of a popular audience and accepting some of the 'diffuse tendencies, general ideas and mental images which were widely spread in lower cultural levels'.[62] But not all *halsingod* were scriptural digests: some were poignant prayers and meditations,[63] others focused on the 'piety and virtue' of eminent saints,[64] and almost all of them were obsessed with the theme of mortality and judgment. In reminding the sons of Adam of the fateful day of reckoning, the word 'repento', however often repeated, never lost its cutting edge. And in stressing the horrors of the tomb and the torments of hell, authors appreciated the mnemonic value of monotonous, plodding repetition, even if the finished product was often couched in the sorriest verse.[65] Very few *halsingod* omitted such ominous expressions as 'graves are at the ready', 'Judgment Day is coming' and 'take heed'.

As might be expected from verses written and performed by members of the church, *halsingod* were shot through with an unwavering faith in the established church and the monarchy. But this loyalty did not preclude social criticism. Clergymen who chose to be dumb dogs, forsaking their spiritual duties for the ephemeral pleasures of the tavern, were condemned as blind shepherds leading their flocks on the road to damnation.[66] Knowing one's alphabet, claimed one author tartly, did not make a minister an apostle of godliness and virtue.[67] Similar

---

[60] Christopher Hill, *The World turned Upside Down* (1972), p. 213.
[61] Geraint Bowen identifies some of these authors in *T.H.S.C.*, 1945, pp. 85–90.
[62] See the instructive article by Georges Duby, 'The Diffusion of Cultural Patterns in Feudal Society', *P & P*, 39 (1968), 3–10.
[63] *Yr Eurgrawn*, 1941, p. 63.
[64] Saunders, p. 33.
[65] For some examples see N.L.W., Cwrtmawr MS. 45A, *passim*.
[66] University of Liverpool MS. 2.69, p. 31; Samuel Williams, *Pedwar o Ganueu ar amryw Desdunion* (1718), p. 11.
[67] N.L.W., Cwrtmawr MS. 45A, p. 107.

arrows of protest penetrated deeply into the corpulent flesh of wealthy landowners. Samuel Williams kept his printed criticisms of men of property discreetly enigmatic but could not resist hinting that the appropriate cap should be worn by each wrong-doer.[68] There was clearly widespread resentment over the oppressions of unmerciful 'great men' and rapacious stewards who trampled like Pharaoh on the houses, lands and possessions of vulnerable and less affluent citizens. Their only comfort was that death would overtake such tyrants in due course, bringing their wealth and mansions tumbling down about their ears; and whereas they would be called to account for their misdeeds on earth, the godly poor, whose guiding light was faith, would inherit eternal bliss.[69]

It has been argued that *halsingod* represent the efforts of orthodox clergymen to fill the gaping breach left within society by the decline of the cherished mysteries and habits of Roman Catholicism.[70] They would seem very much more, however, to be deliberate attempts to ensure the percolation of puritan values in intelligible form. The first extant *halsing* in manuscript is dated 1622, but they remain few in number until 1662, when they begin to multiply rapidly, reaching a high-water mark around 1677 but falling away again until the Revolution, when a further increase survives the turn of the century and continues until around 1722 before declining again towards the mid-eighteenth century.[71] *Halsingod* were thus essentially a phenomenon that spanned the period from the Restoration to Methodism. Their relative confinement to this historical period is significant; the actual timing counts. What must surely be evident is that this self-generated form of religious, biblical and moral education does not square with the traditional historical portrait of a general spiritual ebb in this period. At grass-roots level, resolute and conscientious ministers joined with earnest parishioners in seeking to compensate for the dearth in some places of formal instruction within the church by supplementing the practice of holding one service only on the Sabbath. Just as zealous puritans had

---

[68] *Pedwar o Ganueu*, sig. A1v.
[69] N.L.W. MS. 5A, pp. 102, 211; N.L.W. MS. 609A, pp. 79, 82–5, 107; University of Liverpool MS. 2.69, pp. 54–5, 109.
[70] G. Bowen, *T.H.S.C.*, 1945, p. 83.
[71] Ibid.

sought to fill the spiritual void created by an impoverished and inflexible church by holding 'prophesyings' in the rural market towns of Elizabethan England,[72] so did puritanically-minded clergymen and laymen in this period strive to satisfy the spiritual thirst of the members of their communities in south-west Wales. Early Methodism derived much of its initial vigour and strength from these very communities, and it should be borne in mind that Daniel Rowland figured among those clergymen who saw the value of composing *halsingod* and that Williams, Pantycelyn, adopted the *halsing* as a pattern for some of his hymns.[73]

V. BALLADS

Of the 104 books of Welsh religious verse and sayings published between 1710 and 1730, some 90 per cent were ballads. Ballads of course had been highly popular in oral tradition long before this period,[74] but few had been written down, and the first printed collection of Welsh ballads (as far as is known) was that published by Thomas Jones of Shrewsbury in 1699.[75] It is probable, however, that those printed editions that are extant after 1710 are merely the tip of an iceberg and that only a small proportion of the ballads of the day has survived. The most popular editions were probably those that left fewest extant copies, and where no copies survive the consumption is likely to have been at its greatest. This does not mean that contemporaries regarded ballads as 'ephemeral' literature since, unlike modern bibliographers, they did not belabour the distinction between bound and unbound books.[76]

With the exception of those published by Nicholas Thomas at Carmarthen in the 1720s, Welsh ballads were largely

---

[72] Patrick Collinson, *The Elizabethan Puritan Movement* (1967), pp. 168–76.

[73] E. D. Jones, 'Some Aspects of the History of the Church in north Cardiganshire in the Eighteenth Century', *J.H.S.C.W.*, I (1953), 107; *C.C.H.M.C.*, XXXIII (1948), 12–16; *T.H.S.C.*, 1945, p. 102.

[74] J. H. Davies (ed.), *A Bibliography of Welsh Ballads printed in the Eighteenth Century* (1911), p. viii.

[75] *Pedwar math o faledau Cymraeg*, advertised in Thomas Jones, *Newyddion Mawr oddiwrth y Ser* (1699), sig. C8v. Jones also published the earliest known folio Welsh ballad. Thomas Miles, *Carol o goffadwriaeth am ryfeddol ryddhad Dassy Harry* (1701) (for a photostat copy see N.L.W. MS. 16162D).

[76] Cyprian Blagden, 'Notes on the Ballad Market in the second half of the seventeenth Century', *Studies in Bibliography*, VI (1954), 164.

composed, printed and distributed in north Wales.[77] Th
major focus was Shrewsbury, where John Rhydderch an
Thomas Durston ensured that ballads became the backbon
of their publishing trade. The vast majority of these ballad
were original works and much of their popularity stemme
from the fact that they were written to be sung. Melodi
(usually English) were affixed to each ballad, bearing exoti
names like *Loath to Depart*, *Heavy Heart*, *Crimson Velvet* an
Janthee the Lovely. Religious reformers tended to keep ballads
arm's length; most of them cherished a profound suspicion
potentially frivolous literature, judging that corruption withi
society was fanned by the 'lewd ungodly songs and ballad
which for the devil's catechisms are industriously disseminate
among all orders of rich and poor'.[78] But although man
critics found this kind of literature intolerably shallow, mo
of the ballads in this period, although often light-hearted an
gay affairs, were strongly tinged with a distinct moral flavou
    Legendary tales, current scandals, weird and sensation
events, tragedies and criminal deeds, strange visions an
dreams were all common themes in ballads. But each them
bore an element of social didacticism. 'Even the commo
love-songs', wrote Iolo Morganwg, 'have generally a mor
cast, we very seldom find any wherein some moral sentimer
is not introduced.'[79] Thus, when Thomas Buttry sang the tal
of a young man whose lover had borne him a son out
wedlock and then refused to nurse the child, his motive was t
stress the sanctity of marriage and the evils of bastardy.[8]
Ballads which focused on the terrible misfortunes which stemme
from outbreaks of fire were designed to remind men not onl
to take every possible precaution against similar tragedie
especially since these were pre-insurance days, but also to as
themselves why providence had treated them so cruelly.
Tales of murderous deeds always showed how the culpr

[77] Thomas Parry, *Baledi'r Ddeunawfed Ganrif* (1935), p. 24.
[78] Erasmus Saunders, *A Domestick Charge* (1701), p. 135; Ellis Wynn
Gweledigaetheu'r Bardd Cwsc (1703), p. 23; Clement, p. 152.
[79] N.L.W. MS. 13121B, p. 476.
[80] Thomas Buttry, *Dwy o Gerddi Newyddion* (1724); cf. Richard Parry, *Agori
Carwriaeth* (1714); E. Williams and T. Gabriel, *Dwy o Gerddi Newyddion* (1718).
[81] Huw ap William and William Humphreys, *Cywir Hanes ynghylch Drychineb
Cholled* (1730); *Rhybydd i'r Cymru mewn Tair Can Newydd* (1730–1).

eventually came to an untimely end, and his cries of remorse on the gallows were meant to send shivers of apprehension down the spine of every reader.[82]

A sizeable number of ballads also preached moral imperatives directly, and often with great gusto. Solidly scaffolded with scriptural references, such ballads warned against current social evils, notably insobriety and vain swearing.[83] Ballad-mongers never hesitated to remind habitual sinners of the dire consequences of their misdeeds and some of their more grisly cautionary tales were deliberately designed to bring men to their senses.[84] However, few ballads laid any great claims to subjectivity in their focus on moral and spiritual affairs. Pious men like Owen Gruffydd and Nicholas Thomas strove hard to inject currents of personal experience into ballads by guiding 'prodigal sons' back to 'the path of Sīon', by making poignant appeals to men's hearts and by dwelling single-mindedly on the crucial importance of a fruitful and active faith.[85] But on the whole the most constructive contribution made by Welsh ballads to the reformist campaign was to preach moral virtues in a modest way and in simple, direct language.

It is impossible to tell how far the didactic element in ballads was submerged by the striking tales that formed the major themes. In small, sheltered communities bereft of newspapers, radios and televisions, ballads provided news and entertainment, and readers might well have ignored the moral sentiments in favour of their craving for romance, the spectacular and the unusual. In spite of the inhibiting homilies of the church, the lower orders in particular retained a great love for spontaneous enjoyment and took great delight in telling what James Owen derisively called 'lying old tales' and 'monkish fables' around the fireside at night during the long winter months.[86] It is worth remembering, too, that the

---

[82] John Rhydderch, *Cyffes Ymadrodd* (1717); *Dwy o Gerddi Newyddion* (1723).
[83] John Thomas *et alia*, *Tair o Gerddi Newyddion* (1718); Dafydd Thomas, *Cerdd Newydd* (1720); *Tair o Gerddi Newyddion* (1720); D. Thomas and G. Edward, *Ymddiddanion rhwng y Cybydd ar Oferddyn* (1724).
[84] Richard Parry, *Drych Angau* (1714); *idem*, *Rhybudd Benywaidd* (1727); *Cerydd i'r Cymru* (1722).
[85] Nicholas Thomas, *Newyddion Da ir Dynion Gwaetha* (1717); Owen Gruffydd and Humphrey Owen, *Chwech o Gerddi Duwiol ar amryw Achosion* (1717); *Gwahoddiad Taer i Sion* (1725).
[86] James Owen, *Trugaredd a Barn* (1715), sig. A4v.

agricultural cycle exercised a restrictive hold over men's habits and leisure time. Moreover, the subordination of children, servants and apprentices involved a large measure of social discipline and constraint. Some of the most popular literature disseminated among the lower orders in France at this time were the sensational news-sheets, tales and ballads that were judged 'useful employment for the bemused minds of the common poor'.[87] Similarly in Wales, some palliatives and diversions from social tensions were clearly necessary, and the more spectacular ballad tales did offer some temporary relief and amusement for the man whose occupation was a matter of subjection to the grey, mundane necessities of life. Essentially escapist in character, a good many ballads offered a retreat into the world of imagination far removed from the monotony of daily toil. But whatever men looked to find in ballads, there was no doubt of their popularity: brief in content, easy to sing and cheap to buy, ballads were assured of brisk sales and a warm reception.

VI. RELIGIOUS AND MORAL SAYINGS

This final group comprises a small number of works which used pithy sayings, proverbs and epigrams to convey Christian doctrine and morality. William Meyrick did not need to urge his readers never to despise old proverbs and sayings,[88] for the tradition was deeply-rooted and capable of exercising a powerful influence. John Owen, the epigrammatist, and Morgan Llwyd, the mystic, had both been experts in framing striking proverbs, and there was never any doubt in many reformers' minds that this *genre* was an effective didactic device, especially when sayings were strongly based on scriptural truths. Succinct and penetrating maxims were widely used to spell out the doctrines of the Reformation in simple yet strikingly memorable terms.

Among the popular aphorisms that proved peculiarly congenial to the Welsh psyche were the epigrams of the 'aged and reverend' puritan minister, John Dod. Dod's standing

---

[87] Pierre Goubert, *The Ancien Régime. French Society 1600–1750*, tr. Steve Cox (1973), p. 268.
[88] William Meyrick, *Pattrwm y Gwir Gristion* (1723), p. 12.

among early puritans was based on his appeal as a 'patriarchal utterer of memorable wise sayings'.[89] His apothegms survived his death in 1645, becoming especially popular in the Restoration period when hawkers sold sheets of 'old Mr. Dod's sayings' in epigram and verse form.[90] In 1688, Stephen Hughes, whose thirst for reviving the works of his puritan forebears was unquenchable, published forty-two of Dod's sayings in Welsh, and the same work was swiftly reprinted in 1692, together with three poems taken from Rees Prichard's work (a pairing that surely carries a certain *justesse*), showing that Dod's earthy common sense had struck a familiar chord among the Welsh reading public.[91] Dod himself had been an affable, witty character blessed with a happy knack for hitting the right nail on the right head with the right hammer in all his sermons and sayings.[92] His most pungent maxims were always scrupulously frank; strongly Calvinist in tone, they embodied a sound practical morality, focusing sharply on the fallen state of man, the power of sin, the machinations of the devil, and the paramount importance of a speedy repentance. Since he always preached and wrote words of solace for the poor, his spiritual ministry left an indelible impression on ordinary people, and long after his death his published sayings continued to explain the mysteries of religion to those best able to digest spiritual and moral maxims.[93]

Dod has his Welsh counterpart in this period: Rees Prydderch (d. 1699), Independent minister and schoolmaster, doyen of Welsh epigrammatists and a fiercely penetrating social critic. Prydderch is best known for his collection of some 700 proverbs, epigrams and maxims, which were edited and published after his death by William Evans in 1714.[94] Prydderch based most of his material on the scriptures, though many proverbs were also drawn from the rich alluvial deposit of Welsh proverbial tradition. As a native of

[89] William Haller, *The Rise of Puritanism* (1938), pp. 60–1.
[90] *Old Mr. Dod's Sayings* (1667; 1671); *A Second Sheet of old Mr. Dod's Sayings* (1670); *Old Mr. Dod's Sayings, composed in verse* (1678).
[91] *Ymadroddion hen Mr. Dod* (1688; 1692).
[92] Samuel Clarke, *A General Martyrology . . . whereunto is added a large collection of Lives* (1770), pp. 469–71.
[93] The Welsh translation of *Symptoms of growth and decay to Godliness* (1672), published in 1694 and 1721, belongs to the same *genre* as Dod's sayings.
[94] William Evans (ed.), Rees Prydderch, *Gemmeu Doethineb* (1714).

Ystradwallter, near Llandovery, he was also undoubtedly familiar with the catchy poems of Rees Prichard, and a good many of his own punchy epigrams and crisp sayings are firmly embedded in the same tradition. Like Prichard, Prydderch's ultra-puritanical bent made him an uncompromising enemy of sin. Many of his sayings warned of the tendency of sin to seep insidiously into man's veins and eventually dominate his actions. 'There are many', he grieved, 'who are trampled upon by sin, but few trample upon sin.'[95] His trusty blade cut deeply into the pretensions of those hypocrites and simulators who professed an 'outward shell of holiness'. Self-righteousness, too, inflamed his passions: 'nothing keeps men more in folly', he observed, 'than their own wisdom.'[96] Much may also be read into his perceptive, if despairing, comment that 'many listen to the truth but few listen in truth.' But Rees Prydderch had more to draw on than a well-stocked repertoire of indictments; he was never disposed to minimise the supreme goodness of grace and salvation. Justifying faith was a cardinal theme in his work, and so were the good works born thereof. Placing one's faith in Christ was the crux: 'for Christ', he declared, 'was better without the world than the world was without Christ'.[97]

Rees Prydderch was a man of both intense moral earnestness and high passions. Although some of his more lurid indictments were painted in pastel shades by his editor, there can be no doubt that his strictures reflected the puritan moral code at its most rigorous. One gets the impression that his brow—at least during his younger days—was forever furrowed with some anxiety, and his trenchant attacks on cockfighting, mixed dancing and long hair were strongly redolent of William Prynne's onslaughts on early-Stuart morality.[98] But Prydderch was also deeply sensitive to more basic social and economic problems. Convinced that the family was the most important unit in the puritan commonwealth, Prydderch vented his spleen on covetous landowners who, making their daughters

[95] Ibid., pp. 71, 84.
[96] Ibid., pp. 11, 27, 78.
[97] Ibid., pp. 11, 16, 30, 47, 49, 51, 82, 100.
[98] Ibid., pp. 107–116, 148–9; cf. P. W. Thomas, 'Two Cultures? Court and Country under Charles I', Conrad Russell (ed.), *The Origins of the English Civil War* 1973), pp. 179–81.

slaves to their own appetites for gain, contrived marriage settlements in order to amass more property; he poured vitriol, too, on the gentry's fondness for the practice of fosterage by which male infants were placed under the care of foster-parents outside the family circle; and it was the same concern for discipline within the home that led him to despise the efforts of charitable bodies to instil the practice of conducting family prayers in the English tongue within monoglot Welsh circles.[99]

Prydderch's broadsides against the unbridled appetites and general callousness of the gentry reflected his profound suspicion of the growing commercialism of his day. Although public opinion by the Restoration period was tolerant of usury that was not oppressive,[100] Prydderch shared the views of early puritans like Adams, Bolton and Sibbes in denouncing the evils of lending for gain.[101] Similarly, in castigating the heriot as the fag-end of a superstitious rite, he not only voiced the grievances of many helpless victims but also declaimed against predatory landlords who exacted their pound of flesh with merciless relish.[102] Prydderch's sayings also revealed him as a champion of those who suffered most from economic privation. Many of his best-known maxims were suffused with words of comfort for the poor. 'Better a lowly state in the love of God', he told them, 'than the highest state without it.' 'It is better', he assured them endearingly, 'to be saved in the brine of affliction than to rot in the honey of ease.' Bolstering the confidence of the uninstructed, he comforted them with the assurance that the unlettered might understand God's Word where those able to read it could not.[103] In a sense, therefore, Prydderch was perpetuating the old medieval notion that linked godliness with poverty and softening the burdens of those who lay at the mercy of current economic forces. The underprivileged folk who read and heard his words of comfort must have found it refreshing to find concern for their welfare

[99] Ibid., pp. 117–9, 124–30, 131–3.
[100] Richard B. Schlatter, *The Social Ideas of Religious Leaders, 1660–1688* (1940), p. 221.
[101] *Gemmeu Doethineb*, pp. 120–4; C. H. George, 'English Calvinist Opinion on Usury, 1600–1640', *Journal History of Ideas*, XVIII (1957), 455–74.
[102] *Gemmeu Doethineb*, pp. 134–7; cf. A. H. Dodd, *Studies in Stuart Wales* (1952), p. 20.
[103] *Gemmeu Doethineb*, pp. 6, 14, 43, 46, 74, 179.

couched in such compassionate terms, especially when se
against the chilly utilitarianism which so often provoked th
interest of charitable bodies in the poor.

'There is no end', confessed Rees Prydderch at the end of hi
anthology, 'to the truth of wise sayings',[104] and it is clear tha
the *genre* embracing religious verse and maxims fulfilled
valuable spiritual, didactic and social rôle. There is the tal
of a distressed old woman in mid-eighteenth century Englan
who maintained that she would have been driven to utte
distraction from losing her husband had it not been for 'ol
Mr. Dod's sayings'.[105] The same could well have been th
reaction of many to Vicar Prichard's homely verses, soaked i
biblical allusions and practical advice, to the forthright mora
and social lessons set out in free-metre carols, ballads an
almanacs, to the awkward and laboured *halsingod*, saturate
with guides to repentance and warnings to sinners of impendin
woe, and to the vivid epigrams and sayings of Rees Prydderc
and his ilk. At parish-pump level, many underprivileged peopl
depended on these works not only for biblical instruction
spiritual sustenance and moral guidance, but also for comfor
and consolation.

---

[104] Ibid., p. 106. Prydderch's popularity was paralleled in England by Joh
Mason, rector of Water Stratford. See *D.N.B.* and John Mason, *Select Remai*
(1839), a collection of practical sayings and sententious maxims which reputedl
provoked 'an inward relish and taste of the truth'.
[105] William Haller, op. cit., p. 59.

VII

WORKS OF CONTROVERSY

t has been shown that the vast majority of Welsh books
ublished in this period were chiefly concerned with presenting
ıe basic tenets of Protestantism in the most intelligible form.
'he consensus of opinion was that simple, practical works of
evotion and didacticism were best suited to the needs of the
Velsh reading public. In general, authors studiously avoided
ontentious issues, speculative notions and mysterious doctrines.
)nly thirty-four (6·2 per cent) works of controversy emerged
·om the Welsh press in this period, and these works were
imed mainly at a particular audience, comprising for the most
art gentlemen, clergymen, ministers and the educated
ıiddling sorts. Some of the most bitter theological disputes
·ere symptoms of the growth of sectarianism. Disputants were
cutely aware that there were profound issues at stake, issues
·hich touched upon the very deepest emotions and assump-
ons. Indeed, since both sides felt that their very existence was
nder threat, most literary battles were bathed in an atmos-
here of fear and recrimination. As tempers ran high,
isputants deliberately overstated their respective cases,
ıffused their arguments with tedious minutiae and petty
ophistry, and took great delight in demeaning rivals of lower
ocial status with sneers of derision and contempt.

. ANGLICANISM AND THE CHALLENGE OF DISSENT

n spite of the social and economic limitations that sapped the
rength of the established church, it remained an object of
enuine and sincere affection throughout this period. Fulsome
·ibutes flowed easily from the pens of zealous churchmen.[1]
Ihurch historians waxed lyrical on its antiquity, making much

---

[1] See, for instance, anon., *Cred a Buchedd Gwr o Eglwys Loegr* (1710); John
hydderch, *Datcuddiad or un peth mwya' angenrheidiol, neu pa un yw'r Grefydd Orau*
724).

of the traditions that had been refined and hallowed b
centuries of use.[2] Holy, catholic and apostolic, it was hailed a
'the best and purest church upon earth', the most authenti
in the whole of Christendom. In doctrinal terms, its faith wa
sober and not given to extremes; steering a cautious *via medi*
between the runaway enthusiasm of Genevan-inspired sect
and the gross errors of Popery and superstition, the church wa
viewed as a visible and indomitable pillar of the true Christia
faith.[3] 'God help this poor Church of England'[4] was thus
sentiment shared by all those who viewed it as the uniqu
dispenser of the means of salvation and who believed that th
challenge posed by Dissent was provoked by treachery, malic
and deceit.

At all costs, therefore, the established church was to b
defended from external attacks, even to the extent of relyin
on the coercive power of the state. With the Act of Uniformit
of 1662, the established church had once more become th
handmaiden of the state, a powerful bastion of the social orde
and both civil and ecclesiastical authorities were determined t
ensure that pressure of persecution remained a prickly thorn i
the flesh of sectarian bodies. However, when the civil powe
granted toleration to Dissenters in 1689, the sands of Anglica
persecution gradually ran out. Even so, many clergyme
doubted the wisdom of this act, claiming that toleration gav
men the freedom to reject their authority and thus, implicitl
the authority of God. Ignoring the concrete realities c
toleration, many Anglicans simply refused to believe tha
Dissent had come to stay. It was a delusion, claimed Lewi
Evans in 1711, to believe that Parliament could declare leg:
that which God had ordained as sinful.[5] High churchmen sti
conceived of the established church as an undivided an
indivisible body, a living, structured organism whose ver
existence was now in dire peril. 'The flagrant sin of schism'
aroused particular anger among the clergy. Perfervid churchme

[2] Richard Smallbrooke, *Our Obligations to promote the Publick Interest* (1724), p. 1
[3] Edward Samuel, *Bucheddau'r Apostolion a'r Efengylwyr* (1704), sig. A2r–
idem, *Gwirionedd y Grefydd Grist'nogol* (1716), p. 6.
[4] U.C.N.W.L., Bangor, Mostyn Correspondence, vol. VI, letter from Phili
Fowke to Thomas Mostyn, dated 20 April 1689.
[5] Lewis Evans, *Llythyr oddi wrth Weinidog o Eglwys Loeger* (1711), no paginatio
[6] Griffith Jones, *A Letter to a Proselyte of the Church of Rome* (1731), p. 24.

like Ellis Wynne and Theophilus Evans felt a profound sense of loss as they witnessed zealous sectarians undermining the beauty of holiness.[7] Arguing the merits of unity, they saw schism as a major factor in dissolving obedience and breeding tumult and sedition. 'From schism', wrote John Copner, 'come all suspicions, jealousies, whisperings, backbitings, & all other instances of uncharitableness.'[8] Such fears, moreover, might reach panic levels whenever the bogey of Popish invasion weighed heavily on clerical minds: for every true Protestant knew that Britain's disunity was Rome's opportunity.

Those clergymen who remained a constant prey to such fears seldom examined the motives of their challengers. Dissent was invariably equated with hypocrisy and cant, the severance of its ministers from the church was provoked by pride, prejudice and self-interest, and its ministrations were clearly the 'devilish enchantments' of false prophets.[9] Ever mindful of the social upheavals of the late civil wars, clergymen strongly disputed the right of uninstructed and socially inferior *parvenus* to expatiate on high matters of doctrine. They cherished their traditional powers to enjoy authority over a given parish and its inhabitants, and were determined to obstruct the efforts of unordained or base-born elements to trespass on their freehold. Combing their Bible for crude metaphors that likened sectarians to a variety of predatory animals,[10] they reinforced these with a strong tincture of social contempt. Let carpenters and the like, sniffed Rondl Davies disdainfully, pursue their daily trades and leave preaching and pastoral work to properly educated and ordained divines.[11] Was not Cromwell, asked John Burchinshaw, with a cheerful disregard for Oliver's true lineage, a brewer's son?[12] Common sneers of this kind in clerical circles meant that the spectre of millers-turned-Roundheads would not easily be laid to rest.

---

[7] Ellis Wynne, *Gweledigaetheu y Bardd Cwsc* (1703), pp. 31–9; Theophilus Evans, *Drych y Prif Oesoedd* (1716), p. 268.
[8] N.L.W. MS. 2905A, p. 141. Cf. *Cred a Buchedd Gwr o Eglwys Loegr* (1710), pp. 59–60; Samuel Williams, *Undeb yn Orchymynedig i Ymarfer* (1710), *passim*.; Moses Williams, *Llaw-lyfr y Llafurwr* (1711), p. 55.
[9] Edward Samuel, *Bucheddau'r Apostolion*, p. 146.
[10] Rondl Davies, *Profiad yr Ysprydion* (1675), sig. A1v–A3v; John Morgan, *Llythyr Tertulian at 'Scapula* (1716), p. 4.
[11] Rondl Davies, op. cit., p. 105.
[12] U.C.N.W.L., Bangor MS. 402, p. 257.

Shorn of such calumnies, the issues that divided Anglican and orthodox Dissenters were essentially doctrinal. Almost instinctively, the educated churchman would defend his religion by a threefold resort to scripture, tradition and sound learning. Filled with an acute sense of despair as he witnessed what he believed to be a deliberate attempt by malignant elements to overthrow the most sacred institutions of society, Theophilus Evans hailed Anglicanism as the orthodox 'national' church, based on the scriptures and the primitive apostolic church.[13] Both scriptural and apostolic authority legitimised the church hierarchy, with the episcopacy as the pinnacle of that order. Bishops themselves were 'the offspring of the apostolic seed' and there was no authority in the Bible, primitive antiquity or ecclesiastical history to prove that their status had changed since apostolic times.[14] Moreover, the whole structure of the Anglican church was stiffened and enhanced by 'the most excellent liturgy in the whole Christian world'.

Dissenting ministers, led by the Presbyterians, were unimpressed by Anglican blandishments, and they grasped every opportunity to expose the vulnerability of church doctrines and to defend themselves from hostile attacks. Translations of Enosh Mophet's *Appendix to Delaune's Plea* (1708) in 1720 and Charles Owen's *Plain Dealing* (1715) in 1724 were published so that sectarians might supply themselves with tart rejoinders to some of the prickly insinuations of the Anglican clergy.[15] Dissenters argued that schism had been forced upon them by the severe terms of conformity offered in 1662.[16] Whilst recognising that the Anglican church was a church established by law, they insisted that the Toleration Act of 1689 legally sanctioned their separation. Nor were they slow to point to the non-juror schism which the Revolution of 1688 had occasioned within the ranks of the clergy. 'You can't', submitted Charles Owen, 'condemn the English Dissenters without damning the Scots Episcopals and all the Episcopal Nonjurors in England.'[17]

[13] Theophilus Evans, *The History of Modern Enthusiasm* (1752), p. 35.
[14] Griffith Jones, *Golwg Byrr o'r Ddadl ynghylch Llywodraeth yr Esgobion* (1721) *passim.*
[15] Enosh Mophet (*pseud.*), *An Appendix to Delaune's Plea: neu Lyfr newydd yn cynnwys Ymddiddanion Buddiol* (1720); Thomas Lewis, *Rhesymmau Amlwg* (1724).
[16] James Owen, *Moderation still a Virtue* (1704), p. 19.
[17] Charles Owen, *Plain-Dealing* (1715), p. 26.

But the basis of the Dissenting case was the argument that if a Christian came, by the dictates of conscience, to the conclusion that the church to which he belonged had departed from the truth, it was his duty to secede from that church. It was acknowledged that such a step was not to be taken lightly and indeed it seldom was. 'I do desire of God that he will help me', wrote an anguished John Power of Plas Power, as he strove to shed his Anglican upbringing, 'for I am in a strait between two.'[18] The Toleration Act was thus merely the outer shell which afforded political protection to the inner kernel of religious conviction.

There were, of course, issues on which churchmen and Presbyterians found common ground—their hatred of Rome, their loyalty to the Crown, and their subscription to most of the Thirty-nine Articles[19]—but there remained major stumbling-blocks. Few Dissenters had a good word to say for the Anglican liturgy and they remained wedded to their belief that most church ceremonies had, in the first instance, issued forth from Papal Rome, the cesspit of Europe and the fount of all impurities.[20] The most sensitive and divisive issue, however, was ordination. The chief spokesman for the Presbyterian cause on this issue was the learned academy tutor, James Owen, a man of iron will in matters of doctrinal dispute.[21] The cornerstone of Owen's thesis, from which he never budged either in oral or written dispute, was that 'presbyter and bishop are identitive, both as to name and office'.[22] He argued that the New Testament made no distinction between bishops and presbyters and thus claimed the right of Presbyterians to exercise their ministry without first having been episcopally ordained. Showing the full weight of his scholarship, Owen remorselessly pointed out each obstacle which prevented Dissenters from returning to the bosom of the established church.

[18] N.L.W., Rhual MS. 87.

[19] James Owen, *Moderation a Virtue* (1703), p. 15.

[20] Simon Thomas, *Hanes y Byd a'r Amseroedd* (1718), p. 159.

[21] For an account of a conference held at Oswestry in September 1681 between James Owen, Philip Henry and Jonathan Roberts for the Dissenters, and William Lloyd, Humphrey Humphreys and Henry Dodwell for the Church, see J. B. Williams (ed.), Matthew Henry, *The Life of Philip Henry* (1825), p. 86; M. H. Lee (ed.), *Diaries and Letters of Philip Henry* (1882), p. 309.

[22] Matthew Henry, op. cit., pp. 192–8; James Owen, *A Plea for Scripture Ordination* (1694).

Even though Dissenters still had to overcome the civil disabilities imposed by the Test Act of 1673, they knew full well that the Toleration Act of 1689 had hammered the final nail into the coffin of the old ideal of a single, broad and uniform established church. Welsh Dissenters were thus able to strengthen their organisation by increasing their membership and by building chapels. By 1715 their numbers represented some six per cent of the total population.[23] This minority still remained vulnerable to the bludgeonings of intolerant diehard high churchmen who strove assiduously to keep them at arm's length, but such animosities were steadily declining. At local levels, ties of neighbourliness, the anxiety to avoid fractious disputes, and the common desire to raise the spiritual standards of parishioners, meant that most clergymen adopted a more conciliatory and sympathetic attitude toward Dissenting brethren.

II. THE BAPTIST CHALLENGE

With the possible exception of the Quakers, no sect was imbued with a stronger sectarian consciousness than the Baptists. This sense of identity was allied to a resolute spirit that made doctrinal strife inevitable wherever and whenever their numbers were growing and their interests challenged. From 1690, when their total number of members was around 550, the growth of the Baptist faith in Wales was steady rather than spectacular, finding its firmest roots among the sturdy middle ranks of society in the anglicised towns of the south and the borderland and among the small farmers, cottagers and labourers of the south-west.[24] The latter area, focusing largely on the 'famous and excellent'[25] church of Rhydwilym in Pembrokeshire, was a particularly fruitful ground for Baptist evangelists and their successes provoked a wave of indignation and anxiety among the weakened neighbouring Independent churches.[26] These developments prompted the

[23] R. T. Jenkins, *Hanes Cymru yn y Ddeunawfed Ganrif* (1928), p. 50.
[24] T. M. Bassett, 'Ymgais at Ystadegaeth', *Trafodion Cymdeithas Hanes Bedyddwyr Cymru*, 1972, p. 51; E. G. Bowen, 'Bedyddwyr Cymru tua 1714', ibid., 1957, pp. 5–14.
[25] Joshua Thomas, *A History of the Baptist Association in Wales, 1650–1790* (1795), p. 41.
[26] Thomas Richards, 'Eglwys Rhydwilym', *Trafodion Cymdeithas Hanes Bedyddwyr Cymru*, 1938, pp. 93–9; B. G. Owens, 'Trichanmlwyddiant Rhydwilym', ibid., 1968, pp. 50–9.

Independents to engage the services of the experienced polemicist, James Owen, to espouse the cause of infant baptism in print. Consequently, the latent doctrinal disputes that were fermenting in the south-west burst into literary circles when Owen published *Bedydd Plant or Nefoedd* in 1693.[27]

On the issue of infant baptism, Independents and churchmen stood shoulder to shoulder. Members of the established church believed that adult baptism presented a fundamental challenge to the cherished concept of a national church which, through the rite of paedobaptism, received every single subject of the state into its fold. Early baptism was held to be crucially important not only because it tightened and perpetuated adherence to a unified church community, but also because the heavy infant mortality rate of the times threatened thousands of newly-born babes with the prospect of eternal perdition. Independents, too, believed that adult baptism was a revolutionary rite fraught with peril. They considered Baptists to be social incendiaries and remained highly suspicious of the potentially subversive effect of Baptist doctrine on property rights, political stability and social authority. Moreover, they were clearly anxious to ensure that Dissent of all kinds was not tarred with the brush of Baptist 'Bolshevism'. Owen's work was permeated with social undercurrents of this nature. Doctrinally, however, his thesis was based on the claim that baptism belonged only to the faithful and their children, to the seed of Abraham. Baptism was the natural corollary of God's old covenant with man: it represented a movement from the old dispensation to the sacramental basis of the New Testament. Infant baptism was the antitype of circumcision; just as Jews circumcised all male children in their infancy, so would Christians baptise their infants. Moreover, the scriptures made it plain that it was the will of Christ that the appropriate method of administering the sacrament was by sprinkling or affusion, and not by total immersement.[28]

None of the prominent Welsh Baptists of the day felt sufficiently equipped to cross swords with so formidable an

---

[27] G. H. Jenkins, 'James Owen versus Benjamin Keach: a controversy over Infant Baptism', *N.L.W.J.*, XIX (1975), 57–66.
[28] James Owen, *Bedydd Plant or Nefoedd* (1693), *passim*.

adversary as James Owen.[29] An invitation was thus issued to
the Buckinghamshire tailor and preacher, Benjamin Keach, to
take up the gauntlet flung down by Owen. Deeply embroiled
in similar doctrinal struggles in England,[30] Keach was only too
happy to accept. However, since he neither read nor understood Welsh, the curious situation arose of Owen's book having
to be translated into English and Keach's reply, presumptuously
entitled, *Light broke forth in Wales, expelling Darkness* (1696), then
being translated into Welsh by Robert Morgan, Baptist
minister of Llandeilo Talybont.[31] Keach launched a typically
acerbic attack on Owen's thesis and duly denounced infant
baptism as a human rite, a dangerous and unsubstantiated
custom, a product of 'the antichristian apostasy'. Keach
argued that it was not the covenant of grace that gave the right
to baptism, but the unimpeachable command and will of
Christ. The true inheritance was by faith, for baptism was the
outward seal that blessed those adult converts who had
become new creatures in Christ. Moreover, in obedience to
New Testament teaching, the correct method of baptism was
by immersion and not by affusion. The dispute petered out
following the publication of a rejoinder by James Owen in
1701 in which he retraced his arguments and doggedly refused
to budge an inch from his original thesis.[32]

This controversy highlighted some of the major social and
religious issues that divided the two camps. One of the major
burdens which Baptists were forced to carry was the accusation
that they were the descendants of sixteenth-century Anabaptists. The very word 'Anabaptist' had become a pejorative
epithet bestowed on those groups which threatened to be
totally disruptive of the established order in religion, politics
and society.[33] Viewed in this light, the merits and demerits of
paedobaptism became highly contentious issues, touching of

[29] In 1694, however, a Welsh translation of John Norcott's *Baptism discovered
plainly and faithfully* (1670) was published, though not in direct response to Owen's
work.
[30] William E. Spears, 'The Baptist Movement in England in the late seventeenth
century as reflected in the Work and Thought of Benjamin Keach, 1640–1704
(unpubl. Univ. of Edinburgh Ph.D. thesis, 1953), p. 95.
[31] *Goleuni gwedi torri allan Ynghymry gan ymlid ymmaith dywyllwch* (1696).
[32] James Owen, *Ychwaneg o Eglurhad am fedydd plant bychain* (1701).
[33] Claus-Peter Clasen, *Anabaptism. A Social history, 1525–1618* (1972), p. 14.

the very deepest emotions, raising irrational fears and correspondingly violent passions. Once James Owen's appetite for controversy was whetted, his arguments were prone to lapse to the level of personal denigration and vendetta. Reviving some of the more bizarre charges laid against sixteenth-century Anabaptists, he invoked the tawdry ploy of insisting that adult baptism was a direct violation of the sixth and seventh commandments.[34] Such charges, especially those of immorality, were all the more damaging in view of the fact that the excesses and degradation which had allegedly characterised the activities of the Anabaptists of Münster in the early-sixteenth century—the espousal of polygamy and sexual communism[35]— had been widely publicised and had become a convenient stick with which to beat those who denied the absolute necessity of infant baptism.[36]

There was also a prominent vein of social snobbery involved in this vendetta, reflecting largely the different social and educational background of the various protagonists. The pattern had been set in the preliminaries to this literary fray when John Thomas, an Oxford graduate and Independent minister at Cilcain, pitted his learning against the wits of a self-educated Baptist farmer and minister, John Jenkins of Rushacre, in a preaching contest at Pen-y-lan in 1692.[37] According to oral tradition, when Jenkins asked to see Thomas's sermon notes, the latter contemptuously replied that since they were written in Greek they would certainly be beyond the comprehension of a rustic Baptist.[38] Similarly, James Owen took perverse delight in exposing Keach's pedantry, dismissing his adversary's work as a ramshackle hodge-podge of plagiarisms and firing sarcastic volleys at his pretensions to great learning. The self-educated tailor's book, he maintained caustically, purported to contain 'great light', but beneath the sickly tediousness of his verbosity there lay only jet-black darkness.[39] Adult baptism was thus anathema to the orthodox,

---

[34] James Owen, *Bedydd Plant*, pp. 175–88.
[35] John Cairncross, *After Polygamy was made a Sin. The Social History of Christian Polygamy* (1974), pp. 1–30.
[36] For a similar attack, see *Bedydd Plant yn cael ei ymddiffyn* (1732), p. 59.
[37] Joshua Thomas, *Hanes y Bedyddwyr ymhlith y Cymry* (1778), pp. 421–3.
[38] *Monthly Repository*, I (1806), 400.
[39] James Owen, *Ychwaneg o Eglurhad*, pp. 5–16.

and paedobaptists showed scant concern for hurt feelings or wounded pride in delivering their strictures. When Edmund Jones, the Independent minister of Pontypool, implored the Almighty to 'prosper not Anabaptism, but let it wither daily',[40] he was voicing the deeply-seated hopes and fears of the majority of society.

III. THE QUAKER CHALLENGE

Faced with the pressing need to spread the Quaker gospel more widely, Welsh Friends in the Restoration period were forced to consider the value of the press as a powerful instrument for propagating their doctrines in the vernacular.[41] During the first yearly meeting of Welsh Friends in 1682, members made it clear that an intensive literary campaign was required in order to cement the Quaker faith in Welsh-speaking strongholds and also to attract new followers.[42] Hitherto, Welsh Quakers had lacked a tradition of expression in the Welsh language and this major shortcoming severely hampered their evangelising programmes. Their aspirations in this field also suffered from the debilitating effects of the twin phenomena of persecution and emigration. Although the persecution of Friends prior to the Toleration Act was fitful, tending to coincide with periods of national crisis or reflect the excessive zeal of local magistrates and informers, no other religious body suffered more severely from the rigours of the penal code. True to their character, Quakers retained an unshakable conviction in the rightness of their cause, but the malice of their enemies nonetheless took its toll: it disrupted the network of travelling ministers, it thrust leaders into foul, damp prisons for long periods, it robbed the Quaker gentry of their wealth, and it deterred potential members from entering their fold.[43]

If persecution effectively thinned out Quaker ranks in Wales, from 1682 onwards their numbers were further depleted when groups of virile, independent, Welsh-speaking Friends chose to leave the major Quaker bastions in Wales to establish a holy

---

[40] N.L.W. MS. 7026A, p. 117.
[41] For a fuller discussion of this theme see G. H. Jenkins, 'Quaker and anti-Quaker Literature in Welsh from the Restoration to Methodism', *W.H.R.*, VII (1975), 403–26.
[42] G.C.R.O., D/DSF 2, p. 483.
[43] G. H. Jenkins, *W.H.R.*, 1975, pp. 406–7.

Christian community, under the leadership of William Penn, in the 'good and fruitful land' of Pennsylvania.[44] This comparatively sudden exodus of a substantial proportion of the Quaker *élite* was a bitter blow to Quaker hopes in Wales. Many of those who resisted the temptation to cross the Atlantic despaired of ever being able to re-fill the cultural and spiritual vacuum within their localities, and there was a growing tendency by the end of the seventeenth century for Welsh Quakerism to lapse into a brooding introspection and 'a spirit of ease' which spread, according to John Kelsall of Dolobran, 'like a hidden leprosy'.[45] From the point of view of the Quaker publishing campaign, the loss was brutally severe. At best there was never a large number of Friends able to provide financial support for Welsh books, and those who were most likely to have responded to appeals for patronage or to have bought books regularly or even to have offered their services as translators were precisely those groups which had sailed to America.

At the turn of the century, a more vigorous campaign was launched to instruct old and new members in the tenets of Quakerism through the medium of Welsh printed books. Subscriptions collected in eleven Welsh counties facilitated the publication of Welsh versions of current Quaker best-sellers in 1703–4.[46] The Quaker gentry of Merioneth were made responsible for translating these popular treatises, which included William Penn's *A Key opening a way to every common understanding* (1692), John Crook's *Truth's Principles* (1662), and Chandler, Pyott and Hodges's *Brief Apology in behalf of the People in derision call'd Quakers* (1693).[47] Such works were not only intended to set out the major doctrines of Quakerism, but were also concerned to sift the pure wheat of Quaker doctrine from the chaff of their opponents' misrepresentations. Even so, the publication of these translations proved an enormous strain

[44] A. H. Dodd, 'The Background of the Welsh Quaker Migration to Pennsylvania', *Journal of the Merioneth Historical and Record Soc.*, III (1958), 111–27.
[45] R. T. Jenkins, *Hanes Cynulleidfa Hen Gapel Llanuwchllyn* (1937), p. 31; E. S. Whiting, 'The Yearly Meeting for Wales, 1682–1797', *Journal Friends Hist. Soc.*, 47 (1955), 65; Friends' House Library, Kelsall MSS., vol. 2, letter dated 8 mo. 1701.
[46] G.C.R.O., D/DSF 2, pp. 525, 529; D/DSF 320, pp. 109–10, 114–5.
[47] Owen Lewis, *Agoriad yn agor y ffordd i bob Dealltwriaeth Cyffredin* (1703); Thomas Cadwalader, *Gwyddorion y Gwirionedd* (1703); Humphrey Owen, *Amddiffyniad Byrr tros y Bobl (mewn Gwawd) a elwir Qwakers* (1704).

on the hard-pressed resources of Welsh Quakers, and the
paucity of funds and capable translators meant that subsequent
publications in the early-eighteenth century were not only
small in number but also pitifully brief in content. Moreover,
the rigorous process of correction and censorship which
preceded the publication of Quaker literature meant that
many manuscripts never reached the printing press.[48] The
contribution of Welsh Quakers to the astonishing increase in
the number of Welsh books in this period was modest and
infrequent, and must be accounted as a major factor in the
steady decline of Quakerism in the eighteenth century.

If Welsh Quaker books lay thin on the ground, the response
that their preaching and publishing evoked was both swift and
bitter. Opposition to Quakers, especially in the days of
persecution, ranged over a wide spectrum of doctrinal beliefs.
Most Dissenters avoided them like the plague and invariably
took a strong line when launching their attacks orally and in
print. At times, the mere presence of a Quaker could provoke
the mildest of them to furious rage: that normally benign and
even-tempered puritan, Stephen Hughes, was moved to strike
one of their more offensive brethren in 1659, whilst James
Owen, smarting under Quaker taunts, replied in kind by
chronicling the most lurid tales of how innocent folk might be
duped by the insidious charms of the Quakers' principal agent,
the devil.[49] Quakers were even more ruthlessly hounded by
Anglicans. Churchmen knew that the Quaker doctrine of the
inner light was, by its very subjectivity, the furthest removed
from the conception of a visible established church. It automatically entailed a major reappraisal of the traditional
conception of the Trinity, the efficacy of the sacraments, and
the paramount importance of biblical authority. It also
produced unacceptably radical attitudes towards existing
social values and conventions. Quaker denunciations of
clergymen as 'hireling priests', and their scornful objections
to the payment of tithes as 'an antichristian practice' were

[48] For details see *W.H.R.*, VII (1975), 412–5.
[49] Thomas Richards, 'Nonconformity and Methodism', in J. E. Lloyd (ed.),
A History of Carmarthenshire (2 vols., 1935–9), II, 152; James Owen, *Ychwaneg o
Eglurhad am fedydd plant bychain* (1701), pp. 120–1; *idem*, *Trugaredd a Barn* (1715),
pp. 8–14.

widely considered to be direct threats to the clerical order. Their refusal to swear oaths—apart from smacking of Popery—was interpreted as stubborn irreverence to secular magistrates, whilst their distinctive mode of speech and their refusal to remove their hats was considered by their social superiors to be an insidious breach of the code of deference. Once Quakers had been recognised as potential threats to the social fabric it became easier to swallow rumours that their missionaries were, in fact, Jesuits or crypto-Papists seeking to further the cause of Roman Catholicism by fomenting strife. Such fears were fiercely articulated whenever Quakers sought to turn the tables on their opponents by pointing derisively to the links between the Anglican priesthood and the religion of Rome. By tarring Protestants with a Popish brush, Thomas Wynne of Caerwys was bound to raise the ire of his clerical adversary. 'For what reason', thundered William Jones, 'had he to herd Protestants among Beasts of prey? or to worry us . . . between the Lions and the Bears.'[50] Scant wonder, then, that churchmen considered Quakers to be not only an extremely dangerous threat to the well-being of the established church, but also to social harmony and political stability.

Most Anglican clergymen in the persecuting decades were, therefore, uncompromising foes of Quakerism.[51] But rather than vent their spleen through physical coercion, most of them preferred to use the printing press to voice their grievances and fears. Few of those who did so managed to write with any detachment, especially when their existing prejudices were hardened by the effect of Quaker proselytising within their own localities. Burdened by the anxieties caused by Quaker infiltrations under the patronage of the Lloyds of Dolobran, and further disgruntled on hearing of his daughter's plans to marry the local Quaker blacksmith in defiance of his wishes, Rondl Davies, vicar of Meifod in Montgomeryshire, devoted a generous section of his *Tryall of the Spirits* (1675) to anti-Quaker diatribes, urging his flock neither to fraternise with Friends nor

---

[50] William Jones, *Work for a Cooper* (1679), p. 16.
[51] Richard Davies of Cloddiau Cochion never forgot the 'hard-heartedness and cruelty we found from unmerciful and persecuting bishops and clergy.' *An Account of the Convincement, Exercises, Services and Travels of . . . Richard Davies* (1710), p. 244.

heed their blandishments.[52] Haunted by the spectre of the late
puritan régime, Davies's work was shot through with an intense
burning fear of the social implications of Quaker doctrines.
Similarly, William Jones's assault on Thomas Wynne, the
Quaker barber-surgeon of Caerwys, so redolent of the merciless
ribaldry associated with Martin Marprelate,[53] was drenched in
torrents of social prejudice. Jones insisted that Wynne, a
former cooper, was better equipped 'to mind his axe and saw . .
than to open intricate and abstruse places'.[54] Only at their
peril would churchmen allow base-born creatures of this kind
to 'bubble poor, weak and simple people' with doctrine that
threatened to undermine the most cherished institutions of
society. Clerical attacks were thus heavily studded with petty
sneers and squalid innuendos as they strove to express their
loathing of these malignant intruders. Their most bitter
criticisms ranged from the devastating banter and mordant
sarcasm of satirists like Ellis Wynne of Lasynys to the brooding
sulphurous comments of diehards like Theophilus Evans of
Llandygwydd.[55]

It is clear, then, that members of the established church,
particularly in pre-toleration days, were convinced that no sect
presented a more dangerous threat to established religion and
to social and political order than Quakerism. This led them to
expound at length the baneful effects of that 'tainted' faith and
to portray Friends as noxious hypocrites and cheats, 'fanatic
and mad-men', 'giddy-brain'd . . . railrags to the church',
dealers in witchcraft, and 'sgabby brothers' who babbled
heresy and sedition at every turn and whose evil machinations
could lead to disaster.[56] Even so, as Welsh Quakerism lapsed

---

[52] Thomas Richards, *Wales under the Penal Code, 1662–1687* (1925), p. 62.
Davies's domestic worries are revealed in his will: Probate records of the diocese of
St. Asaph, 1696; *Profiad yr Ysprydion, neu Ddatcuddiad Gau Athrawon, a rhybudd iu
gochelyd* (1675).

[53] William Jones's *Work for a Cooper* calls to mind the Marprelate tract directed
against Bishop Cooper of Winchester, *Hay [ha' ye] any worke for the Cooper* (1589);
Patrick Collinson, *The Elizabethan Puritan Movement* (1967), p. 392.

[54] William Jones, op. cit., p. 20.

[55] Ellis Wynne, op. cit., pp. 31–2, 47; Theophilus Evans, *Galwedigaeth Ddifrifol
I'r Crynwyr i'w gwahawdd hwy ddychwelyd i Grist'nogaeth* (1715); *idem, Drych y Prif
Oesoedd* (1716), p. 167; *idem, The History of Modern Enthusiasm* (1752), pp. 35–7, 42.

[56] Thomas Wynne, *The Antiquity of Quakers* (1677), p. 13; *Work for a Cooper*
(1679), p. 30; N.L.W., Church in Wales Records, SD/Archdeaconry of
Carmarthen/Churchwardens' Returns 1684/no. 79; Richard Davies, op. cit.,
p. 49; N.L.W., Plas Nantglyn MS. 2, pp. 104–12; E. D. Jones, 'Nonconformity in
Merioneth, 1675', *N.L.W.J.*, VIII (1953–4), 118–9.

into a state of 'lukewarmness and indifference' during the early decades of the eighteenth century,[57] attitudes towards Friends changed. John Kelsall's diary indicates a shift of mood, revealing a change in the climate of intolerance and vindictiveness. Clergymen and common people[58] were becoming distinctly more civil and tolerant towards Welsh Friends who, in turn, now found that the world about them was not so much hostile as indifferent. This shift of temper was symptomatic not merely of an acceptance of the fact that persecution would never bring people to love the religion of the persecutor, but also of the fact that Welsh Quakerism was becoming increasingly innocuous. Gravely weakened by losses occasioned by persecution and emigration, bereft now of their early crusaders, notably John ap John and Richard Davies,[59] the Quaker cause in Wales had lost its early zeal and missionary spirit.[60] Moreover, the introduction of clannish marriage customs, together with rules demanding the expulsion of delinquents, exacerbated any hope of swelling their numbers. In the period before the Industrial Revolution, Welsh Quakerism suffered a slow erosion, surviving in depleted, scattered groups, isolated and insulated from the world by their own distinctive patterns of behaviour.

IV. CONGREGATIONALISM, PRESBYTERIANISM AND ARMINIANISM

Since both Congregationalists and Presbyterians were commonly tarred with the same 'non-conformist' brush after 1662, it was natural that they should gravitate towards each other to a much greater degree than during their puritan hey-day. But although the distinction between 'Independents' and 'Presbyterians' became increasingly blurred in the Restoration period,[61] there were still concrete doctrinal differences separating them. Congregationalists believed in the democracy of church government and argued that the final authority lay

---

[57] M. Fay Williams, 'Glamorgan Quakers, 1654–1900', *Morgannwg*, V (1961), 53; H. G. Jones, 'John Kelsall: a study in religious and economic history' (unpubl. Univ. of Wales M.A. thesis, 1938), p. 111.
[58] Friends' House Library, Kelsall MSS., vol. 2, letter to George Lewis, dated 14/7 mo/1722.
[59] John ap John died in 1697 and Richard Davies perished in 1708.
[60] Friends' House Library, Kelsall MSS., vol. 2, letter to Richard Lewis dated 21/1 mo/1723–4.
[61] R. Tudur Jones, *Hanes Annibynwyr Cymru* (1966), p. 99.

with each local church rather than with either episcopal o ministerial authority. Since 1660, moreover, although the maintained a rigid adherence to the doctrine of election, thei outlook was generally broad and evangelical. Presbyterians too, had realised that the old classical polity of organisin their flocks into classes, synods and assemblies was no longe feasible, even though Philip Henry's stolid objections to 'th Independent way' remained as firm as ever.[62] Generally however, Presbyterians had begun to shed their stodgy conservative image, and, heavily influenced by the moderatio of Saumurian theology, they became more liberal in thei outlook, elevating the doctrine of justification above th harsher demands of predestination and election.[63]

Even so, the Restoration climate laid rather less stress o narrow doctrinal differences than on wider and more genera principles. Efforts to bring the two bodies closer togethe eventually culminated in the 'Happy Union' or Heads c Agreements of 1691, to which between eighty and a hundre ministers subscribed.[64] The Union proved short-lived, breakin up in an atmosphere of mutual mistrust and acrimony followin the posthumous publication of Tobias Crisp's sermons.[6] According to Joshua Thomas, Wales was not 'much disturbed by the flurry of 'warm contests' that ensued,[66] but the issue which divided both sides soon reared their ugly heads a Henllan Amgoed in Carmarthenshire.[67] On the death c David Lewis of Cynwyl Elfed in 1705, a dispute broke ou regarding the choice of his successor at Henllan. The candidac

---

[62] M. H. Lee, op. cit., p. 277.

[63] Peter Toon, *The Emergence of Hyper-Calvinism in English Nonconformit 1689–1765* (1967), p. 28.

[64] C. G. Bolam and others, *The English Presbyterians from Elizabethan Puritanis to Modern Unitarianism* (1968), pp. 101–2.

[65] Peter Toon, op. cit., pp. 49–66.

[66] Bristol Baptist College MSS. Joshua Thomas, 'An Ecclesiastical History c the Principality of Wales' (2 vols., *c.* 1779–80), II. p. 470. But see the secession tha occurred at Wrexham in 1691. A. H. Dodd (ed.), *A History of Wrexham* (1957 p. 173; and the venomous pamphlet war involving Daniel Williams, Isaa Chauncy and Thomas Edwards of Rhual. N.L.W., Rhual MSS. 75, 84; Thoma Edwards, *A Plain and Impartial Enquiry into Gospel-Truth* (1693); *idem, The Paraseler dismantled of her Cloud. Or, Baxterianism Barefac'd (1699)*; Daniel Williams *Crispianism unmask'd* (1691); *idem, An End to Discord* (1699).

[67] The following paragraphs are based on R. T. Jenkins (ed.), Jeremy Ower *Golwg ar y Beiau, 1732–1733* (1950), Introduction; Thomas Richards, 'Non conformity and Methodism', pp. 164–70; R. Tudur Jones, 'Trefniadaet Ryngeglwysig yr Annibynwyr', *Y Cofiadur*, 21 (1951), 30–5.

f a high Calvinist, Lewis Thomas, a farmer-cum-elder of Bwlch-y-Sais, was strongly pressed, but the claims of the low Calvinist candidate, David John Owen, also a farmer of Pwll-hwyaid and a man of influential connexions, won the support of the majority. The doctrinal differences which divided the two camps also reflected a sociological cleavage: the low Calvinists, deriving their theological sustenance from the moderation of Baxterianism, were generally well-educated, well-to-do and sober men, inclined to eirenic compromise rather than angry contention. Conversely, the high Calvinists comprised local ministers, who carried some small stake in farming property; generally poorly-educated, their outlook was one of stolid conservatism nourished by a self-sustaining certainty that they were appointed by God to preserve 'the faith once delivered by the saints'.

The tensions implicit in these differences inevitably led to conflict and secession. Fearful of internal crisis and the threat imposed by the high Calvinism of Lewis Thomas, David Owen, presumably at the end of his tether, was unwise enough to invoke publicly the relevant verses from Lamentations iii 64–66, which called on the Lord to 'persecute and destroy them in anger'. Appalled by such inflammatory language, Lewis Thomas broke camp, led his disaffected flock from the Henllan fold in 1707, and established a Congregational meeting house at Rhydyceisiaid in the parish of Llangynin. In October 1710, David Owen died and his son, Jeremy, was elected to replace him. The new minister had barely settled in before Matthias Maurice, son of a tailor of Llanddewi Felffre and an outspoken member of the Henllan congregation, began blowing the high Calvinist trumpet in the locality. News of Maurice's 'harsh expressions' and 'ill conduct' carried as far as Exeter, where it caused a few hearts to flutter among the United Brethren of Devon and Cornwall.[68] As in Lewis Thomas's case, synods were called to judge the issue and the eventual decision to debar the fiery Maurice from local pulpits provoked the guilty party to lead a further secession to Rhydyceisiaid in 1711.

---

[68] Geoffrey F. Nuttall, 'Northamptonshire and the Modern Question: A Turning-Point in Eighteenth-Century Dissent', *Journal of Theological Studies*, XVI, Part 1 (1965), 109.

These acrimonies were revived in 1727 when Matthias Maurice published his version of the secessions in a bid to bolster the flagging spirits of high Calvinists by reminding them of the rightness of their cause.[69] Maurice was characteristically waspish in his aspersions. He poured vitriol on the Presbyterians' fondness of judgment by synods, claiming that they were unwarranted breaches of the Christian's liberty. Mischievously deriding his adversaries, he condemned the autocracy of Henllan, its rickety doctrines, its loose discipline and anachronistic values. Low Calvinists were outraged to find Maurice reopening old sores in such a provocative manner. Setting out his version of the affair in *Golwg ar y Beiau* (1732–3) the affluent, academy-trained, articulate and unyielding Jeremy Owen took up the cudgels with thinly-disguised relish. The main virtue of the Henllan polity, he maintained, was that it steered a judicious *via media* between two extremes. Defending synods with skill, precision, and a wealth of scriptural and historical knowledge, Owen claimed that their rôle was consultative rather than autocratic. Accusing Maurice and his disciples of unwarranted schism, Owen could not resist delivering a stinging reference to his adversary's less favourable connexions, smugly deriding him as a poor tailor's son, a self-styled prophet whose conscience allowed him to poach from his neighbour's flock and deliver unfair judgment on dead men who could not answer back.[70]

In sustaining these theological disputes, ministers and educated laymen were fortified by solid reading-matter in both Welsh and English. Maurice's account reveals that he and his fellow-secessionists leaned heavily on the twin juggernauts of their Independent forebears: Edward Fisher's *Marrow of Modern Divinity* (1645), published in Welsh in 1651,[71] had run through nine English editions by 1699, and was closely rivalled by Thomas Goodwin's *Christ set forth . . . as the cause of justification and object of justifying faith* (1642). Maurice himself

[69] Matthias Maurice, *Y Wir Eglwys yn cyrchu att y nod nefol . . . Att yr hyn chwanegwyd byr hanes Eglwys Rhydyceished yn eu nheulltuad o Henllan, 1708* (1727). This account is reproduced in *Y Cofiadur*, 3 (1925), 41–9.

[70] Jeremy Owen, *Golwg ar y Beiau*, pp. 38, 63. Maurice later returned to the dispute in his preface to *Byrr Hyfforddiad yn Addoliad Duw, a Discyblaeth Eglwysi Testament Newydd* (1734).

[71] John Edwards, *Madruddyn y Difinyddiaeth Diweddaraf* (1651).

was anxious to see many of the tracts which had emerged during the Crispian controversy in the 1690s in a Welsh garb,[72] and he himself made a positive contribution to that end by publishing, in 1711, his translation of Isaac Chauncy's *The Doctrine which is according to Godliness* (1694).[73] Next to the Bible, however, their most popular touchstone was Eliseus Cole's *Practical Discourse of God's Sovereignty* (1673). Translated into Welsh by Howell Powell in 1711,[74] this 'famous book' became a bulwark of the High Calvinist faith in Wales. Woven almost exclusively from scriptural evidence, Cole's work set out the five basic principles of Calvinist doctrine: the absolute sovereignty of God; the redemptive sacrifice of Christ as the fulfilment of a divine purpose; man's inability to do good whilst in a state of sin; the effectiveness of the work of the Holy Spirit in revealing to the heart the power of Christ's sacrifice; and, finally, the irrevocable reconciliation of the redeemed soul to his Redeemer and his perseverance in faith and holiness. Many Welsh Methodists sharpened their doctrinal teeth on Cole's work,[75] and it is significant that the second edition of Powell's translation in 1760 and the fifth edition of 1842 were published, respectively, by two of the staunchest pillars of Welsh Calvinism, Peter Williams and John Elias.

The over-riding dominance of Calvinism, however, was under threat in Wales by the 1720s. From the Restoration period onwards, the elevation of rational principles as preached by Cambridge Platonists and Anglican Rationalists had been guiding men towards the Arminian concept of universal redemption, the co-operative rôle of divine grace, and the will of the individual in the process of conversion. This obviously entailed a denial of the hallowed doctrines of original sin and predestination. Arminianism meant that Everyman was Adam unto himself: it was his moral responsibility to respond to the bestowal of God's grace.[76] In the same period, Lockean thought

---

[72] Matthias Maurice, *Y Wir Eglwys*, p. 47. Maurice also hoped to see the works of John Owen and Samuel Annesley in the vernacular. Matthias Maurice, *Ymddiddan rhwng Dau Gristion, Cywir a Ffyddlon, ynghylch Ail-Enedigaeth* (1730), p. viii.

[73] *Yr Atrawiaeth y sydd yn ol Duwioldeb* (1711).

[74] *Traethawd-Ymarferol am Gyflawn-Awdyrdod Duw, a'i Gyfiawnder Ef* (1711).

[75] Dafydd Cadwaladr of Bala read the whole work nine times. *Ychydig Gofnodau am Fywyd a Marwolaeth Dafydd Cadwaladr* (1836), p. 22.

[76] J. Gwili Jenkins, *Hanfod Duw a Pherson Crist* (1931), pp. 39–40.

penetrated the swiftly-growing Dissenting academies and served to encourage a greater emphasis on reason and freedom of inquiry.[77] The academy at Carmarthen, headed by the liberal Thomas Perrot, strongly advocated a 'catholic' system of education and offered students freedom for theological manoeuvre and independence of thought.[78] This atmosphere liberated those students who were repelled by the harshness of high Calvinist doctrines, and, by laying emphasis on the rational interpretation of scripture and the need for charity and mutual tolerance, many of them committed themselves to the Arminian faith.

One of Perrot's brightest pupils, Jenkin Jones, emerged as the 'apostle of Arminianism' in Wales when he established the first Arminian congregation in the Principality in a farmhouse at Penybanc in 1726 and later built the Arminian chapel of Llwynrhydowen on his own land in 1733.[79] His cause was greeted by Calvinists with a mixture of acute anxiety and utter contempt. Both sides embarked on an ill-tempered war of attrition that ranged from local pulpits to the printing press.[80] Baptists, too, were becoming increasingly uneasy at the success of Arminianism in worming its way through the interstices of the Calvinist monopoly. Acrimony centred largely on the churches of Hengoed and Newcastle Emlyn. At the former church, after working in harmony for some years with his Calvinist colleague, Morgan Griffith, Charles Winter led an Arminian secession of thirty members in 1730.[81] Among the Baptists of Newcastle Emlyn, the Calvinist, Enoch Francis, met with Arminian opposition from his second-cousin, Abel Francis, and from a former Calvinist schoolmaster, Rees David. These disputes were brought before the Baptist Association at Hengoed in 1730 where, much to the dismay of Calvinists, Charles Winter argued the case for universal redemption and free will. Winter's forthright stand caused an uproar and only

[77] Irene Parker, *Dissenting Academies in England* (1914), pp. 125–6.
[78] H. P. Roberts, 'Nonconformist Academies in Wales, 1662–1862', *T.H.S.C.*, 1928–9, p. 89.
[79] T. Oswald Williams, *Hanes Cynulleidfaoedd Undodaidd Sir Aberteifi* (n.d.), pp. 58–60.
[80] For an anti-Arminian sermon preached in September 1729 by James Lewis, minister at Pantycreuddyn, see N.L.W. MS. 11076A, pp. 164–75. The printed works involved were Jenkin Jones, *Cyfrif Cywir o'r Pechod Gwreiddiol* (1729), and James Lewis and Christmas Samuel, *Y Cyfrif Cywiraf o'r Pechod-Gwreiddiol* (1730).
[81] 'Yr Ymraniad yn Hengoed', *Yr Ymofynydd*, 1845–8, pp. 149–50.

the timely intervention of David Rees of London persuaded him to remain in amicable harness with Morgan Griffith and prevent a further split in Baptist ranks.[82] Abel Francis, however, refused to change his colours and continued to spread Arminian doctrines on itinerant preaching tours.[83] Calvinists frantically manned the battlements in a bid to ward off Arminian onslaughts, and their general unease was summed up at the Baptist Association meeting at Llanwenarth in 1731, when members recalled 'how happy the ancient Britons were till the errors of Pelagius and Arminius came in like a flood'.[84] Their anxieties were not unfounded: by 1742 there were six Arminian churches in Jenkin Jones's neighbourhood, and the seeds of modern Unitarianism had been safely planted.[85]

V. THE POPISH THREAT

In Restoration Wales, Roman Catholicism entered its sunset years. The Religious Census of 1676 revealed that there was one Papist to every four Protestant Dissenters, and one Papist to every 140 members of the Church of England. Of 1,122 Catholics estimated to be in Wales, almost half—541—were resident in 'the greatest stronghold of Papistry in Southern Britain', Monmouthshire.[86] Here, a hard core of gentry and yeomen, together with a fair representation of craftsmen in towns, supported by wives, spinsters and widows, resolutely sustained the old faith.[87] In Wales as a whole, however, Roman Catholicism was largely unmilitant in character, a 'sleepy, dust-laden', unreflecting allegiance to an age-old faith.[88] These dormant habits owed little to Jesuit evangelisation and were far removed from the crusading passions of the Counter-Reformation.

[82] Joshua Thomas, *Hanes y Bedyddwyr*, pp. 203–4, 212–4; idem, *History of the Baptist Association*, p. 46.

[83] Joshua Thomas (ed.), *Nodiadau ar Bregeth Mr. Abel Francis* (1775).

[84] *History of the Baptist Association*, p. 45.

[85] J. Gwili Jenkins, op. cit., p. 39.

[86] Thomas Richards, 'The Religious Census of 1676', *T.H.S.C.*, Supplement, 1925–6, pp. 99, 118; Emyr Gwynne Jones, *Cymru a'r Hen Ffydd* (1951), p. 87.

[87] J. H. Matthews, 'Monmouthshire Recusants, 1719', *Publications of the Catholic Record Society*, VII (1909), 246–54. See also the returns made of Catholic recusants in parts of the diocese of St. David's. N.L.W., Church in Wales Records, SD/RC/1–20.

[88] A similar situation obtained in the remoter provinces of England. Angus McInnes, 'The Revolution and the People' in G. Holmes (ed.), *Britain after the Glorious Revolution, 1689–1714* (1969), pp. 81–2.

Nevertheless, side-by-side with this passive drowsiness there existed small groups of militant Catholics who were anxious to disseminate their doctrines as widely as possible. The state made their task as difficult as possible: the printing of Catholic literature was proscribed and, as a result of the tightly-regulated control of the press, few Popish books printed either abroad or secretly in Britain escaped the government's dragnet. As far as is known, only three Welsh editions slipped through during this period: *Drych Cydwybod* (1661), an incomplete translation of Francisco Toledo's treatise on moral theology, *Summa Casuum Conscientiae*[89]; *Allwydd neu Agoriad Paradwys i'r Cymru* (1670), a devotional work by John Hughes which raised Protestant eyebrows with some bitter indictments of the enemies of the Church of Rome[90]; and, finally, the publication of Hugh Owen's translation of Thomas à Kempis's celebrated *De Imitatione Christi* in 1684.[91] Denied unfettered access to the printing press, many Catholic authors were forced to disseminate their literature privately in manuscript form. The most industrious of them was William Pugh, a native of Penrhyn Creuddyn in Caernarvonshire, a lay member of the Benedictine order, a physician and a poet. Having laboured unstintingly for the ancient faith throughout the revolutionary period, Pugh emerged unscathed in the Restoration years as the most vigorous defender of the Catholic literary tradition. In 1674, he translated *The Jesus Psalter* into Welsh, and two years later he compiled a Welsh and Latin Catechism, *Crynodeb or Athrawiaeth Gristnogawl*, which, designed specifically for young people, was clearly a desperate attempt to secure the allegiance of the next generation to a swiftly-diminishing faith.[92] Since none of these manuscripts, however, was transferred on to the printed page, hopes of a Catholic revival were necessarily slender. For an assortment of fragile manuscripts, peddled secretly within small circles, could never hope to compete with the power of the printed word.

[89] B.L., Lansdowne MS. 808, f. 19; *Y Traethodydd*, XXXI (1876), 38–40; G. Bowen, 'Fersiwn Cymraeg o Summa Casuum Conscientiae Francisco Toledo', *J.W.B.S.*, X (1968), 5–35.

[90] This work is analysed by G. Bowen in *T.H.S.C.*, 1961, pp. 80–160.

[91] John Hughes (ed.), Hugh Owen, *Dilyniad Christ* (1684).

[92] G. Bowen, 'Gwilym Pue "Bardd Mair", a Theulu'r Penrhyn', *Efrydiau Catholig*, 11 (1947), 11–35.

Although the persecution of Catholics was usually haphazard and fitful under the penal code, their ranks were nevertheless clearly denuded. At times of political tension, old religious hatreds and personal animosities often intertwined to bring anti-Popish feeling to a hysterical peak. When Titus Oates published fabricated evidence in 1678 of an elaborate plot to murder the king and replace him with the Popish duke of York, the concomitant of which would be a wholesale massacre of Protestants and a French invasion of Ireland, a massive priest-hunt was organised by the government, the repercussions of which were swiftly felt in the Catholic oasis of Monmouth-shire.[93] In the autumn of 1678, Herbert Croft, bishop of Hereford, armed with a warrant from the House of Lords, set forth to wipe out, at one fell swoop, one of the leading Papist strongholds on the border, St. Francis Xavier's 'College' at Cwm. Nestling in a remote, sheltered valley, this seminary had served as a 'spiritual fountain-head' for the Catholic cause in Wales since its foundation in 1622, affording in particular a welcoming haven for Jesuit priests and a storehouse for Catholic literature.[94] The raiding bishop not only unearthed 'priestly foxes' but also found 'a great store of divinity books . . . written by the principal learned Jesuits', together with small Popish catechisms and 'some Welsh Popish books lately printed'.[95] The ransacking of Cwm was unquestionably a cruel blow to the evangelising programme of Welsh Catholics insofar as it shattered the frail unity of the small côterie of priests resident there. Moreover, a mounting wave of local hatred toward Papists[96] inevitably accelerated the number of defec-tions to Protestantism. The ensuing priest-hunt claimed the lives of several martyrs: a secular priest, John Lloyd, was burned at Cardiff in 1678 and, in the following year, two Jesuit priests, Father Philip Evans and Father David Lewis,

[93] M.M.C. O'Keefe, 'The Popish Plot in South Wales and the Marches of Hereford and Gloucester' (unpubl. Univ. of Galway M.A. thesis, 1969), pp. 22–4. In 1684, Thomas Jones, the publisher, produced a Welsh account of various versions of the Popish Plot in *Y Gwir er Gwaethed Yw* (1684). For the fears of Welsh poets, see N.L.W. MS. 263B, pp. 28–9; N.L.W. MS. 527A, pp. 116–7.

[94] Donald Attwater, *The Catholic Church in Modern Wales* (1935), pp. 26, 170–1; Martin Cleary, 'The Catholic Resistance in Wales, 1568–1678', *Blackfriars*, vol. 38 (1957), 122.

[95] Herbert Croft, *A Short Narrative of the Discovery of a College of Jesuits, at a Place called the Come, in the county of Hereford* (1679).

[96] Anon., *The Popes down-fall at Abergavenny* (1679).

were barbarously put to death at Cardiff and Usk respectively.[97] These harrowing events may possibly have served to stiffen the faith of the remaining priests and their followers, but they also signalled the impending decay of Catholicism as a living force in the religious life of Wales.

It is scarcely surprising that the volume of Welsh Protestant literature written against the doctrines of Catholicism far outnumbered apologiae for the Papist faith in this period. Not only was the Protestant author able to take full advantage of his freedom to use the printing press, but he was also morally bound to anathematise the doctrines of the Church of Rome. Countless sermons and tracts argued that Catholicism was essentially a perversion of Apostolic Christianity, a lewd debasement of the teaching of Christ.[98] Neither churchmen nor Dissenters could feel any affinity with the doctrines of Rome and nothing was more calculated to ruffle the feathers of a dour Protestant than to be designated a secret Popish sympathiser.[99] This vigorous anti-Roman sentiment was inextricably bound up with the Protestant theory of the early British church. The Reformation was essentially an appeal to the past; it involved an appeal to history and a denial of innovation. Striving feverishly to erect a water-tight *rationale* of the historicity of their faith, Protestants marshalled their evidence from the twin authorities of the scriptures and the Church Fathers. The Bible was inevitably the supreme touchstone. 'Where was your religion before Luther's time?', asked a Popish priest of David Williams, vicar of Llanfrynach. 'In the scriptures', replied Williams crushingly, 'where your religion has never been.'[100] Superimposed on the scriptural argument was a general aversion to the claim of the Roman Church to be the authentic 'old faith'.[101] Welsh Protestant historians from the days of

---

[97] J. H. Matthews (ed.), *Records of the County Borough of Cardiff* (6 vols., 1898–1911), II, 174–5; IV, 156–9; T. P. Ellis, *The Catholic Martyrs of Wales, 1535–1680* (1933), pp. 119–23, 129–40.

[98] Robin Clifton, 'Fear of Popery' in Conrad Russell (ed.), *The Origins of the English Civil War* (1973), p. 146.

[99] When Benjamin Keach was indiscreet enough to impute Popish sympathies to James Owen (*Light broke forth in Wales* 1696, pp. 234, 250), the latter almost choked with rage in replying to his 'ignorant' Baptist calumniator (*Ychwaneg o Eglurhad am fedydd plant bychain* 1701, p. 83).

[100] N.L.W. MS. 13089E, p. 137.

[101] *Cred a Buchedd Gwr o Eglwys Loegr* (1710), pp. 94–113; anon., *Golwg Eglur o'r Rhagoriaeth sydd rhwng Ffydd y Protestaniaid a Ffydd y Papistiaid* (1715), *passim*.

William Salesbury and Richard Davies to those of Theophilus Evans and Simon Thomas formed a critical tribunal that not only arraigned Papist shortcomings but also argued vigorously that Romanism was the new learning and Protestantism the old. Whereas the early apostolic church had been pure and undefiled, the shackles of Popery had imprisoned Welshmen in new-fangled corruptions and errors from which they only escaped when the rebirth of Protestantism offered them a new opportunity to avail themselves of the true faith.

Welsh Protestants objected violently to the ritualism, pageantry and authoritarianism of the Roman church. Whilst Rondl Davies and Simon Thomas launched strident assaults on the graceless ways of past incumbents of the see of Rome,[102] Ellis Wynne indulged in mincing satire, poking fun at the privileged sons of Lucifer and their specious institutions.[103] More serious was their plea that all men should be free to study God's Word. Nothing was more cruel, mourned John Thomas, than to lock away the scriptures and press men to mumble scores of Ave Marias and Pater Nosters in an unknown tongue.[104] 'That which we plead for against the Papists', challenged Thomas Edwards of Rhual, 'is that all men have eyes in their heads as well as the Pope.'[105] It was, therefore, a constant theme among Protestants that their countrymen should take a proper pride in having the Bible in their own tongue, since, by mastering the scriptures, they would fortify the Protestant cause in Wales and quash the lingering hopes of Catholic evangelists.

Behind the smirks of contempt and the acid invective there lurked a deeply-rooted fear of Catholicism not only as an abhorrent faith but also as a political menace. From Elizabethan times onward, hatred of Catholics had become almost part of the national ideology, incubating deeply in Protestant souls. Just as the stereotype 'great fear' in twentieth-century Germany has been the Jewish conspiracy, so in England and Wales the 'collective emotion' of the seventeenth century focused on the dreaded 'Popish Plot'.[106] Not only did Roman Catholicism

[102] Rondl Davies, op. cit., pp. 58–60; Simon Thomas, op. cit., p. 159.
[103] Ellis Wynne, op. cit., pp. 16–17, 32–4, 68–9.
[104] John Thomas, *Unum Necessarium* (1680), p. 7.
[105] N.L.W., Rhual MS. 74.
[106] H. R. Trevor-Roper, *The European Witch-Craze of the Sixteenth and Seventeenth Centuries* (1969), p. 93.

become the national scapegoat for the Gunpowder Plot of 1605, the civil wars, the great fire of London in 1666, and the Popish Plot of 1678, but at provincial levels, too, wild stories of 'Catholic plots' swept periodically through towns and villages causing widespread alarm and confusion.[107] The result was that Popery was constrained to do penance for every ill-deed that befell the seventeenth century and, at moments of political crisis, it was regarded as a standing threat to Protestantism, Parliament and the nation as a whole. In times of war and social upheaval, it could revive that 'almost insuperable anxiety'[108] which gave Elizabethans so many sleepless nights. When William Lloyd, bishop of St. Asaph, fulminated against the Popish threat on the seventy-fifth anniversary of the Gunpowder Plot, he voiced fears which weighed heavily on the minds of Protestants:

> I would tell them, if they were present, your country is afraid of you. She does as it were beg you to be gone. For a hundred years she hath been in danger of you. She hath not suffered but some way or other on your account. The Spanish Invasion was for Popery, the Gunpowder Treason was for Popery. One Civil War was in great measure occasioned by Popery. She is in danger of another Civil War by Popery. . . . Why should you not be gone, and free her from her fears?[109]

How far fears of Popery preyed on the ordinary Welshman's mind is difficult to assess. Much of the hysteria which surrounded political crises like the Popish Plot was largely a 'metropolitan phenomenon'[110] and most people had learnt to distinguish between Popery as a dreaded political force on the continent and the quietly-practised, inoffensive Catholicism which some of their neighbours embraced as their faith. Even so, it is unlikely that they would remain impervious to the veritable barrage of anti-Papist propaganda which emerged regularly from the press. Scanning the past, Welsh authors made every effort to keep Popish 'cruelties' squarely in the

[107] Robin Clifton, 'The Popular Fear of Catholics during the English Revolution', *P & P*, 52 (1971), 23–55.
[108] Carol Z. Wiener, 'The Beleaguered Isle. A Study of Elizabethan and early Jacobean Anti-Catholicism', *P & P*, 51 (1971), p. 29.
[109] William Lloyd, A *Sermon preached before the House of Lords, on November* 5, *1680* (1680), p. 37.

public eye. Martyrdoms suffered under the iron yoke of Rome received special attention, with Charles Edwards's *Y Ffydd Ddi-ffvant* (1677) teeming with dramatic exemplars of the most horrifying 'cruelties' perpetrated in the name of Catholicism. Edwards succeeded in popularising John Foxe's *Book of Martyrs* in a Welsh garb, arousing and canalising antipathy towards Rome by reliving the horrors of Smithfield in gruesome detail.[111] He and his colleagues left the reader in no doubt whatsoever that a revival of Catholic fortunes would mean more burning of Protestants.

Apart from their obsession with Popish 'crimes' in the past, Protestant authors also shared strongly-felt sentiments regarding the present political situation in Europe. They were particularly disturbed by the grand imperial concepts nursed by 'the self-styled champion of Catholicism'[112] in Europe, Louis XIV of France. More than anything, men feared the imposition of a 'Frenchified Popish' monarchy, especially after 1685 when Louis revoked the edict of Nantes and ravaged the Palatinate. As late as 1717, Jeremy Owen recalled the time when the king of France had filled 'the prisons, the dungeons, and the galleys with . . . cries and groans' of Huguenot captives.[113] The popular Welsh almanacs of Thomas Jones, too, were suffused with a relentless francophobia which focused largely on dire prognostications of King Louis's eventual fate.[114] Even the distinguished polymath, Edward Lhuyd, was provoked to draft a series of *englynion* in which he urged Death to employ its trustiest servant—smallpox—to engineer the speedy departure of the French monarch from this life.[115] Descanting a variant on the myth of the Norman yoke, James Owen warned that the nation could hardly 'expect better treatment from the present French King than our ancestors did from the Norman Bastard'. 'Will not his little finger', he asked rhetorically, 'be heavier than the other's loins?'[116]

The traditional fear of Catholicism as an aggressive, scheming

[110] John Kenyon, *The Popish Plot* (1972), p. 239.
[111] Charles Edwards, *Y Ffydd Ddi-ffvant* (1677), pp. 122–48.
[112] John Miller, *Popery and Politics in England, 1660–1688* (1973), p. 67.
[113] Jeremy Owen, *The Goodness and Severity of God* (1717), p. 26.
[114] See, for example, Thomas Jones, [*Almanac*] (1691), sig. A7r.
[115] E. D. Jones, 'The Brogyntyn Welsh Manuscripts', *N.L.W.J.*, VIII (1953), p. 28.
[116] James Owen, *Salvation Improved* (1696), p. 28.

and cruel power was further revived when the abortive
Jacobite rebellion of 1715 ushered in a flood of anti-Roman
literature. In an encomium to the new Hanoverian king,
Philip Phillips conjured up horrific images of Papists as
wicked rabble-rousers and unmerciful barbarians.[117] 'Is it
possible', asked Jeremy Owen, 'for us to forget all their
massacres, in so many several countries, at so many different
times, in which they have slain thousands and myriads of great
and small, yea the children sometimes, and the sucking
infants of a span long with their pitiful mothers?'[118] His uncle,
James Owen, agreed wholeheartedly: 'whoredom and cruelty',
he rasped, 'constitute her character'.[119] Indeed, throughout
this period, the view expressed by Bishop Richard Smallbrooke
that 'Popery . . . still retains the same barbarous disposition as
ever, and indeed can only be supported by the methods of
force and violence',[120] was an axiom which never staled by
repetition.

Even so, authors never wearied of reminding their readers
that the fall of Antichrist, i.e. the Pope, as foretold in the Book
of Revelations, would not long be delayed. God's deeds,
claimed Jeremy Owen, were tangible proof of His avowed
promise 'to pour forth all the vials of his wrath upon her, and
to destroy her utterly to the very foundation'.[121] Millenarian
fervour in the heady days of the revolutionary period had
moved Morgan Llwyd to forecast the downfall of Belzeebub
and the Pope, the two powers that had made 'Christendom
their slaughterhouse, the church their dancing school'; and
with the reprinting of *Llyfr y Tri Aderyn* in 1714 the batteries of
his forebodings were once more recharged.[122] Hitching his
wagon to the same star, Simon Thomas forecast that 'Babylon'
would soon be tumbling down into the dust.[123] 'God speed that
day',[124] added Matthias Maurice fervently. These expectations,

[117] Philip Phillips, *Ufudd-dod i Lywodraeth a Chariadoldeb* (1716).
[118] Jeremy Owen, op. cit., p. 27.
[119] James Owen, *The History of Images and of Image-Worship* (1709), sig. A3r.
[120] Richard Smallbrooke, *Our Obligations to promote the Publick Interest* (1724),
p. 25.
[121] Jeremy Owen, op. cit., p. 27.
[122] T. E. Ellis and J. H. Davies (eds.), *Gweithiau Morgan Llwyd* (2 vols., 1899–
1908), I, 19, 151–266; Morgan Llwyd, *Dirgelwch i rai i'w Deall* (1714).
[123] Simon Thomas, op. cit., p. 168.
[124] Matthias Maurice, *Y Wir Eglwys*, pp. 30–3; cf. Ellis Pugh, *Annerch ir Cymru*
(1721), pp. 102–6.

however, did not absolve men from their personal responsibility to strive 'unto blood against Popery'. Every true Welsh Protestant might play his part in contributing to the downfall of the common enemy by vigilance, courage and earnest prayer.[125]

---

[125] Jeremy Owen, op. cit., p. 27; Thomas Wynne, *The Evidences of an Over-ruling Providence, in Defeating the Conspiracies of Cunning and Ungodly Men* (1722), p. 22.

VIII
AUTHORS AND THEIR WORLD

I. THE SOCIAL BACKGROUND OF WELSH AUTHORS

The number of authors of Welsh books whose names are known and who spent all or part of their lives within the period 1660 to 1730 totals 140. Most of these were born and bred in north, west and mid-Wales. Twenty-seven authors hailed from Merioneth, 20 from Carmarthenshire, 16 from Cardiganshire, 16 from Denbighshire and 11 from Montgomeryshire. Of the remaining counties, Anglesey provided nine authors, Caernarvonshire seven, Monmouthshire five, Pembrokeshire four, Flintshire and Breconshire three each, Glamorgan two, and Shropshire one. One other author, William Wotton, was born in Suffolk, whilst the home county or residence of fifteen more authors remains unknown. The geographical distribution of these authors reveals a distinction that was more marked between east and west than between north and south: 83 authors were natives or residents of six western counties whilst 40 only hailed from the seven eastern counties. This pattern reflects several factors, the most important being that the western counties of Wales had retained not only their Welshness but also a powerful literary tradition which was now being fully utilised by Protestant reformers. The religious affiliation of all but six authors is known: 93 were members of the established church, 25 were Congregationalists or Presbyterians, 8 were Quakers, 6 were Baptists, and the Roman Catholic and Arminian faiths each claimed one author.

Eight authors regarded themselves as gentlemen-farmers, whilst five others, including three yeomen, a drover-cum-farmer and a husbandman, also earned their living from the soil. Two bishops and forty clergymen represented Anglican interests, whilst the Dissenting cause was served by twenty-two ministers. Six schoolmasters were joined by two academy tutors (both of whom were ordained ministers) and one Roman Catholic priest. Of the remainder, four were weavers, three were printers, two were sextons, one a museum-keeper, one a master of a hospital, one an apothecary, another a barber-surgeon, one a stone-mason, another an almanacer, and one other, whose occupation is unknown, served as a parish clerk but died a pauper. Only one author, James Davies (Iaco ab Dewi), made an attempt, at least for a time, to scrape a living as a professional translator and copyist. The social status of a further thirty-seven authors remains unknown, but since the bulk of them were amateur ballad-mongers it is more than likely that they were small farmers or craftsmen.[1]

Although patronising Welsh culture was still a natural reflex on the part of many of the Welsh gentry, the twin forces of anglicisation and alienation meant that those who were themselves capable of becoming authors of Welsh books were now a small minority. Four authors of gentle stock, all church-men, fall into the same social bracket as the middling gentry. Elis Lewis of Llwyn-gwern owned fairly substantial property in the parishes of Llanuwchllyn and Llanycil in Merioneth,[2] whilst the lay subsidy rolls of 1663 placed his neighbour, Rowland Vaughan of Caergai, among the moderately affluent gentry. A former sheriff of Merioneth, an ardent royalist, the stoutest of high churchmen, a fluent and prolific translator and poet, Vaughan had endured great depths of economic and personal suffering during the revolutionary period. The civil wars left an incurable psychological scar on his personality, leaving him moody and irritable, and planting within him an abiding antipathy towards Dissent and a fastidious distaste for low breeding.[3] Among the smaller gentry, William Lewes was a gentleman sheep-farmer who held the lands of Llwynderw and Pen-y-Gaer in the parish of Llangeler, Carmarthenshire, on a twenty-nine-year lease. An inventory of his goods, totalling £74 7s. 0d., gives some indication of his worldly goods: his possessions included 280 sheep, 15 cows, 4 yoke of oxen, 14 small beasts, 10 working horses, a colt, a filly, a riding horse, swine, poultry, corn and hay.[4] But Lewes did not confine himself to the bucolic habits of most landowners: like many of

---

[1] Thomas Parry, *Baledi'r Ddeunawfed Ganrif* (1935), p. 21.
[2] *D.W.B.*; P.R.O., Prob/10/Box 936.
[3] N.L.W. MS. 18162D, p. 96. Cf. Gwyn Thomas, 'Rowland Vaughan', in Geraint Bowen (ed.), *Y Traddodiad Rhyddiaith* (1970), pp. 231–46.
[4] N.L.W., Archdeaconry of Carmarthen P.R. 1723; D. E. Jones, *Hanes Plwyfi Llangeler a Phenboyr* (1899), pp. 126–7.

the smaller squires of south-west Wales, he was a man of some erudition, deeply sensible of the richness of the Welsh literary heritage, widely-esteemed as a first-rate genealogist and antiquary, and the author of two translations published soon after his death in 1722.[5]

The most striking fact regarding Welsh authors of gentle birth is that four of the eight were Quakers. The publishing campaign of Welsh Friends had suffered heavily as a result of the emigration of so many relatively affluent families to Pennsylvania, and the burdens of authorship thus fell on the shoulders of a small number of literary squires from Merioneth. These families, having chosen to face the storm of persecution, had retained much of their wealth in spite of constant harassment and potentially ruinous distraint. Bound together by their disciplined life of inner certainty, gravity and selflessness, they took advantage of the more peaceful climate in post-toleration days to furnish their brethren with reading matter. Thomas Cadwalader, a 'well-esteemed' gentleman-farmer, administered his estate at Llannerch and devoted time to translating and correcting Quaker tracts.[6] More affluent than he was Humphrey Owen of Llwyn-du, Llangelynin, whose possessions were valued at £627 13s. 0d. in 1715.[7] That same wealth came to his neighbour, Owen Lewis of Tyddyn-y-garreg, near Dolgellau, translator of Penn's *Key* in 1703, on the occasion of his marriage in 1717 to Anne, daughter of Humphrey Owen. Not only did Lewis inherit this substantial patrimony but he also safeguarded his acquired wealth by making swift provision for the future of the lands united by his marriage.[8] At a time when the cause of Quakerism was beginning to wane, Welsh Friends relied more and more on the literary skills and patronage of such squires in major Welsh-speaking strongholds like Merioneth.

[5] These works were *Maddeuant i'r Edifairiol* (1725–6) and *Dwy Daith i Gaersalem* (1728). Lewes was assisted in the first by the fourth gentleman-author, his father-in-law, Evan Pryce of Rhyd-y-benau, Llangeler. See N.L.W., Archdeaconry of Carmarthen P.R. 1732.

[6] G.C.R.O., D/DSF 379, p. 110; T. A. Glenn, *Welsh Founders of Pennsylvania* (2 vols., 1911), I, 18–20.

[7] N.L.W., Bangor P.R. 1715.

[8] N.L.W., Bangor P.R. 1744; *D.W.B.* *Sub* Lewis and Owen of Tyddyn-y-garreg and Humphrey and Owen of Llwyn-du. The fourth Quaker gentleman was a poet, Thomas Lloyd of Penmaen. See G. H. Hughes, 'Llyfrau a Llenorion y Crynwyr', *J.W.B.S.*, IX (1959), 75–7.

The established church made a more weighty contribution, supplying 30 per cent of the total number of authors in this period. The fact that only two bishops took to translating books into Welsh is scarcely surprising, since so many of them were unfamiliar with the Welsh language. Both prelates, in turn, occupied the see of St. Asaph, a bishopric whose reputed value was £280 in 1660. On his appoinmtent in that year, George Griffith, a member of the Griffith family of Carreg Lwyd in Anglesey, clearly felt hardly done by, and successfully petitioned to be allowed to hold additional preferments which effectively trebled his income. Griffith was passionately committed to the task of making religious literature in Welsh more widely available. He contributed to the compilation of the Act of Uniformity in 1662, took responsibility for the 1664 edition of the Welsh Prayer Book, and published a list of errors and omissions contained in editions of the scriptures published before 1660. Nearly twenty years after his death, his discourses on the Lord's Prayer were collected and published by William Foulkes, rector of Llanfyllin.[9] But whereas Griffith was a zealous and effective bishop, one of his later successors was a horse of very different colour. Edward Jones, a native of Forden, Montgomeryshire, and a former bishop of Cloyne, succeeded William Lloyd in 1692 and was fortunate in that his predecessor had not only increased the revenues of the bishopric but had also set new standards of order and discipline within his diocese. Jones, however, proved a man of straw. Weak-minded, ineffectual, and a constant prey to corrupt practices, he was found guilty of simony in 1701, suspended for six months, reinstated in 1702 only to die within a year.[10] One of the few virtues of his ignoble tenure was his collection of several hundred prayers taken from the church catechism, an edition which, according to his scornful chancellor, Robert Wynne, 'stood his Lordship in fifteen shillings'.[11]

[9] G. M. Griffiths, 'The Restoration in St. Asaph: the Episcopate of Bishop George Griffith, 1660–1666', *J.H.S.C.W.*, XII (1962), 10; *idem*, 'Some Extra Diocesan Activities of Bishop George Griffith of St. Asaph, 1660–1666', *N.L.W.J.*, XII (1962), 298–301.

[10] O. W. Jones, 'The Case against Bishop Jones of St. Asaph', *J.H.S.C.W.*, 19 (1964), 58–65. For Jones's will, see P.R.O., Prob/10/1373.

[11] Robert Wynne, *A Short Narrative of the Proceedings against the Bishop of St. Asaph* (1702), p. 68. A copy of the work is included in Wynne's pamphlet on pp. 81–4.

The value of the livings of clerical authors ranged from £20 to £90, with the median value generally lying between £30 and £60. Yet, at the top of the scale most well-connected, university-trained clerics had well-developed appetites for additional lucrative preferments. Edward Wynn's livings comprised the rectorship of Llangeinwen and Llangaffo, valued at £100, the rectorship of Llangybi and Llanarmon (£80), the rectorship of Llanllechid (£80), notwithstanding the revenues which accrued to him as canon of St. Asaph and chancellor of the cathedral at Bangor.[12] More affluent than most was David Maurice who, after 1684, received a special dispensation to hold the livings of Abergele (£70) and Betws yn Rhôs (£60), together with the living of Llanasa (£60) which he had held since 1666. From 1696, too, Maurice was vicar of Llanarmon-yn-Iâl (£60). By his death in 1702, he owned lands, messuages and tenements which, bound up in mortgages, were worth £1,500.[13] Several clerics, even those with comfortable parish livings, were engaged in agricultural pursuits over and above the cultivation of their own glebe. Like Henry Fielding's Mr. Trulliber, a man in this position was 'a parson on Sunday but all the other six might more properly be called a farmer'.[1] One who conformed to this type was Henry Rowlands, who held the livings of Llanidan, Llanddaniel-fab, Llanedwen, Llanfair-yn-y-cwmwd and Llanfairpwll from 1696 to 1723 but who spent much of his time cultivating his valuable estate at Plasgwyn, Llanedwen.[15]

At lower levels, clerical authors who earned less than £20 per annum were distinctly impoverished. It was imperative for these to farm their glebe or find some supplementary means of income. It was surely poverty which forced Samuel Williams, vicar of Llandyfriog (£20), allegedly to occupy himself with the menial tasks of 'a common labourer in hedging, ditching

[12] The yearly value of Wynn's livings is based on the valuation of parishes and dignities in the diocese of Bangor made in the 1680s. Bod., Tanner MS. 146, f. 74
[13] Lloyd-Baker MSS., Letter no. 22; Bod., Tanner MS. 146, f. 23; Tanner MS. 32, f. 69; N.L.W., St. Asaph P.R. 1703.
[14] Cited in Alan Smith, *The Established Church and Popular Religion, 1750–1850* (1971), p. 10.
[15] W. Garel Jones, 'The Life and Works of Henry Rowlands' (unpubl. Univ. of Wales M.A. thesis, 1936); N.L.W., Bangor P.R. 1724. For the wills of other clerics in comfortable circumstances see George Lewis, Abergwili, N.L.W. Archdeaconry of Carmarthen, P.R. 1709; John Langford of St. Martin's, St. Asaph P.R. 1713; Ellis Wynne of Llanfair-juxta-Harlech, Bangor P.R. 1734.

ploughing, reaping, threshing, sowing . . . corn . . . with many other like servile, indecent employments unbecoming a minister'.[16] Simon Jones, perpetual curate of Llandysilio, was so incensed and frustrated by his miserable stipend of £8 per annum that, in language both poignant and rhetorical, he drew the attention of Francis Hare, bishop of St. Asaph, to the critical lack of prospects for advancement among poor curates. With Maecenases at a premium, he complained (paraphrasing Martial), it was little wonder that the wretched poverty of the church stifled the literary aspirations of potential Virgils.[17] But although poverty cast a dark shadow over the well-meaning aspirations of promising clergymen, many of them refused to neglect their studies. Alban Thomas, the many-sided curate of Blaenporth, left goods valued at only £4 18s. 10d. on his death in 1737, but was remembered for his devotional tracts, ballads and elegies.[18] Similarly, although John Morgan received only £15 per annum as vicar of Aberconwy (1697–1701) and was laid low by ill-health, he remained devoted to his parishioners, worked hard to publish melancholy tracts for the benefit of his countrymen, and passionately vowed his determination to shore up the Welsh language.[19] Incentives to publish were not automatically related to wealth. Poverty did not necessarily deter penurious clerics whilst, at the same time, it was not prosperity alone which prompted their well-heeled colleagues to write and publish Welsh books.

The passionate commitment of Dissenting ministers to their faith, together with their personal courage and integrity, steeled their resolve to strengthen their cause in spite of the rigours of penury and persecution. Few of them, however, found it easy to write and publish books without patronage of some sort. William Jones, the ejected minister of Denbigh, was fortunate enough to secure the patronage of the Trevors of Trefalun, who offered him refuge on land valued at £20 per annum at Plas Teg in Flintshire, thus enabling him to indulge his flair for translation in relative comfort and security.[20] Other

[16] N.L.W., Ottley Papers, no. 126.
[17] Simon Jones, *Dr. Wells's Letter to a Friend* (1730), sig. A2r.
[18] N.L.W., Archdeaconry of Carmarthen P.R. 1737. Thomas is noticed in *D.W.B.*
[19] U.C.N.W.L., Bangor MS. 421; *D.W.B.*; J. T. Jones, 'John Morgan, Ficer Aberconwy', *Y Llenor*, XVII (1938), 16–26.
[20] Calamy, II, 713–4.

ministers made signal contributions under the protective aegis of the Welsh Trust. Following his ejection from the living at Llanrhaeadr-ym-Mochnant in 1660, Charles Edwards, the son of a Llansilin gentleman, chose to spend the rest of his career as an author and editor of Welsh books in Oxford and London.[21] However, the loss of his living, coupled with his wife's estrangement and subsequent years of loneliness in cheerless lodgings, eventually induced a mental breakdown. His autobiography, a work of extreme pathos published in the year of his death in 1691, reveals that he was assailed by so many mental and physical tempests that he was no longer capable of behaving rationally. His final work, tragically, was the testimony of a paranoiac.[22] In many ways, too, Stephen Hughes's commitment to the publication of Welsh books was carried out in the teeth of persecution and considerable personal sacrifice. Even so, Hughes was blessed with certain advantages: he was the son of a relatively prosperous silk-mercer; he was, to some extent, financially dependent on his wife, Catherine, a self-effacing woman whose indomitable resilience contributed largely towards his 'comfortable subsistence and future usefulness'; and finally, his sweet temper, personal warmth and complete honesty were capable of disarming most of his enemies.[23] Many of the Anglican gentry saw that his cultural aspirations transcended the bounds of party or doctrine and succumbed to his charming and persuasive tongue. Although Hughes was able to draw on funds accumulated by the Welsh Trust, much of his private income, derived from his wife and his smallholding, together with his labours as minister and schoolmaster, was expended on his literary ventures.[24] On his death in 1688, his worldly goods were valued at £30 10s. 0d., half of which was the value of his books.[25] It is unfortunate that many of Stephen Hughes's achievements, notably his yeoman service in publishing religious literature and thrusting literacy rates

[21] D. L. Morgan, 'A Critical Study of the Work of Charles Edwards (1628–1691?)' (unpubl. Univ. of Oxford D.Phil. thesis, 1967), pp. 1–30.

[22] Charles Edwards, *An Afflicted Man's Testimony concerning his Troubles* (1691).

[23] N.L.W. MS. 12357E, f. 1441; R. T. Jones and B. G. Owens, 'Anghydffurfwyr Cymru, 1660–1662', *Y Cofiadur*, 32 (1962), 35–7; Calamy, II, 718.

[24] A third of his personal savings financed the publication of *Tryssor i'r Cymru* and *Cyfarwydd-deb i'r Anghyfarwydd* in 1677. Stephen Hughes (ed.), *Tryssor i'r Cymru* (1677), sig. A2r.

[25] N.L.W., Archdeaconry of Carmarthen P.R. 1688.

upwards, have often been over-shadowed by the more obvious successes of Griffith Jones's educational movement. It is worth remembering that few seventeenth-century ministers were more revered than Hughes. The affection which his followers reserved for him bordered on pure adulation, and even those who did not share his views were prepared to admit that his was a life of rare quality and achievement.

By the time of Stephen Hughes's death, Welsh Dissent, gathering its own momentum, was nurturing a new breed of ministers whose independent means enabled them to devote time and energy to literary work. Some were heirs to substantial estates: Christmas Samuel, the pious and melancholy minister of Pant-teg, inherited land in the parish of Abergwili and used his wealth not only to patronise Welsh literature and education but also to better the lives of the poor.[26] Jenkin Jones of Llanwenog, the son of a gentleman-blacksmith, was sufficiently prosperous to be able to buy land on which was built the first Arminian chapel in Wales in 1733.[27] More typical of the enterprising and self-sufficient farmers who entered the ministry was David Lewis, Presbyterian minister at Henllan. Lewis owned land in four parishes, and an inventory of his possessions, totalling £43 7s. 2d., reveals that he owned two oxen, a bull, four steers, eleven cows, three heifers, sixteen small cattle, a mare, a colt, five working horses, 46 ewes and lambs, 101 sheep, pigs and poultry.[28] Other ministers were often craftsmen or sons of craftsmen. Simon Thomas practised the trades of silk-mercer and printer at Hereford,[29] whilst Matthias Maurice of Llanddewi Felffre, a tailor's son, achieved a position of some prosperity by entering into a marriage bond of £800, £300 of which was to be laid towards portioning his children.[30] Finally, some ministers, largely through their fashionable appearance, cut an elegant figure in their localities. Thomas Baddy, Presbyterian minister at Denbigh, was 'a gentleman of family and substance' who,

[26] *D.W.B.*; N.L.W., Archdeaconry of Carmarthen P.R. 1765; J. D. Owen, 'Dechreuadau Panteg a Christmas Samuel', *Y Dysgedydd*, CXV (1935), 360–5, CXVI (1936), 10–15.
[27] R. J. Thomas, 'Jencin Jones, Llwynrhydowen', *Baner ac Amserau Cymru*, 27 May 1942, p. 5.
[28] N.L.W., Archdeaconry of Carmarthen P.R. 1705.
[29] *D.W.B.*
[30] *D.W.B.*; Northamptonshire Record Office, P. R. 1738.

resplendent in his dashing clothes and silver spurs, shared the sartorial insignia of the well-to-do.[31]

Although little is known of the social and economic status of schoolmasters and academy tutors, the most capable among them were erudite men of letters anxious to use their skills in translating religious literature. Lewis Evans, Anglican schoolmaster at St. Clears, earned £20 per annum and was highly thought of as 'a very honest and diligent man', whose chief *métier* was his skill as a grammarian.[32] Some of the early Dissenters worked in less comfortable circumstances. Richard Jones, the ejected minister of Denbigh, a man of 'ingenuity, considerable learning and noted piety', kept a private school at Henllan but died in sadly straitened circumstances in 1673, leaving his major assets—his books—to his son, Stephen, on condition that he applied himself to his studies.[33] Conversely, the Independent minister and schoolmaster, Rees Prydderch, who owned lands at Ystradwallter near Llandovery, lived rather more comfortably. A man of solemn mien, Prydderch was imbued with such a strong sense of rectitude that even the most light-hearted frivolity was anathema to him. But this 'respected Gamaliel' was also amply endowed with a fund of shrewd common sense and it was this quality, coupled with his flair for attracting talented pupils, which enabled him to maintain an outstandingly successful school at Ystradwallter for over forty years.[34]

One of Prydderch's brightest pupils was William Evans, schoolmaster and minister at Pencader and subsequently a vigorous academy tutor at Carmarthen. During the 1690s, Evans lived on the margin of subsistence, sustained only by his wife's private income and his meagre salary as schoolmaster. Gradually, however, he built up some capital and his success as a tutor enabled him to bequeath £140 to his daughter and £100 to each of his sons. An exceptionally gifted preacher and preceptor, Evans's reserves of energy and boundless capacity

[31] Edmund Jones, *A Relation of Apparitions of Spirits in the Principality of Wales* (1780), p. 46; *H.P.N.*, pp. 301–2; *D.W.B.*
[32] N.L.W., Ottley Papers, no. 62. See also Thomas Jones's view of him in *Boreual a Phrydnawnol Weddiau* (1711), p. 30.
[33] Calamy, II, 844; N.L.W., St. Asaph P.R. 1673.
[34] *D.W.B.*: Calamy, II, 720; William Evans (ed.), Rees Prydderch, *Gemmeu Doethineb* (1714); G. D. Owen, *Ysgolion a Cholegau yr Annibynwyr* (1939), pp. 11–12.

for work made him, in Jeremy Owen's words, 'a public blessing' in the eyes of his contemporaries.[35] Evans's reputation, high though that might be, did not rival that of James Owen of Oswestry. A former pupil of Samuel Jones, Brynllywarch, and a protégé of Stephen Hughes, Owen had earned a name for himself as a minister of uncommon industry and resilience. In 1690, he had opened a Dissenting academy at Oswestry, which he took with him on his removal to Shrewsbury ten years later. Contemporaries marvelled at his talents as a Bible theologian and as a formidable disputant, and although he was a man of brilliant intellectual gifts he carried his enormous learning with ease. Diligent and painstaking, seldom less than inspiring, James Owen had few equals as a tutor, remaining utterly devoted to the welfare of his students who, in turn, appreciated his tolerant and affectionately paternal authority.[36]

At a time when medical science was still in its rudimentary stages, apothecaries and barber-surgeons were the most proficient medical practitioners in eighteenth-century Wales. However, apothecaries were often little more than shop-keepers with a flair for doctoring, whilst many barber-surgeons were disreputable souls whose techniques ranged from the bizarre to the barbaric.[37] On the other hand, medical men were held in some esteem in Quaker circles owing to the humanitarian nature of their calling. Two Quaker authors who were also members of the medical profession in this period may well have been much more sensitive to suffering and eager to fight peasant obscurantism than their more notorious colleagues. One of the leading lights among Monmouthshire Quakers was Elisha Beadles, a literary-minded apothecary of Pontypool. Beadles owned a copyhold estate in the parish of Llanfihangel Ystum Llewern, and the inventory of his goods, valued at £691 6s. 6d. in 1734, shows him to have been a prosperous man.[38] The other

[35] *D.W.B.*; Alexander Gordon, *Freedom after Ejection* (1917), pp. 144–5; N.L.W., Archdeaconry of Carmarthen P.R. 1718; R. T. Jenkins (ed.), Jeremy Owen, *Golwg ar y Beiau 1732–3* (1950), p. 65.

[36] Charles Owen, *Some Account of the Life and Writings of . . . James Owen* (1709), pp. 87–91; Matthew Henry, *A Sermon preach'd at the Funeral of . . . James Owen* (1706), p. 38; G. D. Owen, 'James Owen a'i Academi', *Y Cofiadur*, 22 (1952), 3–36.

[37] G. Penrhyn Jones, 'Folk Medicine in Eighteenth-Century Wales', *Folk Life*, VII (1969), 60–74.

[38] *D.W.B.*; T. M. Rees, *A History of the Quakers in Wales* (1925), p. 76; N.L.W., Llandaff P.R. 1734.

Quaker, Thomas Wynne, barber-surgeon of Caerwys, Flint-shire, was a self-made man. Largely through his own patient studies and some tuition at Shrewsbury, Wynne was granted a licence to practise surgery in 1659–60. In spite of having to suffer the trials of persecution and imprisonment for non-payment of tithes, he continued to practise his skills in bone-setting, bleeding and purging 'with good success'.[39] But his enthusiastic oral and literary campaigns on behalf of Quakerism led to such relentless harassment that the possibilities implicit in William Penn's proposed 'Holy Experiment' proved irresistible to him.[40] In 1681, in con-junction with John ap John, Wynne purchased 5,000 acres of 'good and health-ful land' in the Welsh Tract of Pennsylvania, some of which was then dispersed among less prosperous Quakers who were bent on crossing the Atlantic.[41] Unlike his co-purchaser, however, Wynne himself undertook the haz-ardous voyage, sailing, in a mood of high optimism, on the *Welcome* with Penn in September 1682.[42] Wynne swiftly established a reputation in Pennsylvania, becoming personal physician to the founder himself, being appointed speaker of the Third Provincial Assembly of Pennsylvania, figuring prominently at the meetings of Philadelphian Friends, and subsequently being appointed associate justice of Sussex county and its representative at the Legislative Assembly in Phil-adelphia.[43] Although Wynne's departure from Wales allowed a certain Roger Hughes—'a villain', according to Wynne, 'as is hardly to be found unhanged in a country'[44]—to distrain his property at Bron Fadog, Ysceifiog, Wynne feathered a comfortable nest for himself in Pennsylvania, erecting a lavish mansion at Lewes where a servant and three negro slaves ministered to his needs. On his death in 1692, his estate was

[39] Thomas Wynne, *An Antichristian Conspiracy Detected* (1679), pp. 40–2.
[40] Thomas Wynne, *The Antiquity of Quakers* (1677); William Jones, *Work for a Cooper* (1677); Thomas Wynne, *An Antichristian Conspiracy;* Wynne was presented before the great sessions on several occasions in the 1670s. N.L.W., Wales 4/988/6–10; 989/1–8; 990/1–3; N.L.W., SA/Misc/1485.
[41] Historical Society of Pennsylvania, Penn Papers, deed dated 15 September 1681.
[42] N.L.W., Rhual MS. 106; George E. McCracken, *The Welcome Claimants proved, disproved and doubtful* (1970), pp. 560–87.
[43] Department of Records, Philadelphia. Philadelphia Monthly Meeting Minute Book, vol. 1, 1682–1714. References to Thomas Wynne from 1682 to 1684, and from 1688 to 1692; T. A. Glenn, *Merion in the Welsh Tract* (1896), pp. 268–71.
[44] N.L.W. MS. 11594E.

valued at £430 1s. 3d. Few Welsh authors in this period achieved the rags-to-riches progress of this remarkable Quaker physician, who died, 'ripe in years and rich in respect', in the mellow comforts of Penn's New Jerusalem.[45]

Many Welsh authors were craftsmen by trade. Literate, skilled and self-sufficient men, they were bound together by a common system of values and style of life. Their culture was dedicated to the self-improvement which stemmed from stressing the values of self-discipline, moral seriousness and piety. Some of them had some stake in farming: Huw Morys, universally acclaimed as the leading Welsh poet of his day, spent part of his youth as an apprentice tanner at Overton, Flintshire, before returning to assist his father on his prosperous farm at Pont-y-meibion, Llansilin, in Denbighshire.[46] Similarly, that winsome Quaker orphan, Ellis Pugh of Brithdir, Merioneth, abandoned his trade as a stone-mason on his emigration to Pennsylvania in 1686, choosing instead to farm the lush pastures of Gwynedd.[47] Others led remarkably versatile careers: Thomas William of Mynydd Bach, Carmarthenshire, was a self-educated weaver, a faithful deacon and subsequently a minister, a talented poet, an ardent antiquary, and one who wrote and edited numerous Welsh books in a hand that is sheer copper-plate.[48] Although it is not possible to be precise about the social origins of ballad-mongers, many of them were craftsmen of unusual attainments. Owen Gruffydd of Llanystumdwy, Caernarvonshire, was a sprightly weaver, genealogist, antiquary and poet, who, despite rapidly fading eyesight, cheerfully practised his many talents until his death in his eighty-eighth year in 1730.[49] Richard Parry of Dyserth, Flintshire, a weaver by trade, achieved distinction as a schoolmaster and poet,[50] whilst John Thomas, also a weaver

---

[45] Department of Records, Philadelphia, will no. 79, 1692; *The Friend*, XXVII, no. 29, p. 228.

[46] *D.W.B.*; David Jenkins, 'Bywyd a Gwaith Huw Morys, Pont-y-meibion' (unpubl. Univ. of Wales M.A. thesis, 1948).

[47] *D.W.B.*; T. M. Rees, op. cit., p. 161.

[48] *D.W.B.*; J. Peter and R. J. Pryse, *Enwogion y Ffydd*, (4 vols., n.d.), III, 114; E. Lewis Evans, *Capel Isaac* (1950), pp. 56–8; *Y Cofiadur*, XVII (1947), 27–9.

[49] *D.W.B.*; Gwyn Thomas, 'A Study of the Changes in the Tradition of Welsh Poetry in North Wales in the Seventeenth Century' (unpubl. Univ. of Oxford D.Phil. thesis, 1966), pp. 336–43.

[50] Dafydd Jones, *Cydymaith Diddan* (1766), p. 82; William Rowlands, *Cambrian Bibliography* (1869), p. 337.

of Bodedern, Anglesey, was a prolific ballad-monger who cast aside his love of tippling as he became increasingly aware of his religious obligations.[51] On the other hand, the pleasures of the tavern were a more enduring attraction to Dafydd Jones of Trefriw, Caernarvonshire, best-known as a poet, printer and publisher, but one who at some time during his chequered career followed the various occupations of schoolmaster, sexton, constable and miller.[52]

Some Welsh printers and publishers were protean men. John Rhydderch of Shrewsbury was a prolific printer and publisher, a successful author, poet and ballad-monger, a capable grammarian and a zealous patron and organiser of *eisteddfodau*.[53] John Jones, a respectable Dissenting gentleman, farmed his thirty-eight acre estate at Caeau, Wrexham and also owned substantial property in the town whence he distributed Welsh almanacs from 1702 onwards.[54] Forced to endure a barrage of reproaches from his great rival, Thomas Jones of Shrewsbury, John Jones nonetheless soon became accustomed to such tantrums and one suspects that he bore them with dignity and forbearance. Thomas Jones's judgments were always heavily tinged with paranoia, and the Wrexham almanacer was not so much the unprincipled villain he made him out to be as a shrewd businessman anxious to peddle his wares among the ever-widening market of Welsh readers. Much more is known about the career and character of Thomas Jones.[55] A former tailor, Jones filled the rôles of printer, publisher, author, almanacer, poet and grammarian. He was an immensely resourceful man, born with a quick wit but also a forthright tongue, blessed with a flair for business but also a burning hatred of all rivals. If his hugely entertaining almanacs are any indication, his life was a round of furious quarrels. At any rate, his personal life was singularly unhappy: an irremediable

[51] D. Wyn Wiliam, 'Y Traddodiad Barddol ym Mhlwyf Bodedern, Môn' (unpubl. Univ. of Wales M.A. thesis, 1970), p. 111.

[52] *D.W.B.*; G. J. Williams, 'Llythyrau at Ddafydd Jones o Drefriw', *N.L.W.J.*, Supplement, series III (1943), 30, note 22.

[53] *D.W.B.*; Gwyn Thomas, op. cit., pp. 384–416.

[54] A. N. Palmer, *History of the Town of Wrexham* (1893), p. 152; N.L.W., Smallwood Collection (unscheduled), deeds involving John Jones of Caeau, dated 15–16 April 1734, 31 October 1734, 13–14 September 1736. I owe these references to Mr. A. J. Roberts.

[55] For a convenient summary see *D.W.B.* Jones's career is discussed more fully in chapter nine.

hypochondriac, Jones's major ailment, the sweating sickness, coupled with the flood of libellous scorn poured on him by his enemies, induced ungovernable fits of depression and bad temper.[56] Even so, he was sufficiently resilient to weather most storms, managing to remain on an even economic keel. An inventory of his goods, drawn up on his death in 1713 and valued at £48 6s. 6d., was made up largely of books and papers, presses and letters, brass and pewter ware, napery, iron, upholstery, joinery and coopery ware.[57]

Professional farmers who developed a taste for writing books were never numerous in this period. Those who did were often described as 'yeomen', but this was an idiosyncratic term, rarely used with any consistency, and one which glossed over fairly broad social and economic differences. The celebrated Quaker apostle, John ap John of Ruabon, Denbighshire, achieved the status of yeoman largely through his marriage to Catherine Edwards, widow of David ap Edward of Plas Efa, Trevor, which facilitated the consolidation of freehold properties at Plas Efa, Trevor and Rhuddallt. Such was his relative affluence that he was able to make a joint purchase, with Thomas Wynne of Caerwys, of 5,000 acres in Pennsylvania at a cost of £100.[58] More typical of the country yeoman-farmer of Anglican persuasion was Foulke Owen of Nantglyn, Denbighshire, a modest landowner who edited *Cerdd-lyfr* in 1686 and who counted 'The Black Book of Basingwerk', a precious manuscript dating from the fourteenth century, as one of his most treasured literary possessions.[59] A rarer breed was represented by Edward Morris of Perthi Llwydion, Cerrig-y-Drudion, Denbighshire: he was a farmer of substance, a widely-travelled drover, a translator and a poet of some esteem. Morris was a staunch Anglican, a fervent patriot well-versed in his nation's literature, a man with both a searching conscience and a nice sense of humour, and one

---

[56] Thomas Jones, *Newyddion mawr oddiwrth y Ser* (1699), sig. A2r–A5v; *Morris Letters*, I, 98, II, 129; cf. the virulent manuscript notes written in a copy of *Y Gymraeg yn ei Disgleirdeb* (1688) in N.L.W. (W.S. 50).

[57] Lichfield Record Office, P.R. 1713.

[58] Historical Society of Pennsylvania, Penn Papers, deed dated 15 September 1681; Charles Morton Smith MSS., vol. 3, no. 1, deed dated 14 February 1682; N.L.W. MS. 1116D, pp. 116–9; T. M. Rees, op. cit., p. 17.

[59] *D.W.B.*; N.L.W., St. Asaph P.R. 1693.

whose instincts in economic matters were refreshingly humanitarian. His fame was such that, on his death somewhere on his travels in Essex in 1689, five of his fellow-poets, mourning his passing in elegy, lavished unstinting praise on his life and works.[60]

Literate husbandmen who wrote Welsh books were also something of a rarity in this period. At this social level, husbandmen were preoccupied largely with their daily tasks of back-breaking labour, and their sole representative (so far as is known) was Roger Jenkin, the translator of one of the monitory tracts of the Quaker, John Barcroft.[61] Jenkin rented tenements and parcels of land in the parish of Llanfrechfa, Monmouthshire, and, together with his brother, Thomas, he became involved in a complex and protracted dispute over tithes, during which both brothers spent long periods in Monmouth gaol and Fleet Prison.[62] The literary work of this faithful and generous Friend was thus ground out in the face of badgering creditors, public hostility and social pressure. Even so, the inventory appended to his will in 1728 reveals that he survived his ordeal over tithes: debts owed to him in the form of mortgages, bills and bonds totalled £235 3s. 0d., and the remainder of his goods, valued at £28 16s. 0d., comprised his household possessions, tools, three cows, ten sheep, a horse, a pig, corn and hay, cheese, books (worth fifteen shillings) and two guineas in ready cash.[63] The fact that Jenkin was able to endure heavy losses of goods suggests that he was a good deal more prosperous than most Welsh husbandmen and underlines the danger of using elastic terms like 'husbandman' and 'yeoman' in the hope that they will consistently reflect social reality. At any rate, we can be sure that few Welsh authors came from the very bottom of the social scale,

[60] *D.W.B.*; Gwenllian Jones, 'Bywyd a Gwaith Edward Morris, Perthi Llwydion' (unpubl. Univ. of Wales M.A. thesis, 1941), chapter one.

[61] G.C.R.O., D/DSF 320, p. 172; Friends' House Library, Kelsall MSS. Diaries, IV, p. 58.

[62] G.C.R.O., D/DSF/325, dated 4/8 mo/1699; D/DSF/2, pp. 63, 80, 87, 95; D/DSF/351, dated 7/6 mo/1717; D/DSF/2, p. 153; D/DSF/352, dated 10/12 mo/ 1726; Friends' House Library, MS. Minutes of Meeting for sufferings, vol. 15, Monmouthshire, p. 116, dated 16 July 1711 (I owe this reference to Mr. Malcolm Thomas); G. Eyre Evans, 'Gleanings from Original Friends' Registers at Somerset House', *Journal Friends Histor. Soc.*, 1 (1904), 83.

[63] N.L.W., Llandaff P.R. 1728.

and the only pauper among them was Robert Evans, ballad-monger and sometime parish clerk of Meifod, who died a poor man in the local almshouse.[64]

II. THE EDUCATIONAL BACKGROUND OF WELSH AUTHORS

Virtually nothing is known of the early education of Welsh authors in this period. James Owen, Moses Williams and possibly Stephen Hughes were sometime pupils at Carmarthen grammar school, whilst Westminster School, one of the most exclusive and well endowed schools in the kingdom, attracted two future bishops of St. Asaph, George Griffith and Edward Jones. Most authors, however, particularly those who became clergymen, attended grammar schools within Wales or the borderland before moving on to university. Others took advantage of the modest education offered in local 'petty' schools, whilst a good many at the lowest levels were self-taught.

The Catholic author, John Hughes, was something of a rarity inasmuch as he studied abroad. Although his studies at the English College in Rome cost his father £200, the discipline he gained there moulded him into an upright, ascetic, puritanical soul, and steeled him for the trials which would confront a Jesuit priest in a hostile world.[65] Sons of gentlemen and clergymen, on the other hand, progressed naturally from grammar school to the university of Oxford or Cambridge. The universities were still regarded as indispensable seminaries for the training of clergymen and, at a time when the intake of undergraduates was declining markedly,[66] the high number of Welsh graduates holding benefices in Wales was a factor which augured well for the established church. There were 71 graduates (61 per cent) out of 116 clergymen in the diocese of St. Asaph in 1710, and 72 graduates (63 per cent) out of 115 clergymen in the diocese of Llandaff in 1726. The ordination lists for the diocese of Bangor reveal a high number of ordinands, drawn from gentle, clerical and merchant stock, who were

[64] Richard Williams, *Montgomeryshire Worthies* (1884), p. 27. For the career of another parish clerk-cum-sexton, Humphrey Dafydd ab Ifan, poet of Llanbrynmair, see ibid., p. 52 and N.L.W. MS. 10249B.

[65] G. Bowen, 'Allwydd neu Agoriad Paradwys i'r Cymrv. John Hughes, 1670', *T.H.S.C.*, Part 2, 1961, pp. 88–94.

[66] H. Kearney, *Scholars and Gentlemen. Universities and Society in pre-industrial Britain, 1500–1700* (1970), p. 142.

graduates, whilst of 265 clergymen in the impoverished, rambling diocese of St. David's in 1714, 87 (32 per cent) were graduates.[67]

It is highly significant, therefore, that of forty graduates of Oxford and Cambridge who became authors of Welsh books in this period thirty-six were clergymen. This is not to say that this privileged clerical *élite* consistently set high standards. Some of the best-educated clergy, struck with a paralysis of lethargy and boredom, were capable of modest exertions only. Bishop William Lloyd of St. Asaph confessed to Archbishop Sancroft in 1686 that of those whom he had ordained, 'the graduates have not been always the best scholars. I have more than once seen them shamefully outdone by men that never saw the university.'[68] John Morgan, vicar of Matchin, knew of talented clerics who hid their lights under bushels of diffidence and modesty. Writing to Moses Williams in 1714, he urged the recipient to encourage young Welsh clerics to bestir themselves and set about translating books into Welsh. 'I don't question', he insisted, 'but there are many . . . that might be more useful to their country, were it not for an excess of modesty.'[69] Self-effacement, however, was scarcely a charge which could be levelled against a man like Theophilus Evans, who not only published his classic *Drych y Prif Oesoedd* (1716) without having sampled the fruits of a university education, but also did so at the youthful age of twenty-three.[70] Similarly, a cleric like Henry Rowlands of Plasgwyn, Llanedwen, had proved thoroughly recalcitrant at school but, having been 'put to plough, which by no means relishing with him, he (to the surprise of all) took wonderfully to his learning, but never went again to school'. This literary squarson, cheerfully boasting of never having ventured further than twenty miles from Anglesey, was yet sufficiently perceptive and imaginative to produce a series of impressive works relating to the environment and antiquity of his native county.[71]

[67] N.L.W., SA/V/3; Ll/VC/3; SD/VC/7; A. I. Pryce, *The Diocese of Bangor during three centuries* (1929), pp. xxxviii–xxxix.
[68] Bod., Tanner MS. 30, f. 124r.
[69] N.L.W. MS. 17B, p. 13.
[70] *D.W.B.* Evans was not ordained priest until 9 November 1718. A. H. Williams, 'Theophilus Evans, Chaplain', *N.L.W.J.*, XVI (1970), 264–71.
[71] J. Loveday, *Diary of a Tour in 1732* (1890), p. 26; Henry Rowlands, *Idea Agriculturae* (1764); idem, *Mona Antiqua Restaurata* (1723).

Many authors fortunate enough to receive a university education, especially those outside the ranks of the propertied *élite*, went up to university under the sponsorship of a bishop or the local gentry.[72] Thirty-three authors matriculated at Oxford, and two others, Elis Lewis of Llwyn-gwern and Rowland Vaughan of Caergai, are known to have spent some time at that university.[73] Twenty-one authors were domiciled at the traditional home of Welsh students, Jesus College, whilst Christ Church, Hart Hall and St. Albans each claimed two Welsh students. Balliol, Brasenose, Oriel, Queen's, St. Mary and Exeter, and University College each received one prospective author.[74] Of the total number of 33, 26 graduated B.A., 19 graduated M.A. (three of whom, including Edward Lhuyd, received their first degrees at Cambridge), and four became Doctors of Divinity. Of the latter, Evan Evans, former curate of Wrexham, made a name for himself as the crusading rector of Philadelphia from 1700 to 1721;[75] George Griffith was bishop of St. Asaph from 1660 to 1666;[76] William Lewis, sometime Fellow and Provost of Oriel College, Oxford, held the post of master of the Hospital of St. Cross near Winchester from 1627 to 1643, lost his preferments during the revolutionary period, but resumed them again from 1660 until his death in 1666;[77] and finally, David Maurice, vicar of Abergele, was so widely considered 'a very worthy man' that William Lloyd recommended him to Archbishop Sancroft as a fitting successor to his see at St. Asaph.[78]

Of seven Welsh authors who matriculated at Cambridge, six graduated B.A. and then proceeded to their Master's degree. Three studied at Jesus College and one each at Catharine Hall, Christ's, Trinity and Queen's.[79] Two first-rate

[72] Walter Price, vicar of Llangwm, publicly thanked twelve eminent dignitaries for acting as his benefactors at Oxford. *Godidowgrwydd Rhinwedd ac Effaith yr Efengyl* (1707), sig. a1r–v. Cf. Robert Lloyd, *Cyssur i'r Cystuddiedig* (1723), sig. a1v.
[73] *J.W.B.S.*, VIII (1954), 82; Gwyn Thomas, 'Rowland Vaughan' in *Y Traddodiad Rhyddiaith*, p. 231.
[74] This section is based on Joseph Foster, *Alumni Oxonienses, 1500–1714*, (2 vols., 1891).
[75] *D.W.B.*
[76] *D.W.B.*
[77] *D.N.B.*; P.R.O., Prob. 10/1002; J. C. Morrice, *Wales in the Seventeenth Century* (1918), pp. 171–2.
[78] Bod., Tanner MS. 32, f. 69; Tanner MS. 31, f. 294.
[79] This is based on J. Venn and J. A. Venn, *Alumni Cantabrigienses*, Part 1, (4 vols., 1927).

scholars among them were Doctors of Divinity: Edward Wynn chancellor of Bangor and canon of St. Asaph, assisted in the review of the Prayer Book of 1662, founded a school at Holy head, wrote and distributed religious literature among hi parishioners, and made bequests for the maintenance of Welsh students at, and for the adornment of, Jesus College;[80] William Wotton, the Suffolk-born scholar and controversialist, wa sufficiently stimulated by his study of Celtic languages a Catharine Hall that he went on to learn Welsh, to preach in that language, and also to assist Moses Williams in the publication of a Welsh translation of the Laws of Hywel Dda.[81]

Dissenters, for their part, were debarred from the universitie in the Restoration period, although three ejected puritans Charles Edwards, Richard Jones and William Jones, had each graduated at Oxford prior to 1660. Henceforth Dissenter gained their education at the learned academies which were swiftly burgeoning in spite of the rigours of persecution and a dearth of funds.[82] Of eleven Dissenting ministers who were authors in this period, eight were educated at Welsh academies James Owen sat at the feet of Samuel Jones at the first Welsh academy at Brynllywarch, and six others—Rees David, Jenkin Jones, James Lewis, Matthias Maurice, Christmas Samuel and John Pugh—were educated under William Evans at Carmarthen between 1704 and 1718. Thomas Baddy attended Richard Frankland's celebrated academy at Rathmell, York shire, whilst Howell Powell pursued his studies at Saffron Walden under Thomas Payne. Simon Thomas, minister a Hereford, was also evidently a product of a Dissenting academy although there is no indication of where he studied.[83] What i clear, however, is that Dissenting academies played a vital rôle in nurturing a galaxy of bright young ministers.[84]

[80] U.C.N.W.L., Penrhos (1), MS. 523, pp. 43–9.
[81] D.W.B.; Moses Williams and William Wotton, Cyfreithjeu Hywel Dda a Eraill (1730).
[82] Irene Parker, Dissenting Academies in England (1914), and H. McLachlan English Education under the Test Acts (1931).
[83] For all these ministers, except John Pugh, see D.W.B. For Pugh, see Thoma Rees and John Thomas, Hanes Eglwysi Annibynol Cymru (4 vols., 1871–5), III, 340
[84] H. P. Roberts, 'Nonconformist Academies in Wales', T.H.S.C., 1928–9 pp. 1–98.

III. THE MOTIVES OF WELSH AUTHORS

Although a variety of considerations induced authors to write and translate Welsh books in this period, each one was invariably subordinate to the religious motive. The very fact that over five hundred books, the vast majority of which were religious and didactic in character, were published in this period is manifest proof of a consensus among authors that the salvation of man was their primary aim. Each author might emphasise certain theological and doctrinal niceties, but their general concern was to dispel ignorance and raise levels of literacy, to instil the fundamental doctrines of Protestantism, to establish a wider respect for the moral laws of Christianity, to outline the right direction of Christian devotional life, to establish the techniques of self-analysis and self-scrutiny, and, finally, to safeguard the social and political fabric.

Religious motives were clearly infinitely more important than any other, but it is also striking that a strong flavour of patriotism should have tinged the concern of authors for the souls of their countrymen. Love of country gave an added spur to their passion for saving men's souls, and the techniques which the more able among them used to illustrate these twin motives were often more penetrating and imaginative than those of less talented authors. Charles Edwards, for instance, was a brilliantly perceptive stylist whose major classic, *Y Ffydd Ddi-ffuant* (1677), was coruscated with a wealth of dazzling images. Edwards was anxious to impress upon his countrymen the need to recapture the pure, evangelical faith and the quality of spiritual life which had distinguished their worthy ancestors. Drawing heavily on Old Testament texts which revealed God's claim upon a nation, Edwards invested the rôle of providence with a particular significance for Welshmen. He often pursued as his theme the comparison between the social and religious condition of the Israelites as shown in scripture and the welfare of his benighted countrymen. Just as the Israelites regarded themselves as the elect nation, a people chosen by God and vouchsafed divine guidance as long as they remained true to His command, so too did Charles Edwards view his own nation as standing in a special relationship with the Creator.[85]

[85] Charles Edwards, *Y Ffydd Ddi-ffuant* (1677), pp. 198–214.

In sharp contrast, that equally masterly writer of prose, Ellis Wynne, used his juggler's brilliance with words to mock, parody and satirise the moral laxity, the foibles and affectations, the hypocrisy and pretensions of his countrymen. His *Gweledigaetheu y Bardd Cwsc* (1703) is probably the most penetrating and effective piece of satire in the Welsh language.[86] Culling some of his basic ideas from the satirical works of the Spaniard, Quevedo, as translated into English by Sir Roger L'Estrange, and also the 'Cockney School of Writers of Burlesque', Wynne lashed the moral and social turpitude of his day with considerable vigour and verve. How far Wynne's censoriousness was a reflection of his own personality is difficult to judge: he was no doubt a prudent, fastidious man, not without a dry sense of humour, but one who would brook no lapses from the proprieties implicit in the puritan moral code. Wynne, after all, was a reforming cleric, and in his mischievous and sometimes savage portraits of his contemporaries, one catches the ring of a man who was no respecter of persons and not averse from telling home truths in the most outspoken terms. At any rate, successive generations of readers up to the present day have found not only his scandalous humour and scathing sarcasm, but also his lively and rhythmic prose, compulsive reading.

The reforming zeal and patriotism of Moses Williams took a different form. He was a man of unusually strong human sympathies and his aspirations were more rounded and far-seeing than those of most of his fellow-authors. His pungent sermon to the members of the Society of Antient Britons in 1718, an outspoken attempt to galvanise prosperous London-Welshmen into charitable activity, was a most penetrating diagnosis of the social ills of his nation and a mirror which reflected his burning concern for the welfare of the deprived orders of society. Williams urged the affluent to raise churches, print godly books, establish universities, and build charity schools, hospitals and almshouses, and also dilated passionately on the almost limitless possibilities of social and economic development within Wales.[87] But his plans, like many of his

---

[86] The standard study of Wynne is Gwyn Thomas, *Y Bardd Cwsg a'i Gefndir* (1971).

[87] Moses Williams, *Pregeth a barablwyd yn Eglwys Grist . . . yn 1717* (1718).

more ambitious literary ventures, met with a shabby response. Williams's passionate fondness for his native land, coupled with his outspoken reluctance to defer to rank, made him *persona non grata* in ecclesiastical circles, and, as his talents went unrewarded, his sense of disenchantment progressively grew.[88] Unable to fulfil many of his cherished ambitions, his later years were marked by great personal loneliness and frustration.

Authors with a passion for antiquarianism were invariably fired by ardent patriotism, especially those who were pre-occupied with the nation's 'glorious origins'. Experienced scholars, zealous antiquaries, popular ballad-mongers and poets all took up the cudgels in defence of the *Brut* tradition as outlined in Geoffrey of Monmouth's *Historia Regum Britanniae* (1136).[89] Although the historicity of the *Brut* had come under heavy fire from the sixteenth century onwards, Geoffrey's romantic farrago had stubbornly maintained its lustre in Wales. Blind to the new spirit of critical detachment and inspired by love for their nation and its past, Welsh authors deplored those who dismissed Geoffrey's tale as 'a mere chimera',[90] choosing instead to cling to fabrications which had long since foundered on the rocks of critical scholarship. But it is perhaps rather too easy to be contemptuous of their values: it should be borne in mind that Welsh historians were cut off from archival material and were untrained in the handling of available documents and in methods of criticism and analysis. These methodological shortcomings, moreover, were aggravated by an intensely fervent patriotism which served only to cloud the image of historical truth. Theophilus Evans's *Drych y Prif Oesoedd* (1716) is a classic example of a work vitiated by incorrigible romanticism and uncritical handling of sources.[91] Medieval fables and legends, the

---

[88] John Davies, *Bywyd a Gwaith Moses Williams (1685–1742)* (1937), chapter seven.

[89] This voluminous literature includes Thomas Jones (ed.), *Ymadrodd Gweddaidd ynghylch Diwedd y Byd* (1703); Theophilus Evans, *Drych y Prif Oesoedd* (1716); Ellis ab Ellis, *Hanes y Cymru* (1717); Henry Rowlands, *Mona Antiqua Restaurata* (1723); Thomas William, *Oes Lyfr* (1724). See also B.L., Add. MS. 14874, pp. 83–4; N.L.W., Cwrtmawr MS. 45B, p. 214; Cwrtmawr MS. 189A, p. 5; Cwrtmawr MS. 211A. Cf. B. F. Roberts, 'Ymagweddu at Brut y Brenhinedd hyd 1890', *B.B.C.S.*, XXIV (1971), 122–38.

[90] As did Simon Thomas in *The History of the Cymbri* (1746), p. 135. Cf. William Lloyd, *An Historical Account of Church-Government* (1684), sig. A8v.

[91] David Thomas, 'Ffynonellau, Arddull a Chymeriad Gwaith Llenyddol Theophilus Evans' (unpubl. Univ. of Wales M.A. thesis, 1937); G. H. Hughes (ed.), *Drych y Prif Oesoedd 1716* (1968), Introduction.

testimony of Church Fathers, early Welsh manuscripts and current theological polemics were all grist to Evans's mill as he prepared this vivid and widely-read book. A victim of his own youthful prejudices, Evans spurned current standards of historical scepticism in favour of his ardent patriotism. His inflexibility was also apparent in his religious views: a dourly conservative high churchman, Evans strove desperately throughout his life to douche the fires of enthusiasm. Where Ellis Wynne flashed a devastating rapier, Theophilus Evans wielded a heavy broadsword whenever schismatics were a target for his spleen. Dissenters and Methodists alike were forced to suffer his unabated virulence,[92] and it was surely filial piety alone which prompted his grandson to describe him as a man filled with the milk of human kindness,[93] for the overwhelming impression one gains of Theophilus Evans is of a waspishly contentious bigot totally devoid of human warmth.

Bound up with the attachment of authors to the past was their affection for the Welsh language. It is too often argued that hard-headed puritan reformers looked upon language in purely utilitarian terms, as a medium of communication and no more. A good deal of evidence suggests that many of them thought it vital that a language which had 'so unaccountably lasted hitherto through all changes'[94] should be preserved and enriched. The decline of the Welsh language in terms of status and prestige was a perennial theme for lament.[95] Here was a language, mourned Griffith Owens of Pwllheli, 'lately overgrown . . . with thorns and briars', a tongue wanting for nothing 'to make it famous save a king to speak it'.[96] Never purblind to the antiquity, etymology and fluency of the language, grammarians waxed discontentedly at the lapses from linguistic purity in the Welshman's vocabulary and published dictionaries and grammars to stiffen 'the old and

[92] Theophilus Evans, *Galwedigaeth Ddifrifol J'r Crynwyr* (1715); idem, *Cydymddiddan rhwng Dau Wr yn ammau ynghylch Bedydd-Plant* (1719); idem, *Prydferthwch Sancteiddrwydd yn y Weddi Gyffredin* (1722); idem, *The History of Modern Enthusiasm* (1752).

[93] Theophilus Jones, *A History of the County of Brecknock* (3 vols., 1909–11), II, 248.

[94] Jeremy Owen, *The Goodness and Severity of God* (1717), p. 10.

[95] Thomas Jones, *Newydd oddiwrth y Seer* (1684), sig. A1v–A2r; Simon Jones, *Dr. Wells's Letter to a Friend* (1730), sig. A2r; N.L.W. MS. 17B, p. 22; John Prichard Prŷs, *Difyrrwch Crefyddol* (1721), sig. A3r–v; U.C.N.W.L., Bangor MS. 421, p. 331.

[96] U.C.N.W.L., Penrhos (VII), MS. 933.

most excellent British language'.[97] Earnest attempts were made to extol the virtues of the language. Arguing a seductive case for its primaeval dignity, Thomas Jones of Shrewsbury maintained that Welsh was the language 'that God himself spoke to Adam and others for about two thousand years after the creation'.[98] Romantic lucubrations of this kind, thinly-substantiated but thick with passion, were considerably stiffened by the publication of the Abbé Pezron's *L'Antiquité de la nation et la langue des Celtes* (1703), which argued that the language was one of the mother tongues of Europe.[99] Pezron's work exercised a powerful influence on patriotic Welsh scholars, notably Moses Williams, Henry Rowlands, William Wotton and Edward Lhuyd. The latter, in particular, was a much venerated figure in scholarly circles.[100] Indeed, no other Welsh author of this time could rival this asthmatic, penurious scholar in breadth of scholarship. The illegitimate son of a Llanforda squire, Lhuyd had swiftly made his way in the academic world, being appointed keeper of the Ashmolean Museum, Oxford, in 1690–1. By dint of careful and minute observation, tireless energy, and an ability to treat a broad range of complex subjects in a learned and perceptive fashion, Lhuyd established himself as the foremost authority on the Celtic languages. Although his studies were pursued, according to Thomas Hearne, 'purely out of love to the good of learning and his country', his scientific approach to a variety of topics provided an important corrective to the romantic amateurism of his counterparts in Wales. It is one of the tragedies of Welsh history that his brilliant career was cut short by his death from pleurisy at the age of forty-nine.

A host of personal reasons compelled Welsh authors to write books. Conscious of the brevity of man's sojourn on earth and the grinding inevitability of death, many reformers were anxious to provide their countrymen with permanent reminders of the cardinal Christian truths which they preached

---

[97] Thomas Jones, *Y Gymraeg yn ei Disgleirdeb* (1688); John Rhydderch, *The English and Welch Dictionary* (1725), idem, *Grammadeg Cymraeg* (1728); William Gambold, *A Welsh Grammar* (1727).
[98] Thomas Jones, *Newyddion oddiwrth y Seer* (1684), sig. A8v.
[99] P. T. J. Morgan, 'The Abbé Pezron and the Celts', *T.H.S.C.*, Part 2, 1965, pp. 286–95. Pezron's work was translated into English in 1706.
[100] Frank Emery, *Edward Lhuyd F.R.S., 1660–1709* (1971), *passim*.

from day to day.[101] Various maladies provoked others to put
pen to paper. Laid low by illness, David Maurice compensated
for his inability to carry out his pastoral duties by translating
devotional books and financing educational schemes in his
locality.[102] Although the effects of tuberculous laryngitis
turned John Morgan's natural melancholy and introspection
into active misery, he remained thankful that he was still able
to commit his convictions to the printed word.[103] Some authors
were animated by the entreaties of friends, some wished to
present fellow-parishioners with tokens of their gratitude, and
others sharpened their quills, like Edward Samuel, lest they
'should be tired with idleness'.[104] One motive which authors
did not share with many of their modern counterparts,
however, was their willingness to write and publish without
recompense for their labours. Only one author, Iaco ab Dewi,
could claim that translating books and copying manuscripts
was 'his chief subsistence', and it is perhaps significant that this
talented but mysterious semi-recluse lived a 'poor and obscure
life', partly through choice and partly through circumstances,
on the very margins of penury.[105] On the other hand, it was
common for those who were commissioned by various trusts or
charitable bodies to receive some remuneration for their work.
Thomas Baddy of Denbigh was paid seven guineas by the
trustees of the Dr. Williams's Fund for translating and correcting
Daniel Williams's *Vanity of Childhood and Youth* (1691) in
1729.[106] The S.P.C.K., too, sometimes rewarded Welsh
authors with payment in kind: Thomas Richards of Llanfyllin
was presented with fifty copies of his translation of Edmund
Gibson's *Pastoral Letter* in 1727.[107] In the provinces it was usual
for booksellers and publishers to buy copyrights from authors,
arrange for printing and its costs, and then gather in the

[101] Stephen Hughes (ed.), *Tryssor i'r Cymru* (1677), sig. A2r-v; Edward Lloyd,
Egwyddor i rai Jevaingc (1682), sig. A4v.
[102] David Maurice, *Cwnffwrdd i'r Gwan Gristion* (1700), p. 3.
[103] John Morgan, *Bloedd-nad ofnadwy Yr udcorn diweddaf* (1704), p. 2.
[104] Thomas Williams, *Ymadroddion Bucheddol ynghylch Marwolaeth* (1691), sig.
A2r; Edward Lloyd, *Egwyddor i rai Jevaingc*, sig. A5r; Bod., MS. Ashmole 1817A,
f. 425.
[105] G. H. Hughes, *Iaco ab Dewi, 1648–1722* (1953), p. 16.
[106] W. A. Evans, 'Thomas Baddy ac Ymddiriedolwyr Cronfa Dr. Daniel
Williams', *Y Cofiadur*, 27 (1957), 21.
[107] Clement, p. 229.

profits. At best, a small minority of authors might receive a few pounds for their endeavours,[108] but most had little or no hope of cash rewards.

IV. AUTHORS AND THEIR PATRONS

Prior to publishing their works, Anglican authors were often disposed to secure the imprimatur of some eminent Maecenas.[109] This was partly a natural progression from the praises traditionally offered by Welsh bards and authors to men of status; but it was also a stereotype much used by their English counterparts. Dissenters, for their part, tended to disdain the rhetorical embellishments and fulsome testimonies that marked epistles and dedications as fawning insincerities.[110] Behind the rhetorical sycophancy and favour-currying prose, however, there lay important motives for such dedications. For impoverished or pusillanimous authors, it was vital in terms of social prestige. Securing the approval of a local dignitary clearly helped to invest a book with enhanced status and increased the likelihood of sales. Books blessed by men who counted within a community would undoubtedly be regarded as prestigious objects to be kept and cherished. Apprehensiveness also stimulated authors to seek the commendation of some influential figure, for some were pathological in their fear of slanderous attacks. Thomas Jones yearned despairingly to be rid of the 'scurrilous aspersions' of 'brutish clowns', whilst Samuel Williams was always mindful of the need for 'generous foster-fathers' or 'brave defenders' lest his books should fall foul of some acerbic Momus.[111]

In many ways, dedications were a reciprocal arrangement: for certain favours or for the promise of patronage, authors often promised to enshrine the memories of their patrons in the most laudatory terms.[112] Both Edward Samuel and Moses

---

[108] Jenkin Jones of Llwynrhydowen clearly gained small profits. See *J.W.B.S.*, I (1914), 230.

[109] Theophilus Evans, *Drych y Prif Oesoedd* (1716), sig. A2r–v.

[110] See the scornful comments of Simon Thomas in *The Arminian Heresy* (1742), pp. i–ii.

[111] Thomas Jones, *An Astrological Speculation of the late Prodigy* (1681), sig. A3r; *idem*, *Y Gymraeg yn ei Disgleirdeb*, sig. A4v; Samuel Williams, *Amser a Diwedd Amser*, sig. A2r; N.L.W., Llanstephan MS. 146E. no pagination.

[112] Evan Evans dedicated his *Y Llyfr Gweddi Gyffredin*, *Y Cydymmaith Gorau* (1693) to Sir John Wynn of Wynnstay, whilst Abel Morgan dedicated his *Cyd-Gordiad Egwyddorawl o'r Scrythurau* (1730) to David Lloyd, chief justice of Pennsylvania.

Williams invoked Robert Price of Giler as a fitting paradigm.[113] Price had been appointed attorney-general for south Wales in 1682 and his subsequent progress in the legal profession was meteoric: in 1702 he was made a baron of the exchequer and in 1726 one of the judges of the court of Common Pleas. But one particular deed of his had already endeared him to Welshmen. In 1695, Price had won the universal gratitude of his countrymen for successfully opposing in Parliament the grant of the lordships of Denbigh, Bromfield and Yale by William III to his Dutch favourite, the earl of Portland. Price assumed the rôle of spokesman for the nation and his eloquent arguments against this rash and exorbitant royal whim won him a secure place in the hearts of Welshmen.[114] Such a 'bold Briton' was clearly the ideal patron and Welsh authors knew full well that any book dedicated to Price would be guaranteed a favourable reception among the reading public.

Just as dedicating books to influential patrons was a well-established literary convention, so were gestures of self-abnegation an age-old trait among authors.[115] Fear of criticism or an adverse reception could lead to quite genuine self-effacement and humility.[116] But self-deprecation or mock-modesty was also often a ploy to ward off potential snipers. 'An unshapely and imperfect abortion' was Moses Williams's description of his *Cofrestr* in 1717, whilst Alban Thomas apologised profusely for his 'coarse jacket' in 1722.[117] Joshua Thomas blushed at the thought of his clumsy translations, while Jenkin Jones coyly styled himself an unscholarly, unskilful and unproficient Welshman.[118] Sometimes, of course, humility was feigned in order to gloss over literary deficiencies: Benjamin Meredith declared that he could boast of nothing save his poverty and weakness, whilst John Harri, mindful of his shortcomings, confessed that his offering, like the widow's

---

[113] Moses Williams, *Pregeth* (1718); Edward Samuel, *Prif Ddledswyddau Christion* (1723).

[114] *D.W.B.*; Edmund Curll, *The Life of the late Honourable Robert Price* (1934), pp. 11–13.

[115] H. S. Bennett, *English Books and Readers, 1475 to 1557* (1969), pp. 55–6.

[116] See, for example, the prefatory verses in Thomas William, *Oes Lyfr* (1724), sig. A3v.

[117] Moses Williams, *Cofrestr* (1717), p. 3; Alban Thomas, *Dwyfawr Rym Buchedd Grefyddol* (1722), sig. A4r.

[118] Joshua Thomas, *Llyfr Du y Gydwybod* (1723), sig. A1v; *idem*, *Golwg ar Destament Newydd* (1728), p. vi; Jenkin Jones, *Llun Agrippa* (1723), p. 2.

contribution in the scriptures, was a mere two farthings among so many good things.[119] Their timidity was countered by a small minority who were always prepared to put their critics to the sword. Thomas Jones's instinctive reaction to his detractors was to challenge them to emulate his achievements, whilst John Thomas vented the feelings of many of his colleagues by claiming that if carping critics were allowed to rule the roost no author would ever summon up enough courage to put pen to paper.[120]

V. AUTHORS AND THEIR BOOKS

It should be borne in mind that the task of writing and translating books in this period was not, in a physical sense, the comfortable task it can be today. Only gentlemen, clergymen and ministers would have had adequately-lit studies, and most authors were ill-equipped with quill pens, muddy ink and poor quality paper. Even though the majority of Welsh books were practical tracts of no great length, authors seldom dragged their feet in producing their manuscripts.[121] Not unexpectedly, the most prolific authors were clergymen, ministers and printers—men who had obvious vested interests in the publishing trade. Among the clergy, the average production was two or three books per author, though Edward Samuel and Thomas Williams published respectively four and five fairly substantial volumes. Dafydd Lewys was the author of five tracts, including his trail-blazing scientific *pot-pourri*, *Golwg ar y Byd* (1725), whilst Robert Lloyd, rector of Hirnant, keeping a weather eye on the morals of his flock, translated six small devotional books. Others were endowed with almost frenetic energy: Theophilus Evans, one of the most skilled and sensitive translators of his time, published sixteen editions (including reprints) of his works within his lifetime. Few, too, possessed the vigour of Moses Williams: his versatility as author, translator, editor, antiquary, rescuer of scarce literature,

[119] Benjamin Meredith, *Pechadur Jerusalem yn Gadwedig* (1721), Preface; John Harri, *Rhai Datguddiadau o'r Nefoedd Newydd* (1725), p. xvii.
[120] Thomas Jones (ed.), *Llyfr o Weddiau Duwiol* (1707), p. 280; John Thomas, *Unum Necessarium* (1680), sig. A1r.
[121] Bod., MS. Ashmole 1817A, ff. 424, 428; *Y Cofiadur*, 1957, pp. 28–30; Clement, pp. 131, 294–5.

and copyist was such that, by simply attempting too much, his own development as an original scholar of character and sympathy was considerably stunted.[122]

Literary-minded Dissenters like Charles Edwards and Stephen Hughes were able to publish freely under the auspices of the Welsh Trust, and their output was thus exceptional. Among their successors, James Owen and Thomas Baddy each contributed five tracts, whilst the vigorous patronage offered by the squirearchy of south-west Wales made possible the publication of seven major translations by Iaco ab Dewi between 1714 and 1719, and a further posthumous publication in 1730. Printers and publishers were naturally in a position to exercise their literary talents. Thomas Jones sustained a regular flow of Welsh almanacs, printed and distributed Welsh and English newspapers for a brief period, collected editions of poetry and prayers, compiled a dictionary, and translated a wide range of very different books. His successor, John Rhydderch, was hardly less industrious, being responsible for writing, translating or editing at least twenty-one books, ten of which were ballads.

Apart from learned antiquaries, very few Welsh authors published English books in this period. Most of them clearly considered that their primary responsibility was to save the souls of the monoglot majority. Those who did write in English were generally men who had received the benefits of higher education. Prior to his election to the see of St. Asaph, George Griffith had involved himself in a vitriolic oral and printed controversy with Vavasor Powell during the Commonwealth years, and later, as bishop, he contributed towards the revision of the Prayer Book of 1662, but never lived to see the publication of his *Plain Discourses on the Lord's Supper* in 1684.[123] An unsuccessful candidate for the see of St. Asaph in the 1690s, David Maurice, published one of his most winsome sermons 'for the support of weak Christians' in 1700, whilst Griffith Jones, successively rector of Bodfari and Denbigh, indulged his penchant for sabre-rattling by publishing four polemical tracts

[122] John Davies, op. cit., pp. 139–41.
[123] George Griffith wrote *A Bold Challenge of an itinerant preacher modestly answered by a local minister* (1652); *A Relation of a Disputation* (1653); *A Welsh Narrative Corrected* (1653). Cf. *N.L.W.J.*, XII (1962), 298–301.

in English between 1720 and 1735.[124] The many-sided rector of Llanfyllin, Thomas Richards, hailed by his Oxford tutor as the best Latin poet since Virgil and saluted by the Quaker, John Kelsall, as 'a pretty fair man', published some of his English sermons, translated several popular English ballads, favoured the establishment with a fulsome elegy (in Latin hexameters) on the death of Queen Caroline, and defended his nation from the calumnies of Edward Holdsworth with a characteristically shrewd piece of satire.[125] On a more popular plane, Thomas Jones served his apprenticeship as an astrologer in London by venturing his version of the significance of Halley's Comet in 1681 and the astrological significance of moles in 1684.[126]

Significantly, those Dissenting authors who lapsed into the English tongue were men who spent an appreciable part of their lives in England. During his sojourn in London, Charles Edwards compiled his *Fatherly Instructions* (1686), a collection of extracts from patristic writings, a prickly sermon, *Gildas Minimus*, designed to dissuade men from apostasy, and the tragic tale of his own life in 1691.[127] James Owen had moved to Oswestry in 1676 where, some fifteen years later, he established an academy which he took with him on his departure to Shrewsbury in 1700. Throughout this period, Owen immersed himself in current doctrinal squabbles, establishing a high degree of expertise in the thorny questions of ordination, paedobaptism and occasional conformity, publishing ten English books and leaving three others in manuscript.[128] Matthias Maurice's removal to England was more fortuitous: in 1712 an act of malice by one of his enemies betrayed him into the hands of a press-gang at Haverfordwest, which frog-marched him to its naval frigate and set sail for Woolwich. Maurice was eventually released and, from 1714

[124] David Maurice, *The Bruised Reed* (1700); Griffith Jones wrote *A Short View of the Controversie about Episcopacy and our Church Communion* (2nd ed., 1720); *A Sermon preach'd at St. Hilary's chapel in Denbigh* (1728); *A Letter to a Proselyte of the Church of Rome* (1731); *Popish Objections against Protestants briefly answer'd* (1735).
[125] Clement, p. 120n; Friends' House Library, Kelsall MSS. Diaries, IV, 35; Richard Williams, op. cit., pp. 119–20; Thomas Richards, *The Nativity of Christ* (1728) and *The Happiness of Good Christians after Death* (1733). See also Richards's *Hoglandia, or, a description of Hampshire* (1709), in answer to Edward Holdsworth's *Muscipula* (1709).
[126] Thomas Jones, *An Astrological Speculation* (1681); *The Famous Fortune-Teller, or the Manifestation of Moles* (1684).
[127] D. L. Morgan, op. cit., pp. 363–412.
[128] Charles Owen, op. cit., pp. 100–111.

until his death in 1738, he served, with remarkable success, as pastor of Rothwell in Northamptonshire. During his career in Wales, Matthias was often his own worst enemy, allowing his volatile, abrasive manner to give deep offence to those authors who differed from him. Never a man to be crossed lightly, he seldom softened his resentments in doctrinal struggles and he continued, during his ministry in England, to drum out the doctrines of high Calvinism, notably in his most celebrated work, *Social Religion Exemplify'd* (1759).[129] Finally, the career of Simon Thomas is shrouded in mystery: a native of Cardiganshire, this angular, egocentric and fiercely learned polemicist was established in Hereford by 1711 as a Presbyterian minister and silk-mercer, who made use of a private press to launch bitter attacks on the Prayer Book and Pelagianism, and to chip away at the mouldering edifice of the *Brut* tradition.[130]

Most Welsh authors bought English and Welsh best-sellers with some constancy, and the careful stress which they laid on the disposal of their books and manuscripts in their wills is eloquent testimony to the value which they attached to their literary possessions. The clergy were especially solicitous, rarely allowing their books to slip outside their family circle. Rondl Davies, vicar of Meifod, bequeathed all his books and papers to his son, William, and John Morgan, vicar of Matchin, made the bequest of his books to his brother, Edward, the very first item in his will.[131] Samuel Williams, vicar of Llandyfriog, bequeathed all his books, valued at the enormous sum of £41 2s. 6d., to his son, Moses, who added them to his own superb specialist collection.[132] Some clerical wills were also hedged around with certain conditions. William Gambold, rector of Puncheston, left his books and manuscripts to his son, John, charging him with the duty of paying £3 apiece to his brothers and sisters should he determine to publish any of his manuscripts.[133] John Morgan, vicar of Aberconwy, bequeathed

---

[129] *H.P.N.*, p. 303–5.

[130] *D.W.B.*; *The Arminian Heresy* (1742); *Remarks upon a small Treatise entitl'd The Beauty of Holiness in the Book of Common Prayer* (1734); *The History of the Cymri* (1746).

[131] N.L.W., St. Asaph P.R. 1696; Essex Record Office P.R. 1733, D/ABW 90/30.

[132] N.L.W., Archdeaconry of Cardigan P.R. 1722.

[133] N.L.W., Archdeaconry of Cardigan P.R. 1728. For some of Gambold's manuscripts, see N.L.W. MS. 3488A and N.L.W., Llanstephan MSS. 189B, 190B, 191A.

the works of Richard Allestree and Henry Hammond's commentary on the New Testament 'to the public use of the Cathedral-Church of Bangor, to be laid there on a desk with chains to them', whilst Walter Price, vicar of Llangwm, insisted that his books should be 'well-looked-after and kept without wasting' at the home of the vicar of Pembrey, Carmarthenshire, for his own personal use and also for the benefit of the vicar of Llanelli.[134] Dissenting authors made similar arrangements: the bulk of the books in Stephen Hughes's study, valued at £15, was bequeathed to his son, Stephen, and twenty other books to his daughter, Jane.[135] Similarly, William Evans, academy tutor at Carmarthen, divided his books between his sons, William and Daniel, and allowed his daughter, Margaret, twelve books to be chosen for her.[136] Having dedicated no small part of their lives to writing and translating books of their own, and buying, borrowing and reading the labours of others, it was fitting that Welsh authors should, in their final hour, ensure that their literary possessions be securely bequeathed and lovingly handled by their descendants.

[134] N.L.W., Bangor P.R. 1702; St. Asaph P.R. 1738.
[135] N.L.W., Archdeaconry of Carmarthen P.R. 1688.
[136] N.L.W., Archdeaconry of Carmarthen P.R. 1718.

IX

THE PRINTING AND PUBLISHING TRADE

I. THE GROWTH OF THE PRINTING PRESS

The printing press, claimed Lewis Morris enthusiastically in 1735, was 'the Candle of the World, and the Freedom of Britain's sons'.[1] Such rhapsodies had been commonplace in Tudor England and were not unknown in the tiny handful of early printed books in Welsh. But literate Welshmen were rather more tardy than most in being able to achieve their ambition of seeing Welsh books flowing regularly from the press. Even so, it must be borne in mind that Welsh was one of the few small European languages in which serious effort was made to print books. Prior to 1695, the licensing laws laid down that books might be published only in London, Oxford or Cambridge. Printing and publishing Welsh books outside Wales, an ordeal which had taxed even the most resilient of their Renaissance forebears, still posed daunting problems to Welsh authors. The paramount problem was that London compositors were unfamiliar with the Welsh language and their products, therefore, were invariably grievously disfigured by printing errors and infelicities. A good many prefaces to Welsh books published in the Restoration period were suffused with face-saving apologies by contrite authors for the flaw-ridden products of the English press.[2] Having begged the reader's indulgence, it became fashionable to urge him to consult the errata (usually equally hastily compiled) and make the necessary corrections himself.

The aspirations of Welsh authors and publishers were constantly frustrated not only by the poor workmanship of printers and booksellers in London, but also by their parsimony and perversity. During his campaign to publish a new edition

---

[1] Lewis Morris, *Tlysau yr Hen Oesoedd* (1735), p. 3.
[2] See, for instance, John Hughes, *Allwydd Paradwys* (1670), p. 481; Rondl Davies, *Profiad yr Ysprydion* (1675), sig. Hh2r–v.

of the Welsh Bible in the 1670s, Stephen Hughes indulged in several tirades against their niggardliness and fraudulence,[3] and would doubtless have subscribed to Aubrey's judgment of them as 'Jews and blockheads'.[4] Few authors, whether Welsh or English, were in a position to bargain with them. As Isaac Chauncy pointed out to Thomas Edwards of Rhual, 'if a man gives anything to the bookseller to print, they stand upon taking as many copies as will answer their gains, while if anyone prints at his own charge they will sell no copies for him'.[5] It was into this world of incompetence and sharp practice that the 'father of Welsh publishing' emerged in the late-1670s. Thomas Jones, son of a Corwen tailor, abandoned his father's trade soon after his migration to London around 1666.[6] The capital had always offered young men of humble parentage a wide range of opportunities to discover a life true to their talents and sensibilities, and Jones chose bookselling as his ladder to fame. From the outset, he nursed fond hopes of distributing Welsh books of high technical quality at cheap rates, but he swiftly found that all books were subject to the stringent laws of profit, supply and demand. Like his predecessors, Jones became increasingly frustrated by the unreliability, bumbling inadequacies and fraudulent practices of printers and publishers in London.[7] Some of the distributors of his almanacs, moreover, proved to be shameless cheats, and as early as 1681 he was forced to sue John Braynton and John Jackson, haberdashers of Cateaten Street, London, in order to recover money on his first batch of almanacs.[8] In Wales, corrupt pedlars and shopkeepers like Evan Lloyd of Haverfordwest—'a pox-ridden, saturnine rogue'—feathered their nests by covertly raising the price of his books and making off

[3] Stephen Hughes (ed.), *Gwaith Mr. Rees Prichard*, IV, (1672), sig. A4v.
[4] Cited in J. Williams, 'An Edition of the Correspondence of John Aubrey with Anthony à Wood and Edward Lhuyd, 1667–96' (unpubl. University of London Ph.D. thesis, 1967), p. 218.
[5] B. E. Howells (ed.), *A Calendar of Letters relating to North Wales* (1967), p. 260.
[6] Thomas Jones is noticed in *D.W.B.* For fuller accounts, see Thomas Shankland, 'Joseph Harris a Chychwyniad Llenyddiaeth Gyfnodol yng Nghymru', *Trafodion Cymdeithas Hanes Bedyddwyr Cymru*, 1912–3, pp. 10–19; D. R. Phillips, 'Thomas Jones the Almanacer', *J.W.B.S.*, 1–2 (1915–8), 239–44, 97–104; Ll. C. Lloyd, 'The Book Trade in Shropshire', *Trans. Shropshire Archaeological and Natural History Soc.*, 1935–6, pp. 131–9.
[7] Thomas Jones, *Y Gymraeg yn ei Disgleirdeb* (1688), sig. X7r–X8r.
[8] Thomas Jones, *An Astrological Speculation of the late Prodigy* (1681), p. 10.

with the profits.[9] Moreover, the slow rhythm of communications, the unreliability of carriers, and the spiralling costs of distributing his products aggravated his disillusionment. With the change in the licensing laws in 1695, Thomas Jones was offered greater freedom of manoeuvre, and his finely-tuned commercial instincts took him to Shrewsbury, where he established his own printing-office at Hill's Lane.

Thomas Jones's choice was no accident, for Shrewsbury was the ideal centre for an aspiring publisher of Welsh books: a nodal point for a whole network of cross-road posts and linked by water to the Severn valley, the capital of Shropshire was a populous and flourishing market town so much frequented by Welshmen that Defoe believed that on market day 'you would think you were in Wales'.[10] Once established, Jones swiftly ensured that Shrewsbury became the centre of the Welsh printing trade, a pre-eminence that persisted throughout the eighteenth century.[11] The catalogue of misfortunes which dogged his career in London, however, did not cease with his removal to the provinces. Many of his troubles began in the early 1680s as a result of his uncompromising interpretation of the royal grant which vested in him a monopoly for the publication of Welsh almanacs.[12] From then on, Jones kept an eagle eye open for rival publications, warning his readers to shun the counterfeit piracies of 'predatory misers' and offering rewards for secret information.[13] But once he had moved to the provinces, his monopoly was thrown into jeopardy, since potential rivals could argue that his copyright had expired, if not at the death of Charles II, then certainly when printing restrictions were lifted in 1695. By the turn of the century, Thomas Jones's worst fears were confirmed when John Jones, a Dissenter of Caeau near Wrexham, began publishing an annual Welsh almanac from 1702 onwards. Having only

[9] Thomas Jones, *Newydd oddiwrth y Ser* (1683), sig. C4v; *idem, Newydd oddiwrth y Seer* (1684), sig. C5v–C8r; *idem, Newyddion mawr oddiwrth y Ser* (1691), sig. C7v.

[10] E. Bowen, *Britannia Depicta or Ogilby Improv'd* (1720), p. 127; J. B. Blakeway and H. Owen, *A History of Shrewsbury* (2 vols., 1825), I, 511–2; Daniel Defoe, *A Tour thro' the whole Island of Great Britain* (3 vols., 2nd ed., 1738), II, 313–4.

[11] Eiluned Rees, 'Developments in the Book-Trade in Eighteenth Century Wales', *The Library*, XXIV (1969), 33.

[12] Jones published a copy of his authority, for the benefit of his rivals, in his *Almanac* for 1703, sig. A8r–B1r.

[13] Thomas Jones, *An Astrological Speculation*, p. 10; *idem, Newydd oddiwrth y Ser* (1685), sig. A2r; *idem, [Almanac]* (1708), sig. C7v–C8r.

recently recovered from a series of debilitating illnesses, Thomas Jones did not find his morale fortified by this untimely competition, since it gravely imperilled one of his major sources of income. His spirits were further dampened when a dishonest and querulous apprentice in his employ, Ellis Edward, conspired with John Jones to hire printing equipment, formerly owned by Randle Holme of Chester, which Thomas Jones had bought.[14] On finding that his claims for an increase in wages were constantly refused, Edward had lapsed into a morose dilatoriness, employing a variety of 'knavish tricks' to defraud his master and, save for one occasion when Thomas Jones boxed his ears for spitting contemptuously in his face, the Shrewsbury printer could scarcely handle his cunning and fleet-footed apprentice. Edward went on to smuggle sheets of his employer's almanacs from his printing-house so that John Jones might publish a counterfeit almanac in London.

Henceforward, the two Joneses became involved in a running feud which persisted until Thomas Jones's death in 1713. Since few of John Jones's almanacs have survived, his side of the story is less clear than that of his voluble rival. But since Thomas Jones was paranoid in his fear of competition, the version which he presented in his almanacs was certainly distorted.[15] His egocentricity, irascibility and devastating candour prompted him to dub all his rivals, however innocent and well-meaning, shameless mountebanks, liars and rogues. But, for all his faults, Thomas Jones was a remarkably industrious and versatile figure in the printing world. He broke new ground in many fields. Never afraid to experiment, he devised as one of his most notable schemes a plan for publishing newspapers in Welsh and English. In his almanac for 1691, Jones promised to send a monthly digest in Welsh of all the news published in England during the previous month. His scheme evoked only lukewarm response within Wales, with many shopkeepers and dealers claiming that local news was rather more popular in the

---

[14] This lively tale, presented in a heavily loaded way by Thomas Jones, is printed in his *Almanac* for 1703, sig. A5r–A8r. Some of the issues are discussed in Eiluned Rees and Derek Nuttall, 'Baddy Vindicated, or Jones v Jones', *J.W.B.S.*, X (1970), 127–34.
[15] Thomas Jones, [*Almanac*] (1704), sig. F1r–v; *idem, Y Cyfreithlawn Almanacc Cymraeg* (1706), sig. C8v; *idem,* [*Almanac*] (1708), sig. C8r; *idem,* [*Almanac*] (1712), sig. B8r–v.

localities and that anyway few would be able to afford his monthly bulletins.[16] Nothing daunted, Jones launched a similar venture in 1706 for the benefit of English readers in the provinces. This entailed the publication of a weekly English newspaper—'A collection of all the material News'—a digest of news, costing 2d., culled largely from London papers.[17] Thomas Jones clearly hoped to play a part in the general growth of provincial newspapers at the turn of the century, but undertakings of this sort were inevitably hampered by financial and organisational problems and also by the attenuated market at his disposal.[18] Not surprisingly, therefore, his second project died of inanition.

Nevertheless, the wide range of books which flowed steadily from his press indicates that Thomas Jones was assured of brisk sales. Despite his claims that profit was not his motive, he was a businessman to his finger-tips. He made a real effort to keep his prices to a minimum, assuring his readers that their 'old servant' provided books 'without hazarding your money but his own, and at cheaper rates than ever you'll have them of others'.[19] The remarkable range of his publications testifies to his extraordinary energy and his determination to provide his countrymen with edifying reading material. The love which he professed towards his native tongue rings true, and the bardic fraternity, grateful for the opportunity of seeing their work in print, sang his praises gladly.[20] But since Thomas Jones had an unfortunate faculty for making enemies, the paeans of poets were less frequent than the brickbats of his antagonists. Many of his contemporaries, rightly or wrongly, cared little for him. The aggrieved tone which Jones adopted in many of his prefaces may account for this impression, but it is nonetheless true that his paranoid pursuit of rivals made him fair game for mockery and scorn. Scholars like Moses Williams,

[16] Thomas Jones, *Newyddion mawr oddiwrth y Ser* (1691), sig. A2v; *idem, Y mwyaf o'r Almanaccau* (1692), sig. A1v.

[17] Thomas Jones, *Y Cyfreithlawn Almanacc Cymraeg* (1706), sig. C7r; T. W. Hancock, 'The First Shrewsbury Newspaper', *Bye-Gones*, 25 May 1881, p. 240.

[18] G. A. Cranfield, *The Development of the Provincial Newspaper (1700–1760)* (1962), pp. 25, 50.

[19] Thomas Jones, *Y Gymraeg yn ei Disgleirdeb*, sig. a4r; *idem*, [*Almanac*] (1708), sig. C8r.

[20] For some examples see Thomas Jones, *Newydd oddiwrth y Ser* (1683), sig. A4r–v; *idem, Y Gymraeg yn ei Disgleirdeb*, sig. X8r; N.L.W., Llanstephan MS. 15A, p. 31.

horrified by his plagiarism, boastfulness and penchant for gratuitous insults, abused him as 'Tom the Tailor' and, more piercingly, 'Tom-ass';[21] the Welsh gentry bristled on reading his outspoken comments on their greed, oppression, and fondness for things English;[22] his rivals in the printing trade found him a belligerent competitor and a sedulous bearer of grudges;[23] and many of his readers, possibly frustrated by his delphic weather forecasts and his ill-tempered reactions to well-meaning advice, turned their backs on him and opted for the almanacs of John Jones.[24] Even so, there is no doubt that Thomas Jones was utterly dedicated to his profession, and the spur which his activity gave to the growth of literacy in Wales is hard to exaggerate. No one did more than he to ensure that Welsh printed books were disseminated in the most remote rural areas and also that those readers who bought his publications came from lower down the social scale than had been true before. Huw Morys and Owen Gruffydd both paid tribute to his achievement in planting the urge within children to learn to read, whilst Dafydd Manuel sang his praises for sending thousands to their Bibles.[25] Finally, even William Morris of Anglesey, who made the Shrewsbury printer's career the subject of much banter, paid him a sincere, if grudging, tribute: Thomas Jones, he admitted, was 'an old fellow, who, in spite of his ignorance, did a lot of good'.[26]

Thomas Jones's successors were less colourful but no less industrious as printers. His business was largely taken over by Thomas Durston who, as printer and bookseller in Shoemaker's Row from 1711 to 1767, became the most prolific and successful printer in Shrewsbury during the first half of the century.[27] Durston had earlier collaborated with the poet and grammarian

---

[21] See the libellous annotations made by Williams on his copy (N.L.W.,W.S. 50) of *Y Gymraeg yn ei Disgleirdeb* (1688).

[22] In his almanac for 1693 (sig. A1v) Jones unashamedly confessed that he had not learnt to 'compliment the gentry' and indeed had been 'too saucy' to some of them.

[23] Thomas Jones, [*Almanac*] (1704), sig. F1r–v.

[24] N.L.W., Llanstephan MS. 15A, pp. 120–1; Thomas Jones, [*Almanac*] (1710), sig. A2r.

[25] Thomas Jones, *Newyddion mawr oddiwrth y Ser* (1699), sig. C7v; *idem, Almanac* (1708), sig. B2v; *idem*, [*Almanac*] (1704), sig. F2v. Manuel also penned Jones's elegy. N.L.W. MS. 1244D, pp. 49–55.

[26] *Morris Letters*, I, 198.

[27] Ll. C. Lloyd, op. cit., pp. 101–3. Durston's will is in Lichfield Record Office, P.R. 1767.

of Cemaes, John Rhydderch, who eventually set up on his own as printer and publisher in Shrewsbury in 1715.[28] In the period from 1713 to 1730, the fact that most Welsh books were issued from the respective presses of Durston and Rhydderch, together with their readiness to accommodate authors and ballad-mongers of all shapes and sizes, won them many eulogies from grateful clients.[29] Receptive they might have been to the wishes of Welsh authors; as printers, however, they were versatile but neglectful, well-meaning but prone to error.[30] On his arrival at the Welsh borders, Thomas Jones had been mortified to find himself in 'a country not furnished with journeymen printers',[31] and the almost indecent haste with which his successors issued and distributed their books betrayed lack of experience and was achieved only at the price of shoddy and careless composition. William Wynn of Llangynhafal despaired of achieving 'any correctness' at Shrewsbury, whilst Lewis Morris shuddered at the thought of placing manuscripts in Durston's 'dirty hands'.[32] Having examined a succession of prayer books printed at Shrewsbury, his brother, William, was equally withering in his criticisms: he found them 'intolerable—bad paper, bad print, bad orthography, bad everything except the subject matter'.[33] On the other hand, it should be remembered that the printing standards required by the Morrises of Anglesey were considerably higher than those which the ordinary reading public had come to expect. Pressed by impatient authors and expectant readers, Shrewsbury printers could scarcely hope to produce books of meticulous print and lavish binding. Never ones to burden themselves with scruples, they made their main reputation by peddling counterfeit material rather than by any aesthetic qualities.[34]

---

[28] Bob Owen, 'Siôn Rhydderch yr Almanaciwr, 1673–1735', *J.W.B.S.*, III (1930), 275–90.

[29] See, for instance, Richard Parry, *Drych Angau* (1714), no pagination.

[30] Ll.C. Lloyd, op. cit., p. 86. But see a more favourable judgment by Brynmor Jones, 'Argraffwyr Cymreig y Gororau', *J.W.B.S.*, X (1970), 120–1.

[31] Thomas Jones, [*Almanac*] (1703), sig. A7v.

[32] *Morris Letters*, II, p. 338; G. J. Williams (ed.), 'Llythyrau at Ddafydd Jones o Drefriw', supplement to *N.L.W.J.*, III (1943), 16.

[33] *Morris Letters*, I, 82.

[34] J. H. Davies, 'Early Welsh Bibliography', *T.H.S.C.*, 1897–8, pp. 14–15; Eiluned Rees, 'Welsh Publishing before 1717', *Essays in Honour of Victor Scholderer* (1970), pp. 333–4.

In spite of the infelicities and piracies which marked the printing trade in Shrewsbury, the demand for printed literature continued to grow. Once commercial letterpress printing was established in Chester from 1712 onwards, Welsh authors in north-east Wales, notably Thomas Baddy of Denbigh, took advantage of the new facilities on their doorstep.[35] The same demand created the first official printing press on Welsh soil at Trefhedyn, near Newcastle Emlyn in south Cardiganshire, in 1718.[36] Here Isaac Carter, a native of Carmarthenshire, printed five Welsh books before moving to Carmarthen in 1725 where he printed five more by 1733.[37] In the meantime, Nicholas Thomas, a native of Cenarth who had served his apprenticeship as a printer in Shrewsbury (probably under John Rhydderch), had established his own press at Carmarthen in 1721, and though his typographical equipment was distressingly sub-standard, the largesse of local squires enabled him to satisfy the thirst for printed books in the communities of the south-west.[38] The location of these presses is readily explained. In this area, a virile literary tradition, centred on the Teifi valley but spanning the three counties of Cardigan, Carmarthen and Pembroke, had flourished since the days of the *penceirddiaid* (chief poets).[39] The traditional love of poetry and prose, now injected with a vigorous religious flavour, galvanised Anglicans and Dissenters alike to sustain local printing presses in a bid to maintain those traditions and to foster the growth of literacy. Moreover, Carmarthen itself was the commercial capital of south-west Wales, a town of some three thousand inhabitants who were reputedly 'the wealthiest and politest' in the Principality.[40] Like Shrewsbury, Carmarthen was also an important centre of communications by land and water, whilst the existence of a well-established grammar school and a flourishing Dissenting academy meant

---

[35] Derek Nuttall, *A History of Printing in Chester from 1688 to 1965* (1969), p. 15.
[36] J. Ifano Jones, *Printing and Printers in Wales and Monmouthshire* (1925), p. 34.
[37] Ibid., pp. 34–5, 39–40; David Jenkins, 'Braslun o Hanes Argraffu yn sir Aberteifi', *J.W.B.S.*, VII (1953), 176–7.
[38] Eiluned Rees, *The Library*, 1969, p. 35.
[39] J. Ifano Jones, op. cit., pp. 35–8; G. J. Williams, 'Daniel Ddu o Geredigion a'i Gyfnod', *Y Llenor*, V (1926), 48; G. Bowen, 'Traddodiad Llenyddol Deau Ceredigion, 1600–1850' (unpubl. Univ. of Wales M.A. thesis, 1943), *passim*.
[40] E. Bowen, op. cit., p. 245; Defoe, op. cit., II, 284–5; Harold Carter, *The Towns of Wales* (1965), p. 29.

that there were always sufficient clients to support the printing industry and book trade in general.

In the early-1730s, an attempt was made by Lewis Morris to establish a Welsh press at Llannerch-y-medd in Anglesey. Morris established contact with John Rhydderch, who had abandoned his business at Shrewsbury in mysterious circumstances (having possibly fallen victim to lawyers whom he later disparaged as 'oppressive' and 'lustful' ravens)[41] and removed to London around 1728. Clearly in a situation of extreme loneliness and despair, Rhydderch was considerably cheered by Morris's invitation to set him up as a printer in Anglesey.[42] Morris, in fact, cherished grandiose ideals, and his prospectus, issued in 1732, envisaged the establishment not merely of a Welsh press but also of a free school, a Welsh bookshop, a national library and a museum.[43] Thrilled by these exciting prospects, Rhydderch returned to his native land and settled in Anglesey, only to find that Morris's aspirations were not shared by a recalcitrant and penny-pinching gentry on whom such an ambitious venture inevitably depended for its success.[44] Sadly disillusioned by what he considered to be many fine but unfulfilled words, Rhydderch shook off the dust of Anglesey and moved south to Carmarthen where, welcomed by bards and littérateurs of sympathy and good-will, he successfully used Nicholas Thomas's press to publish the first Welsh almanac to be printed in Wales in 1734.

II. THE SUBSCRIPTION METHOD

The practice of financing literature by subscription, first begun in 1617, had become a relatively common feature of the book trade in late-seventeenth-century England.[45] The prime virtue

[41] John Rhydderch, *Newyddion oddiwrth y Ser* (1735), sig. b3r; *idem*, *Newyddion oddiwrth y Ser* (1736), sig. B1r.
[42] Hugh Owen (ed.), *Additional Letters of the Morrises of Anglesey (1735–1786)*, Part I, (1947), pp. 4–5.
[43] B.L. Add. MS. 14911.
[44] Hugh Owen, op. cit., pp. 23–4; John Rhydderch, *Newyddion oddiwrth y Ser* (1734), sig. A1v.
[45] Sarah L. C. Clapp, 'The Beginnings of Subscription Publication in the Seventeenth Century', *Modern Philology*, 29 (1931–2), 199–224; *idem*, 'The Subscription Enterprises of John Ogilby and Richard Blome', *ibid.*, 30 (1932–3), 365–79; Winifred E. Risden, 'New Ventures in Publishing between 1680 and 1700', (unpubl. Univ. of Oxford B.Litt. thesis, 1969), *passim.*; F. J. G. Robinson and P. J. Wallis, *Book Subscription Lists. A Revised Guide* (1975).

of this practice was that it enabled publishers 'to promote books of a great bulk, which cannot be printed otherwise'.[46] In Wales, this method was used by Thomas Gouge and Stephen Hughes in their venture to publish a new edition of the Welsh Bible, which appeared in 1677–8. Both elicited funds from the nobility, bishops, gentry, clergy and merchants of Wales, and promised to reimburse subscribers from the proceeds, though it is not clear whether this scheme of short-term subsidy was in fact undertaken.[47] The chief publisher of Welsh books in the last two decades of the seventeenth century, Thomas Jones, was distinctly chary of putting his readers' cash at risk, and in his early years as a printer, he tended to shun the subscription method.[48] By the turn of the century, however, Welsh authors were beginning to adopt the practice of circulating 'proposals' prior to publication:[49] these proposals normally described the author's intentions, gave a brief synopsis of the contents of the proposed book and an estimate of its price. Some of these advertisements often promised more than they delivered, but those involved in the Welsh publishing trade were rapidly coming to the conclusion that publishing by subscription was an economic necessity.

Although different authors and publishers employed various methods of collecting subscriptions, the general pattern was very similar. Subscribers were usually called upon to pay half the cost of the book when subscribing in advance, and the remaining half upon receipt of the book.[50] Editions which required more than the usual amount of capital or which involved an element of risk were hedged around with more stringent conditions: subscribers to *Ysbrydol Bererindod o'r Aipht i Ganaan* in 1722 paid 6*d.* on deposit, but only a further 4*d.* on delivery.[51] When, in 1727, William Gambold advertised a proposed English-Welsh Dictionary made up of ninety-six

---

[46] The phrase belongs to Thomas Hearne. Cited in S. L. C. Clapp, 'Subscription Publishers prior to Jacob Tonson', *The Library*, XIII (1933), 158.

[47] *Gwaith Mr. Rees Prichard*, IV (1672), sig. a5r.

[48] Thomas Jones, *Almanac* (1708), sig. C8r.

[49] See Edward Samuel's plans in Bod., MS. Ashmole 1817A, f. 426. Subscription schemes especially commended themselves to Welsh Quakers. For details see G. H. Jenkins, 'Quaker and anti-Quaker Literature in Welsh from the Restoration to Methodism', *W.H.R.*, VII (1975), 409–10.

[50] Dafydd Lewys, *Bwyd Enaid* (1723), sig. C8r; *anon.*, *Cyfoeth i'r Cymru* (1731), sig. A3v.

[51] *Anon.*, *Cerydd i'r Cymru* (1722), title-page.

sheets, divided into two parts and published in folio, his terms
were more detailed:

> [It] will be sold to subscribers in sheets at three-half-pence
> a sheet, whereof 10s. to be paid in hand, the remainder on
> delivery of the copies. But if any choose to subscribe for single
> parts, they must be content to pay at the rate of seven farthings
> a sheet, whereof 8s. in hand for the English–Welsh part, and
> 3s. 6d. for the Welsh–English.[52]

Distinct advantages accrued to the subscriber as opposed to
the normal purchaser, particularly if he bought in bulk.
Jenkin Jones's proposed *Yr Eglwys yn y Tŷ* would have cost
subscribers 4d., a penny less than the normal price, whilst those
who subscribed for twelve copies received a baker's dozen.[53]
When John Rhydderch began advertising his *English and
Welsh Dictionary* (1725) in 1719, individual copies were priced
at 1s. 8d., but subscribers were offered a discount of 2s. per
dozen.[54] Similarly, when Moses Williams announced his
intention of publishing a collection of Welsh literature from
the earliest times down to the sixteenth century, he hoped to
sell 250 copies at 5s. each, half of which sum was to be paid in
advance and the remaining half on receipt of the book. Those,
however, who subscribed for copies on royal paper paid 10s.,
and if the total number of subscribers reached 300, Williams
promised to deduct from the second payment one-fifth of the
full price of each volume.[55]

The number of books bearing subscription lists and published
in England multiplied rapidly during the early decades of the
eighteenth century. Before 1701, only 35 subscription lists had
been published, but this figure rose to 89 between 1711 and
1721, and to 222 during 1721–31[56] The same period saw a
growing number of lists published in Welsh books: eighteen
were published between 1707 and 1731.[57] The larger,

---

[52] William Gambold, *A Welsh Grammar* (1727), sig. B3v.
[53] W. R., *Rhai byrr ac eglur Rhesymau* (1722), p. 14.
[54] John Rhydderch, *Newyddion oddiwrth y Ser* (1719), sig. A8v.
[55] Moses Williams, *Proposals for printing by subscription a Collection of Writings in
the Welsh Tongue to the beginning of the Sixteenth Century* (1719).
[56] P. J. Wallis, 'Book Subscription Lists', *The Library*, XXIX (1974), 273.
[57] See the analysis in chapter ten. Moses Williams also collected, but did not
publish, a subscription list for a proposed Collection of Triads in 1717: N.L.W.,
Llanstephan MS. 65B. For another unpublished list of subscribers for 134 copies of
Thomas Williams's *Cydymaith i Ddyddiau Gwylion* (1712), see N.L.W. MS. 1963D.

antiquarian tomes of Edward Lhuyd, Henry Rowlands and William Wotton were published in Oxford, Dublin and London respectively, whilst Theophilus Evans's discourse on infant baptism was also published in London. John Rhydderch printed eight lists between 1716 and 1727 at Shrewsbury, and most of his other publications were probably financed by subscription. Nicholas Thomas of Carmarthen published four lists between 1723 and 1727, the first of which, included in *Llun Agrippa* (1723), was the first subscription list to be printed in Wales. Two lists were also published in books published by the Chester press. Of these eighteen books, three were works of antiquarianism, whilst Thomas William's *Oes Lyfr* was a scriptural memory-book interlarded with a wealth of antiquarian material. Ten of the religious books were by Anglicans and two were published by Dissenters. John Rhydderch's *English-Welsh Dictionary* and William Gambold's *Welsh Grammar* complete the list. Almost without exception, subscription lists published in the eighteenth century were written in English.[58] This was partly because subscription methods had originated in England and were used as prototypes by Welsh authors, and partly because an element of snobbery was involved. The latter was certainly true of those arch-middle-class snobs, the Morrises of Anglesey, whose instincts for the observation of the niceties of social distinction were always highly sensitive.[59] Constantly aware of each man's qualifications and place in the social hierarchy, publishers adhered keenly to social categories in formulating their lists.

The geographical distribution of patrons depended on several variables: the nature of the book concerned, the co-operation which existed between author and printer, the system of 'proposals' adopted, the energy and perseverance of the publisher, the number of agents and contacts available in surrounding counties, and the extent of literacy in particular areas. Several authors drew support from relatives and acquaintances before casting their nets to wider circles. Included among Edward Samuel's subscribers were his sister,

---

[58] For a convenient summary see Eiluned Rees, 'Pre-1820 Welsh Subscription Lists', *J.W.B.S.*, XI (1973–4), 85–119.
[59] *Morris Letters*, I, 187; G. J. Williams, Supplement to *N.L.W.J.*, III (1943), 16; G. Melville Richards, 'Yr Awdur a'i Gyhoedd yn y Ddeunawfed Ganrif', *J.W.B.S.*, X (1966), 13–26.

his eldest son and his five daughters.[60] Jenkin Jones also benefited from the patronage of his relatives: his father, John Jenkins, subscribed to *Dydd y Farn Fawr* (1727), as did his sister, Esther, who married the affluent Richard Lloyd of Coedlannau Fawr, Llanwenog, whose name also figured in Jones's list of subscribers.[61] Generally, however, authors and publishers widened their horizons. Although their aspirations often foundered in a sea of apathy, most of them were indefatigable in their search for patrons. The ageing Thomas Gouge traversed the country annually in the early-1670s, wheedling funds from friend and foe alike;[62] Edward Samuel covered the twin dioceses of north Wales on horseback in his search for subscribers and sent earnest letters to Oxford scholars begging financial assistance;[63] the squire of Mathafarn, William Pugh, 'left no stone unturned' in the neighbourhood of Llanwrin and 'at some distance' in eliciting subscriptions on behalf of Thomas Williams of Denbigh;[64] with begging bowl in hand, Moses Williams displayed an abundance of spirit and stamina in his bid to secure support for the ventures of the S.P.C.K. and especially for the campaign to publish the Welsh Bible of 1717–8.[65]

In the last resort, however, most authors drew the bulk of their support from their native counties, relying on agents to secure wider aid. John Prichard Prŷs drew enormous support for his *Difyrrwch Crefyddol* (1721) from patrons in his native Anglesey, but he was also able, through a network of booksellers, grocers and mercers who acted as agents on his behalf, to secure subscribers in seven other counties. The collector of subscriptions for *Defosiwnau Priod* (1720) received the support of 33 men of substance from Anglesey and a further 199 subscriptions from ten parishes in Anglesey and Caernarvonshire; he also drew 30 subscriptions from Denbighshire, 60

---

[60] Edward Samuel's sister, Dorothy, subscribed to *Holl Ddyledswydd Dyn* (1718), *Prif Dd'ledswyddau Christion* (1723) and *Athrawiaeth yr Eglwys Gristnogol* (1731). His son and five daughters also subscribed to the latter work. For details of this family, see John Edwards, 'Edward Samuel: ei Oes a'i Waith' (unpubl. Univ. of Wales M.A. thesis, 1925), vol. I, pp. 7–8; vol. 2, Appendix, pp. 1–5.

[61] N.L.W. MS. 12357E, p. 1498.

[62] Calamy, II, 9.

[63] Bod., MS. Ashmole 1817A, f. 427.

[64] N.L.W. MS. 1963D.

[65] Mary Clement, *The S.P.C.K. and Wales, 1699–1740* (1954), pp. 32–8.

from Flintshire, 21 from Merioneth, and 3 from Shropshire. Similarly, although the preponderance of subscribers to Edward Wynn's *Trefn Ymarweddiad* (1723–4) were natives of Anglesey and Caernarvonshire, support was also forthcoming from Denbighshire, Flintshire, Merioneth and Cardiganshire. In the south, Theophilus Evans, rarely venturing beyond clerical and gentry patronage, confined his subscribers to the diocese of St. David's, whilst William Gambold called on support from his native Pembrokeshire and contiguous counties. Although Jenkin Jones relied on subscriptions from Dissenting ministers in five counties in south Wales, he was almost exclusively dependent for the backbone of his support, especially for *Dydd y Farn Fawr*, on the inhabitants of rural parishes in south Cardiganshire and north Carmarthenshire. The 21 subscribers to *Oes Lyfr* (1724) all came from neighbouring villages and parishes in Carmarthenshire: six came from Talyllychau, five from Llandyfeisant, two each from Abergorlech, Gwynfe and Llanfynydd, and one each from Llanfihangel Rhos-y-Corn, Llan-newydd and Maenordeilo. This subscription list only hints at the total number of subscribers for this venture, and authors were well aware of the large potential public of buyers which existed in the closely-knit and inter-related communities in which they themselves moved.

III. BOOK EDITIONS AND PRICES

The most bulky editions of Welsh books were generally published by charitable organisations like the Welsh Trust and the S.P.C.K. Editions published in London ranged from 500 to 10,000 copies, though latter editions normally comprised Bibles only. Even so, the Welsh Trust managed to finance substantial editions of devotional literature: in 1675, the Trust distributed 500 copies of *Holl Ddyledswydd Dyn* (1672) and 2,500 copies of Rowland Vaughan's *Yr Ymarfer o Dduwioldeb* (1675).[66] By the time of the S.P.C.K., moreover, the system of securing subscribers and the pattern of distributing books had been refined, and their editions, especially of small, cheap, practical works, were consequently much larger. The St. David's Day

---

[66] M. G. Jones, 'Two Accounts of the Welsh Trust, 1675 and 1678', *B.B.C.S.*, IX (1937), 73.

sermon preached by George Lewis in 1714 was published in an edition of 4,000 copies. Similarly, members of the Society of Antient Britons subscribed to 1,200 copies of Philip Phillips's sermon in 1716. Devotional books and catechisms were in even greater demand: Moses Williams printed a thousand copies of his *Catecism* in 1715; 2,000 copies of the Welsh translation of Gibson's *Pastoral Letter* were printed at a cost of less than ten shillings per hundred; and the edition of Thomas Richards's translation of Gibson's *Serious Advice to persons who have been sick*, published in 1730, numbered 4,000 copies at a total cost of £12.[67]

In the provinces, the size of editions in the early-eighteenth century was generally smaller. Only when authors like Thomas Baddy were commissioned (in his case by Dr. Williams's Trust) to translate works could local printing presses cope with relatively large editions. Thus, Baddy was able to print a thousand copies of *Gwagedd Mebyd a Ieungctid* at Chester in 1728 at a cost of £10 for printing and £9 for binding in sheep leather.[68] At Shrewsbury, editions of Welsh books normally comprised a minimum of 500 copies, with small devotional tracts often running to editions of a thousand or more. Welsh Quakers, for instance, were able to strike a bargain with John Rhydderch to print, at a cost of £2, 1,500 copies of Roger Jenkin's translation of Barcroft's *Faithful Warning* (1720).[69] Within Wales itself, the early Welsh presses at Trefhedyn and Carmarthen, hampered by inexperience and penury, were less ambitious and rarely aspired to print editions of more than 500 copies.

Every effort was made to keep the price of books, especially those designed to improve the morals and devotional habits of the lower orders, within reasonable bounds. Much obviously depended on the willingness of charitable bodies and private individuals to subsidise editions and organise the distribution of books. It is clear that Welsh books printed and sold in London were rather more expensive than those produced in the provinces.[70] High printing costs in the capital made it

[67] Sir Thomas Jones, *The Rise and Progress of the most Honourable and Loyal Society of Antient Britons* (1717), p. 16; Clement, pp. 82, 283, 297, 306.
[68] W. A. Evans, 'Thomas Baddy ac Ymddiriedolwyr Cronfa Dr. Daniel Williams', *Y Cofiadur*, 27 (1957), 20–33.
[69] Friends' House Library, Kelsall MSS. Diaries, IV, 50–1.
[70] See, for instance, the book prices listed by Thomas David in 1703–4. Bod., MS. Ashmole 1814, f. 366–7.

extremely difficult for Stephen Hughes to keep down the price of his early publications. The collected poems of Rees Prichard, published in 1672, cost 3s. 6d. bound, and *Holl Ddyledswydd Dyn*, published in the same year, cost the same amount.[71] But once the finances of the Welsh Trust were made available to Hughes, he was able to reduce his prices markedly. Thus, *Cyfarwydd-deb i'r Anghyfarwydd*—a work of some 282 pages— and *Tryssor i'r Cymru* (242 pages), both published in 1677, were remarkably cheap at 2d. each, whilst Hughes's edition of *Taith y Pererin* was made available in 1688 at 3d. per copy.[72] Significantly, too, Hughes was able to produce the cheapest Welsh Bible in octavo hitherto published: his Bible of 1677–8 was sold at 4s. 2d., almost a third cheaper than the previous edition of 1654, and 'much cheaper than any English Bible was ever sold that was of so fair a print and paper'.[73] With the advent of the S.P.C.K. and the burgeoning of the provincial press, Welsh books were made available in greater numbers and at cheaper prices. Even so, some economic ceiling plainly existed for different sections of the reading public. Few besides clergymen, gentry and the wealthiest yeomen would have been able to afford copies of devotional works like *Rheol Buchedd Sanctaidd* (1701) and *Cydymaith i Ddyddiau Gwylion* (1712), both of which cost 4s. each.[74] But the purse-strings of solid, well-to-do yeomen, substantial tenant farmers, artisans and craftsmen could certainly have opened to buy copies of *Yr Ymarfer o Dduwioldeb* at 1s. 6d., *Carolau a Dyriau Duwiol* (1696) at 1s. 6d., and *Pattrwm y Gwir Gristion* (1723) at 1s. 4d.[75] Men of the same social status, but mainly of Dissenting stock, were also more than ready to pay a shilling subscription for *Llun Agrippa* (1723) and sixpence more for *Dydd y Farn Fawr* (1727) and *Y Cywyr Ddychwelwr* (1727).[76]

[71] Edward Arber, *The Term Catalogues, 1668–1709* (1903–6), I, 107; *Llyfr y Psalmau . . . Testament Newydd* (1672), Advertisement.
[72] See the inventory of goods sold by the Carmarthen mercer, Dawkins Gove, in N.L.W., Archdeaconry of Carmarthen P.R. 1692.
[73] M. G. Jones, *B.B.C.S.*, IX, 77; John Tillotson, *A Sermon preached at the funeral of the Reverend Mr. Thomas Gouge . . . with a brief account of his life* (1682).
[74] See the price list in Robert Lloyd, *Llyfr-gell y Cristion Ifaingc* (1713), *passim*.
[75] See the price lists compiled by Thomas Jones, *Newyddion mawr oddiwrth y Ser* (1701), sig. C7v–C8r, and by Thomas William of Mynydd Bach between 1732 and 1734. C.C.L., Cardiff MS. 2.139.
[76] The N.L.W. (Summers Room) copy of *Llun Agrippa* (1723) is the very copy for which a subscriber, John Thomas, paid a shilling; Jenkin Jones, *Dydd y Farn Fawr* (1727), title-page; *anon.*, *Y Cywyr Ddychwelwr* (1727), title-page.

What is more important is that popular devotional works and catechisms were sold at prices within the economic range of all except the most deprived orders of society. Translations of Bunyan's works sold at a shilling per copy in the early-eighteenth century;[77] simple latimers of devotion like *Arweiniwr Cartrefol* (1700) and *Dwysfawr Rym Buchedd Grefyddol* (1722) were available at 6*d*. each; cheaper still, at 2*d*. each, were devotional manuals like *Trefn o Ddefosion* (1700), *Cynghor y Bugail* (1700) and *Anogaeth fer ir Cymun Sanctaidd* (1710).[78] Books of religious verse and epigrams were also cheaply produced: two of Dafydd Lewys's most popular works, *Flores Poetarum* (1710) and *Bwyd Enaid* (1723) cost 4*d*. and 3*d*. respectively, whilst readers eager to buy Rees Prydderch's wise sayings were charged 6*d*.[79] The price of Rees Prichard's poems lessened considerably when published at Shrewsbury: Stephen Hughes's editions of 1672 and 1681 had cost 3*s*. 6*d*. and 2*s*. 6*d*. per copy respectively, but in the early-eighteenth century Thomas William was able to buy *Canwyll y Cymry* at much cheaper rates: his three copies cost 2*s*., 8*d*. and 6*d*. respectively.[80] Cheapest of all were the enormously popular primers, horn books, almanacs and ballads. The ever-popular ABC-cum-catechisms which emerged regularly from the Shrewsbury and Carmarthen press, together with horn-books sold at less than ½*d*. in mercers' shops, were essential arms in the war against illiteracy.[81] At popular levels, too, almanacs and ballads, normally 2*d*. each, were guaranteed ready sales among the reading public.[82]

[77] C.C.L., Cardiff MS. 2.139.

[78] Ibid.; Bod., MS. Ashmole 1814, f. 366–7; Thomas Jones, *Newyddion mawr oddiwrth y Ser* (1701), sig. C7v–C8r; Robert Lloyd, op. cit., *passim*. Other book-prices in this range included *Trugaredd a Barn* (1687) at 9*d*., see Stephen Hughes (ed.), *Taith neu Siwrnai y Pererin* (1688), sig. A3v; Richard Jones's *Galwad i'r Annychweledig* (1677) at 8*d*., see Owen Griffith, *Abraham's Prospect* (1681); Moses Williams's *Pregeth* (1718) cost 6*d*. as did William Wotton's *Sermon* (1723); *Teg Resymmau Offeiriad Pabaidd wedi eu Hatteb* (1686) cost 4*d*., see William Wynne, *The History of Wales* (1697), p. 416; so too did Alban Thomas's *Llythyr Bugailaidd* (1729), title-page.

[79] Dafydd Lewys, *Golwg ar y Byd* (1725), p. xxiii.

[80] Arber, op. cit., I, 107; Stephen Hughes (ed.), *Canwyll y Cymru* (1681), title-page; C.C.L., Cardiff MS. 2.139.

[81] Thomas Jones, *Newyddion mawr oddiwrth y Ser* (1701), sig. C8r; Marjorie Plant, *The English Book Trade* (2nd ed., 1965), p. 239; D. R. Thomas, *The History of the Diocese of St. Asaph* (3 vols., 1908–11), I, 151. See also the inventories of John Price, Ruthin. N.L.W., St. Asaph P.R. 1684 (I owe this reference to Mr. Gareth Evans) and John Lloyd, Denbigh, St. Asaph P.R. 1742.

[82] Thomas Jones, *Newyddion mawr oddiwrth y Ser* (1691), sig. C7v. The scarcity and costliness of imported paper from France forced Jones to raise the price of his almanacs after 1691. *idem*, *Newyddion mawr oddiwrth y Ser* (1694), sig. C8v.

IV. THE DISTRIBUTION OF BOOKS

A report published by the Welsh Trust in 1675 stated that mercers were the only traders in books in both north and south Wales.[83] Prior to the growth of the provincial press, few men were classified as booksellers *per se*, and most books published after 1660, especially those published under the auspices of the Welsh Trust, were placed in the hands of mercers. Mercers at this time were general dealers who sold a wide miscellany of goods, ranging from fine cloths to sandpaper, tobacco to nutmeg, watches to snuff boxes, and gunpowder to salt.[84] What is significant is that they were persuaded that selling books was also a worthwhile proposition. In the early-1670s, Stephen Hughes secured the assistance of respectable, well-to-do mercers in four major market towns in Wales—Abergavenny, Bridgend, Carmarthen and Swansea.[85] Hughes's principal distributor was Dawkins Gove, royalist, philanthropist, and twice mayor of Carmarthen. On his death in 1692, Gove's inventory, valued at £104 16s. 4d., included hundreds of best-selling Welsh and English books to the value of £26 9s. 1d.[86] Hughes's books were also distributed and sold in the Welsh border towns, notably Chester, Llanfyllin, Oswestry and Wrexham, and also in the hinterland of north Wales.[87] When Thomas Williams, a mercer of Pwllheli, died in 1681, his stock, valued at £265 1s. 4d., included books worth £58 10s. 0d.[88] Further east, John Price, a prosperous mercer of Ruthin, died in 1684 leaving goods valued at the impressive sum of £321 7s. 6d. and including 3½ dozen horn-books, 4 dozen primers, 21 grammars, 20 psalters, a dozen testaments, 9 prayer books, 11 Bibles, 4 copies of Charles Edwards's *Y Ffydd Ddi-ffvant* (1677), 6 vocabularies, a copy of *The Whole*

---

[83] M. G. Jones, op. cit., pp. 72–3.

[84] George C. Boon (ed.), *Welsh Tokens of the Seventeenth Century* (1973), pp. 37, 43–75.

[85] Stephen Hughes (ed.), [*Gwaith Mr. Rees Prichard*], III, (1672), sig. a4v.

[86] N.L.W., Archdeaconry of Carmarthen P.R. 1692; William Spurrell, *Carmarthen and its Neighbourhood* (2nd ed., 1779), pp. 175, 202. The other agents were Thomas Vertue of Abergavenny, Matthew Jones of Swansea and Thomas Joseph of Bridgend. For Vertue's will, see N.L.W., Llandaff P.R. 1734; for Joseph see Llandaff P.R. 1673, and Thomas Richards, *Wales under the Penal Code, 1662–1687* (1925), pp. 91, 125.

[87] *Llyfr y Psalmau . . . Testament Newydd* (1672), Advertisement; Stephen Hughes (ed.), *Mr. Perkins His Catechism* (1672), sig. A7v; M. G. Jones, op. cit., pp. 79–80.

[88] N.L.W., Bangor P.R. 1682.

Duty of Man, and a variety of Latin and English books.[89]

During the 1680s, Stephen Hughes's rôle as the major distributor of Welsh books from London was gradually taken over by Thomas Jones. There is no evidence of any liaison between the two, but the fact that Hughes recommended some of Jones's publications suggests that he was delighted to find a fellow-publisher whose anxiety to provide the reading public in Wales with edifying material was equally acute.[90] Thomas Jones's principal agent in London from 1686 onwards was Charles Beard of the Three Blackbirds and Mermaid in Watling Street. Beard sold almanacs, books and patent medicines on behalf of Jones, and he was succeeded after 1688 by John Marsh at the Red Lion in Cateaten Street and by Lawrence Baskerville at the Red Lion in Aldermanbury.[91] Jones's main concern, however, was to establish a network of agents, made up largely of mercers, grocers, butchers and ironmongers, within Wales itself. Only in this way would he be sure that a substantial stock of Welsh books would be consistently available to the bulk of the reading public. His own ambition—by no means a pipedream even at that time—was to see his books and almanacs read in all four corners of Wales, from Abergavenny to Cardigan, and from Wrexham to Holyhead[92].

As a result, in the early-1680s, Thomas Jones took the first step towards fulfilling his dream by securing the assistance of selling agents not only in the borderland market towns used by Stephen Hughes, but also at Bala, Dolgellau, Machynlleth and Welshpool.[93] This network was further expanded on Jones's removal to Shrewsbury in 1695. There he chose Gabriel Rogers, a Shrewsbury bookseller, and Humphrey Page, a Chester bookseller, to supervise the distribution of his books to shopkeepers in north Wales, and also secured Samuel Rogers, a bookseller at Abergavenny, to do likewise in the south.[94] The consequence of this arrangement was that Jones quickly

---

[89] N.L.W., St. Asaph P.R. 1684. Cf. the inventories of Thomas Platt, Wrexham, St. Asaph P.R. 1667; and Edward Davies, Wrexham, St. Asaph P.R. 1681.

[90] *Taith neu Siwrnai y Pererin* (1688), sig. A2v.

[91] Thomas Jones, [*Almanac*] (1686), sig. C8v; idem, *Almanac am y flwyddyn 1688* (1688), title-page and sig. C8v.

[92] C.C.L., Cardiff MS. 2.14, pp. 11–13.

[93] Thomas Jones, *Newydd oddiwrth y Seer* (1684), sig. C8v; idem, *Newydd oddiwrth v Ser* (1685), sig. C3v.

[94] Thomas Jones, *Newyddion mawr oddiwrth y Ser* (1695), pp. 47–8.

succeeded in making his books more widely available. Book-selling agents were established in smaller and remoter towns such as Llanddaniel in Anglesey, Tywyn, Trawsfynydd and Corris in Merioneth, Caersws, Llanidloes, Llanymynech, Montgomery and Newtown in Montgomeryshire, Denbigh and Ruthin in Denbighshire, Mold in Flintshire and Brecon in Breconshire.[95] In fact, Thomas Jones achieved such great success that his arch-rivals in the printing trade swiftly adopted similar methods. John Jones of Caeau established agents in the same market towns and also at Harlech and Minffordd in Merioneth, and Cilfai in Glamorgan, whilst John Rhydderch secured the services of distributors at Llanrwst in Denbighshire, Caio in Carmarthenshire, Llangatwg in Glamorgan, and Pontypool in Monmouthshire.[96]

Clearly, the development of the printing and publishing trade, together with the distribution of books, was closely linked to the growth of Welsh towns. Publishers quickly appreciated the necessity of deploying agents in the important market towns, for they were the thriving foci of rural life and the major trading centres. In turn, butchers, grocers, iron-mongers, mercers and shopkeepers in general were well aware that selling books was a lucrative and worthwhile part of their daily trade.[97] By the early-eighteenth century, however, professional booksellers were increasingly becoming the most vital threads in the publishing and distributive network. Some of the more successful in their ranks were men of some standing. Thomas Jones's chief bookseller in Shrewsbury, Gabriel Rogers, was a yeoman's son who, on his death in 1705, left a personal estate valued at £600.[98] In the north-east, too, Edward

---

[95] Thomas Jones, *Newyddion mawr oddiwrth y Ser* (1698), sig. C8v; *idem, Newyddion mawr oddiwrth y Ser* (1701), sig. C8v; *idem, Newyddion mawr oddiwrth y Ser* (1702), sig. C8r–v; *idem, Y Cyfreithlawn Almanacc Cymraeg* (1706), sig. B5r; *idem, [Almanac]* (1708), sig. C8v; *[Almanac]* (1710), sig. C5v; *idem, Y Cyfreithlawn Almanacc Cymraeg* (1712), sig. B7v.

[96] John Jones, *[Almanac]* (1707), p. 47; *idem, Cennad oddiwrth y Ser* (1720), sig. C8v; *idem, Cennad oddiwrth y Ser* (1721), sig. C7v; John Rhydderch, *Newyddion oddiwrth y Sêr* (1720), sig. C8v. Thomas Baddy of Denbigh also made his books available in 'most of the towns of Gwynedd'. Thomas Baddy, *Pasc y Christion* (1703), title-page; *Pelydr a thywyniad yr Yspryd* (1713), Advertisement.

[97] For the wills of some of these well-to-do agents, see Rowland Hughes, Llanddaniel, N.L.W., Bangor P.R. 1706; William Davies, Newtown, St. Asaph P.R. 1730; Owen Hughes, Oswestry, St. Asaph P.R. 1731; Nathaniel Edwards, Oswestry, St. Asaph P.R. 1746; Michael Parry, Welshpool. St. Asaph P.R. 1752.

[98] Ll. C. Lloyd, op. cit., p. 169.

Wicksteed of Wrexham supplied the needs of gentle families as well as daily callers at his shop.[99] In the south-east, the most prolific and successful bookseller was Samuel Rogers, a well-to-do Presbyterian of Abergavenny, whilst the south-western communities were served mainly by Thomas Lewis and Crispianus Jones at Carmarthen, David John at Newcastle Emlyn, David Evans at Trefhedyn, and Lewis Thomas, a travelling bookseller of Llangrannog.[100]

Booksellers did not merely sell books: most stocked a wide range of functional and exotic wares. Thomas Durston of Shrewsbury not only sold books on divinity, history, law, medicine, mathematics and poetry, but also stationery, prints and maps, pens and quills, inks and pencils, mathematical and navigational instruments, violin and harp strings, sealing wax and snuff boxes, and an assortment of pills, potions and elixirs.[101] Printers and booksellers included within their books advertisements which advised book-collectors where to expect the finest book-binding service. Book-binding grew hand in hand with the printing trade and was a relatively lucrative profession. John Philips of Shrewsbury served the gentry and clergy by binding their books in Turkey or Morocco leather, or in red or blue calf-skin,[102] whilst the Carmarthen bookseller, Crispianus Jones, bound 'all sorts of old and decayed books' in gilt or plain calf, sheep or Morocco leather.[103] It would be facile to pretend, however, that the bindings of provincial book-binders were high in standard. Few of them could boast of being sufficiently well patronised to be able to invest their products with striking aesthetic merit.

[99] N.L.W., Plas Power Deeds and Documents, Vouchers and Accounts, 1727–31.
[100] Bod., MS. Ashmole 1814, f. 367; N.L.W., Llandaff P.R. 1736; Alban Thomas, *Dwysfawr Rym Buchedd Grefyddol* (1722), title-page; anon., *Dull Priodas Ysprydol* (1723–4), p. 8; Enosh Mophet (pseud.), *An Appendix to Delaune's Plea* (1720), p. 81; anon., *Rhybydd i'r Cymru* (1730–1), title-page; Morgan Llwyd, *Llyfr y Tri Aderyn* (1714), Advertisement.
[101] William Meyrick, *Pattrwm y Gwir-Gristion* (1730), Advertisement. Cf. *Llyfr y Psalmau* (1713), Advertisement; J. P., *Cennad oddiwrth y Ser* (1709), sig. C8v; John Rhydderch [*Almanac*] (1718), sig. A5v; Edward Samuel, *Holl Ddyledswydd Dyn* (1718), sig. Ff8r.
[102] Thomas Jones, *Y Cyfreithlawn Almanacc Cymraeg* (1706), sig. C8r; John Rhydderch, [*Almanac*] (1718), sig. A5v; John Prichard Prŷs, *Difyrrwch Crefyddol* (1721), Advertisement.
[103] Anon., *Dull Priodas Ysprydol* (1723–4), p. 8; anon., *Rhybydd i'r Cymru* (1730–1), fly-leaf.

By organising auctions and book sales, booksellers were also able to pander to the liking of littérateurs for buying libraries in bulk. The Chester bookseller, Randall Minshull, advertised a sale for 23 January 1716, issuing beforehand a catalogue of 'choice and valuable' books on divinity, law, physic, mathematics, history, metaphysics, physics, ethics, poetry, plays, romances, novels etc.'[104] Less affluent readers needed to be wooed rather more earnestly, and every bookseller worth his salt regularly marked down in his diary the dates of those markets and fairs which offered him the greatest opportunity for showing his wares. Even whilst in business in London, Thomas Jones frequently travelled to Brecon and Cardiff fairs on 6 and 30 November each year, whilst Shrewsbury printers and booksellers often used the date of a forthcoming fair as a publishing deadline, thereby giving their readers due notice of their plans.[105]

The major drawback implicit in the system of selling books through mercers and booksellers was that readers were required to visit market towns or fairs in order to buy books. By and large, publishers were alive to the necessity of making their books more available in remoter areas. They were scarcely likely to forget that Wales at that time was a cluster of small, dispersed communities, and they would view the itinerant bookseller, carrier, pedlar, hawker and country chapman as an indispensable link between isolated farmhouses and hamlets in dispersed rural areas and the outside world. The S.P.C.K., in particular, made extensive use of the facilities offered by carriers who, leaving London on fixed days for the provinces, left their parcels of books at shops and inns to be duly transferred to Welsh carriers who completed the process of distribution.[106] Distributing books by carrier, however, was a system fraught with problems. Complaints of negligence and irresponsibility on their part are legion, and when John Lloyd muttered caustically, 'the carrier plays the rogue with us all', many heads doubtless nodded their assent.[107] In fairness to

[104] Randall Minshull, *Bibliotheca Miscellanea* (1715).
[105] Thomas Jones, *Almanac am y Flwyddyn 1693* (1693), sig. C4v; John Jones, *Cennad oddiwrth y Ser* (1731), sig. C8v.
[106] Mary Clement, *The S.P.C.K. and Wales*, p. 79; Thomas Delaune, *Angliae Metropolis: or, The Present State of London* (1690), p. 434; *Arch. Camb.*, 3rd series, VI (1860), 246.
[107] Bod., MS. Ashmole 1816, f. 209; B.L. Birch Add. MS. 4274, f. 38.

carriers, however, their life as travellers was often a succession of hazards: roads were often soft and miry, barely suitable for cattle let alone horsemen or foot-travellers, and the most difficult Welsh terrain, always susceptible to floods, snow and ice, was virtually impassable in winter to all except the most hardy and intrepid souls.[108] For these reasons, private individuals and philanthropic bodies often preferred to transport parcels of books by sea to the major ports of north and south Wales. Distribution by sea was often a speedier and less expensive process, except when inclement weather conditions proved a hazard.[109]

More formal means of circulating books were also devised. From 1703 to 1711, the S.P.C.K. was preoccupied with the concept of establishing libraries. In 1707, 5,000 printed proposals were published and distributed throughout England and Wales announcing plans to establish lending libraries in market towns and parochial libraries for the benefit of poorer ministers in each impoverished living in Wales.[110] As a result, between 1708 and 1711, diocesan lending libraries, stocked with books to the value of some £60, were established at Bangor, Carmarthen, Cowbridge and St. Asaph. Books were made available for loan to 'any clergyman or schoolmaster inhabiting within ten miles of the said town . . . or to any of the trustees . . . or to any . . . who shall contribute the sum of ten shillings or give any book or books of that value to or for the use of the said library'.[111] Theological works formed the backbone of these libraries, though works on history, archaeology, classics, philosophy, natural science, law and medicine, were also present to some degree. Folio books could be borrowed for a period of two months and other books for a month. None could borrow more than two books at the same time, except those who wished to furnish themselves with material for publishing works that might be 'useful to religion or learning or . . . conducive to the public good'. Prospective authors who borrowed books were allowed a maximum of six works for a

[108] Joan Parkes, *Travel in England in the Seventeenth Century* (1925); Virginia A. LaMar, *Travel and Roads in England* (1960).
[109] N.L.W., Picton Castle MS. 1664; Mary Clement, op. cit., pp. 78–80.
[110] B.L. Egerton MS. 2882, f. 277.
[111] Maura Tallon, *Church in Wales Diocesan Libraries* (1962), *passim*.

period of four months and, in return for the special privileges granted to them, they were expected to donate to the library a printed copy of their book on its publication.[112]

The diocesan lending libraries were supplemented at grass-roots level by a host of smaller parochial libraries. Drawing their inspiration from vigorous proposals outlined by Thomas Bray,[113] libraries of this nature, stocking books valued at around £20, were set up in parishes where the living was valued at less than £30 per annum. Even then, each parish anxious to secure a library was asked to contribute the sum of £5 towards the total cost of the venture.[114] Both diocesan and parochial libraries, however, were designed to benefit only a small section of the community. They were exclusive rather than inclusive, and the dissident voice of John Vaughan of Derllys soon aired general unhappiness at the confinement of such luxuries to men of the cloth and schoolmasters. Vaughan believed that priority should be given to establishing lending libraries for the benefit of 'the inhabitants of every parish', especially householders and children. The Carmarthenshire squire also pressed his claim that saving knowledge should not be denied to those held captive in Welsh prisons, and though this part of his dream was not fulfilled in his lifetime, constant badgering by Thomas Price of Merthyr eventually persuaded the S.P.C.K. of the merits of this scheme. By April 1725, copies of each Welsh book added to the stocks of the headquarters of the S.P.C.K. were sent to all prisons in Wales.[115]

In both formal and informal ways, it was common for clergymen and ministers who were concerned for the welfare of their literate parishioners and those who aspired to literacy, to subscribe for books on their behalf and to disperse them as widely as possible. The far-flung networks established by the S.P.C.K. were heavily dependent on the readiness of clergymen to act as agents and distribute tracts among 'their meaner parishioners'.[116] Men of the cloth were intimately acquainted

---

[112] N.L.W., Elwes MS. 1589. For a full discussion see Eiluned Rees, 'An Introductory Survey of 18th Century Welsh Libraries', *J.W.B.S.*, X (1971), 240–50.
[113] Neil Ker (ed.), *The Parochial Libraries of the Church of England* (1959), pp. 18–20.
[114] See, for example, N.L.W., SA/Misc/709; SA/Misc/720.
[115] Clement, pp. 21–3, 26, 28, 30, 260, 294.
[116] Ibid., *passim*.

with members of their flock and were thus able to ensure that books reached those persons who were in most need of them. Many were prepared to lend their own books. John Jones, dean of Bangor, lent a variety of theological and classical books to a host of friends and acquaintances, ranging from the bishop of Bangor to the squirearchy of Penrhos and Baron Hill, and from a Welsh author like John Morgan, vicar of Aberconwy, to the poor prisoner whom he visited at Bangor gaol and left to ponder the merits of *The Whole Duty of Man*.[117] Hugh Lloyd, vicar of Mold, raised spiritual standards within his parish by lending catechisms and commentaries to members of his flock,[118] and countless other clerics did likewise with often striking results. The doyen of Welsh interlude-writers, Twm o'r Nant, learnt to read and write by borrowing books from a lay pastor, Siôn Dafydd of Pentrefoelas, a remarkable man whose various attainments ranged from labouring to clog-making.[119] The outstanding example of one who was obsessively aware of the need to provide the most deprived elements in society with saving knowledge was the Dissenting minister, Edmund Jones of Pontypool. Ever impoverished but always ungrudgingly generous, Jones expended most of his income on books and gave a substantial proportion of them away to 'objects of charity' in his locality.[120] Without the liberal spirit and selfless attitude of men of Edmund Jones's character, the task of distributing books and eliminating illiteracy would have been so much harder.

[117] N.L.W. MS. 9102A.
[118] N.L.W. MS. 598E, p. 4.
[119] G. M. Ashton (ed.), Thomas Edwards, *Hunangofiant a Llythyrau Twm o'r Nant* (1948), p. 31.
[120] N.L.W. MS. 7023A.

X

SUBSCRIBERS AND BOOK-OWNERS

The gauging of literacy is one of the most urgent and difficult tasks facing Welsh historians. Even the word 'literacy' defies precise definition. Nowadays we judge the man who can read and write to be literate, but the meaning of literacy 'changes according to the context'[1] and thus varies from century to century and from place to place. In this period, contemporaries made a clear distinction between the ability to read and to write, and were generally agreed that the former was of crucial importance.[2] Indeed, one of the most striking features of the time was the intensity with which the illiterate were exhorted to learn to read. Religious reformers went to some pains to point out to the unlettered that the ability to read was a vital accomplishment. To be illiterate, warned George Bull, was to be in the most 'unhappy circumstances'.[3] Ignorance and illiteracy, claimed David Maurice, were synonymous with blindness of the mind, whilst John Morgan, choosing to hector rather than coax, despised the unlettered as 'stubborn, ignorant, stupid yokels'.[4] Peasant claims of inferiority and impoverishment received short shrift from Lewis Morris: 'these', he insisted, 'are merely empty excuses which the devil thrusts before you so that you might live in blindness forever'.[5] 'A hard case', agreed Richard Steele, 'if you cannot spare two or three shillings [to buy books] in a whole year for God and your

---

[1] R. S. Schofield, 'The Measurement of Literacy in Pre-Industrial England' in Jack Goody (ed.), *Literacy in Traditional Societies* (1968), p. 314.
[2] V. E. Neuburg, 'Literacy in Eighteenth Century England: a Caveat', *Local Population Studies*, 2 (1969), 44.
[3] Robert Nelson (ed.), George Bull, *Some Important Points of Primitive Christianity maintained and defended* (1713), p. 430.
[4] David Maurice, *Cwnffwrdd ir Gwan Gristion* (1700), pp. v–vi; John Morgan, *Bloedd-nad ofnadwy yr udcorn diweddaf* (1704), pp. 88–90. See also the exhortations and pleadings of John Griffith, rector of Llanelian (U.C.N.W.L., Bangor MS. 95), of the poet, Ifan Gruffudd (N.L.W. MS. 6900A, p. 101), and of Thomas Jones in *Newydd oddiwrth y Seer* (1684), sig. A3r–v.
[5] Hugh Owen (ed.), *The Life and Works of Lewis Morris, 1701–65* (1951), p. 330.

souls.'[6] Warnings and exhortations of this kind reflected the acute concern of reformers that men should acquire a new dimension to their lives by becoming able to read and thereby understand issues pertaining to their salvation.

This chapter is concerned with the humblest definition of literacy—the ability to read, and the relationship between book-reading and the prevailing social structure. Books and their distribution, after all, reflect the condition of society and, in particular, the nature of supply and demand. Literacy, moreover, varies according to need and aspiration. Among poorer orders, for instance, literacy involves not only the *desire* to read books but also the *opportunity* to fulfil that desire. Much clearly depended on the standards of life in a particular community: the degree of social and economic progress; the presence of schools and educational opportunities; the richness of the cultural tradition; and the influence of reformist gentlemen, ministers and literate householders on the unlettered elements in society. Thus, for instance, some of the 'ignorant' parts of the rugged and isolated upland parts of mid-Wales where 'Hengist & Horsa & Rowena' had 'settled their affairs',[7] would contrast sharply with the more agriculturally-advanced Vales of Ardudwy and Teifi where literary traditions stretched back over the centuries.[8] Literacy rates were evidently high in parishes like Cellan in Cardiganshire, where pious middling sorts of craftsmen, artisans and yeomen proved an active leaven in the lump.[9] Similarly, those Dissenting congregations nursed by Stephen Hughes and his successors in rural Carmarthenshire reputedly possessed such 'vast knowledge' that Methodist evangelists thought twice before venturing into their midst.[10] It might be expected, too, that the proportion of literates in Welsh towns would be higher than in rural areas since the ability to read, write and keep accounts was indispensable to shopkeepers, tradesmen and officials in local government.

---

[6] Richard Steele, *The Husbandmans Calling* (1668), p. 263.

[7] Bod., MS. Ashmole 1820A, f. 148. When William Pugh of Mathafarn collected subscriptions in these parts he received 'the coldest reception' and a prevailing 'Laodicean temper'. N.L.W. MS. 1963D.

[8] G. Bowen, 'Traddodiad Llenyddol Deau Ceredigion, 1600–1850' (unpubl. Univ. of Wales M.A. thesis, 1943), *passim*.

[9] Edward Lhuyd, 'Parochialia', Suppl. to *Arch. Camb.*, 1909–11, Part 3, p. 68.

[10] G. J. Williams, 'Yr Annibynwyr a'u Llenyddiaeth' in *Hanes ac Egwyddorion Annibynwyr Cymru* (1939), pp. 148–9.

In an attempt to throw some more detailed light on the nature of the reading public in Wales at this time, this study is constructed from evidence found in the subscription lists which prefaced several Welsh books in the early eighteenth century. Subscription lists have been found in eighteen Welsh books within the period 1707–31. In terms of total subscriptions (excluding those antiquarian works that drew support from outside Wales), it is clear that devotional books attracted the greatest number of subscribers: 689 persons subscribed to Edward Wynn's *Trefn Ymarweddiad Gwir Gristion* (1723–4), 352 subscribed to William Lewis's *Defosiwnau Priod* (1720), 233 gave their support to Edward Samuel's *Holl Ddyledswydd Dyn* (1718) and 265 subscribed to John Prichard Prŷs's collection of devotional verses, *Difyrrwch Crefyddol* (1721). On the other hand, some of the more demanding doctrinal works fared less well. Edward Samuel's *Gwirionedd y Grefydd Grist'nogol* (1716) received 126 subscriptions, and ten more subscribers were found for *Prif Dd'ledswyddau Christion* in 1723. Samuel recruited rather more subscribers—227—for his *Athrawiaeth yr Eglwys Gristnogol* (1731), largely because his son, Edward, had found 59 subscribers among students and fellows at Oxford. Among the Dissenters, the first combined venture undertaken by Jenkin Jones and Nicholas Thomas, *Llun Agrippa* (1723), attracted 85 subscribers, whilst *Dydd y Farn Fawr* (1727) was supported by 212 subscriptions. John Rhydderch, poet, author and printer, had so many contacts throughout Wales that he was able to raise 261 subscriptions for his *English and Welsh Dictionary* (1725).

The subscription lists invariably provided indications of the social status of the patrons concerned, and these fall into seven categories: titled patrons; esquires; 'Mr' and 'Mrs'; higher clergy; parish clergy and ministers; unidentified men and women; and miscellaneous subscribers. Further information on the status of these groups, together with the nature and range of their reading habits, has been accumulated from a variety of manuscript sources, especially probate material. Probate material, however, has its pitfalls: only those with some stake in property would make wills and thus we have no indication of the wealth or reading habits (if such habits existed at all) of a large section of the population. Furthermore,

SUBSCRIBERS TO WELSH BOOKS

Author and Title	Number of Subscribers	I Titled Patrons	II Esquires	III 'Mr'	III 'Mrs'	IV Higher Clergy	V Parish Clergy & Ministers	VI Un-identified Men	VI Un-identified Women	VII Miscellaneous
E. Lhuyd, Archaeologia Britannica (1707)	199	42 21%	91 46%	29 15%	0	8 4%	1	0	0	28 14%
E. Samuel, Gwirionedd y Grefydd Grist'nogol (1716)	126	3 2%	37 29%	32 26%	0	5 4%	41 33%	0	0	8 6%
E. Samuel, Holl Ddyledswydd Dyn (1718)	233	8 3%	27 12%	52 22%	11 5%	6 2%	51 22%	61 26%	4 2%	13 6%
T. Evans, Cydymddiddan ynghylch Bedydd Plant (1719)	36	0	0	10 28%	0	3 8%	20 56%	0	0	3 8%
W. Lewis, Defosiwnau Priod (1720)	352	3 1%	33 9%	51 14%	17 5%	2 1%	27 8%	194 55%	18 5%	7 2%
J. Prichard Prŷs, Difyrrwch Crefyddol (1721)	265	0	14 5%	57 22%	7 3%	0	64 24%	103 39%	3 1%	17 6%
T. Evans, Prydferthwch Sancteiddrwydd (1722)	147	0	30 20%	45 31%	4 3%	5 3%	59 40%	0	0	4 3%
E. Samuel, Prif Dd'ledswyddau (1723)	136	0	26 19%	32 24%	7 5%	7 5%	41 30%	10 7%	1 1%	12 9%
Jenkin Jones, Llun Agrippa (1723)	85	0	1 1%	25 29%	2 2%	0	11 13%	42 50%	1 1%	3 4%

SUBSCRIBERS TO WELSH BOOKS—*continued*

Author and Title	Number of Sub-scribers	I Titled Patrons	II Esquires	III 'Mr'	III 'Mrs'	IV Higher Clergy	V Parish Clergy & Ministers	VI Un-identified Men	VI Un-identified Women	VII Miscel-laneous
H. Rowlands, Mona Antiqua Restaurata (1723)	347	14 4%	96 28%	46 13%	0	29 8%	90 26%	0	0	72 21%
Edward Wynn, Trefn Ymarweddiad (1723–4)	689	2	7 1%	80 12%	25 4%	1	60 9%	424 61%	72 10%	18 3%
Thomas William, Oes Lyfr (1724)	21	0	0	1 5%	0	0	0	19 90%	1 5%	0
J. Rhydderch, The English and Welsh Dictionary (1725)	261	2	33 13%	59 22%	6 2%	1	85 33%	38 15%	1	36 14%
W. Gambold, A Welsh Grammar (1727)	132	7 5%	33 25%	24 18%	1 1%	17 13%	37 28%	0	0	13 10%
Jenkin Jones, Dydd y Farn Fawr (1727)	212	0	1 1%	40 19%	16 8%	0	30 14%	102 48%	20 9%	3 1%
G. Wynn, Ystyriaethau o Gyflwr Dyn (1730)	139	3 2%	53 38%	15 11%	9 6%	5 4%	44 32%	0	0	10 7%
William Wotton, Leges Wallicae (1730)	403	44 11%	134 33%	18 5%	2 1%	42 10%	65 16%	1	0	97 24%
E. Samuel, Athrawiaeth yr Eglwys (1731)	224	1	18 8%	55 25%	5 2%	5 2%	50 22%	7 3%	4 2%	79 36%

appraisers often did not trouble to specify books when compiling inventories and were often disposed to mask the presence of books under the blanket-terms of 'household stuff' and 'other lumber'. It must be said, too, that since there are literally tens of thousands of wills extant in this period, this study perforce is based only on a random sample of them. These conclusions, therefore, represent wide gleanings and much work remains to be done in order to test the model which is presented here.

The first two groups of patrons, and possibly parts of the third, although disparate in terms of wealth and social status, constitute the landed classes. Clearly there was an appreciable difference between titled landowners, armigerous squires and parish gentry, but society nonetheless expected each group to be aware of its social obligations. In pre-industrial times, the landed class represented a powerful, unified *élite* whose rôle it was to govern their communities. Even so, there prevailed a two-way relationship between the landed gentry and their social inferiors. Whilst the former came to expect deference to their exalted status in society, the latter, whose views were voiced in the main by ministers, authors and poets, were not slow to adumbrate those duties which they felt their superiors owed to society as a whole. The more articulate Welsh authors evidently looked upon the landed gentry as the cream of society, an *élite* which had specific obligations to fulfil. Prominent among these obligations was their duty to foster their native tongue and culture. Lacking a centralised court, a natural cultural capital like Dublin, and a national educational system of university, grammar and elementary schools attuned to Welsh circumstances and aspirations, all of which might have bolstered a sagging culture and language, Welsh authors were forced to rely on the gentry as their paternal mentors.

Welsh authors were plainly anxious that men of standing should not only view the Welsh language as a fitting medium for the printed word but also subscribe readily to the products of the Welsh press. Many of them were particularly concerned, therefore, to find that the permeation of English influences meant that many of the gentry were devout worshippers at the altar of pride.[11] Authors knew that there had been a time when

[11] See, for instance, Thomas Jones, *Of the Heart and its Right Soveraign* (1678), p. 242; Thomas Jones, *Newydd oddiwrth y Seer* (1684), sig. A1v; *idem, Newyddion mawr oddiwrth y Ser* (1698), sig. A1v; Ellis Wynne, *Gweledigaetheu y Bardd Cwsc* (1703), pp. 13–18

the gentry's pride included a delight in Welshness and a proper regard for the language; but it was all too evident now that their pride was being shaped and dominated by the values of their English counterparts. Much of the older patriotism and pride had been associated with Geoffrey of Monmouth's so-called 'British History', but the vitality which the *Historia* once possessed had almost totally evaporated in intellectual circles by the end of the seventeenth century. As a result, Welshness and the Welsh language no longer retained the same degree of identity with glorious historical and racial traditions that they had once boasted. Poets, too, acutely conscious that the bardic art was in dire straits, feared that the Welsh gentry, bewitched by things English, now judged the old poetic tradition to be utterly worthless.[12] Both Samuel and Moses Williams pilloried the gentry who had deliberately forgotten the rock from which they had been hewn and who affected to despise an ancient tongue which the peoples of Europe held in the greatest envy.[13] Happy the English, mused Lewis Morris wryly, for not having such a dismal brood in their midst.[14] 'One may prove [oneself] a fool by Latin and Greek as well as by Welsh', commented John Morgan pungently, before advocating a search of 'the ship's cellar [to] see whether there be any Lethean liquors so pernicious to the memory there which make people forget their former habitation, and the breasts that gave them suck.'[15] Wales, so it seemed, was 'over-run by pedigree and pride' of the worst sort.[16]

Even so, by relying too heavily on the dolorous comments of Welsh bards and authors, the extent of anglicisation can be grossly overstated. Although it may be conceded that, in general, the nobility and leading gentry, especially in eastern Wales, were adopting English habits of speech, thought and behaviour, they had not wholly abdicated their responsibilities to their native culture. Subscription lists reveal that not only

[12] Gwenllian Jones, 'Bywyd a Gwaith Edward Morris, Perthi Llwydion' (unpubl. Univ. of Wales M.A. thesis, 1941), p. 57; John Prichard Prŷs, *Difyrrwch Crefyddol* (1721), Preface and pp. 160–4.
[13] Samuel Williams, *Amser a Diwedd Amser* (1707), sig. A3v; Moses Williams, *Cofrestr* (1717), p. 3; *idem, Pregeth a barablwyd* (1718), p. 12.
[14] Hugh Owen, op. cit., p. 332.
[15] N.L.W. MS. 17B, pp. 11–12.
[16] N. Griffith, *The Leek. A Poem on St. David's Day* (1718), p. iii.

were many of the gentry still deeply interested in the literature and antiquity of Wales, but that they were also prepared to subscribe regularly to religious books. It may be argued that their patronage was purely academic, grudging contributions to silence pestering authors or gestures calculated to shore up the established church. But the following evidence suggests that many of them were still Welsh in sympathy and were deeply sensible of their roots and native culture. Many of them cherished the literary treasures of the past, patronised authors and poets, and took great pride in their lineage. Moreover, the consistency with which they subscribed to Welsh books indicates that they were eager to provide society with a respectable body of edifying religious literature. In many ways, social and religious changes in seventeenth-century Wales had also involved a cultural mutation: the patrons of the bards of yore were now concerned to raise spiritual and educational standards within their communities.

One further point needs to be stressed regarding the cultural interests of the Welsh gentry. The fact that they subscribed regularly to Welsh books did not imply a narrowing of tastes. On the contrary, they took enormous pride in amassing a wide variety of books which were housed in well-furnished and often elegant libraries. There were, of course, as in most periods, gentlemen who boasted little or no concern for the things of the mind and who, by their extravagant and loose living, not only endangered rank and property but also earned the scorn of their fellows. But Macaulay's caricature of the Restoration gentleman as a bucolic, boorish, simple-minded creature is scarcely applicable to Wales at this time. For the Welsh gentry had not only retained a great passion for antiquity, genealogy and heraldry, but had also developed a wide range of reading interests which encompassed the classics, history, topography and travel, legal and philosophical treatises, and collections of sermons and works of theology. The landed classes evidently bought, read and profited from many books in languages other than Welsh, and it is possible, at least indirectly, that the values and ideas which they imbibed may have permeated widely among those who were in daily contact with them.

I. TITLED PATRONS

The number of titled patrons who subscribed to Welsh books was small simply because there were few noble families in Wales. Even so, no one was better placed, in terms of affluence and leisure-time, to buy and read books. Antiquarianism was a consuming interest for most of them. The common Welshman, starved of the archival treasures which were locked away in private libraries or dusty vaults, knew little or nothing of antiquity, and authors of this *genre* seldom solicited the support of the lower orders. Works of antiquarianism, moreover, were usually calculated to appeal to fervent antiquaries beyond Offa's Dyke. Edward Lhuyd confessed that his *Archaeologia Britannica* (1707) was 'never intended for the use of the common people but was written at the demand of some of the greatest persons of Wales, and for no small number of the learned nobility and gentlemen of England'.[17] As a result, Lhuyd recruited 42 (21 per cent) titled patrons, mainly from England, as subscribers for his major classic. Similarly, William Wotton's massive edition of the Laws of Hywel Dda in 1730 benefited from the patronage of 41 (11 per cent) titled patrons. More important is the fact that the Welsh nobility, whose connexions with local communities were generally extremely tenuous, judged it obligatory to subscribe also to religious books. In offering their patronage to practical devotional books they were evidently motivated partly by a measure of spiritual conviction, partly by their moral responsibility to cater for the needs of the underprivileged, and partly also because they knew that such books made a point of emphasising the social and political obedience expected of society.

Most counties in north Wales boasted nobles who were regular subscribers. In Anglesey, that mercurial figure, Richard, fourth Viscount Bulkeley of Baron Hill, subscribed to the works of Lhuyd and Wotton, ordered ten copies of Henry Rowlands's study of his native shire, and gave his patronage to three devotional books. In Denbighshire, Sir Robert Salesbury Cotton, third baronet of Lleweni, subscribed to two copies of *Mona Antiqua Restaurata*, to the same devotional works favoured by Bulkeley, and also to *Trefn Ymarweddiad* and

---

[17] Edward Lhuyd, *Archaeologia Britannica* (1707), Preface.

Ystyriaethau o Gyflwr Dyn.[18] Sir William Williams, second
baronet of Llanforda and proud owner of the valuable
collection of manuscripts compiled by the distinguished
antiquary, William Maurice of Cefn-y-Braich,[19] subscribed to
the works of Lhuyd and Wotton, and also to three devotional
books. His son, described simply in early subscription lists as
'Watkin Williams esq.' (later to become the great 'Sir
Watkin'),[20] shared his father's charitable interests and subscribed to four devotional books, Wotton's work, and five
copies of Henry Rowlands's county history. Among the
illustrious Mostyn family of Flintshire, the second baronet,
Sir Thomas Mostyn, a voracious book-collector, genealogist
and antiquary, was much esteemed as a liberal patron of Welsh
literature and poetry, whilst his heir, Sir Roger Mostyn, was
not so wholly preoccupied with parliamentary proceedings and
race-meetings as to be incapable of an aesthetic response to
appeals for patronage from Lhuyd and Wotton.[21] The real
founder of the priceless Mostyn collection, however, was the
fourth baronet, Sir Thomas Mostyn (1704–58). The most
studious of noblemen, Mostyn took such a deep aesthetic
pleasure in collecting a wide variety of books that his library
was a model of good taste, containing 'a most elegant collection
of the classics . . . a numerous collection of books relating to
Greek and Roman antiquities . . . [and a] variety of manuscripts, mostly on vellum, & many of them richly illustrated'.[22]

By contrast, as a result of the transfer of the principal Welsh
manuscripts which had been in the hands of gentle families in
south Wales in the later middle ages to the gentry of north
Wales, the nobility in the south had lost much of their passion
for learning and antiquity by the seventeenth century.[23] In
dedicating his *Archaeologia Britannica* to Sir Thomas Mansel of

---

[18] Both Bulkeley and Cotton are noticed in *D.W.B.*
[19] Eiluned Rees, 'An Introductory Survey of Eighteenth Century Welsh
Libraries', *J.W.B.S.*, X (1971), 207.
[20] Askew Roberts, *Wynnstay and the Wynns* (1876), pp. 10–11.
[21] Lord Mostyn and T. A. Glenn, *History of the family of Mostyn* (1925),
pp. 158–60; R. Alun Charles, 'Teulu Mostyn fel Noddwyr y Beirdd', *Llên Cymru*,
IX (1966), 94–7.
[22] Thomas Pennant, *A Tour in Wales* (2 vols., 1784), I, 11; For a catalogue of
the Mostyn Library around 1692–1713, see N.L.W. MS. 21239B.
[23] A. O. H. Jarman, 'Literature and Antiquities' in A. J. Roderick (ed.),
Wales through the Ages (2 vols., 1960), II, 113.

Margam, Edward Lhuyd believed that if others were to follow Mansel's 'Maecenas-like' example 'the commonwealth of learning would soon enlarge its territories, and in particular the darkness of antiquities would in few years be brought to light'.[24] On balance, however, most titled patrons in south Wales were increasingly channelling their energies into the charitable ventures of societies like the S.P.C.K. Two founders of the Society were Sir John Philipps of Picton and Sir Humphrey Mackworth of Neath. The latter had amassed enormous wealth by exploiting rich mineral deposits in Cardiganshire and Neath and by investing in a series of lucrative commercial transactions, but he always believed that his prosperity and authority carried with them an obligation to provide moral and religious instruction for the poor. Mackworth himself penned several religious tracts and not the least of his concerns was to have the S.P.C.K. distribute literature among 'workmen and labourers' in mining districts.[25] Even so, Mackworth could not rival Sir John Philipps as a religious and social reformer. Sir John ploughed most of his wealth into the major religious and philanthropic movements of his day. Widely respected as that 'great and good man', he cherished interests and zeal for promoting the common good that were boundless.[26] Nor did he confine his industry to any particular branch of activity: he was a member of the Society for the Reformation of Manners, the Society for the Propagation of the Gospel, the East India Mission and the Holy Club. Most important of all, he was 'the spring and guide' of the 'laudable actions'[27] of the S.P.C.K. It was his vigorous enthusiasm that stirred many clergymen (notably Griffith Jones, Llanddowror) and laymen in south-west Wales to build charity schools, establish parochial lending libraries, and distribute thousands of Bibles and 'good books' among the deserving poor.

[24] R. T. Gunther (ed.), *Early Science in Oxford. Life and Letters of Edward Lhuyd* (1945), p. 44.
[25] *D.W.B.*; Clement, p. 251.
[26] Thomas Shankland, 'Sir John Philipps; the Society for Promoting Christian Knowledge; and the Charity-School Movement in Wales, 1699–1737', *T.H.S.C.*, 1904–5, pp. 77–8.
[27] The phrase belongs to Philipps's celebrated protégé, Griffith Jones, Llanddowror. Ibid., p. 178.

II. ESQUIRES

Those who were designated 'esq.' in the subscription lists, i.e. the armigerous gentry, constitute the second group of subscribers. In the Restoration period the term 'esq.' normally denoted an admixture of wealth and ancient descent, and it was still normal practice to find an esquire's position judged largely by 'common estimation'.[28] Wales was generally a land of small proprietors who were nothing like as affluent as English counterparts who sported the same suffix.[29] Most Welsh squires, although differing in their breeding, wealth and intellectual attainments, were men of relatively modest standing. The Denbighshire estates of three squires who subscribed to *Defosiwnau Priod*, John Myddleton of Chirk, Thomas Holland of Teyrdan and John Chambers of Henllan, were valued at £250, £240 and £200 respectively in 1707.[30] Similarly, the Denbighshire estates of six armigerous gentlemen who subscribed to Edward Samuel's *Gwirionedd* in 1716 were valued at sums ranging from £150 to £500.[31] Nevertheless, these were men who occupied a position of leadership in their respective communities, carrying out tasks of local administration, filling the post of high sheriff, and representing the interests of their communities in Parliament.

Like their titled superiors, the Welsh squirearchy had retained an enduring fondness for antiquarianism. Lhuyd, Rowlands and Wotton, respectively, recruited 46 per cent, 28 per cent and 33 per cent of their total subscribers from this group. More striking, however, is the consistency with which they subscribed to religious books, particularly those which made the heaviest intellectual demands on the reader. 38 per cent of the subscriptions to the Welsh translation of Jeremy Taylor's *Contemplation on the state of man*, published in 1730, came from this group, 29 per cent subscribed to Edward Samuel's translation of Hugo Grotius's *De Veritate Religionis Christianae* in 1716, and 19 per cent to the same author's

[28] H. P. R. Finberg and Joan Thirsk (eds.), *The Agrarian History of England and Wales, vol. IV, 1500–1640* (1967), p. 301.
[29] P. R. Roberts, 'The Landed Gentry in Merioneth, circa 1660–1832, with special reference to the estates of Hengwrt, Nannau, Rug and Ynysymaengwyn' (unpubl. Univ. of Wales M.A. thesis, 1963), pp. 3–4.
[30] N.L.W., Wynnstay Documents, Box 106, no. 28.
[31] Ibid. The six subscribers were Robert Davies, Thomas Kyffin, Henry Roberts, Roger Salesbury, John Wynne and Thomas Wynne.

translation of William Beveridge's *The Chief Duties of a Christian* in 1723. This suggests that no special effort was made to recruit subscriptions for such works from the lower orders, and that the squirearchy was not simply concerned with the dissemination of religious literature but provided readers themselves. They were also evidently prepared to subscribe to devotional works of a simpler nature: although as a group they comprised only 12 per cent and 9 per cent, respectively, of the total subscriptions for *Holl Ddyledswydd Dyn* and *Defosiwnau Priod*, their numbers in absolute terms—27 and 33— had not diminished.

Overall, the general linguistic and geographical pattern of squirearchical patronage was confined to counties in north-west and south-west Wales. These were counties which had been least affected by anglicisation and could still boast a strong indigenous literary tradition that had been sustained over the centuries by gentlemanly patronage. The most consistent subscribers among them were the Merioneth gentry who, bound together by ties of kinship, marriage and culture, were not enveloped by the ever-encroaching web of anglicising influences until the end of the eighteenth century.[32] William Wynn of Maesyneuadd, high sheriff of Merioneth in 1714, inherited his father's love of poetry and literature, subscribing to no fewer than eight Welsh books and earning three elegies from appreciative if sorrowing bards on his death in 1730.[33] Robert Vaughan of Hengwrt (*d.* 1751), whose estate was valued at £500 in 1718 and who became high sheriff of his county in 1735, subscribed to five Welsh books which were added to the magnificent collection of Welsh manuscripts and books which he had inherited from his illustrious grandfather and namesake.[34] Some of his neighbours were equally benevolent and cultured squires: William Price of Rhiwlas (*d.* 1774), an Oxford-trained antiquary of taste and discernment who became high sheriff of Merioneth and Caernarvon in

[32] R. T. Jenkins and Helen Ramage, *A History of the Honourable Society of Cymmrodorion* (1951), p. 53.

[33] Bob Owen, 'Maesyneuadd', *Journal Merioneth Hist. & Rec. Soc.*, IV (1961), 77–8. For the elegies see N.L.W. MS. 12732E, pp. 11–12; N.L.W., Cwrtmawr MS. 27E, p. 399; N.L.W., Peniarth MS. 239B, p. 317.

[34] Keith Williams Jones (ed.), *A Calendar of the Merioneth Quarter Sessions Rolls, 1733–1765* (1965), p. 309. For a catalogue of the Hengwrt library *c.* 1659, see N.L.W. MS. 9095B.

successive years, subscribed to four Welsh books,[35] whilst Vincent Corbet of Ynysymaengwyn (d. 1723), a subscriber to three Welsh books, endeared himself to society at large as a kindly, charitable landlord and a generous benefactor to local authors and bards.[36]

In Denbighshire, the readiest patronage came from the Myddelton family of Chirk Castle: Robert Myddelton (d. 1733) subscribed to five Welsh books, including two dozen copies of *Prif Dd'ledswyddau Christion*, and paid a subscription of 18s. 6d. for a dozen copies of *Ystyriaethau o Gyflwr Dyn* before presumably sharing them among members of his family.[37] His brother John (d. 1747) also paid a guinea subscription for copies of Edward Samuel's work, adding them to his superb library—totalling some 3,000 volumes—of classical, theological, philosophical, historical and legal works.[38] The most consistent single patron in this group, however, was a native of Flintshire: Richard Mostyn of Penbedw, near Nannerch, third son of Sir Roger Mostyn, first baronet of Mostyn Hall.[39] Mostyn subscribed to nine Welsh books in this period. Many prominent scholars drew heavily, both directly and indirectly, on his 'great knowledge and curiosity', and none was 'more sensible of his obligations' to Mostyn than the Oxford antiquary and scientist, Edward Lhuyd.[40] Moses Williams, that most voracious collector of Welsh books and manuscripts, also had access to Mostyn's much-envied collection of classical, historical and theological works and also to some of the earliest products of the Welsh printing press in Tudor and early Stuart times. It was fitting, therefore, that Williams should have dedicated his *Cofrestr*, the cornerstone of Welsh bibliography, to this enthusiastic antiquary and patron.[41]

[35] Keith Williams Jones, op. cit., p. 308.
[36] Bob Owen, 'Cipolwg ar Ynysymaengwyn a'i Deuluoedd', *Journal Merioneth Hist. & Rec. Soc.*, IV (1962), 111–2; Arwyn Lloyd Hughes, 'Noddwyr y Beirdd yn sir Feirionnydd' (unpubl. Univ. of Wales M.A. thesis, 2 vols., 1969), II, 929, 936–7.
[37] W. M. Myddelton (ed.), *Chirk Castle Accounts, 1666–1753* (1931), p. 454.
[38] N.L.W., Chirk Castle MSS. A.30–1.
[39] Nesta Lloyd, 'The Correspondence of Edward Lhuyd and Richard Mostyn', *Flintshire Hist. Soc. Pubs.*, 25 (1971–2), 31.
[40] B. F. Roberts, 'Llythyrau John Lloyd at Edward Lhuyd', *N.L.W.J.*, XVII (1971), 101; R. T. Gunther, op. cit., p. 258.
[41] N.L.W., Llanstephan MS. 114B, fly-leaf; Moses Williams, *Cofrestr* (1717), sig. A2r–v. For a catalogue of the Penbedw library, see N.L.W., Peniarth MS. 512.

The squirearchy of south-west Wales was equally in the van of Welsh patrons. The Maecenas *par excellence* here was John Vaughan of Cwrt Derllys, Carmarthenshire. Although his name figures in only two subscription lists in this period, Vaughan was the driving force behind many of the successes of the S.P.C.K.[42] Few Welshmen of his time were as prodigious in energy or as fertile in ideas. Vaughan constantly plied S.P.C.K. headquarters with fresh plans: he encouraged and directed the building of charity schools; he suggested English books worthy of translation, bore the costs of publishing some of them, took local authors under his wing, and industriously disseminated their literature among the deserving poor; he stands out as a pioneer of free libraries; and his genuine regard for the welfare and education of poor children and prisoners was not only a form of social insurance but also a reflection of his sincere humanitarianism. Vaughan was also capable of inspiring and invigorating his neighbouring squires. John Lewis, squire of Gernos, Llangunllo, and sometime high sheriff of Cardiganshire, 'commanded' Moses Williams to translate William Fleetwood's *Companion to the Altar* and financed the venture himself.[43] Similarly, Walter Lloyd, squire of Coedmor, and Stephen Parry, the prosperous owner of Neuadd Trefawr in the parish of Llandygwydd, Cardiganshire, were the moving spirits behind the publication of Alban Thomas's *Dwysfawr Rym Buchedd Grefyddol* in 1722.[44] Having inherited a long and distinguished tradition of gentlemanly patronage, literary squires were still exercising a decisive influence on the intellectual and cultural activities of their communities.

III. 'MR' AND 'MRS'

The third group of subscribers are those designated 'Mr' and 'Mrs' in the subscription lists. Such individuals were often described as 'gentlemen', though this term masked wide

[42] Mary Clement, 'Hanes yr S.P.C.K. yn Sir Gaerfyrddin o 1700 hyd 1750, gyda chyfeiriad arbennig at John Vaughan, Cwrt Derllys, a'i waith' (unpubl. Univ. of Wales M.A. thesis, 1940).
[43] J. Ifano Jones, *A history of printing and printers in Wales and Monmouthshire* (1925), p. 36.
[44] Ibid., p. 37; J. R. Phillips, *A List of the Sheriffs of Cardiganshire, 1539–1868* (1868), p. 24.

social differences: 'gentlemen' might be county landowners, the younger sons of esquires, the descendants of old freeholders, or part of the growing class of commercial people in the towns.[45] At any rate, no other group of subscribers was more consistent and numerous in subscribing to Welsh books. Edward Samuel relied heavily on their support, drawing 25 per cent, 22 per cent, 24 per cent and 25 per cent for the four translations he published between 1716 and 1731. Theophilus Evans drew consistently on their patronage: of the total subscribers to *Cydymddiddan* and *Prydferthwch Sancteiddrwydd*, 28 per cent and 31 per cent came from this group. Recruits were particularly numerous for devotional works: 80 (12 per cent) to *Trefn Ymarweddiad*, whilst John Prichard Prŷs's collection of devotional verses attracted 57 (22 per cent) subscribers.

It is not easy to generalise about the wealth of this group. The social and economic upheavals of the revolutionary period had made the task of Restoration heralds a nightmare, since the fluidity of the land market had resulted in enormous differences in the wealth and status of gentlemen.[46] Moreover, a man's designation had never completely corresponded to his worldly possessions and, in economic terms, some gentlemen might well be substantially worse off than well-to-do yeomen. Even so, such men were never disposed to discard their claims to be of gentle birth. Wales was still considered to be 'good pasture for a herald to bite in', even if some of those who purported to be of gentle stock were somewhat 'ill accoutred' and, in parts of Merioneth at least, 'so humble as to live in cottages and huts'.[47]

Generally, most country gentlemen occupied modest estates over which they exercised direct supervision. Probate material from various parts of Wales suggests that the most prosperous of them were invariably book-owners. George Coytmor of Tŷ Mawr in the parish of Dwygyfylchu, Caernarvonshire, left worldly goods valued at £470 17s. 6d. in 1730; he was a subscriber to *Gwirionedd* in 1716 and owned books valued at

[45] Gareth H. Williams, 'A Study of Caernarfonshire Probate Records, 1630–1690' (unpubl. Univ. of Wales M.A. thesis, 1972), p. 299.
[46] Philip Styles, 'The Heralds' Visitation of Warwickshire, 1682–1683', *Trans. & Proceedings of Birmingham Archaeological Soc.*, 70 (1954), 96–134; *idem*, 'The Social Structure of Kineton Hundred in the reign of Charles II', ibid., 78 (1962), 96–117.
[47] William Richards, *Wallography* (1682), p. 64; N.L.W., SA/RD/21, p. 91.

three guineas.[48] Griffith Roberts of Rhiw Goch, Trawsfynydd, Merioneth, was also wealthy and well-read: he subscribed to *Holl Ddyledswydd Dyn* in 1718, owned books worth £4 and left an estate valued at £813 10s. 4d. in 1725.[49] Prosperous men such as these were joined by those maligned social climbers, estate agents. One notable *parvenu* was Hugh Jones, steward of the estates of Jane Jones of Llanrhaeadr in Denbighshire. It was widely believed in local circles that Hugh Jones's wealth was accumulated by fraudulent means, but he nonetheless left several legacies and annuities for the education and clothing of poor children in neighbouring parishes on his death in 1736. Whether such donations were the product of humanitarian instincts or a guilty conscience we cannot tell, but Welsh authors and poets found him a willing patron of their works: six subscription lists bear his name.[50]

The financial independence of gentlemen-farmers meant that they were in a position to buy a wide range of books. Many of them drew nourishment from English devotional books. Tristram Matthews (d. 1735) of Llansilin, Denbighshire, owned copies of William Beveridge's most popular sermons, Simon Patrick's translation of Grotius's *De Veritate Religionis Christianae*, Thomas Comber's *Short Discourses upon the whole Common-Prayer* (1684), and Peter Nourse's *Practical Discourses* (1708).[51] A list of books in the possession of Morris Oliver of Pennal, Merioneth, in 1711, totalled 196 and included 9 books on law, 32 on medicine, 39 on history, and 61 works of theology and popular religion, including devotional works by Allestree, Bayly, Bunyan and Dent. More significant is the fact that Oliver was a faithful buyer and reader of Welsh literature: he owned 30 Welsh books, having inherited or bought a substantial

---

[48] N.L.W., Bangor P.R. 1730.

[49] N.L.W., Bangor P.R. 1725. Fellow gentlemen-subscribers included Evan Carreg of Aberdaron, Bangor P.R. 1738; Peter Foulkes of Cadwgan, St. Asaph P.R. 1717; John Lloyd of Brynllefrith, Trawsfynydd, who bequeathed to his son 'as many of my books as he shall think fit', Bangor P.R. 1764.

[50] G. M. Griffiths (ed.), 'John Wynne, a Report of the Deanery of Penllyn and Edeirnion, 1730', *The Merioneth Miscellany*, I, 37–8, 42; N.L.W., St. Asaph P.R. 1740. For Ellis Cadwalader's fulsome elegy to Jones in 1738, see U.C.N.W.L., Bangor MS. 3212, pp. 524–30.

[51] N.L.W., St. Asaph P.R. 1735. For other examples of book-owning gentlemen, see William Jenkins, Llanfair Cilgedin, Llandaff P.R. 1719; Thomas Howell, Cynwil Elfed, Archdeaconry of Carmarthen P.R. 1720; Thomas Roberts, Llanfair Dyffryn Clwyd, Bangor P.R. 1729.

number of the most popular Welsh books on the market since 1660.[52] Morris Oliver's tastes were shared by Owen Lloyd of Tan-y-bryn, Llanllyfni, Caernarvonshire. On his migration to London in 1691 to enter the service of Sir William Cranmer, Lloyd left behind him a collection of 67 books, ranging from Tully to Elisha Coles's English Dictionary, and from *Canwyll y Cymry* to Thomas Jones's *Y Gymraeg yn ei Disgleirdeb* (1688).[53]

Subscribers of Dissenting persuasion were generally either smaller gentry or substantial freeholders. Richard Lloyd, brother-in-law of the Arminian author, Jenkin Jones, and a descendant of the ancient family of Castell Hywel, farmed the estate at Coedlannau Fawr, Llanwenog, Cardiganshire. He and his father-in-law, John Jenkins of Llanwenog, a gentleman-blacksmith with a modest stake in property, subscribed to *Dydd y Farn Fawr*.[54] Men of their status made up 29 per cent and 19 per cent of those who subscribed to *Llun Agrippa* and *Dydd y Farn Fawr*, respectively. Jenkin Jones's subscribers also included lay ministers, local dignitaries in public office and merchants. John Corrie, a subscriber to *Dydd y Farn Fawr*, was a Presbyterian silk-merchant of Scottish descent who donated the land on which the church at Heol Awst, Carmarthen, was built.[55] A fellow-subscriber, William Williams, a Carmarthen draper, financed the publication of the second edition of *Y Cywyr Ddychwelwr* in 1727.[56] These subscribers were joined by craftsmen of gentle stock. William Rees, a blacksmith of Cynwyl Gaeo and a subscriber to *Llun Agrippa*, was affluent enough to make small bequests totalling £47 6s. 0d. in his will in 1752.[57] More prominent was John Bradford of Betws Tir Iarll, Glamorgan, a fuller and dyer who subscribed to *Llun*

[52] N.L.W., Esgair and Pantperthog MS.2. For Oliver's will, see Esgair and Pantperthog Deeds and Documents, no. 364.
[53] U.C.N.W.L., Bangor MS. 1218, document no. 17. When he returned to Wales, Lloyd subscribed to John Rhydderch's Dictionary. His estate at Llanllyfni was valued at £780 17s. 10d. in 1734 and his son, Richard, inherited all his books, letters, papers and writings. N.L.W., Bangor P.R. 1734.
[54] For Lloyd, see D. R. and Z. S. Cledlyn Davies, *Hanes Llanwenog: y plwyf, a'i phobl* (1939), p. 74. For his will, see N.L.W., Archdeaconry of Cardigan P.R. 1730. For John Jenkins, see N.L.W. MS. 12357E, p. 1498; N.L.W., British Records Association MS. 898, no. 178.
[55] N.L.W. MS. 12357E, p. 1270; N.L.W., Heol Awst MS. 2; N.L.W., F.C. Winchester Deeds, no. 25; J. E. Corrie, *Records of the Corrie Family, 1802–1899* (2 vols., 1899), II, 292, 298; J. Dyfnallt Owen, *Hanes Eglwys Heol Awst* (1926), p. 18.
[56] Thomas Rees and John Thomas, *Hanes Eglwysi Annibynol Cymru*, III, p. 429.
[57] N.L.W., Archdeaconry of Carmarthen P.R. 1752.

Agrippa as a precocious youth of seventeen. An omnivorous reader from an early age, Bradford was later to become the most articulate of freethinkers and a littérateur of some repute. He exercised an enormous influence on the early career of that prince of literary forgers, Iolo Morganwg, and was later hailed (in suitably hyperbolic terms) by his protégé as 'the most learned man that had for more than 200 years appeared in the principality'.[58]

The wives of county and parish gentry were also fairly numerous as patrons. Charitable work in eighteenth-century Wales owed a good deal to the labours of affluent, well-born women, the most celebrated being Madam Bridget Bevan, daughter of John Vaughan of Cwrt Derllys, who became the financial backbone of Griffith Jones's educational movement.[59] Several patronesses in this period also used their wealth to finance the publication of Welsh books. Mrs. Catherine Anwyl, daughter of Sir John Owen of Clenennau, contributed handsomely towards the cost of publishing *Ystyriaethau Drexelivs ar Dragywyddoldeb* in 1661 and, in return, the translator, Elis Lewis, testified warmly to her generous, open-handed nature and her acute concern for the spiritual welfare of her countrymen.[60] Mrs. Margaret Vaughan of Llwydiarth bore the whole cost of printing Edward Morris's *Y Rhybuddiwr Christnogawl* (1689), for which service both the author and Huw Morys eulogised her as 'the Mother of Wales'.[61] Similarly, Margaret Crowther of Little Shelsley, Worcestershire, was a noted philanthropist who, through her contacts with Erasmus Saunders, supplied funds to provide the Welsh reading public with sizeable editions of devotional books in the early-eighteenth century.[62]

Women of gentle birth were regular subscribers to devotional books. From the later middle ages onwards, pious women had played a prominent part in the spread of popular devotion,

[58] G. J. Williams, *Traddodiad Llenyddol Morgannwg* (1948), pp. 237–9; *idem*, *Iolo Morganwg* (1956), p. 119. For Bradford's will, see N.L.W., Llandaff P.R. 1785.
[59] W. Moses Williams, *The Friends of Griffith Jones* (1939), pp. 24–7.
[60] Elis Lewis, *Ystyriaethau Drexelivs ar Dragywyddoldeb* (1661), sig. A7v–A8v; Glenys Davies, *Noddwyr Beirdd ym Meirion* (1974), p. 171.
[61] Edward Morris, *Y Rhybuddiwr Christnogawl* (1689), p. 2; Huw Morys, *Eos Ceiriog* (2nd ed., 1823), II, 361.
[62] William Evans, *Egwyddorion y Grefydd Gristianogawl* (1707), p. 75; Clement, p. 71n.

and many in this period were keenly aware of the virtues of prayer, devotion and contemplation. Many of the works to which they subscribed were intended for use in the family circle: 25, 17, 11 and 7 wives, respectively, subscribed to *Trefn Ymarweddiad, Defosiwnau Priod, Holl Ddyledswydd Dyn* and *Prif Dd'ledswyddau Christion*. Devotional works such as these were staple literature in rearing sons and daughters. Spinsters and widows found that time hung heavy on their hands and turned to pious literature to relieve them of sheer boredom and to derive comfort during their more cheerless days. Relieved of domestic chores, blessed with a good education,[63] taste and an abundance of leisure, wives of the gentry often took refuge in intense piety and devotion. Mary Myddelton, the well-to-do spinster of Croesnewydd, Denbighshire, drew her comfort from reading Thomas à Kempis, Pascal, and especially William Law's *Serious Call to a devout and holy life* (1728).[64] Devotional books were a constant solace to women of independent means who lived alone. Elizabeth Leyson (d. 1724), a widow of Llantrithyd, Glamorgan, shut herself away in solitude to read the devotional manuals of Thomas à Kempis, Simon Patrick and Jeremy Taylor,[65] whilst Jane Tobias (d. 1745), a widow of Llanfairisgaer, Caernarvonshire, depended on her large Welsh Bible, *Y Llyfr Gweddi Gyffredin, Y Cydymaith Gorau*, and Mandeville's *Travels* for her literary comfort.[66] Anne Jenkins (d. 1686), a spinster of Llandyfodwg, Glamorgan, doubtless found that her sole literary possession, a copy of Stephen Hughes's Bible, helped her to bear her loneliness with noble stoicism.[67] Even at less prosperous levels, women found comfort and reassurance from their sparse libraries: Elinor Lloyd (d. 1677), a widow of Wrexham, Denbighshire, left an old Bible and other small books worth five shillings in an estate valued at £15 3s. 8d., whilst Mary James (d. 1742) of Llanddewi Brefi, Cardiganshire, counted her old cupboard, a desk and a

---

[63] A. H. Dodd, *Studies in Stuart Wales* (2nd ed., 1952), p. 6; N.L.W., Plas Nantglyn MS. 8.
[64] N.L.W., Plas Power Deeds and Documents, Vouchers and Accounts, 1727–31.
[65] N.L.W., Llandaff P.R. 1724. Elizabeth Williams, widow of Dolau Cothi, owned a fine cabinet of books worth fifteen guineas. Archdeaconry of Carmarthen P.R. 1734.
[66] N.L.W., Bangor P.R. 1745.
[67] N.L.W., Llandaff P.R. 1686.

small collection of books worth fifteen shillings as the principal possessions in her estate valued at £3 4s. 6d.[68]

IV. THE UPPER CLERGY

The support offered by the Welsh episcopate towards the publication of Welsh books depended largely on the attitudes and predilections of the individuals concerned. In the pre-toleration period, Laudian values were uppermost in the minds of many Welsh bishops, and some of them consequently made no secret of their disapproval of the literary ventures of Welsh Dissenters. Moreover, sympathy among English bishops was likely to be very much less evident than among native prelates. As a result, although ministers like Stephen Hughes were not prepared to let sleeping dogs lie, particularly if those dogs were indolent and indifferent English bishops,[69] religious reformers took care not to rouse them too sharply from their slumbers.

Before the turn of the century, however, the activities of two Welsh bishops, William Lloyd at St. Asaph (1680–92) and Humphrey Humphreys at Bangor (1689–1701), did much to compensate for the lethargy and obduracy of their stiff-necked predecessors. Lloyd swiftly endeared himself to Welsh reformers by ensuring that Welsh cures were filled with able Welshmen, initiating many worthwhile literary ventures, distributing godly literature throughout his diocese, and taking the trouble to learn the Welsh language.[70] Humphrey Humphreys, too, devoted himself to the spiritual needs of his diocese and to his antiquarian and genealogical pursuits. Humphreys was rated by Edward Lhuyd as 'incomparably the best skilled in our antiquities' and, following Lhuyd's death, it was generally agreed 'on all hands' that Humphreys was 'the best Welshman living'. Local poets and authors waxed lyrical in praise of him as a bishop and patron. Humphreys advised one of his protégés, Edward Samuel, to publish *Bucheddau'r Apostolion* (1704) and

[68] N.L.W., St. Asaph P.R. 1677; Archdeaconry of Cardigan P.R. 1743.
[69] Stephen Hughes (ed.), *Gwaith Mr. Rees Prichard* (Part IV, 1672), sig. a5v–a6r.
[70] U.C.N.W.L., Mostyn Correspondence, vol. 2, no. 68; Bod., Tanner MS. 30, f. 124; B.L., Birch Add. MS. 4274, f. 255 and f. 38; Saunders, p. 40; Gwenllian Jones, op. cit., p. 202; C.C.L., Cardiff MS. 5.30, pp. 154–6; N.L.W. MS. 263B, p. 8.

urged Samuel Williams to print his *Amser a Diwedd Amser* (1707) at speed. It was not mere sycophancy that prompted Ellis Wynne to dedicate his translation of Jeremy Taylor's *Holy Living* in 1701 to Humphreys: he judged no one to be worthier.[71]

The increasing trend towards the intrusion of party politics into episcopal appointments in the early decades of the eighteenth century meant that reformers needed to be even more zealous in reminding prelates of their spiritual and cultural obligations. Although tending to sugar the pill with cloying paeans to his dedicatees, Edward Samuel was never loath to point out their responsibilities to Welsh bishops. John Evans, bishop of Bangor (1702–16) had scarcely settled into his episcopal seat before Samuel successfully persuaded him to honour his *Bucheddau'r Apostolion* with his patronage.[72] Similarly, in 1718, Samuel hailed John Wynne, newly-appointed bishop of St. Asaph, as a mirror and light for the whole kingdom.[73] His *laudatio* was prompted not so much on account of Wynne's much-vaunted learning and wisdom, but largely because he was Welsh-speaking and thus something of a *rara avis* among early eighteenth-century bishops in Wales. John Wynne, moreover, proved to be a signal example of the ideal patron. No other bishop subscribed more consistently to Welsh books: six subscription lists bear his name in this period.

In south Wales, most bishops responded, with varying enthusiasm, to the appeals of the S.P.C.K. for their patronage, although the latter was always 'very tender of doing anything that looks like dictating to the reverend clergy and especially those that are dignified with an episcopal character'.[74] Dissident voices, like that of Philip Bisse, bishop of St. David's (1710–13), refused to subscribe to Welsh books because that would 'obstruct the English tongue which he will endeavour to propagate by erecting charity schools'.[75] Neither his predecessor nor successor needed a second bidding. Bishop George Bull (1705–10) cooperated enthusiastically with the

---

[71] *Arch. Camb.*, XIX (1859), 166; N.L.W., SD/Misc. B/131, p. 83; E. G. Wright, 'Humphrey Humphreys, Bishop of Bangor and Hereford (1648–1712)', *Trans. Anglesey Antiq. Soc. and Field Club*, 1949, pp. 61–76; Samuel Williams, op. cit., sig. A2r–v; Ellis Wynne, *Rheol Buchedd Sanctaidd* (1701), sig. A2r–A3v.

[72] Edward Samuel, *Bucheddau'r Apostolion* (1704), p. 5.

[73] Edward Samuel, *Holl Ddyledswydd Dyn* (1718), sig. A2r–A3v.

[74] Clement, p. 326.

[75] Ibid., p. 42.

S.P.C.K. and strove to establish schools, libraries and a proper distribution of Welsh books in his diocese.[76] Adam Ottley (1713–23), too, was a ready patron of Welsh literature, subscribing to Theophilus Evans's translations in 1719 and 1722, following that celebrated author's adulatory dedication to him in *Drych y Prif Oesoedd* in 1716.[77]

The diligence of cathedral dignitaries often glossed over the deficiencies of alien or absentee bishops. In north Wales, cultural patronage among the cathedral clergy was more forthcoming than in the south, since the former had retained their wealth, income and Welshness to a greater degree than their colleagues in the southern dioceses. As a result, non-residence, absenteeism and the intrusion of non-Welshmen were less pronounced in the dioceses of Bangor and St. Asaph. Two individuals whose fingers were always on the spiritual and cultural pulse of their sees were John Jones, dean of Bangor (1689–1727), and Robert Wynne, chancellor of St. Asaph (1690–1743). Both were among the most assiduous agents for the S.P.C.K., constantly raising subscriptions, arranging parochial and diocesan libraries, and disseminating godly literature among the poor. Widely recognised as a 'beloved foster-father' to his native tongue, John Jones subscribed to five books in this period, but this only hints at the quiet encouragement which he gave Welsh authors to publish their works.[78] Similarly, Robert Wynne, a member of the wealthy Garthewin family whose estates he augmented by discreet purchases and two prosperous marriages, subscribed to no fewer than eight Welsh books.[79] Both were also alive to social realities, refusing to pay lip service to the linguistic policy of the S.P.C.K. by their insistence that the Welsh language was the indispensable medium for charity schools in north Wales.[80] Jones set up a dozen Welsh schools where teaching was carried out entirely through the medium of Welsh, and in his will, in which he donated several hundred pounds to

[76] Robert Nelson (ed.), *The Life of Dr. George Bull* (2nd ed., 1714), pp. 443–53.
[77] Theophilus Evans, *Drych y Prif Oesoedd* (1716), sig. A3v; Rees Prichard, *Canwyll y Cymru* (1721), Preface.
[78] N.L.W., Plasgwyn (Vivian) Papers, MSS. 99, 104–6; N.L.W. MS. 13062B, f. 624r–v; N.L.W. MS. 9102A.
[79] R. O. F. Wynne, 'The Wynne family of Melai and Garthewin', *Denbs. Hist. Soc. Trans.*, V (1956), 81.
[80] Clement, p. 7.

various charity schools, he stipulated that the funds were to be used 'for the instructing of poor children for ever to read Welsh so perfectly as that each of them might be able to read the Bible and Common Prayer Book in Welsh well, and be also taught the Catechism of the Church of England in Welsh'.[81] The many-sided interests of cathedral dignitaries of this quality did much to compensate for the derelictions of their superiors. There is a ring of truth about John Morgan's conviction that the elevation of men of John Jones's calibre to Welsh sees would have speedily dispelled the ignorance of the masses.[82]

V. PARISH CLERGY AND DISSENTING MINISTERS

Unlike many of their superiors, the parish clergy was still largely Welsh in origin and sympathy. Of all the social groups in Wales that enjoyed the benefits of education and a modicum of leisure, this was the only one on which there was an obligation, by calling and profession, to use the Welsh language regularly. The fact that 33 per cent and 28 per cent of the subscribers to John Rhydderch's Dictionary and William Gambold's Grammar, respectively, were members of this group is earnest of the clergy's considerable concern for the Welsh language and educational standards in general. Moreover, in spite of the impoverished lives which some clergymen led, they formed the most consistent and reliable group of subscribers in this period. Not only were they readers themselves but they were also anxious to assimilate Welsh religious literature in order to preach Reformation truths to their flocks. Many of them took it upon themselves to subscribe for a quantity of books which were subsequently either sold among well-to-do parishioners or distributed free to the deserving poor. However, clergymen usually bought books for their own personal reference. In particular, doctrinal works

---

[81] For details of Jones's will, see Thomas Shankland, op. cit., pp. 158–65, and E. G. Wright, 'Dean John Jones (1650–1727)', *Trans. Anglesey Antiq. Soc. and Field Club*, 1952, pp. 34–43.

[82] N.L.W. MS. 13062B, f. 624r–v. Another prominent book-collector in this group was Edward Wynne of Bodewryd, chancellor of the diocese of Hereford. For his collections see N.L.W., Bodewryd MS. 68B; U.C.N.W.L., Penrhos (1) MS. 792–5; Penrhos (VII) MS. 956. Cf. Francis Jones, 'A Squire of Anglesey', *Trans. Anglesey Antiq. Soc. and Field Club*, 1940, pp. 76–92.

which called for certain intellectual powers were always prominent on their book-shelves. Theophilus Evans evidently concentrated heavily on clerical patronage for his vigorous apologiae of the Anglican faith: 56 per cent and 40 per cent of the subscribers to his works in 1719 and 1722 were clergymen. Similarly, Edward Samuel received remarkably consistent support from his fellow-clergy in north Wales: 41 (33 per cent) subscribed to *Gwirionedd*, 51 (22 per cent) to *Holl Ddyledswydd Dyn*, 41 (30 per cent) to *Prif Dd'ledswyddau* and 50 (22 per cent) to *Athrawiaeth yr Eglwys*.

Subscription lists reveal that the most consistent clerical patrons were graduates with better livings than most, men of taste, culture and social standing whose libraries were invariably multilingual. Many of them were authors themselves, consciously uniting in a common bond to support the burgeoning stock of religious literature. The most prolific subscriber was John Jones, vicar of Wrexham (1716–31) and sometime Fellow of Jesus College, Oxford, who subscribed to six books and eventually bequeathed his collection of theological works to his successors at Wrexham.[83] Richard Davies, vicar of Ruabon (1704–46) and a Peterhouse graduate, was an active S.P.C.K. agent, a generous philanthropist, who subscribed to five Welsh books which were housed in his splendidly varied library.[84] William Price, vicar of Llanrhaeadr in Kinmerch (1712–34), subscribed to five books which he absorbed in a collection valued at £2 on his death.[85] Humphrey Foulkes, rector of Marchwiel (1709–37) and a graduate of Jesus College, Oxford, subscribed to four books and was well-known in intellectual circles for his unpublished dissertations on religion, literature, politics and law in the middle ages.[86]

A sample of probate material confirms that it was the most prosperous and best-educated clergymen who owned the greatest number of books. William Anwyl, rector of Ffestiniog and Maentwrog, whose goods were valued at £205 12s. 0d. in

[83] D. R. Thomas, *History of the diocese of St. Asaph* (3 vols., 1908–13), III, 319; N.L.W., Plas Power (1970) Miscellaneous Documents ('A Catalogue of the Revd. Mr. John Jones vicar of Wrexham's books').

[84] D. R. Thomas, op. cit., III, 285–6; N.L.W., St. Asaph P.R. 1747; N.L.W. MS. 7396A.

[85] A. I. Pryce, *The Diocese of Bangor during Three Centuries* (1929), p. 17; N.L.W., Bangor P.R. 1734.

[86] *D.W.B.*; D. R. Thomas, op. cit., I, 348; N.L.W., St. Asaph P.R. 1756.

1730, owned books worth £10, whilst Lewis Lewis, rector of Llangynhafal, whose possessions were worth £261 15s. 4d. in 1728, owned books valued at £8.[87] Stephen Hughes of Swansea, the Anglican son of the celebrated Dissenter, added considerably to the rich library which he inherited from his father and bequeathed a collection valued at £40 in 1708.[88] Thomas Price, vicar of Meidrim (d. 1710), owned books worth £8 among worldly goods valued at £107 12s. 5d., whilst William Howell, vicar of Llandeilo Talybont (d. 1732), boasted a library worth £7 among goods totalling £81 7s. 0d.[89] Affluent clerics in the south-east were no less omnivorous as readers: Thomas Wilkins, rector of St. Mary Church (d. 1699), owned a remarkable collection of books and manuscripts valued at £50,[90] whilst James Harries, the industrious vicar of Llantrisant (d. 1728), owned a study of books which, valued at £30, formed almost a tenth of his total material possessions.[91]

Even so, books were by no means a monopoly of wealthy clerics.[92] Books remained a prominent feature of even the most threadbare inventories of the less well-to-do clergy. In the archdeaconry of Carmarthen, John Parry, vicar of Llandeilo Fawr (d. 1706), owned books worth £1 in material goods valued at £20 9s. 0d.; a fifth of the personal goods of Daniel Jones, vicar of Llangathen, whose inventory totalled £20 0s. 10d in 1729, comprised a study of books, whilst books valued at £5 made up a goodly portion of the sixteen guineas at which the worldly estate of John Griffiths, vicar of Llandingad, was assessed in 1709.[93] Similarly, in the impoverished and economically-retarded archdeaconry of Cardigan, the books owned by Evan Davies, rector of Cellan (d. 1702), valued at £1 10s. 0d., formed nearly a twelfth of the total value of his earthly goods. More strikingly, books worth £1 made up a sixth of the total value of the personal estate of Moses Roberts,

---

[87] N.L.W., Bangor P.R. 1730; Bangor P.R. 1728.
[88] N.L.W., Archdeaconry of Carmarthen P.R. 1708. Hughes's estate was valued at £103 5s. 0d.
[89] N.L.W., Archdeaconry of Carmarthen P.R. 1710; Archdeaconry of Carmarthen P.R. 1732.
[90] N.L.W., Llandaff P.R. 1699. Wilkins's estate was valued at £319 10s. 0d.
[91] N.L.W., Llandaff P.R. 1728. Harries's estate was valued at £340 3s. 2d.
[92] Of fifteen Caernarvonshire clergymen who left inventories between 1630 and 1690, twelve owned books in both Welsh and English, and several owned libraries valued at £10. Gareth H. Williams, op. cit., p. 330.
[93] N.L.W., Archdeaconry of Carmarthen P.R. 1706, 1729, 1709.

vicar of Llanilar, in 1731.[94] It would seem probable, therefore, that most clergymen, whether rich or poor, endeavoured to ensure that their libraries were as well-stocked as their means would allow.

What is clear is that John Eachard's portrait of the Restoration cleric as one who owned scarcely more than 'a budget of old stitched sermons hung up behind the door' is a long way from the truth.[95] Welsh clergymen spent a good deal of their time among their books, not only in order to acquire sermon material but also as a means of stimulating their intellects. The range of reading material in their libraries testifies to cultivated tastes. One of the most under-rated antiquaries of the seventeenth century, Thomas Wilkins, was not only the proud possessor of the 'Red Book of Hergest' and the 'Book of the Anchorite', but also of a wide variety of chronicles, legal treatises and theological works.[96] If the list of books possessed by William Herbert, vicar of Llansanffraid (d. 1734) is representative, the reading matter of clergymen in the archdeaconry of Cardigan was equally high in quality. Herbert's library comprised books ranging from John Locke's *Essay concerning Humane Understanding* (1690) to William Wotton's *Reflections upon ancient and modern learning* (1694); and from Thomas Blount's *Glossographia* (1656) to Simon Thomas's *Hanes y Byd a'r Amseroedd* (1718).[97] On the whole, devotional books, both in Welsh and English, provided the staple nourishment of most middling and less well-to-do clergymen. Morgan Williams, vicar of Myddfai (d. 1732), is a good example: he owned books worth £3, including a Welsh prayer book, copies of *Canwyll y Cymry*, *The Whole Duty of Man*, William Dyer's *Christ's Famous Titles* (1663), William Burkitt's *Expository Notes and Practical Observations on the New Testament* (1700) and Francis Bragge's *Practical Observations upon the Miracles of our Blessed Saviour* (1702).[98]

Unlike their Anglican counterparts, Dissenting ministers

[94] N.L.W., Archdeaconry of Cardigan P.R. 1702, 1731.
[95] John Eachard, *The Grounds and Occasions of the Contempt of the Clergy and Religion enquired into* (1670), p. 87.
[96] N.L.W., Llandaff P.R. 1699. See also Ceri Lewis, 'The Literary History of Glamorgan from 1550 to 1770' in Glanmor Williams (ed.), *Glamorgan County History, vol. IV, Early Modern Glamorgan* (1974), pp. 584–9.
[97] N.L.W., Cwrtmawr MS. 420B.
[98] N.L.W., Archdeaconry of Carmarthen P.R. 1732.

were denied the benefits of a parochial endowment. Inevitably, therefore, they needed to be men of private means. Most of the eleven ministers (13 per cent) who subscribed to Jenkin Jones's *Llun Agrippa* were men of farming stock. Morgan Griffith, the popular Baptist minister at Hengoed (1701–38), farmed a small estate at Argoed, near Caerphilly.[99] Llywelyn Bevan, Independent minister at Cwmllynfell and Gellionnen (1701–23), was a self-styled yeoman whose status as a Dissenting minister rather than his modest estate, valued at £8 13s. 4d. and made up of four cows, two steers, two heifers and two horses, entitled him to bear that suffix.[100] Bevan's co-pastor, Roger Howell of Llangiwg, a man suspected of Arminian tendencies but held in awe for his astonishing biblical knowledge, was a blacksmith-cum-smallholder whose material possessions, including a horse and saddle, wearing apparel and books worth £5, were valued at £13 15s. 0d. on his death in 1742.[101] Other ministers supplemented their income by teaching: William Edwards of Caernarvon was a much-persecuted preacher and schoolmaster,[102] whilst Henry Davies, Independent minister at Blaengwrach (1718–38), a man of catholic spirit and 'a great reader of good books', was a tireless preacher and schoolmaster who did much to ease the passage of early Methodist evangelists in the valleys of Glamorgan.[103]

Thirty ministers (14 per cent) subscribed to Jenkin Jones's second major work, *Dydd y Farn Fawr*, in 1727. Although most of these were Calvinists, Jones also recruited subscribers who shared his own doctrinal sympathies. Men like Roger Howell of Llangiwg, Roger Williams (d. 1730), co-pastor at Cwm-y-Glo and Cefnarthen, and Thomas Perrot (d. 1733), academy tutor at Carmarthen, were strong-willed, flinty, academy-trained Arminians who exercised a powerful religious and cultural influence in their respective localities.[104] More

---

[99] N.L.W. MS. 12357E, p. 1384; *H.P.N.*, p. 310.

[100] N.L.W., Archdeaconry of Carmarthen P.R. 1723; *D.W.B.*

[101] N.L.W., Archdeaconry of Carmarthen P.R. 1742; Rees and Thomas, II, pp. 144, 148–9.

[102] Dr. Williams's Library, Trust Minutes, letter dated 3 January 1744; Rees and Thomas, III, 234.

[103] *D.W.B.* Davies was an avid collector of Morgan Llwyd's works. Roy Denning, 'William Thomas of Michaelston-Super-Ely: the Diary and the Man' in Stewart Williams (ed.), *Glamorgan Historian*, IX, 146.

[104] G. D. Owen, *Ysgolion a Cholegau yr Annibynwyr* (1939), pp. 20–3.

extreme elements also subscribed: Samuel Jones (d. 1764) of Llanedi, sometime schoolmaster at Pentwyn, Llannon, in Carmarthenshire, and Samuel Thomas (d. 1766), a native of Derllysg and one of Perrot's successors at Carmarthen, propagated the more passionate and abrasive tenets of Arianism.[105] Most of Jenkin Jones's patrons, however, were orthodox Calvinists whose independence rested on the wealthy estates which they had either inherited or built up themselves. Philip Pugh (d. 1760), the popular Independent minister at Cilgwyn, Cae'r Onnen and Llwynpiod, inherited from his affluent parents extensive estates in the parishes of Blaenpennal, Llanarth, Llangeitho and Llanina,[106] whilst William Williams (d. 1730) tended to the needs of his Dissenting flock at Newmarket, Flintshire, and the farms which he held jointly in Rhandirisaf in the parish of Llanfair-ar-y-Bryn, Carmarthenshire.[107] Other ministers had elevated themselves socially by marrying wealthy brides: Rees Price, minister at Cildeudy, Bridgend and Betws from 1697 to 1739, a dour Calvinist gentleman who nursed and cossetted his famous son, Richard, from the infections of heresy, was a shrewd businessman who inherited the substantial farmhouse at Tyn-ton and further swelled the contents of his coffers with a large portion on the occasion of his marriage.[108] Similarly, Rees Davies (d. 1767), the crotchety Independent minister of Goitre in the parish of Llanover, Monmouthshire, married well and climbed the ladder of social advancement.[109]

The cultivation of reading habits was considered by Dissenting ministers to be indispensable to a truly Christian and enlightened life. Their sensitivity to the value of books was often revealed by their anxiety to supply their friends and successors with edifying literature so that their strivings for moral and spiritual reformation might lose no impetus by their own passing.[110] Their libraries invariably included classical,

[105] Samuel Jones and Samuel Thomas are noticed in *D.W.B.*
[106] J. H. Davies, 'The Abermeurig family', *West Wales Historical Records*, 2 (1911–2), 154.
[107] Rees and Thomas, IV, 213, 269, 272.
[108] *D.W.B.*; Rees and Thomas, II, 197–8, 205–6; G. D. Owen, op. cit., pp. 6–11; N.L.W., Llandaff P.R. 1739; Roland Thomas, *Richard Price* (1924), pp. 6–11.
[109] *D.W.B.*; Rees and Thomas, I, 32–3.
[110] See the wills of David Edwards of Betws Lleucu in N.L.W., Archdeaconry of Cardigan P.R. 1716; David Penry of Llanedi, in Archdeaconry of Carmarthen P.R. 1722; and Rees Davies of Llanofer, in Llandaff P.R. 1767.

theological, historical, biographical and philosophical works—
bought and read at the academies—together with popular
Welsh and English best-sellers. Some of their collections were
quite outstandingly valuable: Daniel Higgs (d. 1691), among
the most active Independent ministers in Swansea, owned
books worth £20,[111] whilst Thomas Perrot, tutor at Carmarthen, must have taken pride in his massive collection of
books valued at £40.[112] Academy students like Thomas
Morgan, sometime Independent minister at Henllan, collected
a rich miscellany of books ranging from Greek and Latin
grammars to the 'shilling histories' of Nathaniel Crouch, and
from the popular works of Bunyan and Baxter to best-selling
Welsh tracts by James Owen, Samuel Williams and Rees
Prydderch.[113] However, the book-collector *par excellence* among
eighteenth-century Independent ministers, was Edmund Jones
of Pontypool. Jones accumulated his library by several means:
his neighbours clubbed together to provide him with cash to
buy books; open-handed ministers provided him with a wide
range of literature; but most of his books were bought out of
his own pocket at great personal sacrifice.[114] 'The old Prophet'
soaked himself in the sermon literature of the seventeenth and
early-eighteenth centuries, heavily annotating his copies with
damning criticisms of Papists, Arminians, Deists and 'blind
malignant royalists'.[115] Nothing gave him greater pleasure
than to know that 'so many of the good old authors' had
'tumbled from London into the farthest parts of Wales to help
to preserve knowledge among the remnants of the ancient
Britons'.[116] Not many Welsh ministers were as impoverished as
Edmund Jones, but fewer still were as well-read as he.

VI. UNIDENTIFIED MEN AND WOMEN

Even the most cursory examination of subscription lists will
reveal that patrons of Welsh books were not confined to the

---

[111] R. T. Jones and B. G. Owens, 'Anghydffurfwyr Cymru, 1660–1662',
Y Cofiadur, 32 (1962), 27 and *passim*.
[112] N.L.W., Archdeaconry of Carmarthen P.R. 1733; N.L.W., B.R.A. 42–3.
Perrot's estate was valued at £117 4s. 9d.
[113] N.L.W. MS. 5457A, pp. 37–59.
[114] N.L.W. MSS. 7024A–7030A.
[115] N.L.W. MS. 15170B.
[116] N.L.W. MS. 17054D, p. 131.

élite of society. In particular, there are striking figures to show that practical devotional books drew a substantial number of subscribers from a reading public below the level of the parish gentry. *Trefn Ymarweddiad Gwir Gristion* attracted 424 (61 per cent) men and 72 (10 per cent) women subscribers, whilst *Defosiwnau Priod* drew 194 (55 per cent) male and 18 (5 per cent) female subscribers. It is significant that the doctrinally-loaded translations of Theophilus Evans and Griffith Wynn drew no subscribers from this group. Nor did Edward Samuel deem it worthwhile to tap their support for his translation of Hugo Grotius's work in 1716. Two years later, however, the list which prefaced his translation of the enormously popular *Whole Duty of Man* attracted 61 (26 per cent) male and 4 (2 per cent) female subscribers, a larger proportion than any other single group of patrons in that list.

The occupations of subscribers in this group were rarely specified and it is not easy, therefore, to estimate their identity and status precisely. It is, however, possible to identify a number of them from probate material and it may be that these are representative of a larger whole. Sixteen persons who subscribed to *Trefn Ymarweddiad* were yeomen. The exact status of a yeoman in this period is difficult to define and one suspects that the term was now used to describe farmers big and small. Some yeomen owned estates that were more prosperous than those of gentlemen, but they lacked claims to gentility, whilst the social and economic boundary which divided an impoverished yeoman from a husbandman was so fluid that social status was something that depended largely on the opinion of neighbours. At any rate, the economic wealth of yeoman-subscribers to *Trefn Ymarweddiad* ranged over a fairly wide span. Self-styled yeomen such as John Venables of Gwysaney, who made bequests totalling over £400, and Edward Kenrick of Marchwiel, whose estate was valued at £418 16s. 0d., were evidently more affluent than some who described themselves as 'gentlemen'.[117] Among the 'middling' yeomen, Foulke Humphreys of Llanelian possessed material goods valued at £168 8s. 6d., whilst Richard Hughes of Pentraeth supplemented a smallholding valued at £138 19s. 0d.

[117] N.L.W., St. Asaph P.R. 1745; 1746.

with a small smithy.[118] At a much lower level, however, penurious yeoman-subscribers like Richard Davies of Llanrwst, John Foulkes of Cyffylliog and Henry Pugh of Cyffylliog left behind them slender goods that totalled £27 2s. 6d., £16 14s. 6d. and £13 9s. 8d. respectively.[119]

Similarly, at least fourteen from this group who subscribed to *Defosiwnau Priod* were yeomen, many of them farming lands in Anglesey and Caernarvonshire. In these parts, yeomen were distinctly less prosperous: the average value of yeoman estates in Caernarvonshire in the latter half of the seventeenth century was around £26.[120] The richest subscriber in the group was John Prichard of Clynnog, whose estate was valued at £91 3s. 8d.[121] Charles Prydderch of Penmynydd supplemented his farming income by keeping a shop, thereby boosting the value of his estate to over £100.[122] Some of his fellow-subscribers were distinctly less well-off: the value of the estates of yeomen such as William Daniel of Llangeinwen (£20 3s. 0d.), William Moses of Pentraeth (£19 3s. 0d.), Griffith Edward of Clynnog (£18 0s. 6d.) and William Prichard of Holyhead (£7 10s. 0d.) indicates that they were smaller farmers whose livelihood suffered constantly from lack of capital, land taxes and stagnation of agricultural prices.[123] Similarly, a strong yeoman element is evident among 65 subscribers from five parishes in Merioneth who patronised *Holl Ddyledswydd Dyn*. These probably represented the surviving Welsh freeholders who were usually very numerous in pastoral areas. At least

[118] N.L.W., St. Asaph P.R. 1764; Bangor P.R. 1732.
[119] N.L.W., St. Asaph P.R. 1766; Bangor P.R. 1729, 1760. The other yeoman subscribers to *Trefn Ymarweddiad* were Edward Arthur, Llanerfil, St. Asaph P.R. 1760; Richard Conway, Llanfairtalhaearn, St. Asaph P.R. 1755; Robert Edwards, Llanarmon, St. Asaph P.R. 1778; Ellis Jones, Henllan, St. Asaph P.R. 1742; Robert Jones, Corwen, St. Asaph P.R. 1732; John Owens, Llanfairtalhaearn, St. Asaph P.R. 1789; John Roberts, Cyffylliog, St. Asaph P.R. 1736; Robert Thomas, Llannefydd, St. Asaph P.R. 1745; Ambrose Williams, Henllan, St. Asaph P.R. 1752.
[120] Gareth H. Williams, op. cit., p. 313.
[121] N.L.W., Bangor P.R. 1731.
[122] N.L.W., Bangor P.R. 1729.
[123] N.L.W., Bangor P.R. 1758, 1765, 1732, 1732. The other eight yeoman subscribers identified from probate material were: Thomas Barker, Hope, St. Asaph P.R. 1736; John Cadwaladr, Clynnog, Bangor P.R. 1736; Robert David, Llangeinwen, Bangor P.R. 1728; Hugh Hughes, Penrhos, Bangor P.R. 1735; John Hughes, Clynnog, Bangor P.R. 1752; Owen Hughes, Llanddaniel, Bangor P.R. 1749; Thomas Lloyd, Clynnog, Bangor P.R. 1738; Hugh Williams, Clynnog, Bangor P.R. 1735.

eleven subscribers from Llanuwchllyn were yeomen: among them John Hugh, whose estate was valued at £88, was the most prosperous, followed by David Rowland (£67 12s. 8d.) and John Morgan (£34 3s. 0d.).[124] In neighbouring parishes, the estate of Hugh Jones, a Dolgellau yeoman who bequeathed all the books in his study to his son, was valued at £135 7s. 0d., whilst yeomen of Trawsfynydd were best represented by John Rowland, whose earthly goods were worth £89 14s. 0d.[125]

Some of the well-to-do yeomen were able to afford a grammar school and even a university education, and this was often a strong stimulant to them to buy books of quality. John Prichard of Llangyfelach (d. 1695), whose goods were valued at £19 5s. 0d., owned Greek, Latin, English and Welsh books which he bequeathed to his son and daughter.[126] Jenkin Jones of Cardigan (d. 1725), whose estate was worth £30 10s. 0d., left his Greek and Latin books to his nephew.[127] William Morgan Evan (d. 1694), a Swansea yeoman, bequeathed an English Bible and copies of *The Practice of Piety* and Gouge's devotional books to his grandchild.[128] It is striking, too, how many small yeoman farmers in Cellan, Cardiganshire—a parish whose inhabitants were well-known for their religiosity—owned books. David Hugh (d. 1690), whose inventory was appraised at £18 13s. 8d., owned books worth £1 which he desired to be divided among his children; Griffith Hugh (d. 1695) and Rees Griffith (d. 1697) owned books valued at 5s. and 2s., a smaller proportion of their estates valued at £37 13s. 0d. and £32 6s. 4d. respectively; Griffith Hughes (d. 1709) bequeathed his household stuff and books to his wife, whilst Thomas John (d. 1710) owned books worth 5s. among goods valued at £14 15s. 6d.; finally, the worldly estate of David Evan (d. 1716) was valued at £39 7s. 6d., of which clothes, corn and books made up £1 10s. 0d.[129] How far the parish of Cellan was typical is difficult to judge, and it would be unwise to over-estimate the prevalence of book-reading among yeomen. Nonetheless, it is clear that yeomen shared the cultural

[124] N.L.W., St. Asaph P.R. 1741, 1741, 1740.
[125] N.L.W., Bangor P.R. 1736, 1744.
[126] N.L.W., Archdeaconry of Carmarthen P.R. 1696.
[127] N.L.W., Archdeaconry of Cardigan P.R. 1725.
[128] N.L.W., Archdeaconry of Carmarthen P.R. 1695.
[129] N.L.W., Archdeaconry of Cardigan P.R. 1690, 1695, 1697, 1709, 1710, 1716.

interests of the literate, educated classes rather than the peasant culture of the poor. Literacy was fast becoming an economic asset as well as a mark of social pride and cultural status to them, and the relative comfort and privacy of their homes were always conducive to family devotion and private study.

Subscriptions to practical devotional books were also readily forthcoming from craftsmen in both rural and urban areas. Since crafts were woven into the daily pattern of agricultural life, most country craftsmen supplemented their own special trades with income drawn from smallholdings. By having more than one string to their bow, they were able to exercise a decisive influence on the personality and character of their communities.[130] Their economic independence, highly-developed skills, good taste and pride in their craft were often transferred into matters of culture and religion. Moreover, the craftsman's emphasis on industry, probity and moral zeal, and the importance which he attached to literacy, education and general self-improvement made him a man capable of injecting a good deal of vitality into the religious life of his locality. Many Welsh authors, especially ballad-mongers, were craftsmen by trade, whilst a preponderance of Methodist exhorters in early-eighteenth-century Wales were either craftsmen or sons of craftsmen.[131] Prominent among subscribers to devotional books in this period were men like John Prichard of Clynnog and William Hughes of Penmynydd, humble weavers who kept smallholdings, Humphrey Hughes of Llanfachreth, a shoemaker-cum-farmer whose estate was valued at £50 5s. 0d., and Edward Ogden, a corviser who owned small tenements in Mold.[132] Men who later made their way in the world also paid their subscriptions for Welsh books in their youth: Lewis Morris of Anglesey learnt the craft of carpentry from his father before taking up practice as a surveyor and earning a reputation in intellectual circles as a 'proud, scornful, boastful, peppery' scholar and patriot.[133] His more generous and self-effacing brother, Richard, also a

[130] J. G. Jenkins, *Traditional Country Craftsmen* (1965), pp. 2–5.
[131] David Jenkins, 'The part played by craftsmen in the religious history of Modern Wales', *The Welsh Anvil*, VI (1954), 90–7.
[132] N.L.W., Bangor P.R. 1733, 1757, 1723; St. Asaph P.R. 1730.
[133] Hugh Owen, op. cit., *passim*. His unattractive character is described by R. T. Jenkins in *D.W.B.*

subscriber in his teens, followed his grandfather into the cooping trade before migrating to London to work as a clerk and a book-keeper.[134] Subscribers to Dissenting literature tended to come from the 'small merchant-yeoman-artisan social world' that formed the nucleus of early political radicalism in Wales.[135] Dissent found its most virile roots among those who were relatively well-to-do and whose economic independence enabled them to divorce themselves from the social hierarchy of the Anglican establishment and form their own religious views without fear of harassment from the landed *élite*. Most subscribers to Jenkin Jones's works seem to have been small freeholders. Among 42 subscribers (50 per cent) to *Llun Agrippa* were Morgan Harry of Caio and William Harry of Llanfynydd, both freeholders who voted in the Carmarthen election of 1722, joining two other freeholders, Evan David of Llanfihangel Rhos-y-Corn and Rowland Prydderch of Llandeilo, who subscribed to *Oes Lyfr* in 1724.[136] Jones also called on the support of modest yeomen like John Nicholas of Llangynwyd, whose material goods were worth £19 16s. 6d. in 1723, and Morgan William of Neath, whose estate was valued at £57 3s. 10d. on his death in 1743.[137] A substantial number of the 102 subscribers (48 per cent) to *Dydd y Farn Fawr* were also mostly freehold farmers occupying small homesteads in the Llandysul area.[138] The rateable value of these farms ranged between £6 and £8 per annum, and the most typical of these pious small farmers were men like David Morgan and John Howell of Llandysul, who left estates valued at £7 19s. 9d. and £5 0s. 6d. respectively.[139]

Craftsmen, too, were prominent subscribers to Dissenting

[134] *D.W.B.*; T. H. Parry-Williams (ed.), *Llawysgrif Richard Morris o Gerddi* (1931).

[135] Gwyn A. Williams, 'South Wales Radicalism: the First Phase', in Stewart Williams (ed.), *Glamorgan Historian*, II (1965), 32.

[136] 'Poll Book for the 1722 Parliamentary Election', *The Carmarthenshire Historian*, III (1966), 57–83.

[137] N.L.W., Llandaff P.R. 1723, 1724. See also Samuel Flew of Laleston, Llandaff P.R. 1766; Lewis Treharne of Llansannor, Llandaff P.R. 1729.

[138] W. J. Davies, *Hanes Plwyf Llandysul* (1896), pp. 294–8.

[139] N.L.W., Archdeaconry of Cardigan P.R. 1759, 1743. See also David Evan of Pen yr Allt Fawr (N.L.W., B.R.A. 898, MS. 89, 1–2, MS. 64); Evan David and Evan Thomas of Llanfihangel Yeroth in Bettws (*Carms. Historian*, 1966, pp. 57–83); Rees Thomas of Llanfair (J. H. Davies, 'Cardiganshire Freeholders in 1760', *West Wales Histor. Records*, 3 (1913), p. 85).

books.[140] This was entirely in character, for craftsmen formed one of the major pillars of Dissenting causes in eighteenth-century Wales. Most of them were men of many talents. The most protean subscriber to *Llun Agrippa* was Rhys Morgan, carpenter, weaver, harp-maker, poet, quack, deacon and preacher from Pencraig-nedd, a farmhouse in the parish of Cadoxton in the Vale of Neath.[141] Joseph John, a subscriber to *Oes Lyfr*, was a learned craftsman, epigrammatist, author and preacher whose medical skills enabled him to do 'a great deal of good to his neighbours rich and poor, both to souls and bodies'.[142] John subsequently became a Methodist exhorter and, on his death, he bequeathed to Thomas William, author of *Oes Lyfr*, Matthew Poole's twin-volume synopsis of his *Annotations upon the Holy Bible* (1683–5) and Andrew Willet's *Synopsis Papismi* (1592), and also left his nephew copies of Samuel Clarke's *A brief concordance to the Holy Bible* (1696), Arthur Hildersham's *Lectures upon Psalm LI* (1635) and Edward Leigh's *A System or Body of Divinity* (1654).[143] For a humble weaver, Thomas William himself owned an enviable and much-varied collection of books, ranging from Tudor chronicles to English devotional works, and from classic novels like *Robinson Crusoe* to the popular assortments of Nathaniel Crouch. His library of Welsh books, moreover, contained a Bible, a prayer book, three editions of the psalms, copies of devotional books by Edward Samuel, Rowland Vaughan, Iaco ab Dewi, Ellis Wynne, Charles Edwards, James Owen, Alban Thomas and William Meyrick, most translations of Bunyan's works, five catechisms, three copies of Rees Prichard's poems and a copy of John Rhydderch's dictionary.[144]

Dissenting women were just as committed as their bookish

---

[140] For useful parallels, see Peter Laslett, 'Scottish Weavers, Cobblers and Miners who bought books in the 1750s', *Local Population Studies*, 3 (1969), 7–15; R. C. Richardson, 'The Diocese of Chester. Religion and Reading in the late sixteenth and early seventeenth centuries', *The Local Historian*, XI (1974), 15–16.

[141] *D.W.B.*: G. J. Williams, *Traddodiad Llenyddol Morgannwg*, pp. 230–1.

[142] Joseph John's brother-in-law, David Davies, bequeathed him his carpenter's tools; N.L.W., Archdeaconry of Carmarthen P.R. 1734. Thomas William praised his skills as a craftsman in a collection of religious verse by John, *Hymnau Ysgrythurawl* (1765), p. 3; *Y Cofiadur*, XXIII (1953), 37.

[143] N.L.W., Calvinistic Methodist Archives 3005, pp. 3013–4 (I owe this reference to Mr. Emrys Williams); E. Lewis Evans, *Capel Isaac* (1950), p. 123; N.L.W., Archdeaconry of Carmarthen P.R. 1752.

[144] C.C.L., Cardiff MS. 2.139.

husbands to buying Welsh literature. Indeed, it is difficult to exaggerate the contribution of pious women to the growth of early Dissent in Wales. Many of them were wives or widows of freeholders or craftsmen: among the 20 (9 per cent) women subscribers to *Dydd y Farn Fawr* were Gwenllian David, a widow of Pant-y-Defaid, Llandysul, and Elinor Morgan of Llanwenog, who left estates valued at £17 10s. 0d. and £19 2s. 6d. respectively.[145] Such women were in relatively comfortable circumstances and were held in high esteem by ministers for their prudence and piety, their 'good stock of knowledge', their diligence and enthusiasm in attending meetings, their charitable concern for the poor, and their capacity for flourishing 'like the palm tree' to the last.[146] Jane and Elinor, successive wives of Christmas Samuel, Independent minister at Pant-teg, were 'full of good works' and 'great encouragers of ministerial labours', whilst well-to-do spinsters like Lleucu John of Abergwili won repute as 'eminent, zealous, faithful Christians'.[147] When Edmund Jones outlined the virtues of pious Dissenting women in the parish of Aberystruth, he found many 'notable Christians' in their midst, not least of whom was his mother, who was 'lively and zealous in divine things' and of 'very merciful disposition' to the poor.[148] Jones's own beloved wife, Mary, typified the self-effacing commitment of women to the aspirations of their husbands: most of the books that adorned 'the old Prophet's' library were read over by his 'good and dear spouse' and the knowledge and comfort thus gained moulded her into a 'rare excellent Christian' who remained 'strong, faithful and true . . . on the Lord's side'.[149]

VII. MISCELLANEOUS SUBSCRIBERS

The final group of subscribers, labelled 'miscellaneous', is made up of those persons whose occupations were stipulated in

[145] N.L.W., Archdeaconry of Cardigan P.R. 1728, 1761.
[146] See the descriptions of Dissenting women in E. D. Jones, 'Llyfr Eglwys Mynydd-bach', *Y Cofiadur*, 18 (1947), 3–50; *idem*, 'Llyfr Eglwys Pant-teg', *Y Cofiadur*, 23 (1953), 18–70.
[147] *Y Cofiadur*, 1953, pp. 60, 63–5. For Lleucu John's will, see N.L.W., Archdeaconry of Carmarthen P. R. 1720.
[148] Edmund Jones, *A Geographical, Historical and Religious Account of the Parish of Aberystruth* (1779), pp. 112–60.
[149] Newport Public Library MS. 350.012, p. 347.

the subscription lists.[150] Antiquarian works clearly drew the widest range of subscribers in this group. William Wotton was fortunate in being able to enlist the support of thirteen private libraries, state officials, civil servants, university dons, justices and lawyers, and also many London merchants and craftsmen of Welsh extraction. Edward Lhuyd also benefited greatly from the patronage of government officials, university graduates and professional men, whilst Henry Rowlands's list of subscribers was studded with professional Welshmen who held appointments in Ireland and Dublin merchants who traded with their counterparts in his own native county.[151]

It is in this group, engaged in *les professions libérales*, that we find the nascent professional middle-class in Wales. Edward Samuel's works in particular appealed to important social groups such as excisemen and customs officials, doctors and apothecaries, lawyers and clerks, university fellows and schoolmasters. These elements were beginning to impinge slightly on the cohesion and unity that bound the ruling landed *élite* together. Essentially *hommes nouveaux*, they nonetheless aspired to the same style of living as that enjoyed by the gentry, and their education, piety and cultural tastes, together with the dignity of their offices, won them a high degree of respect. Most of them retained a lively interest in native Welsh literature as well as the other intellectual pretensions of the upper classes. Richard Wynne of Garthewin, a London attorney, owned lavishly-bound legal treatises and works on theology, history, geography and travel; but his library was also adorned with Welsh Bibles, Lhuyd's *Archaeologia Britannica*, Langford's translation of *The Whole Duty of Man*, Thomas Williams's translation of Robert Nelson's *Companion for the Festivals and Fasts of the Church of England*, and a copy of the 1696 edition of *Canwyll y Cymry*.[152] The medical profession boasted several enthusiatic devotees of Welsh culture. Rowland Pugh of Rug, a kindly and learned physician who subscribed to four Welsh books in this period, was a well-informed man of

[150] Not every publisher went to the trouble of describing the profession of his subscribers and those who figure in this group therefore need to be fitted into the overall picture.
[151] C. L. Hubert-Powell, 'Some Notes on Henry Rowlands' "Mona Antiqua Restaurata" ', *Trans. Anglesey Antiq. Soc. and Field Club*, 1953, p. 27.
[152] N.L.W. MS. 889E.

taste whose prominence as a patron was readily praised by Welsh bards.[153] Similar esteem was accorded to Richard Evans of Llannerch-y-medd, Anglesey: he was such a master in the fields of genealogy, poetry, grammar and language that John Rhydderch relied heavily on him for advice in compiling his dictionary and Lewis Morris engaged his services in the campaign to establish a Welsh press in Anglesey.[154] Apothecaries, too, were often men whose homes were well-supplied with books. Intermingled with a variety of medical books in the possession of Henry Williams of Clynnog were devotional books like Simon Patrick's *The Christian's Sacrifice* (1671) and John Tillotson's *A Seasonable New Years Gift* (1687), a Welsh prayer book, two English Bibles and a prayer book, and a copy of *The Practice of Piety*.[155]

Miscellaneous subscribers also included shopkeepers and craftsmen, some of whom figured among the most prosperous members of the community engaged in trade or crafts. A butcher, a chandler, a grocer, a mercer and a tanner were among the subscribers to *Trefn Ymarweddiad;* John Prichard Prŷs secured the services of three grocers and three mercers to disseminate copies of his devotional verses; John Rhydderch's shopkeeping subscribers, made up of three grocers and four mercers, probably acted as his agents, together with Edward Wicksteed, the Wrexham bookseller, and John Jones, the almanacer of Caeau. Once retail shops had established themselves in market towns, shopkeepers took on the responsibility of subscribing for, and selling, Welsh books in bulk. Some of these traders were men of some standing: John Foulkes, a grocer of Denbigh, owned lands in four parishes and was sometime burgess, bailiff and alderman of that town;[156] Thomas Bryan of Llannerch-y-medd, a tobacconist-cum-farmer, owned an estate valued at £419 9s. 3½d., whilst Robert Hughes, a grocer of Holyhead, owned goods to the value of £152 10s. 5d.[157] Literacy, moreover, was an indispensable tool

[153] U.C.N.W.L., Bangor MS. 3212, pp. 421-4.
[154] N.L.W. MS. 15C; B.L., Add MS. 14911; J. G. Penrhyn Jones, 'A History of Medicine in Wales in the Eighteenth Century' (unpubl. Univ. of Liverpool M.A. thesis, 1957), pp. 76-7.
[155] N.L.W., Bangor P.R. 1690.
[156] N.L.W., St. Asaph P.R. 1737; W. M. Myddelton, op. cit., p. 237.
[157] N.L.W., Bangor P.R. 1760, 1722.

MISCELLANEOUS SUBSCRIBERS

Book Title	Occupations
Archaeologia Britannica (1707)	12 M.A.s, 7 M.D.s, 4 D.D.s, Ll.B., Ll.D, Principal Secretary of State, Comptroller of Her Majesty's Household, Baron of the Exchequer.
Gwirionedd y Grefydd (1716)	3 Clerks, 2 Schoolmasters, 2 University Fellows, M.D.
Holl Ddyledswydd Dyn (1718)	4 Clerks, 3 Schoolmasters, 3 Excise Collectors, University Fellow, Ironmonger, Bookseller.
Cydymddiddan (1719)	Professor of Theology, Registrar of St. David's, Schoolmaster.
Defosiwnau Priod (1720)	2 Clerks, Supervisor of Excise, Collector of Excise, Excise Officer, Officer of Customs, Innkeeper.
Difyrrwch Crefyddol (1721)	4 Excise Officers, 3 Schoolmasters, 3 Shopkeepers, 3 Mercers, 3 Grocers, Oxford Carrier.
Prydferthwch Sancteiddrwydd (1722)	2 Doctors, Surgeon, Attorney at Law.
Prif Dd'ledswyddau Christion (1723)	2 Attorneys at Law, Attorney at Law-cum-Recorder, Baron of the Exchequer, Bishop's Secretary, M.D., Apothecary, Receiver of Land Tax, Collector of Excise, Officer of Excise, Postmaster, Scotsman [Carrier?].
Llun Agrippa (1723)	2 Booksellers, Blacksmith.
Mona Antiqua Restaurata (1723)	13 Counsels at Law, 10 Dublin Merchants, 6 Attorneys, 6 M.D.s, 5 Booksellers, 4 Captains, 3 Excise Collectors, 3 M.A.s, 2 Senior Fellows of Trinity College, Dublin, 2 School Ushers, 2 Distillers, His Majesty's Surveyor General of Ireland, Deputy-Master of the Revels in Ireland, Deputy-Auditor of Ireland, Standard-bearer to His Majesty's Band of Gentlemen Pensioners, Postmaster General of Ireland, Postmaster, Captain of The Royal Welch Fusiliers, Fellow of Jesus College, Oxford, Surgeon, Dublin Alderman, Doctor, Ll.B, Printer, Excise Officer.
Trefn Ymarweddiad (1723–4)	6 Clerks, 2 Schoolmasters, Officer of Custom and Salt, Excise Officer, School Usher, University Fellow, Apothecary, Tanner, Chandler, Butcher, Grocer, Mercer.

MISCELLANEOUS SUBSCRIBERS—*continued*

Book Title	Occupations
English–Welch Dictionary (1725)	4 Mercers, 4 Tanners, 3 Grocers, 3 Clerks, 3 Excise Officers, 2 Schoolmasters, 2 Surgeons, 2 Bookbinders, 2 Booksellers, Attorney General, Deputy Registrar of St. Asaph, Steward, Almanacer, Weaver, Joiner, Glazier, Ironmonger, Innkeeper, Dyer, Blacksmith.
A Welsh Grammar (1727)	2 Attorneys, 2 Doctors, 2 Captains, 2 Excise Officers, 2 University Fellows, University Principal, Bookseller.
Dydd y Farn Fawr (1727)	Captain in the Militia, School Usher, Bookseller.
Ystyriaethau (1730)	4 Clerks, 3 Counsels at Law, Doctor, Apothecary, School Usher.
Leges Wallicae (1730)	11 M.D.s, 9 University Fellows, 6 Attorneys at Law, 6 Booksellers, 6 University College Masters, 5 D.D.s, 3 M.A.s, 2 Professors, 2 Provosts, 2 Ll.D.s, 2 Lecturers, 2 Principals, 2 Schoolmasters, 2 Justices of Common Pleas, Garter Principal King at Arms, Baron of the Exchequer, Norroy King at Arms, Justice of the King's Bench, Member of His Majesty's Council at Law, Lord Chief Baron of the Court of Exchequer, His Majesty's Solicitor General, Prolocutor of the Lower House of Commons, Chief Justice of Chester, Deputy Auditor of the Principality of Wales, Recorder of Brecon, Secretary of the Royal Society, Clerk of the Parliament, Barrister at Law, President of St. John's College, Oxford, President of Corpus Christi College, Oxford, President of Brasenose College, Oxford, Bodleian Library, Oxford, Brasenose College Library, Oxford, Warden of All Souls, Warden, Balliol College Library, Oxford, The Queens College Library, Oxford, Jesus College Library, Oxford, Trinity Hall College Library, Cambridge, King's College Library, Cambridge, Peterhouse College Library, Cambridge, Trinity College Library, Cambridge, Gonville and Caius College Library, Cambridge, Lincoln Cathedral Library, Doctors–Commons Library, Merchant, Painter, Plumber, Peruke-maker, Hosier.
Athrawiaeth yr Eglwys (1731)	53 Students of Jesus College, Oxford, 3 Fellows of Jesus College, Oxford, 3 Attorneys, 2 M.D.s, 2 Excise Officers, 2 Clerks, 2 Ironmongers, Principal of Jesus College, Oxford, a Student of Balliol College, Oxford, a Student of Oriel College, Oxford, a Scholar of Wrexham, Registrar of St. Asaph, Alderman, Bookseller, Glover, Grocer, Saddler, Mercer, Surveyor.

for tradesmen, because they needed to be able to count and to write, as well as read, in order to compile bills and invoices, make out orders, label goods and parcels, and generally keep their account-books in good working order.

Many book subscribers in this group were either engaged in crafts closely allied to agriculture or were part-time farmers who produced their own raw materials. Settling on the outskirts of towns and drawing their raw material of hides, skins, oak bark and water from the rural hinterland, tanners were particularly prosperous and well-to-do men. The amount of capital required to set up tanning pits and buy raw materials represented a considerable outlay, and tanners' wills and inventories often revealed a substantial amount of property and wealth. Many of them were literate and devout men. The parish of Cellan, for instance, was famous for its pious tanners: around twenty of them practised their trade in that locality in the 1690s and did much to sustain cultural vitality in the area.[158] Among the four tanners who subscribed to John Rhydderch's dictionary were William Roberts of Caernarvon, who left a selection of calf skins, cow hides and sundry goods to his dependants,[159] and John Griffith of Pwllheli, whose estate was valued at £201 7s. 6d. Like many of his fellow-tanners, Griffith was a pious and prudent soul: in his will he revealed an acute concern for his spiritual obligations, charging his wife with the duty of bringing up his three children 'in the fear of God'.[160]

General craftsmen, such as shoemakers, carpenters, smiths, masons, glovers and weavers, found both in rural and urban milieus, were also consistent subscribers in this group. Apart from the constant flow of religious books, utilitarian works such as *Cyfarwyddiad i Fesurwyr*, published in 1715 and 1720, were published specifically to assist craftsmen in their daily work. As we have seen, craftsmen were well to the fore among subscribers to both Anglican and Dissenting literature, and their contribution in particular to the growth of early Methodism is hard to exaggerate. Moreover, the fact that two

---

[158] *Arch. Camb.*, 1909–11, Part 3, pp. 67–8.
[159] N.L.W., Bangor P.R. 1735.
[160] N.L.W., Bangor P.R. 1726. John Parry, a Ruabon tanner, also subscribed to Rhydderch's Dictionary—for his will, see St. Asaph P.R. 1738.

bookbinders, a blacksmith, a dyer, a glazier, a joiner and a weaver subscribed to John Rhydderch's dictionary betokens a healthy regard for linguistic and cultural standards. The degree of literacy and social awareness among them was often very high, for, unlike small farmers and labourers, they could work without 'wetting or tiring' their bodies and 'think and talk of the concerns of [their] soul[s]' without interfering with their work.[161] There must have been many parishes like Cellan which could boast of having smiths, joiners, bookbinders, glovers, weavers, tuckers, harpers and shoemakers who could give a 'very good account of their faith'.[162] Wills and inventories suggest that craftsmen were literate and perceptive men who collected books with discernment and enthusiasm. The inventory of William Rees, a Carmarthen cobbler, totalled a mere £4 17s. 6d. but nevertheless included books worth six shillings;[163] a library of books valued at fifteen shillings figured among the prized possessions of an estate valued at £8 4s. 7d. owned by Isaac Price, a Carmarthen cobbler;[164] a mason from Neath, John Simon, left an estate valued at £10 3s. 8d., but he too owned two Bibles and other books worth five shillings.[165]

VIII. THE POOR

Somewhere between a third and a half of the population of Wales hovered precariously on or below the level of subsistence. Composed largely of husbandmen, cottagers, labourers, servants, paupers, vagabonds and beggars, their unheard voices were those of the unlettered and unpropertied poor. These 'mute common folk' have left few clues as to their religious beliefs and access to books, but in spite of their penury, their limited aspirations and attenuated horizons, they were sentient, reflecting beings who had their own popular and cultural identity.[166] How far reformers had such people in

---

[161] F. J. Powicke, 'The Reverend Richard Baxter's Last Treatise', *Bulletin of John Rylands Library*, X (1926), 184.
[162] *Arch. Camb.*, 1909–11, Part 3, p. 68.
[163] N.L.W., Archdeaconry of Carmarthen P.R. 1732.
[164] N.L.W., Archdeaconry of Carmarthen P.R. 1732. Francis Knoyle, a Swansea blacksmith, owned wearing apparel and books worth ten shillings in his estate valued at £4 7s. 0d. N.L.W., Archdeaconry of Carmarthen P.R. 1736.
[165] N.L.W., Llandaff P.R. 1720.
[166] Margaret Spufford, *Contrasting Communities. English Villagers in the Sixteenth and Seventeenth Centuries* (1974), p. xx.

mind when they referred to 'the poor' is difficult to judge. We know that the Welsh Trust established between three and four hundred schools in Wales between 1674 and 1681 and that by the autumn of 1675 a total of 2,225 children were attending these schools.[167] But nothing is known of the social and economic background of the children concerned. The same may be said of the 96 schools established by the S.P.C.K. in Wales between 1699 and 1740.[168] Both charitable societies claimed to be educating 'the poorer sorts' within their schools and distributing literature among 'the deserving poor'. In 1678, Welsh Trust accounts reveal that 5,186 Welsh books were distributed, mainly in Cardiganshire, Carmarthenshire, Denbighshire and Glamorgan, among 'poor people that could read Welsh'.[169] Similarly, in 1710, Edward Tenison estimated that there were 760 poor people in 29 parishes in the archdeaconry of Carmarthen who were able to read, and these doubtless were the products of charity schools.[170] Modest advances were continuously made in local 'petty' reading schools which, often supported by well-disposed persons and maintained by penurious schoolmasters, curates, spinsters and widows, achieved valuable success in small communities. William Lewis of Margam informed the S.P.C.K. in 1714 that there was hardly a parish in his part of the world 'where there is not a private school for teaching children to read'.[171] Nearly half the parishes in the diocese of St. Asaph in 1738 had some educational facilities, largely in the form of charity schools, free schools or small reading schools.[172]

Nevertheless, the question remains: what was the social and economic status of these 'poorer sorts'? It is hard to believe that many people below the level of tenant farmers and craftsmen would be able to afford (in terms of both time and money) any kind of organised elementary education. Whether the children of cottagers, labourers and paupers were formally educated depended almost entirely on economic considerations.

---

[167] *B.B.C.S.*, IX (1937), 73.
[168] Mary Clement, *The S.P.C.K. and Wales, 1699–1740* (1954), p. 13.
[169] *B.B.C.S.*, IX (1937), 79–80.
[170] N.L.W., SD/Misc. B/131.
[171] Clement, p. 63.
[172] G. M. Griffiths, 'Education in the diocese of St. Asaph, 1729–1730', *N.L.W.J.*, VI (1950), 394–5; *idem*, 'Further notes on Education in the Diocese of St. Asaph, 1738', ibid., VII (1951), 81–4.

Pinned behind the barriers of poverty and deprivation, the mass of unlettered peasants were committed to the daily task of fending off creeping starvation, hardship and despair. Living on the knife-edge margin of penury stifled their aspirations and left them with little more than the bare necessities of life. Ready cash was scarce at these levels. It was common for wage-earning labourers to be paid in kind, and many of the ordinary needs of life were often acquired by direct exchange. At times of harvest failure or economic recession, the problems of raising money to buy books were especially acute. 'Very few of the Welsh people', complained Griffith Jones, Llanddowror, in 1747, 'even of the farmers, and scarce any at all of the labourers, can at present afford to buy books; all the lower ranks of people here being much reduced in their circumstances.'[173]

The implication behind Griffith Jones's remarks is that, in normal times, some labourers might be able to buy books. Least likely to do so were landless labourers whose daily pittance was scarcely sufficient to maintain their families. On the other hand, landed labourers who were rich enough to have inventories made on their death might be expected to have pennies to spare to buy cheap, practical books. John Evan, a Llandysul labourer whose estate, valued at £10, comprised a cow worth £2 15s. 0d., sheep worth £2 10s. 0d., poultry, corn, hay and a swarm of bees, subscribed to *Dydd y Farn Fawr* and owned a collection of books worth five shillings.[174] Farther south, another labourer of the same name, less fortunate in that he languished in Cardiff gaol in 1741 for non-payment of debts, counted an old Welsh Bible and copies of *Holl Ddyledswydd Dyn* and *Canwyll y Cymry* among the most valuable items of his meagre estate.[175] Some of the better-off labourers in the upland and middle regions of Glamorgan owned copies of the scriptures and prayer book.[176] Even so, the great majority of ordinary labourers were unable to read. Since most of them lived in damp, draughty, ill-lit, single-room

---

[173] Griffith Jones, *Welch Piety* (1747), p. 4.
[174] N.L.W., Archdeaconry of Cardigan P.R. 1760.
[175] J. H. Matthews (ed.), *Cardiff Records* (6 vols., 1898–1911), II, 200.
[176] M. I. Williams, 'A general view of Glamorgan houses and their interiors in the seventeenth and eighteenth centuries' in Stewart Williams (ed.), *Glamorgan Historian*, IX (1974), 169.

cottages in which the whole family lived, ate and slept together, they were clearly denied the leisure and privacy that would enable them to learn their letters. Indeed, the environment in which they lived almost certainly conditioned them to believe that books were, at best, inessential commodities and, at worst, irrelevant luxuries.

John Jones, dean of Bangor, believed that 'taxes, want and poverty' were the major obstacles to the growth of literacy among the lowest ranks of society. At certain times in the year, moreover, particularly at harvest-time, impoverished farmers were unwilling to spare their children from the fields. Poor children in Caernarvonshire were sent out 'for ever and anon to beg for victuals' and, at harvest time, their parents often withdrew them from charity schools since 'they had rather they should not be taught at all than be debarred of the use and service of them'.[177] Children were inextricably involved in supplementing the family budget by herding cattle, hay-making, crow-scaring, stone-picking, or performing any other task that might help to keep starvation from the door. The rural peasantry would doubtless have argued that, in contrast to the expanding commercial towns, the attainment of literacy was scarcely a valuable asset in their communities; it seemed to bring neither tangible material dividend nor a sudden change in social status. Consequently, the preoccupation of small farmers and labourers with the hazards of the season and the soil meant that they remained either blandly indifferent or implacably hostile to local schools.

It would seem probable, therefore, that, of those below the level of the gentry, only professional men, substantial farmers, merchants and tradesmen, skilled artisans and craftsmen were consistently able to afford elementary education for their children. Subscription lists and probate material confirm that these were the groups that bought books, created a demand for more books, and set a high premium on literacy. What is most striking is that well-to-do farmers and craftsmen supplied the backbone of Methodist congregations in the eighteenth-century. Early Methodism in Wales fed on the growing literacy of the 'middling sorts', those whom Richard Baxter reckoned to be

---

[177] Clement, pp. 2, 86–7.

'the strength of religion and civility in the land'.[178] Methodist leaders drew their most vigorous support not from the poor but from those 'with a measure of respectability and a stake in property, however modest'.[179]

There is one further key factor which cannot be ignored: the importance of oral culture and informal instruction. Pre-industrial Wales was essentially a collection of small, largely introspective rural communities in which face-to-face contacts were natural and in which men and women shared a culture that was based chiefly on the spoken word.[180] Enmeshed in a web of allegiances that seldom transcended parish or county boundaries, the range of social encounters facing the bulk of society was strictly limited. Society was still attuned to the ear rather than to the eye, and a whole range of images, symbols and meanings existed which a literate world would find difficult to understand.[181] We must beware, however, of equating illiteracy with 'stupidity or mental blankness',[182] for the oral and ritual culture of the peasantry, suffused with popular beliefs and customs, proverbs and myths, folklore and fables, had a vitality of its own.

The growth of Protestantism clearly depended a good deal on the tradition of oral communication. Within small com-munities, the literate oracle of the village performed a variety of tasks, ranging from reading out news to deciphering or writing letters on behalf of unlettered folk. The flood of religious books published in this period, moreover, gave this oral culture a new impetus, providing the literate with new themes to discuss and enabling them to enrich the experience of the illiterate mass by presenting the spiritual message in a dialect and language which their listeners were used to hearing.[183] William Morris recalled his father telling him that the only literate person in the parish of Llanfihangel Tre'r

---

[178] Matthew Sylvester (ed.), *Reliquiae Baxterianae* (1696), p. 89.
[179] Glanmor Williams, *Welsh Reformation Essays* (1967), p. 30.
[180] E. L. Eisenstein, 'Some Conjectures about the Impact of Printing on Western Society and Thought: a Preliminary Report', *Journal of Modern History*, 40 (1968), 30–1; Richard D. Altick, *The English Common Reader* (1963), p. 29.
[181] G. H. Bantock, *The Implications of Literacy* (1966), p. 10.
[182] Pierre Goubert, *The Ancien Régime. French Society, 1600–1750*, tr. Steve Cox (1973), p. 263.
[183] For a useful parallel, see Natalie Zemon Davis, *Society and Culture in Early Modern France* (1975), chapter seven.

Beirdd in Anglesey in the 1680s was a cooper, Siôn Edward, to whom the parish youths, including Morris's father, used to flock to learn to read the work of the Shrewsbury printer and almanacer, Thomas Jones. 'Who knows', mused William Morris to his brother Richard, 'but that you and I would be illiterate were it not for that old fellow of Clorach who taught our father . . . and so started the blessed gift'.[184] Iolo Morganwg also testified to the important rôle played by the 'good-natured neighbour', who spent an hour two or three times a week teaching people to read and presumably involving them in the religious currents of the day.[185] Wakes, festivals and village gatherings were also social occasions when books and ballads were read aloud to the unlettered public. Craftsmen, too, set up informal reading groups in which books were exchanged and discussed orally.[186] Weavers in particular were able to read aloud over their looms. 'I have known many', claimed Richard Baxter, 'that weave in the long loom that can set their sermon-notes or a good book before them and read and discourse together for mutual edification while they work.'[187]

The most effective informal instruction, however, was usually carried out within the privacy of the home. Within the household, the rôle of the literate master or mistress was supremely important, for they were the focal point of a virile oral transmission of religious truths. It was the moral and spiritual duty of the head of the household to read scriptural and devotional works aloud until illiterate members of the household had mastered the art of reading on their own account. Thousands of primers and catechisms were published in this period to help heads of households to teach their children and servants to read. Some parents relied on the Bible as the first reading book, starting always with the large capitals at the beginning of each chapter; others found the verses of Rees Prichard a homely guide, but many more concentrated on getting their children to master the alphabet thoroughly by using horn-books. The horn-book (*Llyfr Corn*) was much-used in schools and households: it was generally a small sheet of paper on which was printed the alphabet, in small and capital letters, the vowels, monosyllabic combinations of vowels and consonants, the Invocation and the Lord's Prayer; the sheet was placed on a small oak tablet protected by a thin transparent sheet of horn and a narrow frame of brass, and held by a handle.[188] This stereotype was often reproduced in many Welsh primers and devotional books and was clearly intended to be read aloud by householders until aspiring readers had familiarised themselves with letters.[189] Men who made their way in the world were often deeply sensible of the debt they owed to their parents. David Evans of Llanfihangel-ar-Arth, Carmarthenshire, who became minister of Pencader church, Delaware, in 1714, recalled his youth when as 'a feeble shepherd' his parents had taught him the value of literacy by sending him to a local weaver's school and always satisfying his longing for books.[190] How far Iolo Morganwg's testimony corresponded with reality is hard to judge, but he nonetheless claimed to have been literate in both Welsh and English, thanks to his mother's tuition, from the very earliest age.[191]

Informal instruction took place even among the lowest orders of society. Erasmus Saunders was impressed by the endeavours of 'common people', including shepherds and servants, to avail themselves of religious knowledge by 'reading or discoursing to instruct one another in their houses'.[192] Knowing that shepherds were blessed with an abundance of unoccupied time, Stephen Hughes strove valiantly in the Restoration period to ensure that they were supplied with scriptural and devotional matter.[193] Some shepherds, like

---

[188] Andrew W. Tuer, *History of the Horn-Book* (2 vols., 1896); D. R. Thomas, *History of the Diocese of St. Asaph*, I, 151; John Fisher, 'The Old-time Welsh Schoolboy's Books', *J.W.B.S.*, II (1921), 193–201; Mitford M. Mathews, *Teaching to Read Historically Considered* (1966), pp. 15–16.

[189] See, for instance, John Morgan, *Bloedd-nad Ofnadwy yr udcorn diweddaf* (1704), pp. 84–8; anon., *Naturiaeth Conffirmasion* (1706), p. 16; William Evans, *Egwyddorion y Grefydd Gristianogawl* (1707), p. ii. A.B.Cs. were published at Shrewsbury in 1700, 1714, 1718 and 1720, and at Carmarthen in 1727. See also John Rhydderch, *Sillafydd yn cynwys Athrawiaeth i'r Anysgedig i Anadlu Geiriau a Sillafau yn gywir* (1718); *Y Brif Addysg i Ddarllain gyntaf* (*c.* 1727–36).

[190] G. Alban Davies, 'Y Parch. David Evans, Pencader—Ymfudwr Cynnar i Pennsylvania', *N.L.W.J.*, XIV (1965–6), 74–96.

[191] Glanmor Williams, 'Language, Literacy and Nationality in Wales', *History*, 56 (1971), 8.

[192] Saunders, p. 32.

[193] Stephen Hughes (ed.), *Gwaith Mr. Rees Prichard* (Part IV, 1672), sig. A3r–v.

Dafydd Cadwaladr, familiarised themselves with the alphabet by comparing letters stamped on their sheep with the letters in the prayer book.[194] Others, like Edmund Jones of Pontypool, developed their innate faculties in spite of the poverty of their circumstances. Writing under the pseudonym, 'Solomon Owen Caradoc', 'the old Prophet' tended to sentimentalise as he recalled his youth through the mists of memory, forgetting the debt which he owed to the informal instruction received within the home and drawing attention largely to the knowledge which he had accumulated by his own efforts. Even so, his evidence highlights the autodidacticism practised by a minority of shepherds and husbandmen:

> He hath been bred up only to husbandry and looking after cattle and sheep, and although he was not in any university or academy, nor was instructed in any of the liberal sciences, yet was a great lover of books, buying and borrowing as much as he could come at. And is well versed in scripture, and very knowing (his circumstances considered) both in divinity and other kinds of knowledge.[195]

Another who raised himself up by his bootstraps was Thomas David, a self-educated day-labourer of Cardiganshire who, troubled with 'the itch of curiosity', set off for London in his youth, became a voracious collector of Welsh books and manuscripts, and a correspondent of Edward Lhuyd whom he kept informed of current Welsh publications in London, Oxford and the provincial presses. By his own testimony, David confessed that he had received no formal schooling but had overcome his disabilities by relying on his own labours and the gifts which God had planted within him.[196] Even among the lowest ranks, therefore, there were always some who, in spite of the many powerful deterrents to the spread of reading habits, set a high premium on literacy and vowed to fulfil their deepest aspirations.

---

[194] *Ychydig Gofnodau am Fywyd a Marwolaeth Dafydd Cadwaladr* (1836), pp. 9–10.
[195] Solomon Owen Caradoc (pseud.), Edmund Jones, *The Leaves of the Tree of Life* (1745), pp. ix–x.
[196] Bod., MS. Ashmole 1814, f. 361r–v; *Arch. Camb.*, V (1859), 251.

XI

CONCLUSION

This study has attempted not only to evaluate the quality of religious life in Wales from 1660 to 1730, but also to throw some light on the beginnings of Methodism. Two explanations of the Methodist revival still hold the field in Welsh historiography. The first is the notion that Methodism arose as a reaction against the abuses within the unreformed Anglican church. This stems very largely from the preoccupation of historians with the dismal portrait of the church painted by Erasmus Saunders in his best-known work, *A View of the State of Religion in the diocese of St. David's* (1721). Saunders ran through the whole gamut of ecclesiastical malpractices in St. David's: lay impropriation, pluralism, absenteeism, non-residence and nepotism. His unhappy conclusion was that 'the doctrines of the Reformation begun about two hundred years ago in England have not yet effectually reached us'.[1] A good deal of what Saunders had to say was true, but his strictures are scarcely applicable to the whole of Wales. As has been shown, the diocese of St. David's was much poorer than the dioceses of Bangor and St. Asaph in this period. Moreover, Saunders drew the bulk of his evidence from the impoverished western fringes of Wales, and it would not be difficult to find dioceses in England, especially in the north, that were in similar straits. We should remember, too, that Saunders himself, resentful and embittered at being refused a bishopric, may well have written in a mood of disillusionment not to say a fit of pique. Nevertheless, the dimissal of this period as one of unrelieved torpor is too narrowly and uncritically based on Saunders's prejudiced evidence. The truth is that the preoccupation of historians with antiquated machinery, meagre endowments and abuses in the church has blinded them to many improvements in the religious life of Wales in this period.

[1] Saunders, p. 37.

The second explanation is the brain-child of Methodist historians. The Methodist revival was hailed by its adherents as nothing less than a rebirth of new passions into the national life of Wales. They believed the revival to be a turning-point in Welsh history and duly dismissed the pre-Methodist period as one of acute moral decadence and spiritual depression. The past was dead, dark and best forgotten. In 1742, Howel Harris claimed that the established church had been in 'an obscure and almost utter darkness of near 80 years',[2] a darkness which Robert Jones, Rhoslan, considered to be 'akin to that of ancient Egypt'.[3] The skilful use of images such as 'light' and 'heat' meant that the *post tenebras lux* theme became the new orthodoxy. This had been a common motif in the writings of Protestant reformers in the sixteenth century, and the same Old Testament images of religious history now became deeply embedded in the Methodist psyche. Methodists believed that the trumpet voice of their leaders had been schooled by providence as a divine means of rousing a slumbering land. According to John Hughes, doyen of nineteenth-century Welsh Methodist historians:

> The true features of the gospel were lost in their midst, and a passive torpor, akin to that in the valley and shadow of death, enveloped the country. . . . But there came a time to be merciful to Sïon, yea, the notable time; God released his Spirit and there was noise and movement among the dry bones; life and light came to the valley of death and the face of the earth was regenerated.[4]

The use of such imagery was, of course, perfectly natural, for Methodists firmly believed that their movement was exclusive and God-given. What is regrettable is that this ideology became an article of faith among subsequent historians. In contrast to the almost embarrassing flood of books and articles on various aspects of eighteenth-century Methodism, the period before 1735 has received the most cursory treatment.[5] In large measure, this lacuna is an index of the preoccupation

---

[2] G. M. Roberts (ed.), *Selected Trevecca Letters (1742–1747)* (1956), 1, p. 65.
[3] Robert Jones, *Drych yr Amseroedd*, edited by G. M. Ashton (1958), p. 27.
[4] John Hughes, *Methodistiaeth Cymru* (3 vols., 1851–6), 11, pp. 1–2.
[5] See R. T. Jenkins and William Rees (eds.), *A Bibliography of the History of Wales* (2nd ed., 1962).

with the 'Methodist' view of history. The sub-title chosen for the recently-published first volume of the official history of Calvinistic Methodism in Wales—*Y Deffroad Mawr* (The Great Awakening)—is eloquent testimony to the tenacity of this tradition.[6]

Three points need to be made regarding this attitude. The first is that much effort has gone into the study of the founding fathers of Calvinistic Methodism in Wales, and this has given rise to a dangerous and misleading mystique about the providentially-inspired rôle of the early Methodist leaders. John Walsh has noted that the disproportionate stress on the contribution of John Wesley to the growth of English Methodism has meant 'a diversion of historical attention from the study of the Revival as a whole, and in particular from the complex of influences which fed it'.[7] This is even more true of Welsh historiography. The second point is that the cataclysmic effect of Methodism has been exaggerated. Whilst it is certainly not the intention of this study to belittle the importance of the revival, it is nevertheless true that Welsh Methodism experienced an ebb and flow during its first three decades: in particular, it made painfully slow progress in North Wales, and suffered a severe setback during the rift between Howel Harris and Daniel Rowland in the 1750s. Indeed, John Hughes believed that Methodism did not truly begin to score the Welsh character until the 1770s.[8]

The third point is that by gazing at pre-revival Wales through Methodist spectacles our understanding of the period is distorted. It becomes difficult to judge it on its own merits. The argument presented here is that the Methodist revival was not a creation *ex nihilo*, but that it grew from roots laid in this period.[9] The very real improvements carried out in the religious, cultural and educational life of Wales at this time deserve more attention.[10] As we have seen, by the eve of

---

[6] G. M. Roberts (ed.), *Hanes Methodistiaeth Cymru: Y Deffroad Mawr* (1973).
[7] John Walsh, 'Origins of the Evangelical Revival', G. V. Bennett and J. D. Walsh (eds.), *Essays in Modern English Church History* (1966), p. 132.
[8] John Hughes, op. cit., 1, p. 52.
[9] Cf. Elie Halévy, *The Birth of Methodism*, tr. and edited by B. Semmel (1971), p. 51; John Walsh, 'Elie Halévy and the Birth of Methodism', *T.R.H.S.*, 25 (1975), 1–20.
[10] A start has been made by M. G. Jones, *The Charity School Movement* (1938) and M. Clement, *The S.P.C.K. and Wales, 1699–1740* (1954).

Methodism, sermons had not only become more frequent in number but also more effective in the range of their content and in the response which they evoked. This improvement was underpinned by an explosive increase in the number of printed books in Welsh which were deliberately geared to engage the sympathy and emotional response of the reading public. The dissemination of the scriptures in large editions encouraged the growth of biblical knowledge, fostered the development of independent thinking and nurtured the spread of literacy in the vernacular. Within the church, a heartening revival, based on 'the sober piety and strong moral emphasis of the Prayer Book and Church Catechism',[11] had been launched. This served to instil the basic fundamentals of Protestantism and began to erode the vestiges of popular rites grounded in ignorance, superstition and magic. The campaign for a moral reformation, based on the puritan gospel of industry and honesty, sobriety, thrift and the proper observance of the Sabbath, achieved a limited degree of success, but had gained considerable ground by the end of the eighteenth century and was triumphant in the nineteenth century. What is important is that laymen were becoming more aware of the standards of morality expected of them and that a growing number of clergymen were striving to ensure that they themselves were morally above reproach. The enormous amount of devotional books published, in prose and verse, did much to foster the virtues of sanctity and holiness, to implant a profound form of individual and collective piety, to awaken a sense of personal conviction and to instil an awareness of the certainty of death and judgment—all features which became an intrinsic part of early Methodism.

Methodist historians were not only preoccupied with the shortcomings of the established church but were also critical of the old Dissenters, whom they believed had become 'dry', fractious and ineffectual. But the present study has shown that many of the seminal forces at work between 1660 and 1730 were attributable to the vitality and commitment of Dissenters. The doctrinal controversies were invariably a symptom of the

---

[11] E. T. Davies, 'The Church of England and Schools, 1662–1774', Glanmor Williams (ed.), *Glamorgan County History, vol. IV, Early Modern Glamorgan* (1974), p. 460.

growth of Dissent, and Methodism is known to have drawn heavily in its formative years on the experience, knowledge and connexions of prominent Dissenters. It augured well for the future, moreover, that so many articulate and conscientious authors of widely differing social, religious and educational background were anxious to create a convincing religious experience among their readers. Their efforts were reinforced by a large-scale attempt to disseminate literature among a wide social and geographical cross-section of the reading public, from wealthy, high-placed noblemen to humble and impecunious peasants. The demand for books was especially great among the active and enterprising middling sort in town and country, independent men of substance who placed a heavy premium on literacy and spiritual conviction, and who eventually became the mainstay of the Methodist movement. Early Methodism in Wales was a complex phenomenon made up of many different forces and impulses, but its success was based on the fact that the groundwork carried out in the period 1660 to 1730 made men more receptive to the revivalist message and more fully prepared to respond to the exciting spiritual experiences which were now close at hand.

BIBLIOGRAPHY

I. CONTEMPORARY SOURCES

(a) MANUSCRIPT COLLECTIONS

National Library of Wales, Aberystwyth (N.L.W.)

(i)   MSS. 3B, 5A, 9A, 10B, 15C, 17B, 24B, 68A, 75A, 79A, 85A, 128C, 263B, 368A, 510A, 527A, 559B, 598E, 609A, 770A, 889E, 1116D, 1244D, 1446A, 1963D, 2026B, 2576B, 2771B, 2905A, 3488A, 4495A, 4710B, 5457A, 5465A, 5920A, 6900A, 7022A–7030A, 7396A, 9070E, 9095B, 9102A, 9167A, 9913A, 10249B, 10254B, 10589A, 10995A, 11030A, 11076A, 11302–26D, 11440D, 11991A, 12298A, 12357E, 12444B, 12732E, 13062B, 13077B, 13089E, 13121B, 15170B, 17054D, 18162D, 21239B.

(ii) *Records of the Church in Wales*
  1. Probate inventories and wills in the dioceses of Bangor, Llandaff, St. Asaph and St. David's.
  2. *Diocese of Bangor*
     (a) Churchwardens' Presentments, 1675–1737.
     (b) Sermons (B/MC/402–452).
  3. *Diocese of Llandaff*
     (a) Consistory Court Papers (Ll/CC/G; Ll/CC/C/G).
     (b) Visitation Books (Clergy) (Ll/V/3).
  4. *Diocese of St. David's*
     (a) Returns of Roman Catholics (SD/RC/1–21).
     (b) Miscellaneous Books (SD/Misc. B/3, 10, 14, 39, 131).
     (c) Consistory Court Papers (SD/CCB/G; SD/CCCm/G; SD/CCCd/G; SD/CCD/G).
     (d) Visitation Books (Clergy) (SD/VC/1–10).
     (e) Presentments (Episcopal and General Visitations); Churchwardens' Declarations.
     (f) Miscellaneous Papers (SD/Misc./1–1400).
  5. *Diocese of St. Asaph*
     (a) Visitation Books (Clergy) (SA/V/1–3).
     (b) Reports on Rural Deaneries (SA/RD/1–26).
     (c) Letters to the Bishop; Miscellaneous Letters (SA/Let/1–1065).
     (d) Miscellaneous Documents (SA/Misc/1–1813).
     (e) Miscellaneous Volumes (SA/MB/5, 9, 10, 23, 57, 58, 63).

(iii) *Deposited Collections*
  Bodewryd MSS. 68B, 69B, 89B, 89C, 90B.
  Bodewryd (Sotheby) Correspondence, nos. 94, 96, 97, 98, 136, 169, 230, 966.
  British Records Association (1955) MS. 898.
  Brogyntyn MS. 905.
  Calvinistic Methodist Archives MS. 3005.
  Chirk Castle MSS. A30–1.

Cwrtmawr MSS. 27E, 45A, 189A, 211A, 253A, 420B, 455B.
E. Francis Davies (1937–8) MS. 216.
Elwes MS. 1589.
Esgair and Pantperthog MS. 2; Deeds and Documents no. 364.
F. C. Winchester Deeds no. 25.
Heol Awst MS. 2.
Llanstephan MSS. 6B, 15A, 23A, 65B, 105B, 107B, 114B, 146E, 189B, 190B, 191A.
Lloyd-Baker MSS. Letters (xerox copies).
Ottley Papers, nos. 89, 100, 126, 139, 1045.
Peniarth MSS. 124D, 325A, 373B.
Penrice and Margam MSS. A98–100, L266, 5555.
Picton Castle MSS. 1664, 1669.
Plasgwyn (Vivian) MSS. 21, 24, 36, 94, 99, 104–6, 144.
Plas Nantglyn MSS. 2, 8.
Plas Power (1970) Deeds and Documents.
Rhual MSS. 74, 75, 84, 87, 106.
Smallwood Deeds and Documents.
Wynnstay MS. 6; Documents, Box 106, no. 28.

University College of North Wales, Bangor (U.C.N.W.)
 (i) MSS. 54, 65, 95, 362, 402, 421, 1218.
 (ii) *Deposited Collections*
      Henblas MSS. 9A, 18A.
      Mostyn Correspondence, vols. 2, 5, 6.
      Mostyn MS. 183.
      Penrhos MSS. 523, 604, 722, 792–5, 933, 956, 975.
Baptist College Library, Bristol
Joshua Thomas, 'An Ecclesiastical History of the Principality of Wales', 2 vols.
      c. 1779–80 (facsimile copy in N.L.W.).
Central Library, Cardiff (C.C.L.)
MSS. 2.14, 2.139, 2.222, 2.225–6, 5.30.
Glamorgan Record Office, Cardiff (G.C.R.O.)
D/DSF/2, 320, 325, 351–2, 364, 379: Quaker records relating to Wales.
Essex Record Office, Chelmsford
D/ABW90/30: Will of John Morgan, Matchin.
Lichfield Record Office, Lichfield
Probate records: Wills of Thomas Jones (1713) and Thomas Durston (1767).
Harold Cohen Library, University of Liverpool
MS. 2.69: A collection of *halsingod.*
British Library, London (B.L.).
Add. MSS. 14866, 14874, 14911.
Birch MS. 4274.
Egerton MS. 2882.
Lansdowne MS. 808.
Dr. Williams's Library, London
MS. 34: Dr. John Evans's List of Dissenting Congregations in England and Wales, 1715.
Trust Minutes, 1743–4.
Friends' Library, Friends' House, London
Kelsall MSS., Diaries, vols. 1–6; Book of Letters; Book of Poems.
Morning Meeting Book, vols. 1–4.

Minutes of Meetings for Sufferings, vol. 15.
Portfolio MS. 6.35.
Lambeth Palace Library, London
MS. 930: correspondence of Archbishop Tenison.
The Public Record Office, London (P.R.O.)
Prob/10/936: Will of Elis Lewis, Llwyngwern, 1660.
Prob/10/1002: Will of William Lewis, Winchester, 1666.
Prob/10/1373: Will of Edward Jones, Bishop of St. Asaph, 1704.
Public Library, Newport
MS. 350.012: Edmund Jones's *Spiritual Botanology*.
Northamptonshire Record Office, Northampton
Probate records: Will of Matthias Maurice, 1738.
Bodleian Library, Oxford (Bod.).
Ashmolean MSS. 1814, 1816, 1817, 1820.
Rawlinson MSS. 94, C743, D317, D376.
Tanner MSS. 29, 30, 32, 34, 36, 40, 45, 146, 282.
Welsh f. 6.
Christ Church Library, Oxford
Arch. W. Epist. 9, 21, 22: correspondence of Archbishop Wake.
Department of Friends' Records, Philadelphia, Pennsylvania
Philadelphia Monthly Meeting Minute Book, vol. 1, 1682–1714.
Department of Records, Philadelphia
Probate records: Will of Thomas Wynne, Philadelphia, 1692.
Historical Society of Pennsylvania, Philadelphia
Charles Morton Smith MSS., vol. 3: Quaker deeds; Penn Papers: deeds relating
to land purchases by Thomas Wynne and John ap John.

(b) PRINTED WORKS

(i) WELSH BOOKS (For a fuller survey readers are referred to my thesis, 'Welsh
Books and Religion, 1660–1730', unpublished University of Wales Ph.D. thesis,
1974). All the printed sources cited here were published in London, unless it is
stated otherwise.
AB DEWI, Iaco, *Llythyr y Dr. Well's at Gyfaill* (Shrewsbury, 1714).
AB DEWI, Iaco, *Llythyr at y Cyfryw o'r Byd* (Shrewsbury, 1716).
AB DEWI, Iaco, *Catecism o'r Scrythur* (edited by William Evans, Shrewsbury, 1717).
AB DEWI, Iaco, *Meddyliau Neillduol ar Grefydd* (1717; 1726).
AB DEWI, Iaco, *Tyred a Groesaw at Iesu Grist* (Shrewsbury, 1717).
AB ELLIS, Ellis, *Hanes y Cymru* (Shrewsbury, 1717).
Ffordd y Gwr Cyffredin (Oxford, 1683).
Teg Resymmau Offeiriad Pabaidd wedi eu hatteb (1686).
Ymadroddion Mr. Dod (1688; 1692).
Hyfforddwr Cyfarwydd i'r Nefoedd (1693; 1723).
*Pregeth ynghylch Godidowgrwydd a Defnyddiaeth neu Lesioldeb Llyfer y Gweddiau
Cyffredin* (1693).
Rhesswmmau Yscrythurawl (1693).
Bedydd Gwedi i Amlygu yn Eglir (1694).
Cyngor y Bugail i'w Braidd (1700).
Testament y Dauddeg Padriarch (Dublin, 1700).
Cristionogrwydd yn Gynnwys (1703).
Cyngor yr Eglwyswr (1703).
Cymorth i'r Cristion (Shrewsbury, 1704).
Cadwyn Euraidd o Bedair Modrwy (1706).

BIBLIOGRAPHY 313

Naturiaeth Conffirmasiwn (1706).
Rhybudd i bob Tyngwr ofer (1707).
Cred a Buchedd Gwr o Eglwys Loegr (1710).
Catechism Sacramentaidd (Shrewsbury, 1711).
Y Psalter neu Psalmau Dafydd yn Gymraeg (1711).
Golwg Eglur o'r Rhagoriaeth sydd rhwng Ffydd y Protestaniaid a Ffydd y Papistiaid (Chester, 1715).
Can ar fesur Triban (Trefhedyn, 1718).
Gair i Gymru (Shrewsbury, 1722).
Cerydd i'r Cymru (Carmarthen, 1722).
Gronyn o Had Mwstard (Carmarthen, 1722).
Dwy o Gerddi Newyddion (Shrewsbury, 1723).
Dull Priodas Ysprydol (Carmarthen, 1723–4).
Gwahoddiad Taer i Sion (Carmarthen, 1725).
Y Cywyr Ddychwelwr (Carmarthen, 1727).
Myfyrdodau Duwiol i'n cymhwyso erbyn awr Angeu (Chester, 1727).
Rhybudd i'r Cymru mewn Tair Can Newydd (1730–1).
Cyfoeth i'r Cymru (Carmarthen, 1731).
AP JOHN, John, *Tystiolaeth o Gariad ac Ewyllys Da* (1683).
AP WILLIAM, Huw and HUMPHREY, William, *Cywir Hanes ynghylch Drychineb a Cholled* (Shrewsbury, 1730).
BADDY, Thomas, *Pasc y Christion neu Wledd yr Efengyl* (1703).
BADDY, Thomas, *Dwys Ddifrifol Gyngor* (Chester, 1713).
BADDY, Thomas, *Pelydr a thywyniad yr Yspryd* (Chester, 1713).
BADDY, Thomas, *Caniad Salomon* (Chester, 1725).
BUTTRY, Thomas, *Dwy o Gerddi Newyddion* (Shrewsbury, 1724).
CADWALADER, Thomas, *Gwyddorion y Gwirionedd* (1703).
DAVIES, John, *Llyfr y Resolusion*, 1632; 1684 (Shrewsbury, 1711; 1713).
DAVIES, Rondl, *Profiad yr Ysprydion* (Oxford, 1675).
E., E., *Ymddiddan rhwng Gwr o gyfraith ar angeu* (1728).
E., T., *Cyngor i Ddychwelyd at yr Arglwydd* (1728).
EDWARDS, Charles, *Y Ffydd Ddi-ffvant* (Oxford, 1677).
EDWARDS, Charles, *Gwyddorion y Grefydd Gristianogol* (1679).
EDWARDS, Charles, *Catecism yn cynnwys Pyngciau y Grefydd Gristianogol* (1682).
EDWARDS, John, *Madruddyn y Difinyddiaeth Diweddaraf* (1651).
EVANS, Evan, *Y Llyfr Gweddi Gyffredin, y Cydymmaith Goreu* (Oxford, 1693; Shrewsbury, 1711).
EVANS, Henry, *Cynghorion Tad i'w Fab* (edited by Stephen Hughes, 1683).
EVANS, Jenkin, *Catecism Byrr i Blant*, 1708 (Carmarthen, 1727).
EVANS, Lewis, *Llythyr oddi wrth Weinidog o Eglwys Loegr* (Shrewsbury, 1711).
EVANS, Theophilus, *Cydwybod y Cyfaill Gorau ar y Ddaear* (Shrewsbury, 1715).
EVANS, Theophilus, *Galwedigaeth Ddifrifol i'r Crynwyr* (Shrewsbury, 1715).
EVANS, Theophilus, *Drych y Prif Oesoedd* (Shrewsbury, 1716).
EVANS, Theophilus, *Cydymddiddan rhwng Dau Wr yn ammau ynghylch Bedydd-Plant* (1719).
EVANS, Theophilus, *Prydferthwch Sancteiddrwydd yn y Weddi Gyffredin* (Shrewsbury, 1722).
EVANS, Theophilus, *Pwyll y Pader* (1733).
EVANS, William, *Egwyddorion y Grefydd Gristianogawl* (Shrewsbury, 1707).
FOULKES, William, *Esponiad ar Gatechism yr Eglwys* (Oxford, 1688).
FRANCIS, Enoch, *Gwaith a Gwobr Ffyddlon Weinidogion yr Efengyl* (Carmarthen, 1729).
FRANCIS, Enoch, *Gair yn ei Bryd* (Carmarthen, 1733; 2nd ed., Cardiff, 1839).

GAMBOLD, William, *A Welsh Grammar* (Carmarthen, 1727).

GRIFFITH, George, *Gueddi'r-Arglwydd wedi ei hegluro* (edited by William Foulkes, Oxford, 1685).

GRUFFYDD, Owen and OWEN, Humphrey, *Chwech o Gerddi Duwiol ar amryw achosion* (Shrewsbury, 1717).

HARRI, John, *Rhai Datguddiadau o'r Nefoedd Newydd ar Ddaear Newydd* (Carmarthen, 1725).

HUGHES, John, *Allwydd neu Agoriad Paradwys i'r Cymru* (1670).

HUGHES, Stephen (ed.), *Rhan o Waith Mr. Rees Prichard* (1658).

HUGHES, Stephen (ed.), *Gwaith Mr. Rees Prichard* (parts III and IV, 1672; 1681).

HUGHES, Stephen (ed.), *Mr. Perkins His Catechism* (1672).

HUGHES, Stephen (ed.), *Cyfarwydd-deb i'r Anghyfarwydd* (1677).

HUGHES, Stephen (ed.), *Tryssor i'r Cymru* (1677).

HUGHES, Stephen (ed.), *Adroddiad Cywir o'r Pethau pennaf* (1681).

HUGHES, Stephen (ed.), *Taith neu Siwrnai y Pererin* (1688).

J., E., *Annogaeth yn erbyn y Pechod o Feddwdod* (Shrewsbury, 1720).

JOHN, Joseph, *Hymau Ysgrythurawl* (edited by Thomas William, Carmarthen, 1765).

JONES, Dafydd, *Cydymaith Diddan* (Chester, 1766).

JONES, Dafydd, *Blodeu-gerdd Cymry* (Shrewsbury, 1779).

JONES, Griffith, *Golwg Byrr o'r Ddadl ynghylch Llywodraeth yr Esgobion* (Shrewsbury 1721).

JONES, Griffith, *Y Llyfr a elwir Holl Ddyledswydd Dyn* (Shrewsbury, 1722).

JONES, Griffith, *Cyngor Rhad yr Anllythrennog* (1737).

JONES, Griffith (ed.), *Pigion Prydyddiaeth Pen-fardd y Cymry* (1749).

JONES, Jenkin, *Llun Agrippa* (Carmarthen, 1723).

JONES, Jenkin, *Dydd y Farn Fawr* (Carmarthen, 1727).

JONES, Jenkin, *Cyfrif Cywir o'r Pechod Gwreiddiol* (Carmarthen, 1729).

JONES, Jenkin, *Llawlyfr Plant* (Carmarthen, 1732).

JONES, John, *Cennad oddiwrth y Ser* (Shrewsbury, 1721).

JONES, Michael, *Attebion i'r Holl Wag Escusion a wnae llawer o bobl yn erbyn dyfod i dderbyn y Cymmun Bendigedig* (Shrewsbury, 1698).

JONES, Michael, *Y Cymmunwr Ystyriol* (1716).

JONES, Richard, *Testun y Testament Newydd* (1653).

JONES, Richard, *Perl y Cymro* (1655).

JONES, Richard, *Galwad i'r Annychweledig* (1659; 1677).

JONES, Richard, *Hyfforddiadau Christianogol* (1675).

JONES, Richard, *Traethawd ar Feddwdod* (1675).

JONES, Simon, *Dr. Well's Letter to a Friend* (Shrewsbury, 1730).

JONES, Thomas, Welsh *Almanacs* from 1681 to 1712.

JONES, Thomas (ed.), *Y Gwir er Gwaethed Yw* (1684).

JONES, Thomas (ed.), *Y Gymraeg yn ei Disgleirdeb* (1688).

JONES, Thomas (ed.), *Ymadrodd Gweddaidd ynghylch Diwedd y Byd* (Shrewsbury, 1703).

JONES, Thomas (ed.), *Llyfr o Weddiau Duwiol* (Shrewsbury, 1707).

JONES, William, *Gair i Bechaduriaid* (1676).

JONES, William, *Principlau neu Bennau y Grefydd Gristianogol* (1676).

JONES, William, *Work for a Cooper* (1679).

LEWES, William and PRYCE, Evan, *Maddeuant i'r Edifairiol* (Carmarthen, 1725–6).

LEWES, William, *Dwy Daith i Gaersalem* (Shrewsbury, 1728).

LEWIS, Dafydd, *Caniadau Nefol* (Shrewsbury, 1714).

LEWIS, Elis, *Ystyriaethau Drexelivs ar Dragywyddoldeb* (Oxford, 1661).

LEWIS, George, *Annogaeth i Gymmuno yn fynych* (1704).
LEWIS, George, *Cyngor Difrifol i Geidwaid Tai* (1704).
LEWIS, George, *Pregeth a bregethwyd . . . yn Eglwys St. Paul* (1715).
LEWIS, James and SAMUEL, Christmas, *Y Cyfrif Cywiraf o'r Pechod-Gwreiddiol* (Carmarthen, 1730).
LEWIS, Owen, *Agoriad yn agor y ffordd i bob dealltwriaeth cyffredin* (1703).
LEWIS, Thomas, *Rhesymmau Amlwg* (Carmarthen, 1724).
LEWIS, Thomas, *Bywyd a Marwolaeth yr Annuwiol dan enw Mr. Drygddyn* (Carmarthen, 1731).
LEWIS, William, *Defosiwnau Priod* (Shrewsbury, 1720).
LEWYS, Dafydd, *Bwyd Enaid* (Carmarthen, 1723).
LEWYS, Dafydd, *Golwg ar y Byd* (Carmarthen, 1725).
LEWYS, Rees, *Holl Dd'ledswydd Christion* (Shrewsbury, 1714).
LHUYD, Edward, *Archaeologia Britannica* (Oxford, 1707).
LLOYD, Edward, *Egwyddor i rai Jevaingc* (1682).
LLOYD, Edward, *Meddyginiaeth a Chyssur* (Shrewsbury, 1722).
LLOYD, Robert, *Duwioldeb ar Ddydd yr Arglwydd* (1698).
LLOYD, Robert, *Llyfr-gell y Cristion Ifaingc* (Shrewsbury, 1713).
LLOYD, Robert, *Ffordd y Cristion i'r Nefoedd* (Shrewsbury, 1716).
LLOYD, Robert, *Llaw-Lyfr y Gwir Gristion* (Shrewsbury, 1716).
LLOYD, Robert, *Cyssur i'r Cystuddiedig* (Shrewsbury, 1723).
LLWYD, Robert, *Llwybr Hyffordd yn cyfarwyddo yr anghyfarwydd i'r Nefoedd* (1682).
MAURICE, David, *Arweiniwr Cartrefol i'r Iawn a'r Buddiol Dderbyniad o Swpper yr Arglwydd* (1700).
MAURICE, David, *Cwnffwrdd ir Gwan Gristion* (Oxford, 1700).
MAURICE, Matthias, *Yr Atrawiaeth y sydd yn ol Duwioldeb* (1711).
MAURICE, Matthias, *Y Wir Eglwys* (1727).
MAURICE, Matthias, *Ymddiddan rhwng Dau Gristion* (1730).
MAURICE, Matthias, *Byrr Hyfforddiad yn Addoliad Duw* (1734).
MEREDITH, Benjamin, *Pechadur Jerusalem yn Gadwedig* (Hereford, 1721).
MEYRICK, William, *Pattrwm y Gwir-Gristion* (Chester, 1723).
MILES, Thomas, *Carol o goffadwriaeth am ryfeddol ryddhad Dassy Harry* (Shrewsbury, 1701).
MOPHET, Enosh (pseud.), *An Appendix to Delaune's Plea: neu Lyfr newydd yn cynnwys Ymddiddanion Buddiol* (Shrewsbury, 1720).
MORGAN, Abel, *Cyd-Gordiad Egwyddorawl o'r Scrythurau* (Philadelphia, 1730).
MORGAN, John, *Bloedd-Nad Ofnadwy, yr Udcorn diweddaf* (Shrewsbury, 1704).
MORGAN, John, *Eglurhad Byrr ar Gatechism yr Eglwys* (1699).
MORGAN, John, *Llythyr Tertulian at 'Scapula* (1716).
MORGAN, John, *Myfyrdodau Bucheddol ar y Pedwar Peth Diweddaf* (Shrewsbury, 1716).
MORGAN, Robert, *Goleuni gwedi torri allan Ynghymry gan ymlid ymmaith dywyllwch* (1696).
MORRIS, Edward, *Y Rhybuddiwr Christnogawl* (Oxford, 1689; 1699).
MORRIS, Lewis, *Tlysau yr Hen Oesoedd* (Holyhead, 1735).
OWEN, Foulke (ed.), *Cerdd-Lyfr* (Oxford, 1686; edited by Thomas Jones and entitled *Carolau a Dyriau Duwiol* (Shrewsbury, 1696).
OWEN, Hugh, *Dilyniad Christ* (edited by John Hughes, 1684).
OWEN, Humphrey, *Amddiffyniad Byrr tros y Bobl (mewn Gwawd) a elwir Quakers* (1704).
OWEN, James, *Bedydd Plant or Nefoedd* (1693).
OWEN, James, *Ychwaneg o Eglurhad am fedydd plant bychain* (1701).
OWEN, James, *Hymnau Scrythurol* (1705).

316 BIBLIOGRAPHY

OWEN, James, *Trugaredd a Barn* (1715).
OWEN, Jeremy, *Golwg ar y Beiau, 1732–3* (edited by R. T. Jenkins, Cardiff, 1950).
OWEN, Jeremy, *Traethawd i brofi ac i gymmell ar yr holl Eglwysi y Ddyledswydd Fawr Efangylaidd o weddio dros Weinidogion* (1733).
PARRY, Richard, *Agoriad Carwriaeth* (Shrewsbury, 1714).
PARRY, Richard, *Drych Angau* (Shrewsbury, 1714).
PARRY, Richard, *Dihuniad Cysgadur* (Shrewsbury, 1723).
PARRY, Richard, *Rhybudd Benywaidd* (Shrewsbury, 1727).
PHILLIPS, Philip, *Ufudd-dod i Lywodraeth a Chariadoldeb* (1716).
POWELL, Howell, *Y Gwrandawr* (1709).
POWELL, Howell, *Traethawd-Ymarferol am Gyflawn-Awdyrdod Duw* (1711).
PRICE, Walter, *Godidowgrwydd, Rhinwedd ac Effaith yr Efengyl* (Shrewsbury, 1707).
PRICHARD, R. and DAFYDD, T., *Y Newydd Dychyrynadwy o Ffraingc* (Shrewsbury, 1721).
PRYDDERCH, Rees, *Gemmeu Doethineb* (edited by William Evans, Shrewsbury, 1714).
PRŶS, John Prichard, *Difyrrwch Crefyddol* (Shrewsbury, 1721).
PUGH, Ellis, *Annerch ir Cymru* (Philadelphia, 1721).
PUGH, John and J. T., *Eglurhad o Gatechism Byrraf y Gymanfa* (Trefhedyn, 1719).
RHYDDERCH, John, *Cilgwth neu Ergyd at Halogedigaeth a Llygredigaeth* (Shrewsbury, 1716).
RHYDDERCH, John, *Dwyfolder Gymmunol neu Ddefosiwnau Sacramentaidd* (Shrewsbury, 1716).
RHYDDERCH, John, *Cyffes Ymadrodd* (Shrewsbury, 1717).
RHYDDERCH, John, *Sillafydd yn cynnwys Athrawiaeth i'r Anysgedig* (Shrewsbury, 1718).
RHYDDERCH, John, *Datcuddiad or un peth mwya' angenrheidiol, neu pa un yw'r Grefydd Orau* (Shrewsbury, 1724).
RHYDDERCH, John, *The English and Welch Dictionary* (Shrewsbury, 1725).
RHYDDERCH, John, *Y Brif Addysg i Ddarllain gyntaf* (Shrewsbury, c. 1727–36).
RHYDDERCH, John, *Grammadeg Cymraeg* (Shrewsbury, 1728).
RICHARDS, Thomas, *Cyngor Difrifol i un ar ol bod yn Glaf* (1730).
ROBERTS, Edward, *Llaw Lyfr yw Ddarllen ir Cleifion* (1754).
ROBERTS, Robert, *A Sacrament Catechism* (no imprint, 1720).
ROBERTS, Robert, *A Du-Glott-Exposition* (Shrewsbury, 1730).
ROWLANDS, Henry, *Mona Antiqua Restaurata* (Dublin, 1723).
ROWLANDS, William, *Hynodeb Eglwysydd Cywir* (1712).
ROWLANDS, William, *Catechism yr Eglwys* (Shrewsbury, 1713).
SAMUEL, Edward, *Bucheddau'r Apostolion a'r Efengylwyr* (Shrewsbury, 1704).
SAMUEL, Edward, *Gwirionedd y Grefydd Grist'nogol* (Shrewsbury, 1716).
SAMUEL, Edward, *Holl Ddyledswydd Dyn* (Shrewsbury, 1718).
SAMUEL, Edward, *Prif Dd'ledswyddau Christion* (Shrewsbury, 1723).
SAMUEL, Edward, *Athrawiaeth yr Eglwys Gristnogol* (Chester, 1731).
THOMAS, Alban, *Dwysfawr Rym Buchedd Grefyddol* (Trefhedyn, 1722).
THOMAS, Alban, *Llythyr Bugailaidd* (Carmarthen, 1729).
THOMAS, Dafydd, *Cerdd Newydd* (Shrewsbury, 1720).
THOMAS, Dafydd, *Hanes y Pla yn Ffraingc* (Shrewsbury, 1721).
THOMAS, Dafydd and GRUFFYDD, Edward, *Ymddiddanion rhwng y Cybydd ar Oferddyn* (Shrewsbury, 1724).
THOMAS, David and Evan, *Hymnau Ysprydol* (Carmarthen, 1730).
THOMAS, John, *Unum Necessarium* (Oxford, 1680).
THOMAS, John, *Tair o Gerddi Newyddion* (Shrewsbury, 1718).

THOMAS, John, *Dwy o Gerddi Newyddion . . . ynghylch y Drudaniaeth Clefydon ar Marwolaethau sydd yn ein plith* (Shrewsbury, 1729).
THOMAS, Joshua, *Llyfr Du y Gydwybod* (Carmarthen, 1723).
THOMAS, Joshua, *Golwg ar Destament Newydd* (Carmarthen, 1728).
THOMAS, Joshua (ed.), *Nodiadau ar Bregeth Mr. Abel Francis* (1775).
THOMAS, Joshua (ed.), *Hanes y Bedyddwyr* (Carmarthen, 1778).
THOMAS, Nicholas, *Newyddion Da ir Dynion Gwaetha* (Shrewsbury, 1717).
THOMAS, Simon, *Hanes y Byd a'r Amseroedd* (Shrewsbury, 1718; 1721).
THOMAS, Simon, *Llyfr Gwybodaeth y Cymro* (Shrewsbury, 1724).
VAUGHAN, Rowland, *Yr Ymarfer o Dduwioldeb*, 1675 (Shrewsbury, 1709, 1713, 1715, 1730).
WILLIAM, Thomas, *Oes Lyfr* (Carmarthen, 1724).
WILLIAMS, E. and GABRIEL, T., *Dwy o Gerddi Newyddion* (Shrewsbury, 1718).
WILLIAMS, John, *Blaenor i Ghristion* (1701).
WILLIAMS, Moses, *Llaw-Lyfr y Llafurwr* (1711).
WILLIAMS, Moses, *Ymarferol-Waith i'r Elusen-Ysgolion* (1711).
WILLIAMS, Moses, *Y Catecism* (1715).
WILLIAMS, Moses, *Cofrestr* (1717).
WILLIAMS, Moses, *Pregeth a barablwyd . . . yn 1717* (1718).
WILLIAMS, Moses and WOTTON, William, *Cyfreithieu Hywel Dda ac Eraill* (1730).
WILLIAMS, Samuel, *Amser a Diwedd Amser* (1707).
WILLIAMS, Samuel, *Undeb yn Orchymynedig i Ymarfer* (1710).
WILLIAMS, Samuel, *Pedwar o Ganueu ar amryw Desdunion* (1718).
WILLIAMS, Thomas, *Ymadroddion Bucheddol ynghylch Marwolaeth* (Oxford, 1691).
WILLIAMS, Thomas, *Pregeth o Achos y Dymmestl Ddinistriol* (1705).
WILLIAMS, Thomas, *Eglurhad o Gatechism yr Eglwys* (1708).
WILLIAMS, Thomas, *Annogaeth Ferr i'r Cymmun Sanctaidd* (1710).
WYNN, Edward, *Trefn Ymarweddiad Gwir Gristion*, 1662 (Shrewsbury, 1723–4).
WYNN, Griffith, *Ystyriaethau o Gyflwr Dyn* (Chester, 1730).
WYNNE, Ellis, *Rheol Buchedd Sanctaidd* (1701).
WYNNE, Ellis, *Gweledigaetheu'r Bardd Cwsc* (1703).
WYNNE, Thomas, *An Antichristian Conspiracy Detected* (1679).
Yr A.B.C. neu y llyfr cyntaf i ddechreu dysgu darllen Cymraeg (Shrewsbury, 1700, 1714, 1718, 1720; Carmarthen, 1727).

(ii) ENGLISH BOOKS AND OTHER PRIMARY MATERIAL IN WELSH

The Life and Death of Mr. Vavasor Powell (1671).
The Condemnation of the cheating Popish priest (1679).
The Popes down-fall at Abergavenny (1679).
North Wales defended or an Answer to an imodest and scurrilous libel, lately published and entitled A Trip to North Wales (Shrewsbury, 1701).
A Large Review of the Summary View, of the Articles exhibited against the Bishop of St. David's (1702).
A Dialogue between the Rev. Mr. Jenkin Evans . . . and Mr. Peter Dobson . . . concerning Bishops (1744).
A Journey to Llandrindod Wells (2nd ed., 1746).
BARROW, Isaac, *Several Sermons against Evil-Speaking* (1678).
BAXTER, Richard, *A Christian Directory* (1673).
BEVERIDGE, William, *The Church Catechism explained* (1704).
BOWEN, E., *Britannia Depicta or Ogilby Improv'd* (1720).
BROWN, Thomas, *Novus Reformator Vapulans: or, The Welch Levite tossed in a Blanket* (1691).

BULL, George, *A Companion for the Candidates of Holy Orders* (1714).

CALAMY, Edmund, *An Account of the ministers . . . ejected after the Restoration in 1660* (2 vols., 1713).

CALVIN, John, *Institutes of the Christian Religion* (edited by J. T. McNeill, 2 vols., 1961).

CLARKE, Samuel, *The Lives of Divers Eminent Divines of this Later Age* (1683).

CLARKE, Samuel, *A General Martyrology* (Glasgow, 1770).

CLEMENT, Mary (ed.), *Correspondence and Minutes of the S.P.C.K. relating to Wales, 1699–1740* (Cardiff, 1952).

CLEMENT, Mary (ed.), *Correspondence and Records of the S.P.G. relating to Wales, 1701–1750* (Cardiff, 1973).

CRADOCK, Joseph, *Letters from Snowdonia* (1770).

CROFT, Herbert, *The Naked Truth, 1675* (edited by H. H. Henson, 1919).

CROFT, Herbert, *A Short Narrative of the Discovery of a College of Jesuits* (1679).

CROSSMAN, Samuel, *The Young Mans Monitor* (1664).

DAVIES, J. H. (ed.), *The Letters of Lewis, Richard, William and John Morris of Anglesey, 1728–1765* (2 vols., Aberystwyth, 1907–9).

DAVIES, Richard, *An Account of the Convincement . . . of . . . Richard Davies* (1710).

DEFOE, Daniel, *A Tour thro' the whole island of Great Britain* (3 vols., 2nd ed., 1738).

DELAUNE, Thomas, *Angliae Metropolis* (1690).

DOD, John, *A Second Sheet of old Mr. Dod's Sayings* (1670).

DOD, John, *Old Mr. Dod's Sayings* (1667, 1671).

DOD, John, *Old Mr. Dod's Sayings, composed in verse* (1678).

EACHARD, John, *The Grounds and Occasions of the Contempt of the Clergy and Religion enquired into* (1670).

EARLE, John, *Microcosmography* (1732).

EDWARDS, Charles, *An Afflicted Man's Testimony concerning his Troubles* (1691).

EDWARDS, Thomas, *A Plain and Impartial Enquiry into Gospel-Truth* (1693).

EDWARDS, Thomas, *The Paraselene dismantled of her Cloud* (1699).

EDWARDS, Thomas, *Hunangofiant a Llythyrau Twm o'r Nant* (edited by G. M. Ashton, Cardiff, 1948).

ELLIS, T. E. and DAVIES, J. H. (eds.), *Gweithiau Morgan Llwyd* (2 vols., Bangor, 1899–1908).

EVANS, John, *Some Accounts of the Welsh Charity-Schools; and of the Rise and Progress of Methodism in Wales* (1752).

EVANS, Theophilus, *The History of Modern Enthusiasm* (1752).

EVANS, William (ed.), *The Welshman's Candle* (Carmarthen, 1771).

FLEETWOOD, William, *A Sermon preach'd before the Lords . . . on January 30th 1695–6* (1708).

FLEETWOOD, William, *The Bishop of St. Asaph's Charge to the Clergy of that Diocese in 1710* (1712).

FLEETWOOD, William, *A Sermon upon Swearing* (1721).

FORTESCUE, Sir John (ed.), *The Correspondence of King George the Third from 1760 to December 1783* (6 vols., 1927).

FOWLER, Edward, *The Principles and Practices of certain moderate divines of the Church of England* (1670).

GOUGE, Thomas, *The Principles of the Christian Religion* (1679).

GRIFFITH, N., *The Leek. A Poem on St. David's Day* (2nd ed., 1718).

GRIFFITH, Owen, *Abraham's Prospect* (1681).

GRIFFITHS, G. Milwyn (ed.), 'John Wynne, a Report on the Deanery of Penllyn and Edeirnion, 1730', *The Merioneth Miscellany* 1 (1955).

HALL, E. Hyde, *A Description of Caernarvonshire* (edited by E. Gwynne Jones, Caernarvon, 1952).

HANCORNE, Thomas, *The Right Way to Honour and Happiness* (Bristol 1710).

HENRY, Matthew, *A Church in the House* (1704).

HENRY, Matthew, *A Sermon preach'd at the Funeral of . . . James Owen* (1706).

HENRY, Matthew, *The Life of the Rev. Philip Henry* (edited by J. B. Williams, 1825).

HOOPER, George, *A Sermon preach'd before the Lords . . . on January 31st, 1703–4* (1704).

HOWELLS, B. E. (ed.), *A Calendar of Letters relating to North Wales* (Cardiff, 1967).

HUGHES, G. H. (ed.), *Rhagymadroddion, 1547–1659* (Cardiff, 1967).

HUGHES, John, *Methodistiaeth Cymru* (3 vols., Wrexham, 1851–6).

HUMPHREYS, Humphrey, *A Sermon preach'd before the House of Lords on . . . 30th day of January, 1695–6* (1696).

JONES, E. D., 'Llyfr Eglwys Mynydd-bach', *Y Cofiadur*, 18 (1947).

JONES, E. D., 'Copi o Lyfr Eglwys Pant-teg, Abergwili', *Y Cofiadur*, 23 (1953).

JONES, Edmund, *The Leaves of the Tree of Life* (Carmarthen, 1745).

JONES, Edmund, *A Sermon preached . . . on the death of Mr. Evan Williams* (1750).

JONES, Edmund, *A Geographical, Historical and Religious Account of the Parish of Aberystruth* (Trevecca, 1779).

JONES, Edmund, *A Relation of Apparitions of Spirits in the Principality of Wales* (1780).

JONES, Griffith, *A Short View of the Controversie about Episcopacy and our Church Communion* (2nd ed., Chester, 1720).

JONES, Griffith, *A Sermon preach'd at St. Hilary's Chapel in Denbigh on occasion of the late General Mortality* (2nd ed., 1730).

JONES, Griffith, *A Letter to a Proselyte of the Church of Rome* (1731).

JONES, Griffith, *Welch Piety* (1740–60).

JONES, M. G., 'Two Accounts of the Welsh Trust, 1675 and 1678', *B.B.C.S.*, IX (1937).

JONES, Robert, *Drych yr Amseroedd* (edited by G. M. Ashton, Cardiff, 1958).

JONES, R. Tudur and OWENS, B. G., 'Anghydffurfwyr Cymru, 1660–1662', *Y Cofiadur*, 32 (1962).

JONES, Thomas, *An Astrological Speculation of the late Prodigy* (1681).

JONES, Thomas, *Of the Heart and its Right Soveraign, or, an Historical Account of the title of our Brittish Church* (1678).

JONES, Sir Thomas, *The Rise and Progress of the most Honourable and Loyal Society of Antient Britons* (1717).

LEE, M. H. (ed.), *Diaries and Letters of Philip Henry* (1882).

LHUYD, Edward, 'Parochialia', Supplement to *Arch. Camb.* (1909–11).

LLOYD, William, *A Sermon preached before the House of Lords, on November 5, 1680* (1680).

LLOYD, William, *An Historical Account of Church-Government* (1684).

LOVEDAY, J., *Diary of a Tour in 1732* (Edinburgh, 1890).

MATTHEWS, J. H. (ed.), *Records of the County Borough of Cardiff* (6 vols., Cardiff, 1898–1911).

MAURICE, David, *The Bruised Reed* (Oxford, 1700).

MAURICE, Matthias, *Social Religion Exemplify'd* (3rd ed., 1759).

MINSHULL, Randall, *Bibliotheca Miscellanea* (Shrewsbury, 1715).

MYDDELTON, W. M. (ed.), *Chirk Castle Accounts, 1666–1753* (Manchester, 1931).

NELSON, Robert, *The Life of Dr. George Bull* (2nd ed., 1714).

NICHOLSON, William, *A Plain, but full Exposition of the Catechism of the Church of England* (1678).

OWEN, Charles, *Some Account of the Life and Writings of Mr. James Owen* (1709).

OWEN, Charles, *Plain-Dealing* (1715).

OWEN, Hugh (ed.), *Additional Letters of the Morrises of Anglesey, 1735–1786* (1947).

OWEN, James, *A Plea for Scripture Ordination* (1694).

OWEN, James, *Salvation Improved* (1696).

OWEN, James, *Moderation a Virtue* (1703).

OWEN, James, *Moderation still a Virtue* (1704).

OWEN, James, *The History of Images and of Image-Worship* (1709).

OWEN, Jeremy, *The Goodness and Severity of God* (1717).

PENNANT, Thomas, *A Tour in Wales* (2 vols., 1784).

PHILLIPS, J. R., *A List of the Sheriffs of Cardiganshire, 1539–1868* (Carmarthen, 1868).

'Poll Book for the 1722 Parliamentary Election', *The Carmarthenshire Historian*, III (1966).

POWELL, Vavasor, *The Bird in the Cage* (1662).

POWELL, William, *Swearing and Drunkenness, the Bane of Society* (Shrewsbury, 1727).

POWELL, William, *A Sermon preach'd at the Visitation of the Lord Bishop of St. Asaph* (1742).

Proposals for reprinting the Holy Bible and Common Prayer Book in the British or Welsh Tongue in Octavo (1714).

REES, David, *A View of the Divine Conduct in the Government of this Lower World* (1730).

RICHARDS, Thomas, *Hoglandia, or, a description of Hampshire* (1709).

RICHARDS, Thomas, *The Nativity of Christ* (1728).

RICHARDS, Thomas, *The Happiness of Good Christians after Death* (1733).

RICHARDS, William, *Wallography* (1682).

SAUNDERS, Erasmus, *A Domestick Charge* (Oxford, 1701).

SAUNDERS, Erasmus, *The Divine Authority and Usefulness of the Pastors of the Christian Church Vindicated* (1713).

SAUNDERS, Erasmus, *A View of the State of Religion in the Diocese of St. David's 1721* (reprinted Cardiff, 1949).

SHEPARD, William, *Camrias Light, being two of Mr. Rees Prichard's Divine Gems* (Shrewsbury, 1716).

SMALLBROOKE, Richard, *Our Obligations to promote the Publick Interest* (1724).

SMALLBROOKE, Richard, *Charge . . . to the Clergy* (1726).

STEELE, Richard, *The Husbandmans Calling* (1668).

SYLVESTER, Matthew (ed.), *Reliquiae Baxterianae* (1696).

Syntagma Thesium Theologicarum in Academia Salmvriensi Variis Temporibvs Dispvtatarvm (2 vols., 2nd ed., Saumur, 1665).

THOMAS, John, *Rhad Rhas* (edited by J. Dyfnallt Owen, Cardiff, 1949).

THOMAS, Joshua, *A History of the Baptist Association in Wales, 1650–1790* (1795).

THOMAS, Simon, *Remarks upon a small Treatise entitl'd The Beauty of Holiness in the Book of Common Prayer* (Hereford, 1734).

THOMAS, Simon, *The Arminian Heresy* (Hereford, 1742).

THOMAS, Simon, *The History of the Cymbri* (Hereford, 1746).

THOMAS, William, *The Bishop of Worcester. His Letter to the Clergy of his Diocese* (1689).

TILLOTSON, John, *A Sermon preached at the Funeral of the Reverend Mr. Thomas Gouge* (1682).

TONG, William, *An Account of the Life and Death of . . . Matthew Henry* (1716).

TYLER, John, *A Sermon preach'd before the Lords . . . on 30 January, 1706–7* (1707).

WILLIAMS, A. H. (ed.) *John Wesley in Wales, 1739–1790* (Cardiff, 1971).

WILLIAMS, Daniel, *Crispianism unmask'd* (1691).

WILLIAMS, Daniel, *An End to Discord* (1699).

WILLIAMS, G. J., 'Llythyrau at Ddafydd Jones o Drefriw', *N.L.W.J.*, Supplement (1943).

WILLIAMS, Moses, *Proposals for printing by subscription a Collection of Writings in the Welsh Tongue* (1719).

WILLIAMS, William, *Marwnad y Parchedig Mr. Gryffydd Jones* (Carmarthen, 1761).

WILLIAMS-JONES, Keith (ed.), *A Calendar of the Merioneth Quarter Sessions Rolls, 1733–65* (Dolgellau, 1965).

WYNDHAM, H. P., *A Tour through Monmouthshire and Wales*, 1774 (2nd ed., 1781).

WYNNE, Robert, *A Short Narrative of the Proceedings against the Bishop of St. Asaph* (1702).

WYNNE, Robert, *Unity and Peace the support of Church and State* (1704).

WYNNE, Thomas, *The Evidence of an Over-ruling Providence* (1722).

WYNNE, William, *The History of Wales* (1697).

YARDLEY, Edward, *Menevia Sacra* (edited by Francis Green, suppl. to *Arch. Camb.* 1927).

II. MODERN WORKS

(i) WORKS OF REFERENCE

ARBER, Edward (ed.), *The Term Catalogues, 1668–1709* (3 vols., 1903–6).

BALLINGER, John and JONES, J. Ifano (eds.), *Catalogue of printed literature in the Welsh Department of the Cardiff Free Library* (Cardiff, 1898).

DARLOW, T. H. and MOULE, H. F. (eds.), *Historical Catalogue of the Printed Editions of the Holy Scriptures* (2 vols., 1903).

DAVIES, J. H. (ed.), *A Bibliography of Welsh Ballads printed in the Eighteenth Century* (1909).

DAVIES, W. Ll., 'Welsh Books entered in the Stationers' Company's registers, 1554–1708', *J.W.B.S.*, II (1921).

DAVIES, W. Ll., 'Short-title list of Welsh Books, 1546–1700', *J.W.B.S.*, II (1921).

FOSTER, Joseph, *Alumni Oxonienses, 1500–1714* (2 vols., Oxford, 1891).

GRIFFITH, J. E. (ed.), *Pedigrees of Anglesey and Caernarvonshire families* (Horncastle, 1914).

JENKINS, R. T. and REES, William (eds.), *A Bibliography of the History of Wales*, 2nd ed., Cardiff, 1962 (and supplements).

JONES, J. Ifano, *Printing and Printers in Wales and Monmouthshire* (Cardiff, 1925).

PETER, J. and PRYSE, R. J., *Enwogion Cymru* (4 vols., n.d.).

POWICKE, M. and FRYDE, E. B. (eds.), *Handbook of British Chronology* (2nd ed., 1961).

RICHARDS, G. Melville (ed.), *Welsh Administrative and Territorial Units* (Cardiff, 1969).

RICHARDS, William, *The Welsh Nonconformists' Memorial* (1820).

ROWLANDS, William, *Llyfryddiaeth y Cymry* (edited by D. Silvan Evans, Llanidloes, 1869).

The Dictionary of National Biography (and Supplements).

The Dictionary of Welsh Biography down to 1940 (1959).

VENN, J. and J. A., *Alumni Cantabrigienses* (4 vols., Cambridge, 1927).

WATT, R. (ed.), *Bibliotheca Britannica* (4 vols., 1824).

WILLIAMS, Richard, *Montgomeryshire Worthies* (Newtown, 1884).

WING, Donald (ed.), *Short-title Catalogue, 1641–1700* (3 vols., Columbia, 1945–51).

WING, Donald (ed.), *A Gallery of Ghosts. Books published between 1641–1700 not found in the Short-Title Catalogue* (New York, 1967).

(ii) PRINTED WORKS

ABBEY, C. J. and OVERTON, J. H., *The English Church in the Eighteenth Century* (2 vols., 1878).

ALTICK, R. D., *The English Common Reader* (Chicago, 1963).

ANDREWS, Stuart, *Methodism and Society* (1970).

Ychydig Gofnodau am Fywyd a Marwolaeth Dafydd Cadwaladr (Bala, 1836).

ASHTON, O. S., 'Eighteenth Century Radnorshire: a Population Survey', *Trans. Radnorshire Soc.*, XL (1970).

ATTWATER, D., *The Catholic Church in Modern Wales* (1935).

BAHLMAN, D. W. R., *The Moral Revolution of 1688* (New Haven, 1957).

BALLINGER, John, *The Bible in Wales* (1906).

BALLINGER, John, 'Vicar Prichard: a study in Welsh Bibliography', *Y Cymmrodor*, XIII (1900).

BANTOCK, G. H., *The Implications of Literacy* (Leicester, 1966).

BASSETT, T. M., 'Ymgais at Ystadegaeth', *Trafodion Cymdeithas Hanes Bedyddwyr Cymru* (1972).

BEHRENS, B., 'The Whig Theory of the Constitution in the Reign of Charles II,' *The Cambridge Historical Journal*, VII (1941).

BELL, H. E. and OLLARD, R. L. (eds.), *Historical Essays 1660–1750 presented to David Ogg* (1963).

BENNETT, G. V., *White Kennett, 1660–1728, Bishop of Peterborough* (1957).

BENNETT, G. V. and WALSH, J. D. (eds.), *Essays in Modern English Church History* (1966).

BENNETT, H. S., *English Books and Readers, 1475 to 1557* (2nd ed., Cambridge, 1969).

BENNETT, H. S., *English Books and Readers, 1603 to 1640* (Cambridge, 1970).

BENNETT, Richard, 'Richard Tibbott (1719–1798)', *C.C.H.M.C.*, II (1916).

BEST, G. F. A., *Temporal Pillars* (Cambridge, 1964).

BEYNON, Tom, *Howell Harris's Visits to Pembrokeshire* (Aberystwyth, 1966).

BEYNON, Tom, 'Howell Harris' Visits to Kidwelly and District (1743–1746)', *C.C.H.M.C.*, XXV (1940).

BIRABEN, Jean-Noel, 'Certain Demographic Characteristics of the Plague Epidemic in France, 1720–1722', *Daedalus* (Spring 1968).

BLAGDEN, Cyprian, 'Notes on the Ballad Market in the second half of the seventeenth century', *Studies in Bibliography*, VI (1954).

BLAKEWAY, J. B. and OWEN, H., *A History of Shrewsbury* (2 vols., 1825).

BOLAM, C. G. and others, *The English Presbyterians from Elizabethan Puritanism to Modern Unitarianism* (1968).

BOSSY, John, 'The Counter-Reformation and the People of Catholic Europe', *P & P*, 47 (1970).

BOSSY, John, 'Early Modern Magic'. *History*, 57 (1972).

BOON, G. C. (ed.), *Welsh Tokens of the Seventeenth Century* (Cardiff, 1973).

BOWEN, E. G., 'Bedyddwyr Cymru tua 1714', *Trafodion Cymdeithas Hanes Bedyddwyr Cymru* (1957).

BOWEN, Geraint (ed.), *Y Traddodiad Rhyddiaith* (Llandysul, 1970).

BOWEN, Geraint (ed.), 'Yr Halsingod', *T.H.S.C.* (1945).

BOWEN, Geraint (ed.), 'Gwilym Pue 'Bardd Mair', a Theulu'r Penrhyn', *Efrydiau Catholig*, II (1947).

BOWEN, Geraint (ed.), 'Llyfr y Resolusion neu Directori Christianogol Huw Owen o Wenynog', *N.L.W.J.*, XI (1959).

BOWEN, Geraint (ed.), 'Rhai o Lyfrau Defosiynol Reciwsantiaid Cymru yn yr ail ganrif ar bymtheg', *N.L.W.J.*, XI (1960).

BOWEN, Geraint (ed.), 'Fersiwn Cymraeg o Summa Casuum Conscientiae Francisco Toledo', *J.W.B.S.*, X (1968).

BOYCE, Benjamin, *The Theophrastan Character in England to 1642* (Cambridge, Mass., 1947).

BUSH, Douglas, *English Literature in the earlier seventeenth century, 1600–1660* (2nd ed., Oxford, 1962).

CAIRNCROSS, John, *After Polygamy was made a Sin. The Social History of Christian Polygamy* (1974).

CARPENTER, S. C., *Eighteenth Century Church and People* (1959).

CARRUTHERS, S. W., *Three Centuries of the Westminster Shorter Catechism* (Fredericton, New Brunswick, 1957).

CARTER, Harold, *The Towns of Wales* (Cardiff, 1965).

CHARLES, R. A., 'Teulu Mostyn fel Noddwyr y Beirdd', *Llên Cymru*, IX (1966).

CLAPP, S. L. C., 'The Beginnings of Subscription Publication in the seventeenth century', *Modern Philology*, 29 (1931–2).

CLAPP, S. L. C., 'The Subscription Enterprises of John Ogilby and Richard Blome', *Modern Philology*, 30 (1932–3).

CLAPP, S. L. C., 'Subscription Publishers prior to Jacob Tonson', *The Library*, XIII (1933).

CLASEN, Claus-Peter, *Anabaptism. A social history, 1525–1618* (Ithaca, 1972).

CLEARY, Martin, 'The Catholic Resistance in Wales, 1568–1678', *Blackfriars*, 38 (1957).

CLEMENT, Mary, *The S.P.C.K. and Wales, 1699–1740* (1954).

CLIFTON, Robin, 'The Popular Fear of Catholics during the English Revolution', *P & P*, 52 (1971).

COLLINSON, Patrick, *The Elizabethan Puritan Movement* (1967).

COMPER, F. M. M., *The Book of the Craft of Dying* (1917).

CORRIE, J. E., *Records of the Corrie Family, 802–1899* (2 vols., 1889).

CRAGG, G. R., *Puritanism in the period of the Great Persecution* (1957).

CRANFIELD, G. A., *The Development of the Provincial Newspaper, 1700–1760* (Oxford, 1962).

CREIGHTON, Charles, *A History of Epidemics in Britain* (2 vols., 2nd ed., 1965).

CURLL, Edmund, *The Life of the late Honourable Robert Price* (1934).

DALE, Bryan, *The Good Lord Wharton* (1906).

DAVIES, D. R. and DAVIES, Z. S. C., *Hanes Llanwenog: y plwyf, a'i phobl* (Aberystwyth, 1939).

DAVIES, G. Alban, 'Y Parch David Evans, Pencader—Ymfudwr Cynnar i Pennsylvania', *N.L.W.J.*, XIV (1965–6).

DAVIES, Glenys, *Noddwyr Beirdd ym Meirion* (Dolgellau, 1974).

DAVIES, John, *Y Lloffyn Addfed* (Swansea, 1852).

DAVIES, John, *Bywyd a Gwaith Moses Williams, 1685–1742* (Cardiff, 1937).

DAVIES, J. H. (ed.), *The Life and Opinions of Robert Roberts, a Wandering Scholar* (Cardiff, 1923).

DAVIES, J. H. (ed.), 'Early Welsh Bibliography', *T.H.S.C.* (1897–8).

DAVIES, J. H. (ed.), 'The Abermeurig family', *West Wales Historical Records*, 2 (1911–12).

DAVIES, J. H. (ed.), 'Cardiganshire Freeholders in 1760', *West Wales Historical Records*, 3 (1913).

DAVIES, W. J., *Hanes Plwyf Llandysul* (Llandysul, 1896).

DAVIS, N. Zemon, *Society and Culture in Early Modern France* (1975).

DODD, A. H., *Studies in Stuart Wales* (Cardiff, 1952).

DODD, A. H., *A History of Wrexham* (Wrexham, 1957).

DODD, A. H., 'Welsh and English in East Denbighshire: an Historical Retrospect', *T.H.S.C.* (1940).

DUBY, Georges, 'The Diffusion of Cultural Patterns in Feudal Society', *P & P*, 39 (1968).

EDWARDS, Lewis, *Traethodau Llenyddol* (Wrexham, n.d.).

EISENSTEIN, E. L., 'Some Conjectures about the Impact of Printing on Western Society and Thought', *Journal of Modern History*, 40 (1968).

ELLIS, T. P., *The Catholic Martyrs of Wales, 1535–1680* (1933).

EMERY, Frank, *Edward Lhuyd F.R.S., 1660–1709* (Cardiff, 1971).

EVANS, A. O., *A Chapter in the history of the Welsh Book of Common Prayer* (3 vols., Bangor, 1922).

EVANS, E. Lewis, *Capel Isaac* (Llandysul, 1950).

EVANS, G. Eyre, 'Gleanings from Original Friends' Registers at Somerset House', *Journal Friends Histor. Soc.*, I (1904).

EVANS, G. Nesta, *Social Life in Mid-Eighteenth Century Anglesey* (Cardiff, 1936).

EVANS, G. Nesta, 'Llanfechell Church, 1734 to 1760', *Trans. Anglesey Antiq. Soc.* (1947).

EVANS, W. A., 'Thomas Baddy ac Ymddiriedolwyr Cronfa Dr. Daniel Williams', *Y Cofiadur*, 27 (1959).

FINBERG, H. P. R. and THIRSK, Joan (eds.), *The Agrarian History of England and Wales, vol. IV, 1500–1640* (Cambridge, 1967).

FISHER, John, 'The Religious and Social Life of Former Days in the Vale of Clwyd', *Denbighshire Free Press*, 10 February (1906).

FISHER, John, 'The Old-time Welsh Schoolboy's Books', *J.W.B.S.*, 11 (1921).

GEORGE, C. H., 'English Calvinist Opinion on Usury, 1600–1640', *Journal History of Ideas*, XVIII (1957).

GEORGE, C. H. and K., *The Protestant Mind of the English Reformation, 1570–1640* (Princeton, 1961).

GLASS, D. V., 'Gregory King's Estimate of the Population in England and Wales in 1695', *Population Studies*, 111 (1949–50).

GLENN, T. A., *Welsh Founders of Pennsylvania* (2 vols., Oxford, 1911–13).

GOODER, A., 'The Population Crisis of 1727–1730 in Warwickshire', *Midland History*, 1 (1972).

GOODY, Jack (ed.), *Literacy in Traditional Societies* (Cambridge, 1968).

GORDON, A., *Freedom after Ejection* (Manchester, 1917).

GOUBERT, Pierre, *Beauvais et le Beauvaisis de 1600 à 1730* (Paris, 1960).

GOUBERT, Pierre, *The Ancien Régime. French Society 1600–1750* (tr. Steve Cox, 1973).

GREAVES, R. L., *John Bunyan* (Abingdon, 1969).

GRIFFITHS, G. Milwyn, 'Education in the diocese of St. Asaph', *N.L.W.J.*, VI–VII (1950–1).

GRIFFITHS, G. Milwyn, 'Eight Letters from Edmund Gibson to Bishop Humphreys, 1707–9', *N.L.W.J.*, X (1958).

GRIFFITHS, G. Milwyn, 'The Restoration in St. Asaph: the Episcopate of Bishop George Griffith, 1660–1666', *J.H.S.C.W.*, XII (1962).

GRIFFITHS, G. Milwyn, 'Some Extra Diocesan Activities of Bishop George Griffith of St. Asaph, 1660–1666', *N.L.W.J.*, XII (1962).

GRIFFITHS, G. Milwyn, 'Glimpses of Denbighshire in the Records of the Court of Great Sessions', *Denbs. Hist. Soc. Trans.*, 22 (1973).

GRIFFITHS, G. Milwyn, 'A Visitation of the Archdeaconry of Carmarthen, 1710', *N.L.W.J.*, XVIII–XIX (1974–6).

GUNTHER, R. T. (ed.), *Early Science in Oxford. Life and Letters of Edward Lhuyd* (Oxford, 1945).

HALÉVY, Elie, *The Birth of Methodism in England*, tr. and edited by Bernard Semmel (Chicago, 1971).

HALLER, William, *The Rise of Puritanism* (New York, 1938).

HANCOCK, T. W., 'The First Shrewsbury Newspaper', *Bye-Gones* (25 May 1881).

HART, A. T., *Bishop William Lloyd, 1627–1717* (1952).

HART, A. T., *The Country Priest in English History* (1959).

HART, A. T., *Clergy and Society, 1600–1800* (1968).

HAVARD, W. T., 'The Eighteenth Century Background of Church Life in Wales', *J.H.S.C.W.*, X (1955).

HILL, Christopher, 'Puritans and The Dark Corners of the Land', *T.R.H.S.*, XIII (1963).

HILL, Christopher, *Puritanism and Revolution* (1965).

HILL, Christopher, *Society and Puritanism in Pre-Revolutionary England* (1966).

HILL, Christopher, *The World turned Upside Down* (1972).

HOLMES, G. (ed.), *Britain after the Glorious Revolution, 1689–1714* (1969).

HOLMES, G. (ed.), *The Trial of Doctor Sacheverell* (1973).

HOSKINS, W. G., 'Harvest Fluctuations and English Economic History, 1620–1759', *Agricultural History Review*, 16 (1968).

HUBERT-POWELL, C. L., 'Some Notes on Henry Rowlands' "Mona Antiqua Restaurata" ', *Trans. Anglesey Antiq. Soc. and Field Club* (1953).

HUGHES, G. H., *Iaco ab Dewi, 1648–1722* (Cardiff, 1953).

HUGHES, G. H., 'Halsingau Dyffryn Teifi', *Yr Eurgrawn*, CXXXIII (1941).

HUGHES, G. H., 'Emynyddiaeth Gynnar yr Ymneilltuwyr', *Llên Cymru*, II (1953).

HUGHES, G. H., 'Cefndir Meddwl yr Ail Ganrif ar Bymtheg: rhai ystyriaethau', *Efrydiau Athronyddol*, XVIII (1955).

HUGHES, G. H., 'Llyfrau a Llenorion y Crynwyr', *J.W.B.S.*, IX (1959).

JAMES, E. O., *Seasonal Feasts and Festivals* (1961).

JAMES, L. J. Hopkin and EVANS, T. C., *Hen Gwndidau, Carolau a Chywyddau* (Bangor, 1910).

JEFFERSON, H. A. L., *Hymns in Christian Worship* (1950).

JENKINS, David, 'Carolau Haf a Nadolig', *Llên Cymru*, II (1952–3).

JENKINS, David, 'Braslun o Hanes Argraffu yn sir Aberteifi', *J.W.B.S.*, VII (1953).

JENKINS, David, 'The part played by craftsmen in the religious history of Modern Wales', *The Welsh Anvil*, VI (1954).

JENKINS, G. H., 'James Owen versus Benjamin Keach: a controversy over Infant Baptism', *N.L.W.J.*, XIX (1975).

JENKINS, G. H., 'Quaker and anti-Quaker Literature in Welsh from the Restoration to Methodism', *W.H.R.*, VII (1975).

JENKINS, J. Geraint, *Traditional Country Craftsmen* (1965).

JENKINS, J. Gwili, *Hanfod Duw a Pherson Crist* (Liverpool, 1931).

JENKINS, R. T., *Hanes Cymru yn y Ddeunawfed Ganrif* (Cardiff, 1928).

JENKINS, R. T. and RAMAGE, H., *A History of the Honourable Society of Cymmrodorion* (1951).

JEREMY, W. D., *The Presbyterian Fund and Dr. Daniel Williams's Trust* (1885).

JOHNSTON, J. A., 'The Impact of the Epidemics of 1727–30 in South West Worcestershire', *Medical History*, XV (1971).

JONES, Brynmor, 'Argraffwyr Cymreig y Gororau', *J.W.B.S.*, X (1970).

JONES, D. E., *Hanes Plwyfi Llangeler a Phenboyr* (Llandysul, 1899).

JONES, E. D., 'Some Aspects of the History of the Church in north Cardiganshire in the Eighteenth Century', *J.H.S.C.W.*, 1 (1953).

JONES, E. D., 'The Brogyntyn Welsh Manuscripts', *N.L.W.J.*, VIII (1953).

JONES, E. D., 'Nonconformity in Merioneth, 1675', *N.L.W.J.*, VIII (1953–4).

326   BIBLIOGRAPHY

JONES, E. Gwynne, *Cymru a'r Hen Ffydd* (Cardiff, 1951).
JONES, Francis, 'A Squire of Anglesey', *Trans. Anglesey Antiq. Soc. and Field Club* (1940).
JONES, G. Penrhyn, *Newyn a Haint yng Nghymru* (Caernarvon, 1963).
JONES, G. Penrhyn, 'Folk Medicine in Eighteenth Century Wales', *Folk Life*, VII (1969).
JONES, J. T., 'John Morgan, Ficer Aberconwy', *Y Llenor*, XVII (1938).
JONES, M. G., *The Charity School Movement* (Cambridge, 1938).
JONES, M. H., 'Emynyddiaeth Gynnar y Ddeunawfed Ganrif', *J.W.B.S.*, III (1928).
JONES, O. W., 'The Case against Bishop Jones of St. Asaph', *J.H.S.C.W.*, 19 (1964).
JONES, R. Foster, *The Seventeenth Century. Studies in the History of English Thought and Literature from Bacon to Pope* (Stanford, 1951).
JONES, R. Tudur, *Hanes Annibynwyr Cymru* (Swansea 1966).
JONES, R. Tudur, 'Trefniadaeth Ryngeglwysig yr Annibynwyr', *Y Cofiadur*, 21 (1951).
JONES, R. Tudur, 'Agweddau ar Ddiwylliant Ymneilltuwyr', *T.H.S.C.* (1963).
JONES, Theophilus, *A History of the County of Brecknock* (3 vols., Brecon, 1909–11).
JONES, Thomas (ed.), *Astudiaethau Amrywiol* (Cardiff, 1968).
JORDAN, W. K., *The Charities of London, 1480–1660* (1960).
KAMEN, Henry, *The Iron Century. Social Change in Europe, 1550–1660* (1971).
KEARNEY, H., *Scholars and Gentlemen. Universities and Society in pre-industrial Britain, 1500–1700* (1970).
KENYON, John, *The Popish Plot* (1972).
KER, Neil (ed.), *The Parochial Libraries of the Church of England* (1959).
LaMAR, V. L., *Travel and Roads in England* (Washington, 1960).
LASLETT, Peter, *The World we have Lost* (1965).
LASLETT, Peter, 'Size and Structure of the Household in England over Three Centuries', *Population Studies*, XXIII (1969).
LASLETT, Peter, 'Scottish Weavers, Cobblers and Miners who bought books in the 1750s', *Local Population Studies*, 3 (1969).
LE BRAS, Gabriel, *Études de Sociologie Religieuse* (2 vols., Paris, 1955).
LE ROY, Ladurie, E., *Les Paysans de Languedoc* (2 vols., Paris, 1966).
LENNARD, R. (ed.), *Englishmen at Rest and Play* (1931).
LESSENICH, R. P., *Elements of Pulpit Oratory in Eighteenth-Century England, 1660–1800* (Koln, 1972).
LEWIS, David, 'A Progress through Wales in the Seventeenth Century', *Y Cymmrodor*, VI (1883).
LEWIS, Henry, 'Perlau Benthyg', *T.H.S.C.* (1930–1).
LEWIS, H. Elvet, 'Emynwyr Cynnar yr Annibynwyr yng Nghymru', *Y Cofiadur*, 8–9 (1932).
LEWIS, Saunders, 'Arddull Charles Edwards', *Efrydiau Catholig*, IV (1949).
LEWIS, Saunders, 'Thomas à Kempis yn Gymraeg', *Efrydiau Catholig*, IV (1949).
LLOYD, J. E. (ed.), *A History of Carmarthenshire* (2 vols., Cardiff, 1935–9).
LLOYD, Ll. C., 'The Book Trade in Shropshire', *Trans. Shropshire Archaeological and Natural History Soc.* (1935–6).
LLOYD, Nesta, 'The Correspondence of Edward Lhuyd and Richard Mostyn', *Flintshire Hist. Soc. Pubs.*, 25 (1971–2).
MALCOLMSON, R. W., *Popular Recreations in English Society, 1700–1850* (Cambridge, 1973).
MARTIN, L. C. (ed.), *Henry Vaughan: Poetry and Selected Prose* (1963).

MATTHEWS, J. H., 'Monmouthshire Recusants, 1719', *Publications of the Catholic Record Society*, VII (1909).

MATHEWS, Mitford M., *Teaching to Read Historically Considered* (Chicago, 1966).

McADOO, H. R., *The Spirit of Anglicanism* (1965).

McCRACKEN, George E., *The Welcome Claimants proved, disproved and doubtful* (Baltimore, 1970).

McLACHLAN, H., *English Education under the Test Acts* (Manchester, 1931).

McNULTY, R., 'The Protestant Version of Robert Parsons' The First Book of the Christian Exercise', *H.L.Q.*, XXII (1959).

MILLER, John, *Popery and Politics in England, 1660–1688* (Cambridge, 1973).

MILLER, Perry, *The New England Mind: The Seventeenth Century* (Cambridge, Mass., 3rd ed., 1967).

MITCHELL, A. F., *Catechisms of the Second Reformation* (1886).

MITCHELL, W. F., *English Pulpit Oratory from Andrewes to Tillotson* (1932).

MORGAN, P. T. J., 'The Abbé Pezron and the Celts', *T.H.S.C.* (1965).

MORGAN, W. T., 'The Consistory Courts in the diocese of St. David's', *J.H.S.C.W.*, VII (1957).

MOSTYN, Lord and GLENN, T. A., *History of the family of Mostyn* (1925).

NEUBURG, V. E., 'Literacy in Eighteenth Century England: a Caveat', *Local Population Studies*, 2 (1969).

NUTTALL, Derek, *A History of Printing in Chester from 1688 to 1965* (Chester, 1969).

NUTTALL, G. F., *The Holy Spirit in Puritan Faith and Experience* (Oxford, 1946).

NUTTALL, G. F., 'Northamptonshire and the Modern Question: A Turning Point in Eighteenth-Century Dissent', *Journal of Theological Studies*, XVI (1965).

OLIVER, John, 'Tywydd Cymru yn y cyfnod hanesyddol', *Y Gwyddonydd*, IV (1966).

OWEN, Bob, 'Siôn Rhydderch yr Almanaciwr, 1673–1735', *J.W.B.S.*, III (1930).

OWEN, Bob, 'Maesyneuadd', *Journal Merioneth Hist. & Rec. Soc.*, IV (1961).

OWEN, Bob, 'Cipolwg ar Ynysymaengwyn a'i Deuluoedd', *Journal Merioneth Hist. & Rec. Soc.*, IV (1962).

OWEN, Elias, 'Churchyard Games in Wales', *The Reliquary and Illustrated Archaeologist*, 1–2 (1895–6).

OWEN, G. D., *Ysgolion a Cholegau yr Annibynwyr* (Llandysul, 1939).

OWEN, G. D., 'James Owen a'i Academi', *Y Cofiadur*, 22 (1952).

OWEN, Hugh (ed.), *The Life and Works of Lewis Morris, 1701–1765* (Anglesey Antiq. Soc. supplement vol., 1951).

OWEN, J. Dyfnallt, *Hanes Eglwys Heol Awst* (Carmarthen, 1926).

OWEN, J. Dyfnallt, 'Dechreuadau Panteg a Christmas Samuel', *Y Dysgedydd*, CXV–CXVII (1935–6).

OWEN, Leonard, 'The Letters of an Anglesey Parson, 1712–1732', *T.H.S.C.* (1961).

OWEN, T. M., *Welsh Folk Customs* (2nd ed., Cardiff, 1968).

OWENS, B. G., 'Trichanmlwyddiant Rhydwilym', *Trafodion Cymdeithas Hanes Bedyddwyr Cymru* (1968).

PALMER, A. N., *History of the Town of Wrexham* (Wrexham, 1893).

PARKER, Irene, *Dissenting Academies in England* (Cambridge, 1914).

PARKES, Joan, *Travel in England in the Seventeenth Century* (1925).

PARRY, Thomas, *Baledi'r Ddeunawfed Ganrif* (Cardiff, 1935).

PARRY-WILLIAMS, T. H. (ed.), *Llawysgrif Richard Morris o Gerddi* (Cardiff, 1931).

PATRIDES, C. A., 'Renaissance and Modern Thought on the Last Things', *Harvard Theological Review*, LI (1958).

PEATE, I. C., 'The Denbigh Cockpit and Cock-fighting in Wales', *Denbighshire Hist. Soc. Trans.*, 19 (1970).

PETTIT, Norman, *The Heart Prepared: Grace and Conversion in Puritan Spiritual Life* (New Haven, 1966).

PHILLIPS, C. S., *Hymnody Past and Present* (1937).

PHILLIPS, D. R., 'Thomas Jones the Almanacer', *J.W.B.S.*, 1–2 (1915–18).

PLANT, Marjorie, *The English Book Trade* (2nd ed., 1965).

POWICKE, F. J., 'The Reverend Richard Baxter's Last Treatise', *Bulletin of John Rylands Library*, X (1926).

PRYCE, A. I., *The Diocese of Bangor during three centuries* (Cardiff, 1929).

PRYCE, W. T. R., 'Approaches to the Linguistic Geography of Northeast Wales, 1750–1846', *N.L.W.J.*, XVII (1972).

RANDALL, H. W., 'The Rise and Fall of a Martyrology: Sermons on Charles I', *H.L.Q.*, X (1947).

REES, Eiluned, 'A Bibliographical note on early editions of Canwyll y Cymry', *J.W.B.S.*, X (1968).

REES, Eiluned, 'Developments in the Book-Trade in Eighteenth Century Wales', *The Library*, XXIV (1969).

REES, Eiluned, 'Welsh Publishing before 1717', *Essays in Honour of Victor Scholderer* (Mainz, 1970).

REES, Eiluned, 'An Introductory Survey of 18th Century Welsh Libraries', *J.W.B.S.*, X (1971).

REES, Eiluned, 'Pre-1820 Welsh Subscription Lists', *J.W.B.S.*, XI (1973–4).

REES, Eiluned and NUTTALL, Derek, 'Baddy Vindicated, or Jones v Jones', *J.W.B.S.*, X (1970).

REES, Thomas, *History of Protestant Nonconformity in Wales* (2nd ed., 1883).

REES, Thomas and THOMAS, John, *Hanes Eglwysi Annibynol Cymru* (4 vols., Liverpool, 1871–5).

REES, T. M., *A History of the Quakers in Wales* (Carmarthen, 1925).

RICHARDS, Gwynfryn, 'Y Plygain', *J.H.S.C.W.*, I (1947).

RICHARDS, G. Melville, 'Yr Awdur a'i Gyhoedd yn y Ddeunawfed Ganrif', *J.W.B.S.*, X (1966).

RICHARDS, Thomas, *Religious Developments in Wales, 1654–1662* (1923).

RICHARDS, Thomas, *Wales under the Penal Code, 1662–1687* (1925).

RICHARDS, Thomas, *Wales under the Indulgence, 1672–1675* (1928).

RICHARDS, Thomas, 'The Religious Census of 1676', *T.H.S.C.*, Supplement, (1925–6).

RICHARDS, Thomas, 'Henry Maurice: Piwritan ac Annibynwr', *Y Cofiadur*, 5–6 (1928).

RICHARDS, Thomas, 'Eglwys Rhydwilym', *Trafodion Cymdeithas Hanes Bedyddwyr Cymru* (1938).

RICHARDSON, R. C., 'The Diocese of Chester. Religion and Reading in the late sixteenth and early seventeenth centuries', *The Local Historian*, XI (1974).

RINGGREN, Helmer (ed.), *Fatalistic Beliefs in Religion, Folklore and Literature* (Stockholm, 1967).

ROBERTS, Askew, *Wynnstay and the Wynns* (Oswestry, 1876).

ROBERTS, B. F., 'Rhai Swynion Cymraeg', *B.B.C.S.*, XXI (1965).

ROBERTS, B. F., 'Llythyrau John Lloyd at Edward Lhuyd', *N.L.W.J.*, XVII (1971).

ROBERTS, B. F., 'Ymagweddu at Brut y Brenhinedd hyd 1890', *B.B.C.S.*, XXIV (1971).

ROBERTS, E. P., 'Hen Garolau Plygain', *T.H.S.C.*, (1952).

ROBERTS, G. M., 'Letters written by David Jones, Dygoed, Llanlluan, to Howell Harris', *C.C.H.M.C.*, XXI (1936).

ROBERTS, G. M., 'Griffith Jones' Opinion of the Methodists', *C.C.H.M.C.*, XXXV (1950).

ROBERTS, G. M., *Selected Trevecca Letters, 1742–1747* (Caernarvon, 1956).

ROBERTS, G. M., *Hanes Methodistiaeth Galfinaidd Cymru* (vol. I, Caernarvon, 1973).

ROBERTS, H. P., 'Nonconformist Academies in Wales, 1662–1862', *T.H.S.C.* (1928–9).

ROBERTS, John, *Ychydig o Hanes y Diweddar Barchedig Lewis Rees* (Carmarthen n.d.).

ROBERTS, P. R., 'The Social History of the Merioneth Gentry, *c.* 1660–1840', *Journal Merioneth Hist. & Rec. Soc.*, IV (1963).

ROBERTS, P. R., 'The Decline of the Welsh Squires', *N.L.W.J.*, XIII (1963–4).

ROBINSON, F. J. G. and WALLIS, P. J., *Book Subscription Lists. A Revised Guide* (Newcastle upon Tyne, 1975).

RODERICK, A. J. (ed.), *Wales through the Ages* (2 vols., Llandybie, 1960).

RUSSELL, Conrad (ed.), *The Origins of the English Civil War* (1973).

SAER, D. Roy, 'The Christmas Carol-Singing Tradition in the Tanad Valley', *Folk Life*, 7 (1969).

SAVIDGE, Alan, *The Foundation and early years of Queen Anne's Bounty* (1955).

SCHLATTER, R. B., *The Social Ideas of Religious Leaders, 1660–1688* (1940).

SCHOCHET, G. F., 'Patriarchalism, Politics and Mass Attitudes in Stuart England', *The Historical Journal*, XII (1969).

SCHOFIELD, R. S., 'Crisis Mortality', *Local Population Studies*, 9 (1972).

SCHÜCKING, L. L., *The Puritan Family* (1969).

SHANKLAND, Thomas, 'Sir John Philipps: the Society for promoting Christian Knowledge; and the Charity-School Movement in Wales, 1699–1737', *T.H.S.C.* (1904–5).

SHANKLAND, Thomas, 'Joseph Harris a Chychwyniad Llenyddiaeth Gyfnodol yng Nghymru', *Trafodion Cymdeithas Hanes Bedyddwyr Cymru* (1912–13).

SHAPIRO, B. J., 'Latitudinarianism and Science in Seventeenth-Century England', *P & P*, 40 (1968).

SMITH, Alan, *The Established Church and Popular Religion, 1750–1850* (1971).

SPUFFORD, Margaret, *Contrasting Communities* (Cambridge, 1974).

SPURRELL, William, *Carmarthen and its Neighbourhood* (2nd ed., 1879).

STANFORD, Charles, *Joseph Alleine: his Companions and Times* (1861).

STEWART, B. S., 'The Cult of the Royal Martyr', *Church History*, XXXVIII (1969).

STOEFFLER, F. E., *The Rise of Evangelical Pietism* (Leiden, 1965).

STRANKS, C. J., *Anglican Devotion* (1961).

STYLES, Philip, 'The Heralds' Visitation of Warwickshire, 1682–1683', *Trans. & Proceedings of Birmingham Archaeological Soc.*, 70 (1954).

STYLES, Philip, 'The Social Structure of Kineton Hundred in the reign of Charles II', *Trans. & Proceedings of Birmingham Archaeological Soc.*, 78 (1962).

SUTHERLAND, James, *English Literature of the late Seventeenth Century* (Oxford, 1969).

SWEET-ESCOTT, Bickham, 'William Beaw: a Cavalier Bishop', *W.H.R.*, I (1963).

SYKES, Norman, *Church and State in England in the Eighteenth Century* (Cambridge, 1934).

SYKES, Norman, *William Wake, Archbishop of Canterbury, 1657–1737* (2 vols., Cambridge, 1957).

TALLON, Maura, *Church in Wales Diocesan Libraries* (Athlone, 1962).

THIRSK, Joan, 'The Family', *P & P*, 27 (1964).

THOMAS, D. R., *History of the Diocese of St. Asaph* (3 vols., Oswestry, 1908–11).

THOMAS, Gwyn, *Y Bardd Cwsg a'i Gefndir* (Cardiff, 1971).

THOMAS, Isaac, 'Y Gronfa Gynulleidfaol ac Annibynwyr Cymru', *Y Cofiadur*, 28 (1958).

THOMAS, Keith, *Religion and the Decline of Magic* (1971).

THOMAS, Keith, 'Work and Leisure in Pre-Industrial Society', *P & P*, 29 (1964).

THOMAS, R. J., 'Jencin Jones, Llwynrhydowen', *Baner ac Amserau Cymru* (27 May 1942).

THOMAS, R. S., *Poetry for Supper* (1958).

TOON, P., *The Emergence of Hyper-Calvinism in English Nonconformity, 1689–1765* (1967).

TREVOR-ROPER, H. R., *The European Witch-Craze of the Sixteenth and Seventeenth Centuries* (1969).

TUER, A. W., *History of the Horn-Book* (2 vols., 1896).

USHER, G. A., *Gwysaney and Owston* (Denbigh, 1964).

WADDINGTON, H. M., 'Games and Athletics in Bygone Wales', *T.H.S.C.* (1953).

WALLIS, P. J., 'Book Subscription Lists', *The Library*, XXIX (1974).

WALSH, J. D., 'Elie Halévy and the Birth of Methodism', *T.R.H.S.*, 25 (1975).

WARNE, Arthur, *Church and Society in Eighteenth-Century Devon* (Newton Abbot, 1969).

WATKINS, O. C., *The Puritan Experience* (1972).

WHARTON, E. R., *The Whartons of Wharton Hall* (Oxford, 1898).

WHITAKER, W. B., *The Eighteenth Century English Sunday* (1940).

WHITE, H. C., *English Devotional Literature, 1600–1640* (Wisconsin, 1931).

WIENER, C. Z., 'The Beleaguered Isle. A study of Elizabethan and early Jacobean Anti-Catholicism', *P & P*, 51 (1971).

WILKINS, Charles, *The History of Merthyr Tydfil* (Merthyr, 1908).

WILLIAMS, A. H., 'Theophilus Evans, Chaplain', *N.L.W.J.*, XVI (1970).

WILLIAMS, G. J., *Traddodiad Llenyddol Morgannwg* (Cardiff, 1948).

WILLIAMS, G. J., *Iolo Morganwg* (Cardiff, 1956).

WILLIAMS, G. J., 'Daniel Ddu o Geredigion a'i Gyfnod', *Y Llenor*, V (1926).

WILLIAMS, G. J., 'Glamorgan Customs in the Eighteenth Century', *Gwerin*, 1 (1957).

WILLIAMS, Glanmor, *The Welsh Church from Conquest to Reformation* (Cardiff, 1962).

WILLIAMS, Glanmor, *Welsh Reformation Essays* (Cardiff, 1967).

WILLIAMS, Glanmor, 'Language, Literacy and Nationality in Wales', *History*, 56 (1971).

WILLIAMS, Glanmor (ed.), *Glamorgan County History, vol. IV, Early Modern Glamorgan* (Cardiff, 1974).

WILLIAMS, J. Gwynn, 'Rhai Agweddau ar y Gymdeithas Gymraeg yn yr Ail Ganrif ar Bymtheg', *Efrydiau Athronyddol*, XXXI (1968).

WILLIAMS, M. Fay, 'Glamorgan Quakers, 1654–1900', *Morgannwg*, V (1961).

WILLIAMS, Robert, 'A history of the parish of Llanfyllin', *Mont. Colls.*, III (1870).

WILLIAMS, Stewart (ed.), *Glamorgan Historian*, X (1974).

WILLIAMS, T. O., *Hanes Cynulleidfaoedd Undodaidd Sir Aberteifi* (Llandysul, n.d.).

WILLIAMS, W. Moses, *The Friends of Griffith Jones* (1939).

WILSON, Charles, *England's Apprenticeship, 1603–1763* (1971).

WILSON, J. L., 'Catechisms and their use among the Puritans', *One Steadfast High Intent*, The Puritan and Reformed Studies Conference (1966).

WRIGHT, E. G., 'Humphrey Humphreys, Bishop of Bangor and Hereford (1648–1712)', *Trans. Anglesey Antiq. Soc. and Field Club* (1949).

WRIGHT, E. G., 'Dean John Jones (1650–1727)', *Trans. Anglesey Antiq. Soc. and Field Club* (1952).

WRIGHT, L. B., *Middle-Class Culture in Elizabethan England* (Chapel Hill, 1935).

WRIGLEY, E. A., 'Mortality in pre-industrial England: the example of Colyton, Devon, over three centuries', *Daedalus* (Spring 1968).

WYNNE, R. O. F., 'The Wynne Family of Melai and Garthewin', *Denbs. Hist. Soc. Trans.*, V (1956).

(iii) UNPUBLISHED THESES AND DISSERTATIONS

BOWEN, G., 'Traddodiad Llenyddol Deau Ceredigion, 1600–1850' (unpublished University of Wales M.A. thesis, 1943).

BRINK, A. W., 'A Study in the Literature of Inward Experience, 1600–1700' (unpublished University of London Ph.D. thesis, 1963).

CLEMENT, Mary, 'Hanes yr S.P.C.K. yn Sir Gaerfyrddin o 1700 hyd 1750, gyda chyfeiriad arbennig at John Vaughan, Cwrt Derllys, a'i waith' (unpublished University of Wales M.A. thesis, 1940).

DAVIES, J. Vyrnwy, 'The diocese of St. David's during the first half of the eighteenth century' (unpublished University of Wales M.A. thesis, 1936).

EDWARDS, John, 'Edward Samuel: ei Oes a'i Waith' (unpublished University of Wales M.A. thesis, 1925).

HUGHES, A. Lloyd, 'Noddwyr y Beirdd yn sir Feirionnydd' (unpublished University of Wales M.A. thesis, 1969).

JENKINS, David, 'Bywyd a Gwaith Huw Morys, Pontymeibion (1662–1709)' (unpublished University of Wales M.A. thesis, 1948).

JONES, Gwenllian, 'Bywyd a Gwaith Edward Morris, Perthi Llwydion' (unpublished University of Wales M.A. thesis, 1941).

JONES, H. G., 'John Kelsall: a study in religious and economic history' (unpublished University of Wales M.A. thesis, 1938).

JONES, J. G., 'The Caernarvonshire Justices of the Peace and their Duties during the Seventeenth Century' (unpublished University of Wales M.A. thesis, 1967).

JONES, W. Garel, 'The Life and Works of Henry Rowlands' (unpublished University of Wales M.A. thesis, 1936).

LEWIS, Mairwen, 'Astudiaeth gymharol o'r cyfieithiadau Cymraeg o rai o weithiau John Bunyan, eu lle a'u dylanwad yn llên Cymru' (unpublished University of Wales M.A. thesis, 1957).

MARSHALL, W. M., 'The Life of George Hooper, Bishop of Bath and Wells, 1640–1727' (unpublished University of Bristol M.Litt. thesis, 1971).

MORGAN, D. L., 'A Critical Study of the Works of Charles Edwards (1628–1691?)' (unpublished University of Oxford D.Phil. thesis, 1967).

O'KEEFE, M. M. C., 'The Popish Plot in South Wales and the Marches of Hereford and Gloucester' (unpublished University of Galway M.A. thesis, 1969).

RISDEN, W. E., 'New Ventures in Publishing between 1680 and 1700' (unpublished University of Oxford B.Litt. thesis, 1969).

ROBERTS, P. R., 'The Landed Gentry in Merioneth, *circa* 1660–1832, with special reference to the estates of Hengwrt, Nannau, Rug and Ynysymaengwyn' (unpublished University of Wales M.A. thesis, 1963).

SPEARS, W. E., 'The Baptist Movement in England in the late seventeenth century as reflected in the work and thought of Benjamin Keach, 1640–1704' (unpublished University of Edinburgh Ph.D. thesis, 1953).

THOMAS, David, 'Ffynonellau, Arddull a Chymeriad Gwaith Llenyddol Theophilus Evans' (unpublished University of Wales M.A. thesis, 1937).

THOMAS, Gwyn, 'A Study of the Changes in the Tradition of Welsh Poetry in North Wales in the Seventeenth Century' (unpublished University of Oxford D.Phil. thesis, 1966).

WILIAM, D. Wyn, 'Y Traddodiad Barddol ym Mhlwyf Bodedern, Môn' (unpublished University of Wales M.A. thesis, 1970).

WILLIAMS, G. H., 'A Study of Caernarvonshire Probate Records, 1630–1690' (unpublished University of Wales M.A. thesis, 1972).

WILLIAMS, J., 'An Edition of the Correspondence of John Aubrey with Anthony à Wood and Edward Lhuyd, 1667–96' (unpublished University of London Ph.D. thesis, 1967).

INDEX

DATE DUE
